The Global South Atlantic

The Global South Atlantic

Kerry Bystrom
and Joseph R. Slaughter
Editors

Fordham University Press
New York 2018

Fordham University Press also publishes its books in a variety of electronic formats. Some content that appears in print may not be available in electronic books.

Visit us online at www.fordhampress.com.

Library of Congress Cataloging-in-Publication Data available online at https://catalog.loc.gov.

Printed in the United States of America

20 19 18 5 4 3 2 1

First edition

CONTENTS

INTRODUCTION

The Sea of International Politics

Fluidity, Solvency, and Drift in the Global South Atlantic

Joseph R. Slaughter and Kerry Bystrom

When Winston Churchill and Franklin D. Roosevelt made their Joint Declaration of "hopes for a better future of the world" from a warship off the coast of Newfoundland on August 14, 1941, they were not thinking about the South Atlantic. They were anticipating a formal North Atlantic Anglo-American military alliance against German aggression and looking forward to a postwar peace that might, in the Charter's words, "afford assurance that all the men in all the lands may live out their lives in freedom from fear and want," based on principles of "sovereign rights and self government" and "the right of all peoples to choose the form of government under which they will live."[1] The Joint Declaration, released to the press by cablegram and delivered to the world by radio operators aboard the ships, was quickly dubbed the "Atlantic Charter," lending the name of the sea that both separated and united the United States and the United Kingdom to oceanic principles of liberty and peace intended to inspire (potential) allies and to reassure others of the justness of their war aims. Within six months, the Charter's grand rhetorical commitments to the rights of "all the men in all the lands" to territorial sovereignty and democratic governance would be cited as the "common program of purposes and principles" for the "Declaration by United Nations" that expanded its scope beyond the North Atlantic and laid the legal foundations for the later Charter of the United Nations in 1945. However, despite its promises and lofty principles for a "New World Order" (as many then described it), the first effect of the Atlantic Charter was to fortify the Anglo-American alliance between the old and new empires, and it ultimately secured the Anglophone North Atlantic hegemony to come.

Yet, while Roosevelt and Churchill may not have had the South Atlantic or other oceans in mind when they issued their statement to the world, many people living in the shadows of empire were already thinking about these North Atlantic promises and oceanic "expectation[s] of national self-determination" (Grovogui 1996, 146). Seeming to "have application to all the peoples of the world," as the British West Indian anti-imperialist George Padmore insisted (Cunard and Padmore 2002, 137), the Charter fanned heated debates about "the legitimacy of colonialism and the shape of post-war internationalism" (Ibhawoh 2014, 835), both in colonial capitals and across the still vast terrains of empires. On his return from the Atlantic conference, Churchill felt compelled to assure his compatriots in Parliament that he intended only to restore self-government to European nations occupied by Germany, but he and Roosevelt soon had to answer questions about the extension of Atlantic Charter principles of self-determination to the great mass of "dependent peoples" still living under European colonial domination. In November 1941, Nnamdi Azikiwe, then editor of the *West African Pilot* and later the first president of Nigeria, cabled Churchill to ask, "Are we fighting for security of Europeans to enjoy the four freedoms while West Africa continues on pre-war status? . . . We respectfully request your clarification of the applicability of the Atlantic Charter regarding Nigeria. This will enable us to appreciate the correct bearing of 21 million Negroes in the sea of international politics" (quoted in Padmore 1942, 236).

On the other side of the North Atlantic, Roosevelt received a letter from Mohandas K. Gandhi pointing out that "the Allied Declaration that the Allies are fighting to make the world safe for freedom of the individual and for democracy sounds hollow, so long as India, and for that matter, Africa are exploited by Great Britain, and America has the Negro problem in her own home" (quoted in Borgwardt 2005, 545). The African American and Caribbean press propelled the anticolonial interpretation of the Charter forward, strengthening transatlantic intellectual and political solidarities throughout what, fifty years later, would become known as the "Black Atlantic" (Von Eschen 1997, 25–28). For example, W. E. B. DuBois was invited, along with future Ghanaian leaders Ebenezer Ako-Adjei and Francis (Kwame) Nkrumah (then students at Lincoln University in the United States), and others, to help prepare a 1942 study by a New York–based Committee on Africa, the War, and Peace Aims that outlined a plan for the application of Atlantic Charter principles of individual rights and collective self-government to a postwar, postcolonial Africa (Committee on Africa 1942).

Efforts to leverage the ideals of the Atlantic Charter proliferated around the globe. The Philippine statesman Carlos Romulo described the document as a "flame of hope," and Algerian nationalist Ferhat Abbas invoked it as support for the cause of independence from France (Klose 2013, 22–25). In the Dumbarton Oaks negotiations that led to the founding of the United Nations, it was Latin American representatives from the old South Atlantic colonies of the Spanish and Portuguese empires who insisted on "amendments relating to the position of dependent peoples and to self-determination"; they cited the Atlantic Charter as an international precedent (Brownlie 1970, 97). Those same principles later helped to consolidate domestic and international opposition to dictatorships across Latin America (Liss 1984, 36). Indeed, as Elizabeth Borgwardt notes, in the wake of the declaration of what became known as the Atlantic Charter, "anti-colonial activists began to demand a 'Pacific Charter,' an 'African Charter,' or a 'World Charter' as companions to the Atlantic one" (2005, 554). This pressure pushed Roosevelt to contradict Churchill in early 1942 by announcing that "The Atlantic Charter applies not only to the parts of the world that border the Atlantic, but to the whole world; disarmament of aggressors, self-determination of nations and peoples, and the four freedoms—freedom of speech, freedom of religion, freedom from want, and freedom from fear" (quoted in Committee on Africa 1942, 30). Writing in 2005, Borgwardt calls this reading of the Joint Declaration "Mandela's Charter" (532), relocating the Charter's spirit to the opposite pole of the Atlantic based on the South African president's later recollection in *Long Walk to Freedom*: "Inspired by the Atlantic Charter and the fight of the Allies against tyranny and oppression, the ANC created its own charter . . . [so that] ordinary South Africans would see that the principles they were fighting for in Europe were the same ones we were advocating for at home" (Mandela 1994, 83–84).

Thus, while the Charter strengthened the transatlantic bonds of imperial and proto-imperial power that came to dominate world affairs (manifested most powerfully in the subsequent formation of the North Atlantic Treaty Organization in 1949), it also internationalized principles that would form part of the legal basis for anti-imperial, anticolonial, and antidictatorial struggles across the Global South (often conducted against the two countries that originally made the Joint Declaration). Indeed, the Atlantic Charter principles of self-determination and territorial sovereignty were later reaffirmed in the Final Communiqué of the Asian-African Conference at Bandung in 1955 and again reconditioned for militant anti-imperialism in the General Declaration of the First Tricontinental Conference (which we might think of as the Global South Atlantic Charter) of the peoples of Africa, Asia and Latin America held in Havana, Cuba, in 1966.[2] Drawing on the language of promises made (and betrayed) in the North Atlantic, those struggles reshaped global politics and postcolonial societies and cultures for the rest of the twentieth century; they not only remade the modes and terms of transnational and trans-regional political association, military alliance, and economic and cultural cooperation (and contest), but they also created new imperatives for renewed forms of associative thinking and comparative study.

The essays collected in *The Global South Atlantic* respond to this imperative to compare in order to trace pathways, networks, transactions, and systems of interchange and imagination that have historically defined the South Atlantic (and that continue to drive its futures) but are obscured or suppressed by the hegemonic North Atlantic orientation of knowledge production and the division of disciplines tasked with producing it. This collection brings together a wide variety of approaches to studying the South Atlantic in order to explore ways to read productively both what is and what is not (or what is no longer) visible even to an oceanic approach like Atlantic studies that too often retreats to a description of systems of transatlantic exchange or that merely documents some relations between regions, primarily Europe and the United States. The frameworks and varied modes of comparison brought to bear on the topic in this volume sometimes complement and sometimes chafe against each other, creating a productive friction that reveals closures not only in Northward-tilted academic formations but also in certain renewed investments (both libidinal and literal) in the Global South and South-South linkages. We ultimately pose the South Atlantic as a problem. It may be a geopolitical *region* (think of, say, a "South Atlantic Rim"), yet at the same time it is also a *vision*, an ideal or aspiration of solidarity and interconnection (whether across the South Atlantic Ocean or between Southern locales, as the Global South imagines the Atlantic) that has come to pass (or not) precisely because of the structural and epistemological impediments that make the

South Atlantic difficult to apprehend as a coherent region. To help establish this bifocal perspective, this introduction draws from the story of the Atlantic Charter and its variegated implications for and uses in the Global South a series of questions about how we might best grasp the heterogeneous space of the South Atlantic historically, conceptually, and methodologically.

New International Formations

The New World Order that followed World War II brought new international institutions, such as the United Nations, and new regional alliances and associations, such as NATO, the Eastern Bloc, and the Non-Aligned Movement among others, along with new contests of power during the era of decolonization and the Cold War. These arrangements had implications not only for geopolitics and economics but also for the liberal arts and sciences, making some new forms of studying and thinking about the world possible while overshadowing and undercutting others. The NATO-centrism that characterized the approach to global affairs among the powerful North Atlantic nations fostered and demanded new academic formations and organizational approaches to knowledge in order to make sense of (and often to better dominate) the new dispensations of the international political order. Just as Oriental and African studies emerged in Europe in the context of imperial pursuits in the nineteenth century, area studies, as is well known, originated in the United States to serve foreign policy interests and military objectives of the new hegemon. In a sense, then, area studies in the North Atlantic was a Cold War enterprise designed to help manage any realization in the Third World of the sorts of promises of self-determination and territorial sovereignty made in the Atlantic Charter—that is, area studies could be understood as the academic mode of containing the troublesome aspirations underwritten by the Atlantic Charter and the international institutions built on its unmoored foundation. (Of course, many scholars housed in area studies centers have resisted the original instrumental impulse that brought the research institutes into being.) And postcolonial studies, world systems analysis, Third World studies, various transnational regionalisms, and oceanic studies could be understood as alternative academic formations that have sought to challenge the alliance between area studies knowledge and neoimperialism. Yet, all of these rubrics emerged as modes of understanding and managing the realignment and redistribution of power, people, resources, and solidarities around the world. Those rubrics had implications for the fields that most concern us in this volume—cultural studies, history, and especially comparative literature—that have changed the way we talk about cultural and social interactions among peoples.

It could be argued that the Atlantic Charter helped to spawn modern oceanic thinking in the postwar era of new internationalism that imagined a sea basin and its rim as both a "physical unity" and a "human unit," as Fernand Braudel described the Mediterranean in his seminal 1949 study (1995, 231).[3] Indeed, according to Bernard Bailyn, the academic field of Atlantic history emerged from the postwar "Atlanticist climate" on both sides of the northern ocean, treating "the Atlantic world" as a single "unit, historically as well as politically" (2005, 15). The task of the Atlantic historian was to document the networks of political, economic, and intellectual transactions across and around the sea that constituted "The Atlantic System," or, as it was more popularly known, "The Atlantic Community" (Hoffman 1945; Davis 1941). However, the Anglo-American military and political alliance affirmed in the Atlantic Charter inflected the ideological bias of much Anglophone Atlantic history. Often propagandistic, serving the interests of North Atlantic geopolitical hegemony, the early Atlantic history that Bailyn identifies as the field's opening salvos promoted a NATO-centric vision of transoceanic commonalities, connections, and interactions across the ocean that emphasized both the exceptionalism of the region and the supposed universality of the ideals that its exceptional history had produced. Thus, for example, as early as 1945, Ross Hoffman, professor of European history at Fordham University, characterized the Atlantic Ocean as "the inland sea of Western Civilization" and as the "citadel" of "British, French, and American ideals of liberty and constitutional government" (Hoffman 1945, 25), eliding at once the history and experiences of perhaps the vast majority of people living along the full stretch of coasts and submerged at the bottom of Western Civilization's sea. The slippage between an (imaginary) oceanic geography and lofty political ideals that we find in the writing of Hoffman and other early Atlantic historians repeated the rhetorical overflow from "the Atlantic . . . to the whole world" in Roosevelt's expansive interpretation of the Atlantic Charter. The sweeping gesture that engulfs the globe will suggest to many in the South Atlantic (and the Global South more generally) that it is not just Atlantic states that need to be free of colonialism; as Luiz Felipe de Alencastro's essay in this volume so pointedly demonstrates, the oceans and their histories also need to be decolonized.

Promise of Oceans

The Atlantic Charter might seem an unlikely point of departure for a collection of essays on the Global South Atlantic, but there are peculiarly oceanic qualities to the charter, its principles, and its history that can help illuminate some of the problems and prospects of studying an undelimitable South Atlantic from the shifting perspectives of the Global South that we are concerned with in this book. As Hester Blum has written, oceanic studies "deriv[es] from the fluidity of its object of study a constitutive position of unboundedness, drift, and solvency" (2013, 152), and these qualities—qualities of fluids—disturb (or disregard) geopolitical demarcations and sociocultural distinctions that are characteristic of traditional transnational analysis that are themselves modeled on the Westphalian fiction of the timeless territorial integrity of nation-states. In the case of the Atlantic Charter, the oceanic qualities of solvency, drift, and unboundedness perhaps become clearer if we approach the historic Joint Declaration through three questions that can also be applied to the South Atlantic as an entity, an ideal, and a rubric: (1) Does it exist, or what is the nature of its existence? (2) What does it imply, and (how) do those implications change? (3) To whom does it apply? In beginning by discussing these three questions in terms of the Atlantic Charter, we want to give a sense of the contours of some modes of oceanic thought that are relevant to studying something so polymorphous as the Global South Atlantic, to which we turn later.

"Atlantic Charter" was the late name given to a radio and cablegram announcement about the Anglo-American alliance that never existed as a legal document—at least not as such. Just as the "Atlantic" originally envisioned by the Joint Declaration was not the whole Atlantic, the "Charter" was not a charter, and questions about its existence and force as a legal document were soon raised by domestic commentators and politicians, especially in the United States, who were against the creation of supranational intergovernmental institutions. Challenged about the Charter's legal status by a hostile American reporter in 1944, President Roosevelt acknowledged, "There isn't any copy of the Atlantic Charter. . . . The nearest thing you will get is the radio operator on the Augusta and on the Prince of Wales. . . . It was signed in substance. . . . There is no formal document—complete document—signed by us both" (quoted in Borgwardt 2007, 38). Nonetheless, as has been typical of the development of international law in the customary mode, the Charter did acquire legal (not just moral) importance by the back door of citation, through subsequent references to it in other international legal texts, namely the "Declaration by United Nations" and the Charter of the United Nations.[4] There is something oceanic about a legal text that is not a text, a Charter flowing in the radio airwaves that carried the announcement of principles, "signed in [watery] substance," to the shores of the Atlantic and beyond. Questions about the existence of a signed document were motivated, of course, not merely by an ontological obsession with original documents but by political interests in validating or invalidating the legitimacy of the law.

These questions about solvency—about what can and cannot be dissolved or absorbed by an idea—are important ones to ask also of any oceanic or regional formation that is being studied as a single system: does the Atlantic, or, for us, the South Atlantic, actually exist, or is it something like an inchoate set of subsequent citations and cross-references still to be assembled by historians and cultural studies scholars from dispersed archives? Or is it something else altogether? In a review of the limits of Atlantic history, Allison Games has provocatively asserted that "if the Atlantic is a less obvious and coherent unit than the Mediterranean, it is also an anachronistic one. Historians have first had to invent the region: the emergence of the Atlantic as a single unit of analysis reflects trends in historical geography" (2006, 742–743). Games suggests that in the case of the Atlantic—and perhaps oceanic regions more generally—the structure that Braudel describes as a "human unit" is the retrospective invention of historians. There is probably a lot of truth to that claim, but it also undervalues the myriad economic, political, and cultural forces that do bring people into social assemblages and sentimental arrangements across a region in something like "real time." After Benedict Anderson's *Imagined Communities: Reflections on the Origins and Spread of Nationalism* (1983), we have become used to thinking about nations and other communities as imaginary structures of feeling among the people who share a sense of political commonality and moral purpose. Famously, for Anderson, it was novels and newspapers that made it possible for people to begin to imagine themselves in relations of community with people whom they would never meet across a large geographical territory. "Print-literacy," he wrote, "made possible the imagined community floating in homogeneous, empty time" (1983/2006, 118). If "floating" is more than a metaphor in Anderson's reconfiguration of Benjaminian time, it suggests that the sense of belonging to a "human unit" is fluid and in flux, subject to change and dependent upon other modes of creating a feeling of being suspended in a sea of shared time. In the traditional Westphalian model of nation-states—and of nationalist sentiment—the sense of community and commonality is fostered not merely by literature, but by the shared mediums of law and language (things that the United Kingdom and the United States had much in common at the time of the Atlantic Charter). In other words, Enlightenment principles about the territorial integrity of the nation-states required a common sentimental attachment to the law, language, and literature produced in the polity.

But oceanic regions are neither communities nor polities (in the Andersonian sense). They do not share a single language, law, or literature—even if there develop common creoles or trade language, sets of maritime and coastal customs, and a circulating literature of the sea. Oceans as human units may not have a single unifying principle, and they do not have a single chronotope, even if the ship—as figure and fact, in Paul Gilroy's "Black Atlantic"—might provide a good starting place for charting sea life. Indeed, the South Atlantic, even more than the North Atlantic, is a multilingual, multitemporal, and multidimensional space. It is, then, an intrinsically comparative and relativized space (perhaps a sea of comparison), united not by a single language or history, but by multiple intersecting, diverging, dissolving, and overlapping languages, laws, cultures, and histories. As such, in this collection of essays, as suggested earlier and as we will discuss further, we do not take it for granted that such a thing as the (Global) South Atlantic exists—or that it does not, or might be imaginary. We are interested in the various historical efforts, undertaken from multiple locations, to bring such an oceanic conceptual or sentimental or material system into being, as well as the many failed attempts to do so. Thus, one goal for this collection is to reflect metacritically on the conditions of possibility and impossibility for the coming into being of discursive spaces like a global "South Atlantic." We are thinking about the terms under which any oceanic or regional formation becomes intelligible to scholars and palpable to (and through) artists, politicians, merchants, and other peoples living within it.

Ocean Promises

There is something poetic about the new international order having been announced by shortwave radio from the decks of British and American ships bobbing at sea, and the commitment to territorial sovereignty and self-government having been declared from the wavy surface of the ocean, which itself has no clear boundaries and knows no sovereign—at least in the Westphalian legal tradition since Hugo Grotius.[5] In the early seventeenth century, Grotius published his famous treatise on the "freedom of the seas," which, despite its titular commitment to liberty (*Mare Liberum*), was nonetheless proffered "in the name of a sea-born empire" as part of a legal justification for Dutch imperialism in the East Indies (Brito Vieira 2003, 377). The insistence on the freedom of the oceans—that the high seas are the navigational media for global free trade and an international space that cannot be claimed as the territory of any nation—has long been bound up with the defense of colonialism in international law. The European notion that the seas should be open for business—colonialism and slave trading included—has much to do with the history of the Atlantic. Indeed, the Atlantic Charter might be understood to continue that tradition (at least in the mind of Churchill), when it declared in its seventh point that any postwar peace "should enable all men to traverse the high seas and oceans without hindrance." In terms of questions of sovereignty, the Charter offers a double vision that is central to the modern international legal system: territorial sovereignty on land, navigational liberty at sea. Thus, it declares a commitment to a new world order of stable self-governing states from the unstable space of Westphalian exception where such nationalist principles do not apply, as if the delimitations of policed state borders only make sense against the unbounded backdrop of international waters. These are liquid promises for littoral ends.[6]

As we have seen, colonial and dependent peoples drew different conclusions about sovereignty and self-government from the Atlantic Charter than those originally intended by Churchill, and perhaps even by Roosevelt. However, like so many other European and American declarations of rights grounded in Enlightenment principles of human dignity and liberty, the fluid nature of the concepts must eventually overspill their container. We might think about this spillage in terms of the oceanic characteristic of drift, the tendency of ideas to flow and change as they move through space and time, but especially in the fluid context of the sea. If it is true, as Blum maintains, that "modes of oceanic thought are themselves predicated on relations whose unfixed, ungraspable contours are ever in multi-dimensional flux" (2013, 151), it is also true that normative principles have oceanic qualities that will themselves produce relations that are unfixed and in flux—position(alitie)s that cannot be pinned down once and for all. Such multidimensional flux can be seen in the slippage between rhetorical intention and tactical usage in Churchill's desire to reduce the Atlantic principles to a geography that covered only Europe (in order not to jeopardize the British Empire) and Roosevelt's politically canny extension of the promise of self-determination to "all peoples" everywhere if one takes an ocean view of international law. In that sense, the Atlantic Charter and, probably more importantly, the uses that colonized peoples made of it globalized an idea of the "Atlantic" as the name of normative principles about dignity, democracy, and freedom. In the process, what was originally framed as a geopolitical alliance became an imaginary ideal; imperial geography turned into anti-imperial aspiration.

If, in the middle of the twentieth century, the Atlantic could imply a promise of self-determination and freedom, the subsequent North Atlantic domination of the terms of its fulfillment and denial in the Global South would ultimately turn much of the South Atlantic into a region of resistance to European and North American imperialism. One set of questions that our collection addresses pertains to that history: What does the South Atlantic imply? What does it imply for peoples around the South Atlantic, and what does it imply for peoples of the Global South? If the "Atlantic" was an ideal that seemed to belong first and foremost to the North Atlantic, is the South Atlantic also an idea or an ideal? Is it formed in response to North Atlantic domination of an Atlantic ideal—an ideal of self-determination that might, nonetheless, be said to belong properly to peoples of the South Atlantic who were often written out of Atlantic history, such as the negro slaves of the Haitian Revolution of 1791–1803, who successfully revolted against their island masters, the French, the British, and the Spanish, as C. L. R. James famously detailed in *The Black Jacobins* in 1938? And what does a focus on the South Atlantic imply about Atlantic studies itself? Is it a new formation, or does it return us to a "longer, more multi-ethnic, and more genuinely international" mode of Atlantic history pursued by C. L. R. James, W. E. B. DuBois, and others—rejoining a discontinuous history that, as David Armitage notes, was "overlooked" by NATO-centric historians such as R. R. Palmer, who failed even to register the Haitian Revolution in his tome *The Age of Democratic Revolutions* (Armitage 2002, 14–15)? As the essays in our volume suggest, there can probably be no definitive or single answer to these questions, since the Atlantic has been imagined from various perspectives in the Global South for a very long time.

Politics of Liquid

Asking after the promises and prospects of a South Atlantic, or of an Atlantic viewed from the Global South, raises other questions about the boundaries and limits of such a geographical and imaginary formation. The Atlantic Charter was couched in rhetorically unbounded terms intended, however, to apply only to a narrow part of the human population. The historical ebb and flow of the category of "all peoples" in the Atlantic Charter (its extension to and withdrawal from shores beyond the North Atlantic) evinces something of the peculiar fluidity of universalizing categories in international law, what Belizean legal scholar, Edward Laing, calls the Charter's "flexible constitutional essence" (quoted in Borgwardt 2007, 44). No matter how "essential" the fluidity of international law may be, we must not lose sight of the fact that the Charter's principles were flexed by the political and moral pressure that colonial peoples put on it and the strategic rhetorical uses they made of it. In a sense, the anticolonial claims made in terms of the principles of the Atlantic Charter reveal what Judith Butler describes as "the promising ambivalence of the norm," the fluid nature of apparently stable universal categories that makes them the objects of politics (Butler's italics, 1997, 91); in turn, the Atlantic itself becomes what Azikwe called a "sea of international politics," both a contested geographical space and an ideal to be fought for.

The history of the waves of political expansion and retraction of the ground and water that the Atlantic Charter might cover is pertinent for thinking about who belongs to the South Atlantic, who is part of it, to whom the term applies? Who might use the term? Indeed, since history is itself a field of contest, "whose Atlantic are we talking about?" (Boelhower 2008, 97). These are both ideological and practical questions about the approach (or approaches) that scholars might take to study the South Atlantic; they are also historical and political questions that have been answered in different ways from different locations. Keeping with the postwar period, we can take the example of a South Atlantic Treaty Organization, the idea of which, "despite being pronounced dead on so many occasions, . . . has simply refused to die," as Andrew Hurrell wrote in 1983 in the wake of the Malvinas/Falklands war (1983, 179). From the mid-1950s through the end of the Cold War, there were multiple efforts by military and political leaders to initiate a South Atlantic pact (on the model of NATO) that would include some combination of Argentina, Brazil, Chile, Great Britain, Uruguay, the United States, and South Africa. Calls for negotiations, especially by the apartheid government (in part to rehabilitate its pariah international status), increased over the 1960s and '70s in response to a growing perception among some of the countries that, as a vice admiral of the South African navy put it in an interview in Rio de Janeiro in 1976, "The Communists are turning the area into a Soviet lake" (quoted in Hurrell 1983, 181). The anticommunist SATO effort to reclaim the "inland sea of Western Civilization" (Hoffman 1945, 25) never materialized, because, although it involved only a few nations of the Southern

Cone and South Africa, "the interests and perceptions of the countries involved are so divergent that it is hard to envisage any kind of closer more tightly-knit system of South Atlantic defence" (Hurrell 1983, 192).

In 1986, a more comprehensive vision of the region was given effect in the "Declaration of a Zone of Peace and Co-operation in the South Atlantic," sponsored by Brazil and passed by the UN General Assembly. Among other things, the Declaration called for international respect of the "sovereignty, independence, and territorial integrity of every State therein," and insisted on "the elimination of apartheid and the attainment of self-determination and independence by the peoples of Namibia."[7] The idea of a fuller South Atlantic alliance was revived in the twenty-first century, picking up some of the dropped threads of the earlier SATO efforts, but spinning them to other ends. In 2006, the first of a series of Africa–South America (ASA) summits met in Abuja, Nigeria, to foster South-South cooperation on economic, social, political and technical fronts across the South Atlantic. Having called for a South Atlantic Treaty Organization to counter NATO, Hugo Chávez hosted the second summit in Venezuela in 2009. The Nueva Esparta Declaration that emerged from that meeting stressed "the deeply historical and cultural ties" between South America and Africa, noting in particular "the active participation of Afro-descendant population in the development of South America as well as the contribution of South American countries to the consolidation of political independence and development on the African continent."[8] These more recent efforts to construct a South Atlantic alliance based on common historical and cultural ties and on mutual circumoceanic political and economic interests parallel developments in the various fields of Atlantic studies, which also have moved toward a more holistic understanding of the region.

Drift of History

The history of Atlantic studies is itself a story of fluidity and drift. The chauvinism of much Anglophone Atlantic history that tilted the topic toward the north for half a century effectively repeated Churchill's reduction of the Atlantic and its history to a story of European peoples on either side of the North Atlantic. The subsequent global rhetorical expansion of the "Atlantic" to a set of principles encompassing "all the men in all the lands" also tracks more recent movements in Atlantic history. One effect of writing the history of the "Atlantic Community" as the progressive realization of liberal principles of good governance in nations around the (North) Atlantic basin was, as we have seen, to relegate the histories of other peoples and other Atlantics to minor factors and bit parts in a glorious European maritime history. As Jorge Cañizares-Esguerra and Benjamin Breen have noted, "such studies merely repackage narratives of American and British exceptionalism against a world stage where other actors appear in a shadowy and undifferentiated guise" (2013, 599). In the name of an oceanic region, NATO-centric histories created a myth of the Atlantic "dominated by a handful of Europeans," obfuscating the roles that "Africans, Amerindians, Creoles of the New World, poor Europeans, and women of all groups" played in "the creation and shaping of the Atlantic World" (Falola and Roberts 2008, x). Indeed, even the recent turn to world systems theory in Atlantic history and transatlantic American literary studies has tended (at its worst) to reinforce the cultural, political, economic, and academic superiority of the Euro-American North Atlantic. Thus, the dominant English-language histories of the region have obscured the roles that other European empires played in the modern history of the Atlantic, at the same time that they rendered invisible other Anglophone histories from below.

In 1993, when Paul Gilroy suggested in *The Black Atlantic: Modernity and Double Consciousness* that "cultural historians could take the Atlantic as one single, complex unit of analysis," he was proposing a subaltern perspective and corrective to the white, Eurocentric, Christian myth of the inland sea of Western Civilization (1993, 15). The influential concept of a "Black Atlantic" opened the field of Atlantic studies to the South by demonstrating the centrality of the slave trade, the African diaspora, and transatlantic black intellectual exchanges and political alliances to any understanding of the "Atlantic World." Yet, even that South was largely situated in the North, around the triangular systems of trade among Europe, North America/Caribbean, and Africa above the equator. Indeed, Gilroy's heuristic of the Black Atlantic that sought to describe a single "system of cultural exchanges" (1993, 14) was itself totalizing—perhaps strategically so. Thus, Gilroy's Black Atlantic was, as Chinua Achebe once quipped (after Hobbes) about history in the English crown colonies, "nasty, British, and short" (1990, 146). It was primarily Anglophonic (not exactly stereophonic, as Gilroy wanted), and it didn't extend geographically to South America or Southern Africa.

Pointing to these limitations in the introduction to a recent collection seeking to open up Black Atlantic studies by expanding it beyond the experience of slavery and its afterlife to include different forms of diaspora, Yogita Goyal underscores the way Gilroy's paradigm "replicated the problematic exclusion of Africa from modernity" (2014, vi); and she argues that in its wake "many scholars in black diaspora studies replicate this omission and continue to read the Atlantic as primarily referring to the movement of people, ideas and objects between Britain and the United States" (ibid).[9] The powerful influence of Gilroy's model may also have helped to keep other colonial and postcolonial histories of the Atlantic World—particularly those from the South Atlantic—from registering in a broader Anglo-American oceanic imagination outside the academy. Indeed, in Henry Louis Gates Jr.'s 2011 book *Black in Latin America*, a companion to a PBS television series by the same name, the famous scholar of African American literature and culture voiced what he imagined would be the surprise of U.S. readers and viewers to learn that many more Africans were transported as slaves to South America than to North, and therefore that there is a long shared history of Black culture and politics that spans the entire ocean: "Between 1502 and 1866, 11.2 million Africans survived the dreadful Middle Passage . . . . only 450,000 arrived in the United States. . . . So, in one sense, the major 'African American Experience,' as it were, unfolded not in the United States as those of us caught in the embrace of what we might think of as 'African American Exceptionalism' might have thought" (Gates 2011, 2). That finding Africa in Latin America (or Latin America in Africa) might come as a surprise speaks powerfully to the North Atlantic Anglophone bias in Atlantic knowledge production (and global knowledge production more generally), since the pursuit of European imperial expansion and the transatlantic slave trade have left historical traces of recorded traffic—of people, goods, ideas, and culture—across, around, and under the entire Atlantic for nearly five centuries.

Gates's *Black in Latin America* is a relative latecomer to the rapidly growing body of Diasporic, Transatlantic, Afro-Latino, and Lusophone Black Atlantic studies that have picked up traces left by the slave trade and expanded the racial compass to reorient our sense of the ocean. To speak only to the last category, the work of Lusophone historian Luiz Felipe de Alencastro, who contributes the opening chapter to this collection, has in the past decade and a half inaugurated a rediscovery of the Portuguese (and occasionally Spanish and Dutch) South Atlantic. De Alencastro's *O trato dos viventes* (2000) charts the major traffic in enslaved humans (along with silver, tobacco, spirits, missionaries, soldiers, and colonial administrators) that crisscrossed what was then known as the "Ethiopic Ocean" from Rio de Janeiro, Bahia, Pernambuco, Buenos Aires, Luanda, and Benguela between 1550 and 1850. While the conditions that led to this massive enforced movement of people shifted rapidly following the closure of the last slave trading routes in 1850, enabling a remarkable kind of amnesia about the Portuguese South Atlantic in the century that followed, legacies of this history remain even as different kinds of South-South relations develop in the second half of the twentieth century (De Alencastro 2015, 9).[10] Such macro-level work is complemented by studies like James H. Sweet's (2013) portrait of the African healer Domingos Alvarez, whose person, ideas and influence followed Atlantic currents from Dahomey to Recife, Rio and finally to Portugal.

More widely, since the publication of Gilroy's *Black Atlantic*, there has been a proliferation of differently colored Atlantics that have taken advantage of the historical and conceptual opening created by his seminal book. Thus, a "Green Atlantic" of the Irish diaspora intertwines with the Black Atlantic (O'Neill and Lloyd, 2009); the "White Atlantic" of the old NATO-centric histories is now said to be "a self-conscious field of study rather than the defining model for all other Atlantic histories" (Armitage 2002, 15); and, there are multiple "Red" Atlantics: the "Red Atlantic" of Indigenous peoples described by Jace Weaver and others (Weaver 2014); the "Red Peril" of the "Soviet lake" feared by proponents of the anti-communist South Atlantic Cold War coalition; and Peter Linebaugh and Marcus Rediker's ocean-based history of capitalism, colonization, and resistance in *The Many-Headed Hydra: Sailors, Slaves, Commoners, and the Hidden History of the Revolutionary Atlantic* that Armitage dubbed "red Atlantic History" (2002, 15; 2001). These color-coded Atlantics, like their linguistic-focused counterparts—the Lusophone already mentioned, Hispanophone, Iberian, and French Atlantics—"push back the boundaries of (trans)atlantic studies," as Thea Pitman and Andy Stafford have noted in oceanic terms, but "they are still limited by an essentially monolingual/monocultural and, at times, monoracial, interest in the field" (2009, 200).

Gilroy's account was not the first subaltern approach to the Atlantic that attempted to integrate the dispersed histories of the African diaspora into a single system. In 1968, historian Philip D. Curtin proposed the idea of the "South Atlantic System" to describe the circular trade among Africa, the Americas, and Europe in which African slave labor in the Americas produced commodities for consumption in Europe (1968, 191). "Social and economic development on the tropical shores of the Atlantic," Curtin maintained, "was a single process, regardless of the theoretically self-contained empires of mercantilist Europe" (1968, 190). The South Atlantic System of colonial exploitation and slavery, as Allison Games has recently explained, may have given the oceanic region "a coherence for almost four hundred years, creating a viable unit of analysis" (2006, 747–748), but that unified space is cross-cut by the intersecting, overlapping, intertwined, complementary, and exclusionary practices of the European empires that competed and colluded for dominance in various Atlantic locations. Thus, as Games also notes, "attempts to write a Braudelian Atlantic history—one that includes and connects the entire region—remain elusive, driven in part by methodological impediments, by the real disjunctions that characterized the Atlantic's historical and geographic components, by the disciplinary divisions that discourage historians from speaking to and writing for each other, and by the challenge of finding a vantage that is not rooted in any single place" (Games 2006, 741). Like many recent scholars of Atlantic history, Games raises central questions about the region that are appropriate for thinking about oceanicity more generally: Is the Atlantic one unit or many? Does it share a single history, or do the plurality of languages, nations, peoples, and empires mean that Atlantic histories are necessarily plural and discontinuous?

Across Divided Waters

While claiming to describe the coherence of a single "Atlantic Community," mid-twentieth century Atlantic history's collusion with Cold War NATO power politics effectively reinscribed old imperial divisions and subdivisions in the oceanic unit that Fernand Braudel himself saw operating in the sixteenth century. In other words, telling a partial and patriotic story of a particular "human unit" of the Atlantic did not finally produce a convincing history of the ocean as a single system; instead, the Atlantic was redivided into the "several Atlantics" that Braudel identified in the age of European exploration and empire, both as subjects of history and as geopolitical regions.[11] "These different Atlantics, linked to national [and imperial] histories, have had no difficulty in finding historians," Braudel noted (1995, 224). Indeed, although Atlantic histories "repeatedly emphasize themes of interconnection, circulation, encounter, and exchange" they still tend to be restricted by "national or linguistic boundaries": "Scholarship on British, Dutch, French, Spanish, and Portuguese Atlantics follow separate trajectories" (Cañizares-Esguerra and Breen 2013, 597). And, only recently has growing awareness of those other national histories of imperial Atlantics effectively managed to relativize the "White Atlantic" story in scholarship produced in the North Atlantic.

However much the idea of a "South Atlantic System" might accurately capture a singular history of the Atlantic, the legacy of rival empires that separated the sea into discrete, if overlapping, imperial geographies remains with us. The old imperial records and resources are themselves distributed in archives scattered around and under the ocean. Like the materials upon which they work, scholars of Atlantic (and more especially South Atlantic) histories and cultures themselves confront multiple centrifugal forces that scatter their efforts: They are often isolated from one another by barriers of their respective colonial languages and distributed among academic departments that are also divided along the linguistic lines of the old European empires (departments of Spanish, Portuguese, French, English, Dutch, not to mention the native languages of Africa and the Americas) and the regional rubrics of Cold War area studies (African, Latin American, or Caribbean studies centers, for example). Thus, although no part of "the Atlantic world contains a past that can be said to belong neatly and exclusively to one or another empire"—since all "Atlantics are the product of multiple 'entangled histories,'" as Cañizares-Esguerra and Breen argue (2013, 600)—the fluid study of the ocean continues to be channeled by littoral geopolitical divisions and linguistic barriers. In this regard, the Atlantic generally, and the South Atlantic more narrowly, might be said to be simultaneously one unit and many, "a space of dispersion, conjunction, distribution, contingency, heterogeneity, and of intersecting and stratified lines and images—in short, a field of strategic possibilities in which the Oceanic order holds all together in a common but highly fluid space," as William Boelhower has argued in his influential 2008 proposal for a "new Atlantic Studies Matrix" (2008, 92–93).

The Global South Atlantic brings together scholars working in Lusophone, Francophone, Hispanic, and Anglophone literary and cultural studies, as well as researchers working in other languages (such as Arabic) that are important components of a Global South Atlantic. Most of the authors are comparatists, working across linguistic and disciplinary boundaries to trace obscured or overlooked sociohistorical linkages and cultural circulations among Latin America, Africa, and the Caribbean. Despite numerous concerted efforts over the past five hundred years to bring the continents of Africa and South America and the Caribbean Islands into purposeful contact with each other—for example, the Portuguese monopoly over the southern slave trade, British schemes for the South Seas Company and for acquiring the Spanish *Asiento*, transoceanic abolitionism, the thwarted South Atlantic Treaty Organization, Tricontinentalism, the OPEC extension to South America and multilateral trade agreements—the South Atlantic has generally not emerged as a particularly coherent social, political, economic, or cultural configuration in world history or geopolitics. Further, despite the rise in oceanic, hemispheric, and regional studies in the past decade, and again despite the institutional formations of transatlantic, Black Atlantic, and diaspora studies, the South Atlantic has also not often emerged as a particularly potent conceptual or analytical configuration in literary, historical or cultural studies (with Lusophone South Atlantic studies an illustrative exception). Yet, each of the chapters in this volume demonstrates one of the many important ways in which people, governments, political movements, social imaginaries, cultural artifacts, goods, and markets do (or sometimes do not) travel the South Atlantic. Together they help to reveal a complex network of cultural, material, and social relations that begins to make visible a multitextured version of a South Atlantic world, even as they also consider the larger structures of knowledge and power that enable or inhibit these flows and may have kept an organized geopolitical space from coming into being or an oceanic orientation from capturing the popular imagination.

One More Atlantic?

The South Atlantic is not singular, although it may be one; it is also not simply the Black Atlantic extended below the equator. Given the multiplicity of overlapping, entangled Atlantic worlds that make up the cultures and histories of the South Atlantic, no single edited collection could exhaust the possibilities and resources for comparative research across the ocean, even one that brings together an array of scholars working in (and across) multiple disciplines and languages as we do. Indeed, any oceanic study must come to terms with the unfixed and, finally, unfixable boundaries of its topic, and our volume is no exception, offering an inherently partial vision of an oceanic space that can never be seen in its totality, but may still be glimpsed from certain vantages. Collectively, we hope to make visible some of the many ways and many forms in which something called the South Atlantic might be said to appear on the conceptual and analytical horizon, as well as to think about what such oceanic organizations of knowledge make it possible to apprehend that otherwise remains dissolved in separate languages, histories, literatures, disciplines, and archives.

While most of the studies in this volume focus specifically on cultural, social, and intellectual transactions and interactions among Africa, Latin America, and the Caribbean—in other words, they respect the cartographic limits of a region initially known as the "Ethiopic Sea" and now called the "South Atlantic"—we have prefixed "Global" to the "South Atlantic" in our title in order not only to signal that we are talking about the Atlantic of the Global South, but also to recognize that the South Atlantic itself has been imagined (and unimagined) from multiple global positions over the course of modern history. "Global" here is not the global of globalization. It does not intend towards the homogenization ordinarily signified by globalization—the integration of the South Atlantic into a singular (if uneven) system of world capitalism (although that is certainly part of its history and configuration). Rather, the "Global" before "South Atlantic" points to the multiplicity of visions and versions of the Atlantic, most especially to those constructed from the Global South. In other words, just as the "South Atlantic" is both one and many, it is also nowhere and everywhere at the same time. Despite all of its global and varied reverberations, the term "South Atlantic" nonetheless designates a kind of historical impossibility (so far) that allows us to think about the social, economic, political, and cultural forces and contingencies that make certain geospecific configurations possible—the conditions that make space imaginable—as well as those that keep a regional orientation (or oceanic feeling) from materializing. Thus, "Global" in the title of the volume is also intended to point to the international, transregional nature of the connections and investments (material and intellectual) that might constitute a functional system of (imaginary) relations called the "South Atlantic." Such connections defy strict geopolitical descriptors as they move amphibiously between water and land, and well beyond the territorial boundaries of the states and seas that comprise the region.

Together, the essays in *The Global South Atlantic* work simultaneously from within two frameworks that we think are intertwined in order to pursue two allied goals: reframing Atlantic studies from the perspective of the Global South and identifying features and modes of South-South interactions that might be unique to South Atlantic studies as its own field. Indeed, one aspiration of the volume is to raise the profile of comparative work across the South Atlantic by demonstrating something of the range and richness of the issues and methods that researchers and teachers are currently pursuing. The essays also explore new models of comparative literary and historical practice for investigating what Françoise Lionnet and Shu-mei Shih (2005) called "minor transnationalisms" that we hope will encourage innovative future work by scholars interested in understanding multilingual relations around the South Atlantic and beyond, in order to challenge the NATO-centric assumptions that continue to dominate comparative and world literature and history today. This is, of course, part of a broader and flourishing discussion about deprovincializing the field of Comparative Literature and rerouting the work of comparison.[12]

Postcolonial, subaltern, and comparative ethnic and third-world cultural studies pioneered approaches and frameworks for studying South-South connections that oceanic, hemispheric, regional, and other transnational studies influential on comparative literature (among other humanities and social science disciplines) have taken up more recently. The impulse for those approaches was to challenge the North Atlantic hegemony, not just in geopolitics but also in intellectual and cultural production, that seemed always to route interactions among peoples and places in the Global South through economic and intellectual centers in the Global North. As Thea Pitman and Andy Stafford have noted, most studies of the Atlantic, even those interested in South-South connections, continue "to assert [or imply] that Europe is the essential mediating 'bridge' through which all transatlantic dialogue must pass" (2009, 200). Intellectual and cultural routings through Europe and North America are often inevitable, just as there are very few direct international flights between South America and Africa and digital communications between the two continents must still either pass through relay satellites or cables crossing the North Atlantic (most of which depart North America within miles of the sea site where Roosevelt and Churchill met, as they did in the 1940s).[13] Indeed, the two high-speed submarine digital cables planned to connect Latin America and Africa—the South Atlantic Express and the South Atlantic Cable System—have yet to be laid. Nevertheless, we think that "Europe might still be bracketed in transatlantic studies" (as many of our contributors do) by studying cases "where African and Latin, or African Americans have themselves deliberately sough to limit the role of Europe in their relationships with one another" (Pitman and Stafford 2009, 200).

There are many ways to organize an anthology of essays. For the sake of a kind of historical narrative trajectory intended to provide some bearing for readers who might be unfamiliar with the region, the chapters in *The Global South Atlantic* are ordered in a loose chronology according to the primary theme each author discusses. As we will detail, the essays grouped together in Part I primarily explore the South Atlantic as a unit forged (or attempted to be forged) through the key processes of colonialism, slavery, abolition, and strategic resource and territorial acquisition by European empires through the early twentieth century. The essays in Part II highlight efforts from the mid-twentieth century or what we might call Cold War modernity to make the region "stand for" something—be it anticommunism, socialist internationalism, third-world liberation, anti-imperialism, or (trans)racial and (trans)regional solidarity. Finally, the essays on contemporary works in Part III look toward the region's future by turning to these pasts.

That said, however, we are even more interested in other nonchronological rubrics that crosscut these essays. In particular, as noted early in this introduction, we wish to flag the problems and prospects of a (Global) South Atlantic understood as region and vision, structures that become legible through thoughtful and substantive acts of comparison. All of the essays collected here engage with the South Atlantic in both of these ways. They treat the South Atlantic as a region with specific distinguishing characteristics and histories of transoceanic interactions, even if none of them presume that the contours of such a unit are given in advance. They also show us, as Edward Said reminds us in *Orientalism* (1978), how regions are always constructed as much by others elsewhere as by anyone on the ground (so to speak), and exist not simply as geographical designations but as historical ideas that comprehend political and economic aspirations along with cultural, social, religious, and racial transactions and visions of solidarity and exclusion.

While toggling between region and vision in their mapping of the imbrications and entanglements of South Atlantic worlds, many of these essays also self-consciously reflect upon the methodology they use to do comparative literary and cultural studies across spaces that have traditionally been treated as incomparable.[14] This brings us back to our earlier categorization of the South Atlantic as the name of a methodological problem. As a discipline, comparative literature, and its traditional practices and points of comparison in "high culture" (which mostly meant Western Europe, but certainly not the "low" culture below the equator), emerged from the context of the nineteenth century's consolidation of the Westphalian nation-state arrangement in Europe. Thus, historically, "comparative literature assumes the existence of a number of states, each with its divergent character and aims" (Saussy 2006, 25), and, ostensibly, a single dominant national language. It was these divergences in language, character, and aims that enabled (even necessitated) acts of comparison in order to pursue national competition and cooperation among states along the Rhine. In other words, comparative literature developed out of riverine politics and land-based polities that understood imaginary state borders to mark the definitive differences that matter between peoples, societies, and cultures. Turning scholarly attention to configurations such as the South Atlantic that do not match the classic features of the Westphalian international order imagined and instituted on the model of (and from) Europe raises new challenges for comparatists and for comparative literature more generally. With that in mind, we want to highlight again the diversity of approaches taken by the authors in this volume for reading the traces of sometimes subtle and submerged networks of relation among peoples, histories, and cultures around the ocean. Each of the essays, in one way or another, wrestles with the Eurocentric legacy of comparative literature as the authors explore various methods that might make the South Atlantic visible as either (or both) a region or a vision and might also reinflect the purposes of comparison.

South Atlantic Imperial Geographies

The essays in Part I, "South Atlantic Imperial Geographies," explore multiple and overlapping configurations of South Atlantic worlds during the long period of European colonialism, the transatlantic slave trade, and abolitionism. Competing imperial interests and the various languages of commerce and culture mean that there is no single shared image or archive of the South Atlantic but rather a number of visions striving for hegemony (or sometimes liberation from imperial hegemony). Each of the essays in this section explores a distinct historical version of the South Atlantic, while reflecting on the difficulties of—and possible comparative methodologies for—reading the traces of histories whose fragmented archives are distributed around the ocean. Together, they begin to sketch a sense of the South Atlantic as what Laura Doyle (2014) has called an "inter-imperial" assemblage.

In "The African Slave Trade and the Construction of the Iberian Atlantic," Luiz Felipe de Alencastro shows in more detail how what we have already noted is the most significant South Atlantic empire to date—that constructed by the Portuguese from the sixteenth to nineteenth centuries—came together from the international trade in African slaves that depended on multidirectional traffic among Europe, Africa, and South America. Jaime Hanneken considers the historical force of an idea of the South Atlantic proffered by the influential disciples of San Simon. Her chapter, "A World Girded: Saint-Simonian Space and Race in the Nineteenth-Century Latin Transatlantic," identifies a nineteenth-century French prehistory for "Latin transatlantic" racial identity (*Latinité*) that emerged from a vision of a South Atlantic stretching from the Suez to the Panama canals, and which was taken up by Creole intellectuals as they tried to shape a "Latin America" out of Spain's New World colonies. Exploring a relatively neglected South Atlantic archive of eighteenth- and nineteenth-century Arab-Islamic slave narratives from the United States, England, Panama, and Senegambia, Jason Frydman traces the importance of Arabic literary forms on the development of Black Atlantic writing and the abolitionist movement in "Scheherazade in Chains: Arab-Islamic Genealogies of African Diasporic Literature." Finally, "Southern By

Degrees: Islands and Empires in the South Atlantic, the Indian Ocean, and the Subantarctic World," by the African literature and Indian Ocean scholar Isabel Hofmeyr, argues that the South Atlantic Ocean was an important, if underappreciated, site for negotiating and consolidating British empire, from the early era of the slave trade to the late scramble for Antarctica. Hofmeyr also maps a series of methodological models, including that of reading for islands and archipelagos, taken up in later chapters.

South Atlantic Cold War Modernities

Each chapter in Part II, "South Atlantic Cold War Modernities," examines a specific effort to forge South Atlantic connections, real and imaginary, beginning from the end of World War II and the simultaneous onset of decolonization and the Cold War. New visions of the South Atlantic, often with roots in pan-African ideologies or inspired by (or even frustrated by) Bandung, emerged during the era of decolonization to challenge the politics of imperial (and neoimperial) fragmentation that separated Latin America from Africa from the Caribbean in order to establish distinct spheres of influence. Through the efforts of various groups, from guerilla fighters to famed novelists and economic migrants, the South Atlantic was reimagined as a rich source of—rather than an oceanic barrier to—solidarity among peoples across the Global South (including African Americans) struggling against racism, colonialism, and the violence of Cold War geopolitics. Indeed, decolonization within the context of the Cold War made possible (if partially and temporarily) revolutionary visions of a South Atlantic where Southern solidarities drew together ideas and people, exchanging books and guns through material and intellectual networks that connected, for example, Santiago to Havana to Harlem to Algiers to Maputo and elsewhere. Such networks, of course, also prompted counter-articulations of authoritarian control and reassertions of empire, themselves visions (if sometimes contradictory) of the South Atlantic as the final watery battleground for "Western, Christian civilization."

In her essay "Beyond the Color Curtain: The Metonymic Color Politics of the Tricontinental and the (New) Global South," Anne-Garland Mahler looks at the South Atlantic as a generative thought-space for understanding how what we now call the "Global South" emerged from forms of solidarity imagined during the periods of decolonization and the Cold War, specifically through the revolutionary cultural production of the Tricontinental (and the journal of the same name) that launched in Cuba in 1966. In "South

Africa, Chile, and the Cold War: Reading the South Atlantic in Mark Behr's *The Smell of Apples*," Kerry Bystrom uses the appearance of a "fictional" Chilean general in a novel by a South African writer to explore a reactionary counterpoint to such revolutionary dreaming. She traces multilateral relationships among "pariah" states across the South Atlantic during the Cold War, which created a network through which repressive techniques and military materiel were exchanged between the Southern Cone of Latin America and the racist regimes of Southern Africa. Revealing the multiplicity of reactionary South Atlantics and illustrating how anti-imperialist and imperialist ideologies can dissolve into each other, Oscar Hemer examines the event that probably brought the South Atlantic to more people's attention in the Global North than any other: the Malvinas/Falklands war (1982). "Islands in Distress: Making Sense of the Malvinas/Falklands War" shows how the islands became projection surfaces for two competing but uncannily doubled visions of nationalism and a nostalgia for South Atlantic empire by reading novels on the topic written in the United Kingdom and Argentina during and after the short war.

If the first three chapters in this section focus on excavating political projects of the Cold War period, then the last two chapters bring to the fore the question of what literary South Atlantic solidarities look like against the background of entangled imperial, neoimperial, and homegrown violence that marks the ocean's history in this era. In "Orientalism and the Narration of Violence in the Mediterranean Atlantic: Gabriel García Márquez and Elias Khoury," Christina E. Civantos traces some of the intertextual relationships between *Majamaʾ al-asrar* (*The Collection of Secrets*), by the Lebanese novelist Elias Khoury, and García Márquez's *Crónica de una muerte anunciada* (*Chronicle of a Death Foretold*), in order to explore the long intertwined histories of Arabic and Spanish cultures in Latin America and the kind of transnational writing strategies novelists forged to respond to structural exclusions of the twentieth century shared across the South Atlantic and the Mediterranean. Taking a more formalist approach, Magalí Armillas-Tisyera considers what it means to write (across) the South Atlantic by identifying a "constellation" of literary devices that connect novels about dictators from different, though interrelated, imperial, geographical, and cultural contexts in Africa and Latin America. "Marvelous Autocrats: Disrupted Realisms in the Dictator Novel of the South Atlantic" shows how the idea of the South Atlantic as a space of dictatorships and banana republics was contested on the ground by literary experimentation and transoceanic influence.

Global South Atlantic Futures

The essays in Part III, "Global South Atlantic Futures," examine how contemporary artists and societies located in the South Atlantic grapple with the legacies of their geopolitical, cultural, and economic positioning—including not only histories of colonialism and slavery but also those of Southern solidarity and socialist internationalism. They also ask what these legacies mean for a future partially constituted in (and against) global neoliberalization. Globalization and the consolidation of neoliberal capitalism in the late twentieth century may have flattened time by expanding their reach, but they have also reinforced old divisions across the South Atlantic while creating new routes of South-South interaction. Coming on the heels of the apparent defeat of the "non-aligned" and Tricontinental movements earlier in the twentieth century, these transformations call to crisis many of the national (and transnational) narratives that shaped societies during the independence struggles and in the postcolonial eras, and trouble linear understandings of chronology and progress or failure,[15] opening space for future-inflected reassessments of the past that might continue to challenge political orthodoxies and to reinvigorate or reinvent the meaning of "minor" South-South flows. These reevaluations demand new modes of scholarly thought on the oceanic methods required to make sense of the multiple geographical and temporal frameworks, scales, and structures of feeling and interaction that make up the historically incoherent (and still largely invisible) space of the South Atlantic. These essays thus echo and expand methodological suggestions posed in earlier sections, including theorizing islands, tracking what Said called "traveling theory" (1983, 226), such as his own idea of Orientalism, and paying close attention to formal concerns—in the process often calling for new ways of understanding temporal as well as geographical interconnections and disjunctions.

In "Postwar Politics in *O Herói* and *Kangamba*," Lanie Millar examines the Cuba-Angola axis of the South Atlantic, considering two important twenty-first-century films about Cuban assistance during the Angolan War of Independence—a major theater of Third World solidarity in the era of decolonization—and asks whether and how such anticolonial internationalism should be recuperated as a template for resistance to global capital in the present. Luís Madureira takes a different approach in an insightful and detailed close reading of a novel from Cape Verde, an important nexus for so many South Atlantic crossings. In "Adrift between Neoliberalism and the Revolution: Cape Verde and the South Atlantic in Germano Alemeida's *Eva*," Madureira considers the tension between memories of transnational anticolonial resistance and the reality of national postcolonial politics as they play out in terms of individual and communal Lusotropical identity formation in the former Portuguese colony. Switching the island standpoint into the Caribbean and looking at how novelist and performance artist Rita Indiana Hernandéz responds to anti-Haitian sentiment and legislation in the Dominican Republic, in "A Sweet Sweet Tale of Terror: Rita Indiana Hernández Writes the Dominican Republic into the Global South Atlantic," Maja Horn constructs a vision of the South Atlantic wrestling with the ongoing repercussions of the Haitian revolution and the legacies of a colonial order underpinned by the still-racialized transnational sugar economy. And finally, Waïl S. Hassan looks at one of the most widely circulating Southern genres, the *telenovela* or Latin American soap opera, to probe contemporary anxieties of transatlantic Brazilian identity as the country emerges as a global economic powerhouse able to reconnect with historical routes that link it to populations across the South Atlantic and beyond. "Carioca Orientalism: Morocco in the Imaginary of a Brazilian *Telenovela*" follows the plot and South Atlantic circulation of the hit drama *O Clono* in order to show how the series transforms classic Orientalism to refashion identities in the Global South.

As neoliberal globalization remakes the world, the 2014 launch of a new publication, *Atlantic Currents: An Annual Report on Wider Atlantic Perspectives and Patterns*, with joint cooperation of the German Marshall Fund of the United States and the OCP Policy Center of Morocco, might suggest that the South Atlantic is a region whose time has come.[16] The essays in that first volume focus primarily on topics such as mineral and agricultural trade around the region, its energy production potential, security possibilities and concerns, the rise of new regional partnerships and dynamics. The volume also contains an overview of "Atlanticism in the 21st Century," by Ian O. Lesser and Karim El Aynaoui. This overview of historical approaches to (and blindnesses of) traditional transatlantic analysis largely follows Lesser's 2010 report to the Brussels Forum on "Southern Atlanticism: Geopolitics and Strategy for the Other Half of the Atlantic Rim," in which he notes (among other things) that a turn to the South Atlantic as a geopolitical concern is, in fact, "a rediscovery of historic patterns" (2010, 4), of, that is, earlier imperial formations of the sorts we have been reviewing in this introduction and that become visible in other forms in each of the chapters of *The Global South Atlantic.* Missing from the German Marshall Fund accounts, not surprisingly, is any deep discussion or understanding of the region as a social, cultural, or intellectual unit (as something more than a potential distributed economic or resource market), and although both the 2014 and 2010 reports are interested in South-South connections, those are given importance primarily in the ways in which "the Other Half" has implications for countries in the Global North.

Our essays here are interested in South Atlanticisms that are likely to remain invisible to these sorts of prospecting studies. Indeed, we believe that the South Atlanticisms that emerge from this collection contribute to the "rediscovery" of histories and sociocultural relations of the South Atlantic as a region and vision that have been suppressed by old imperial interests that erase their own histories, like the ocean rolling over the wake behind a ship. We further hope that these South Atlanticisms might yet be inhospitable to the forces, purposes, and imperatives of the new historical Northern alliances that are turning their attention to oceanic areas and their histories. For these reasons in particular, we suggest that the versions of the South Atlantic offered here are the ones whose time has indeed come—or come again.

NOTES

1. Atlantic Charter, August 14, 1941. Available: http://avalon.law.yale.edu/wwii/atlantic.asp

2. On Bandung, see Romulo (1965) and Tan and Acharya (2008). The General Declaration, resolutions, and executive statements of the Tricontinental Conference are published in issues of the *Tricontinental* from 1966 to 1968.

3. Indeed, Braudel describes the "human unit" of the Atlantic (in comparison to the Mediterranean) as "one of the most vigorous of the present day world" (1995, 231).

4. Borgwardt suggestively describes this process, which is not unusual in the "customary law approach" to international law, as "a way of laundering the Atlantic Charter's status as international law" (2007, 41).

5. The scene is replete with poetic ironies: The transatlantic allies make a joint statement (that is not quite law) about a future commitment to the rule of law from the seas, which have historically been considered lawless, or at least beyond the reach of most national law.

6. The way "liquid promises" are made for littoral ends is even clearer when we consider the effects of the Truman Doctrine as documented by Elizabeth DeLoughrey; the myth of "freedom of the seas" gets quickly revealed as fraudulent in the Cold War "scramble for the seas" in which states claim 200 nautical miles from the shore as national territory to be used mainly for military (or economic) ends (2010, 705).

7. http://www.un.org/documents/ga/res/41/a41r011.htm. See also Davilevicz Pereira.

8. http://www.voltairenet.org/article162310.html

9. See Goyal's (2014) introduction to the special issue "Africa and the Black Atlantic." Goyal's discussion of Gilroy's omission of Africa from the Black Atlantic builds on an earlier seminal discussion by Simon Gikandi in his 1996 "Introduction: Africa, The Diaspora and the Promise of Modernity" (Goyal vi). Goyal, of course, is not the only scholar engaged in opening up the Black Atlantic model; another collection that came out in 2014 is Monica Popescu, Cedric Tolliver, and Julie-Ann Tolliver's "Alternative Solidarities," published as a special issue of the *Journal of Postcolonial Writing*. This collection also aims to decenter slavery as a defining paradigm in black diaspora studies and, focusing on the Cold War era, underscores "the internationalist political engagements and expansive geographic reach of the black diaspora which are often left unexamined in scholarly treatments of black expressive cultures nurtured along the different shores of the black Atlantic" (Tolliver 2014, 380).

10. Alencastro argues that with the end of the slave trade and the shift from sailing to steam vessels, "the close of the South Atlantic network generated a defining geopolitical transformation in 1850. Unlike other maritime networks within trading areas such as the Caribbean or the Indian Ocean, the South Atlantic bilateral exchanges did not unravel progressively in the face of new competitors or resume with different commodities. Rather, these maritime exchanges broke down abruptly and vanished under British diplomatic pressure and naval coercion. From then onward, 'Ethiopic Ocean' turned into an outdated name as the new international division of labor precluded the south-south trade" (2015, 9). The astonishing swiftness of this network's erasure can be seen in 1883 British nautical guide describing the oceanic basin where commerce flourished only fifty years earlier in the following terms: "A large portion of coast lying within the Southern tropics, and the absolutely barren nature of its eastern side, render the commerce in this vast area of water of very small importance compared with other seas of equal magnitude" (cited ibid).

11. Indeed, actual material efforts to break out of the divide-and-conquer regionalization— that is, to establish transnational, transoceanic, and transregional solidarity—were met with strong resistance by the United States and the much of the Global North.

12. See, for instance, Gayatri Chakravorty Spivak's *Death of a Discipline* (2003) and the essays collected in *Comparison: Theories, Approaches, Uses*, especially Shu-mei Shih's "Comparison as Relation" (2013). Following Martinican Édouard Glissant's poetic theory of relation, Shih develops what could be seen as a more robust version of "minor transnationalism," in the form of "relational comparison" that brings "into relation terms that have traditionally

been pushed apart from each other due to certain interests, such as the European exceptionalism that undergirds Eurocentrism" (79). In that regard, we might say that Latin America and Africa have been pushed apart less by the movement of tectonic plates and the inundation of an ocean than by the Eurocentrism of scholarly disciplines, economic globalization, and geopolitics.

13. See the Submarine Cable Map: http://www.submarinecablemap.com.

14. David Armitage has attempted to systemize the methodological approaches to oceanic accounts in the field of history with a "three-fold typology": "*Circum*-Atlantic history," which considers the ocean as a Braudelian unit; "*Trans*-Atlantic history," which puts two or more places around the Atlantic into a comparative framework; and "*Cis*-Atlantic history," which focuses on a single "national or regional history within an Atlantic context" (2002, 17). The approaches that the comparative literature and cultural studies scholars have taken in our volume do not fit neatly Armitage's typology, which perhaps raises interesting questions about the differences between "culture" and "history" as the subject matter for mapping the human relations and interactions of oceanic regions.

15. We think here of Jennifer Wenzel's (2009) argument that "failed" anticolonial movements have afterlives that continue to animate current struggles, creating a field of time that is discontinuous and continuous at once.

16. It is worth noting, given the shape of Atlantic studies to date, that the German Marshall Fund was established by Germany to recognize the assistance that the Marshall Plan provided across the North Atlantic after World War II. Thus, it was historically part of the structures of political, military, and economic cooperation that consolidated the NATO-centrism of the late twentieth century.

PART I

South Atlantic Imperial Geographies

The African Slave Trade and the Construction of the Iberian Atlantic

Luiz Felipe de Alencastro

Scholarly studies of the colonization of the Americas generally focus on the interactions among Europe, the Americas, and Native American peoples. Africans and black peoples tend to appear unconnected from the Atlantic networks, since they were already part of American colonial enclaves. Ignoring the African slave trade in the Americas and the growing predominance of African descendants in most of the New World enclaves, such historical neglect reflects the old idea that the conquest of the Americas was merely an extension of the Reconquista of the Iberian Peninsula, part of reestablishing Iberian social practices and institutions throughout Spain and Portugal. Indeed, the idea that Iberian feudalism "survived" in the structures and practices of agriculture in Latin America (a subject that consumed much of the historical debate in the late twentieth century) gave rise to new terms, such as "semi-feudalism" and "Hispano-American neo-feudalism."[1] Most recently, this theme was revived by Jérôme Baschet, who has proposed the concept of "late feudalism" in order to describe the general shape of the Iberian conquest and domination of the New World.[2]

However, another interpretive approach to the history of colonization in the Americas, as old as the first, regards modern slavery and the slave trade as creating a new historical framework that broke with the Iberian past and inaugurated Atlantic modernity. In fact, this idea was already sketched out in 1554 in the commentaries that Bartolomé de las Casas added to his *Brevísima relación de la destrucción de las Indias* (1552). Considering the first Portuguese discoveries in Africa and Asia, as described by Gomes Eanes de Zurara in *Cronica da Guiné* (1453–60) and by João de Barros in *Décadas da Ásia* (1552–53), Las Casas revisited the subject of the conquest of the Canary Islands. He refuted Portuguese arguments that presented their pillaging along the coast of West Africa as a "just war," and he had withering criticism for the Crown and Portuguese slave traders who "fill the world with Black slaves . . . [until] our Indies are overflowing with them" (1989, 114–125; Esponera Cerdán 2003).[3] According to Las Casas, the extermination of the native inhabitants of the Canaries, the Guanchos, and the routing of the slave trade through the islands set up a transitional process that would lead to the mass deportation of Africans to the Americas.

Modern Slavery and Antislavery in the South Atlantic

While Iberian royal regulations were generally restrictive when it came to the enslavement of Native Americans in the sixteenth and seventeenth centuries, royal and papal justifications for the legitimacy of slavery itself and of the slave trade were in place even before discovery of the Americas.[4] *Romanus Pontifex*, issued by Pope Nicolas V in 1455, offered the first evangelist justifications for a Lusitanian empire overseas and a Portuguese monopoly on the slave trade. The papal bull was proposed by the king of Portugal, Alfonso V, soon after Europeans arrived at the mouth of the Senegal River and made contact with non-Muslim black Africans. Indeed, the Spiritain missionary scholar António Brásio has described the document as the "Magna Carta" of the Portuguese Empire (1959, 147). In it, the King's right to a monopoly over the slave trade was presented as compensation for the costs incurred by the Portuguese in propagating the Catholic faith throughout Africa, Asia, and the Americas. The papal bull also expounded the doctrine of the complementarity of Christian evangelization and the slave trade that was later systemized in the treatise *De Justo Imperio Lusitanorum Asiatico* (1625), written by Father Serafim de Freitas in response to Dutch jurist Hugo Grotius's *Mare Liberum* (1608) (1983, 1:216, 364, 367, and 2:94). The slave trade and slavery were said to be justified insofar as the pagans, captured along the African coasts or born in captivity, were taken to Portugal and "converted to the Catholic Faith" (Brásio 1952, 277–286).[5]

The evangelical argument for the slave trade articulated in *Romanus Pontifex* was reprised by numerous propagandists at the end of the sixteenth century. Around the time when King Philip II of Spain occupied the Portuguese throne in 1580, the system of individual licenses for trading slaves in Spanish America evolved into a single unified contract, *l'Asiento de Negros*. The *Asiento* granted a royal concession for the importation and auction of African slaves to supply the Spanish ports of Vera Cruz, Cartagena, and, occasionally, Buenos Aires. The concession was granted for a limited number of years; Portuguese slavers systematically acquired *asentista* rights between 1595 and 1640. Thus, the *Asiento* became both an important source of revenue for the kingdom and an administrative instrument for colonialism. Just like the Portuguese monarch, the Spanish king came to play an integral part in the pillaging of African populations, even if not always directly.

During this period, the Spanish Jesuit priest Luis de Molina drafted his major work, *De Justitia et Jure* (1593–97), considered to be the most accomplished theological and legal treatise on slavery and the slave trade. Having studied and taught in Coimbra and Evora, and having spent time in Lisbon learning about the slave trade, Molina expounded his eight *disputatio* on slavery, including three points specifically on the African slave trade.[6] He condemned the treatment of blacks and even hoped for an end to slavery, but, ultimately, Molina nonetheless accepted the legality of slavery.[7] Truly, he concluded that a buyer who had purchased slaves in good faith could hold onto them: *in dubio melior sit condition possidentis, quando possessio bona fide incepit* ("in case of doubt, the right of ownership must prevail when the purchase was made in good faith") (Molina 1733, 105–107). In addition, Iberian theologians and jurists devised a second key argument in favor of slavery and the slave trade. They maintained that there exists an inherent legal right of ownership to any item of merchandise that had been taxed by the prince or the state (Monteiro 1993). Such modern reasoning was drawn upon to justify slavery in the United States and Brazil through the second half of the nineteenth century.

Nonetheless, there were some dissenting voices, such as the Portuguese Dominican friar Fernando de Oliveira, who offered a wholesale indictment of the Portuguese slave trade in his *Arte da Guerra do Mar* (1555, 15). Likewise, in Bahia, the Jesuits Miguel Garcia and Gonçalo Leite criticized the fact that the college of the Society of Jesus held American Indians and Africans in captivity. In 1586, their superior in Lisbon, Jerônimo Cardoso, wrote to Claudio Acquaviva, the Superior General of the Society in Rome, to denounce the practice of slavery by the Jesuits in both Brazil and Angola

(1586, 288–289). Amador Arrais, the Bishop of Portalegre, Portugal, and his disciple Pedro Brandão, Bishop of Cap Vert, both Carmelites, attacked the slave trade from a completely different ideological angle. More than anything, they opposed bringing slaves and slavery to Portugal itself. They argued that this practice contributed to the disruption of traditional society and the disintegration of the Portuguese seigneurial system. "In the past, before these scoundrels [the Africans] were brought to the kingdom . . . nobody begged . . . the poor lived with the rich, the rich maintained them, and everyone had what they needed for life," wrote Bishop Arrias in his *Diálogos* (1589).[8]

Such arguments are not abolitionist. Rather, they reflect a conservative vein of antislavery ideology that is frequently misunderstood in accounts of the fight against modern slavery in Europe and the Americas, from the sixteenth to the nineteenth century.

Notwithstanding those critiques, the *Asiento* had, in the meantime, institutionalized the African slave trade. In this regard, it is important to underscore the crucial role that the Jesuits played in the Iberian Atlantic. The Society of Jesus was the only religious order that was continuously present in Angola and the Americas from the sixteenth century until its expulsion from Portugal in 1759 and from Spain in 1767. As a result, the Jesuits, who sold slaves from Angola in Brazil and owned properties tended by slaves on both sides of the ocean, are at the center of the South Atlantic slave network. More than any other religious order, the Jesuits developed moral justifications for slavery and the slave trade during this first era of globalization.[9] For example, the *Sermons* of Father António Vieira (1608–1697), some of which he wrote and revised in Bahia for publication in Lisbon between 1670 and 1690, should be read as the metatexts of this doctrine on the slave trade.[10] The Portuguese Jesuit priest formulated an audacious defense of the slave trade. In his sermons to blacks in the brotherhood of Our Lady of the Rosary in Salvador da Bahia, Vieira preached about the "great miracle" that brought Africans to Brazil and so had rescued them from certain pagan death, offering salvation for their souls in Christian lands in Sermons XIV and XXVII (1993, 733–769 and 1202–1241).

To better understand this argument, we should note that over the course of the seventeenth century, the Jesuits showed less and less enthusiasm for their missions in Angola. In their view, as expressed in "Carta dos padres da companhia ao governador de Angola" (1678), disease, adverse climate, and the volatility of the Mbundu and Bakonga peoples, with whom they had the closest contact in Angola and the Congo, hampered their evangelizing efforts in Africa (reproduced in Brásio 1982, 455–464). Thus, for the salvation of Africans, it was deemed necessary to remove them from Africa, even in bondage; the present captivity of their bodies ensured the future liberation of their souls. This is exactly what Father Vieira preached in Bahia in Sermon XXVII: "The first transmigration (*transmigracão*) in captivity is ordained by Her Mercy [of Our Lady of the Rosary] in order to secure the freedom of the second [transmigration]" (1993, 1205).

As we have seen, Vieira's thesis that slavery could save pagan souls had already been put forward in *Romanus Pontifex*. Nevertheless, Vieira's words reached much farther in the Portuguese Atlantic world than did the papal bull. Thus, half a century later, in *Peregrino da América* (1728)—a book on Christian morality that became a best-seller in colonial Brazil, reprinted five times during the eighteenth century—Nuno Marques Pereira reproduced word for word, and without acknowledgment, Vieira's sermon on the slave trade as a means of evangelization and salvation (1993 148–150).[11] Such religious legitimation of the slave trade harmonized with civil legislation arising from the Crown's system for taxing slavery. In effect, the levy extracted for each African deported from Luanda, who was marked at the point of departure with a hot iron brand bearing the Portuguese royal seal on the body of the slave, constituted official recognition of the legality of chattel slavery and slave trading. From this transatlantic perspective, the debate on the legitimacy of slavery in Brazil and, to some extent, in Iberian America more generally, was of secondary importance. The highest authorities had already sanctioned slavery. Why, then, should the right to own slaves in the Americas be questioned when it had been endorsed by the Crown and the Church at the moment when a slave trader acquired a captive in Angola?

The Preeminence of the Portuguese in the South Atlantic

The intensification of the Atlantic slave trade in the sixteenth and seventeenth centuries had two important effects in Africa. First, the Portuguese *asentistas*—those holding Spanish rights to the slave trade, who were sometimes the governors (or their partners) in Angola—began sending ships more routinely to Luanda. Protected by the currents of the South Atlantic, which cartographers and sailors in the eighteenth and nineteenth centuries considered a separate oceanic system (called the "Aethiopian Sea"), the navigation routes to Luanda also protected the Portuguese from competition with other European slave traders in the ports of Senegambia and the Gulf of Guinea. Having already cornered the Brazilian market, the Portuguese would also dominate the slave trade in the ports of Spanish America, taking almost complete control of the Atlantic trade. Second, the concentration of *asentista* trade in Luanda attracted other European merchant capital to the region, facilitating Portuguese expansion into the hinterlands of Angola. Indeed, a merchant lobby interested in Luanda sought to convince Philip II to expand the slave trade and the occupation of Angola (Cortes Lopez 1991). The coastal forts and settlements at Luanda and Benguela, as well as those of the interior at Massangano, Muxima, and Cambambe, were established or reinforced during the period when the Portuguese held the *Asiento*. The enclaves in the hinterlands of Angola were crucial for the Portuguese in maintaining their presence in the country during the occupation of Luanda and Benguela by the Dutch West India Company (1641–48). Later, control of the ports and outposts of Angola helped the Portuguese to restrict the activities of Dutch slavers—and the French as well—to the Soyo region and the Kingdom of Loango, just south and north of the mouth of the Congo River.

The *Asentista* period, from 1595 to 1640, strengthened the Portuguese presence on both sides of the South Atlantic. Indeed, the conflict between the Portuguese and the Dutch around the Atlantic highlights the geopolitical unity of this oceanic space. So, for example, when the Dutch West India Company seized Pernambuco and the surrounding sugar-producing regions in the northeast of Brazil (1630–54), they then also took Luanda, Benguela, and São Tomé (1641–48). In that offensive, Dutch control over the slave plantations in Brazil was to be secured by seizing the areas of Angola that supplied slaves. Likewise, the counteroffensive of the Portuguese and Brazilian colonists also followed the transatlantic route. The retaking of Luanda and Benguela by a fleet of slavers outfitted in Rio de Janeiro (1648) weakened Dutch West India Company forces, leading to their surrender to the Portuguese at Pernambuco and to their expulsion from Brazil in 1654.

Buenos Aires, with its access routes to the silver mines of Potosí, was another strategic location in the South Atlantic. During the Iberian Union, between 1580 and 1640, illegal slave trading through the Río de la Plata made it possible for the Portuguese to acquire the silver that cemented their commerce with the Far East. In the ports of Cartagena and Veracruz, Portuguese *asentistas* also acquired silver coins, the pieces of eight, which, in the 1620s, became the most lucrative commodity in Portugal's trade with Asia (de Silva 1974, 181–182). After the Portuguese Restoration in 1640 and the war between Lisbon and Madrid, Salvador de Sá approached the Court of Braganza with a plan to invade Buenos Aires in order to attain the mines at Potosí. Coming from a line of governors and powerful property owners in Rio de Janeiro, a three-time governor himself, Salvador de Sá also had family and business associates in Buenos Aires. As the British historian Charles Boxer (1952) has demonstrated in his biography of the man, Salvador de Sá played a key role in the reorganization of Portugal's overseas territories under the Braganza dynasty, following the transatlantic route by later commanding the expedition to retake Angola and taking up the governorship of the African colony (1648–51).[12] Trade, horses, troops, and officers with experience in tropical wars who came from Brazil helped the Portuguese to take control of large parts of Angola, leading Jan Vansina, one of the foremost specialists in West Central Africa, to suggest that by the end of the seventeenth century Angola had become "the first substantial" European colony in Africa (Vansina 1975, 145–146).

Salvador de Sá's Dutch adversary, Nassau-Siegen, also had a similar global vision for the South Atlantic. In 1642, as governor of Recife in Nieuw Holland (Dutch Brazil), which comprised the territories conquered by the West India Company in Portuguese America (1637–44), Nassau-Siegen equipped a fleet to take over Buenos Aires, with the goal of finishing the operation begun with the seizure of Angola in 1641. However, Nassau-Siegen had to abandon the project because of an anti-Dutch revolt in Maranhão and the fear of a general uprising in Pernambuco. Nevertheless, the plan itself reveals the extent to which the stretch of the South Atlantic was a front in the Thirty Years War that ended formally in Europe with the Peace of Westphalia. The history of these confrontations between the Portuguese and the Dutch, in both the Atlantic and the Pacific, demonstrate some of the geopolitical differences between the spice trade and the sugar trade in the sixteenth and seventeenth centuries. The Portuguese lost the "Spice Wars," in which control of Asian trading posts was at stake. They won the "Sugar Wars," fought over control of the plantations in the Americas and the slave ports in Angola. The Portuguese prevailed in the South Atlantic primarily because of the settlements and seaports that they managed to hold onto in Brazil and Angola. Over time, the colonial advantage of the slave-plantation economy (compared to the economic fluctuations of the spice trade) began to become apparent.

The Extension of the Angolan Slave Trade in the Seventeenth Century

The following table, showing the primary zones of deportation in the slave trade to the Americas, compiled from the Trans-Atlantic Slave Trade Database (TSTD), demonstrates the scope of the Angolan slave trade from West

Central Africa in relation to that of the other seven major regions of Africa.[13] In the TSTD, "West Central Africa" essentially designates Angola and, more especially in this period, the port of Luanda, which would become the biggest slave trading port in Africa (Eltis and Richardson 2010, 90). After drawing from the ports of Senegambia, the *asentista* demand had the biggest impact on the port of Luanda, especially from 1611 to 1630. The Portuguese alliance with Jaga-Imbangala mercenaries that extended the slave trade and raids into the hinterlands of Angola also expanded the traffic of captives to Luanda (Miller 1972). Incidentally, we should note that the huge increase in slave deportations from the Gulf of Benin that we see in the last two decades of the seventeenth century was caused by the arrival there of slavers from Bahia.

The export of slaves from West Central Africa increased dramatically during the first period of the Portuguese *Asiento* (1595–1601), as the next graph shows the estimated number of slaves from the area who were sent to Ibero-America. At the receiving end, Cartagena emerges as the most important slave port in Spanish America, followed closely by Vera Cruz. Cartagena was also the base of two of the most powerful Portuguese merchants in Spanish America: Jorge Fernandes Gramaxo (or Gramacho), the agent for the *asentistas* between 1595 and 1610, and Jorge Fernandes de Elvas (or Delvas), the son and, from 1619 to 1622, the agent of the *asentista* Antonio Fernandes de Elvas. Both were Marranos, and they were, along with the Portuguese Jews, persecuted by the Inquisition and governing magistrates (Ventura 2001; Vila Vilar 1979; Chaunu and Chaunu 1955–59, 4:346–347 and 3:1031–1054). From Cartagena, the regional redistribution of African slaves fanned out toward Venezuela, the Antilles, and Lima (via Portobello and Panama), continuing by land to Upper Peru and Potosí. Enriqueta Vila Vilar estimates that this long and tortuous inland route from Cartagena caused more deaths among the captives than the Atlantic crossing (1977, 213–221).

The number of slaves exported to America from Angola spiked again between the years 1617 and 1625. This spike represents the most intense outflow of slaves from a single African region and from a single port of departure, again Luanda, to a single American port since the transatlantic trade began. According to David Wheat, fifty-six boats carried 11,328 captives from Angola and the Congo to Cartagena between 1619 and 1624 (2011, 15–16, 19; 2009, 252–256). After that date, the Dutch West India Company launched its first offensive in the South Atlantic, leading to the occupation of Bahia (1624–25) and the temporary blockade of Luanda, which disrupted the activity of the *Asiento*. On the other side of the Atlantic,

TABLE 1. Primary zones of deportation in the slave trade to the Americas.

	Senegambia and offshore Atlantic	*Sierra Leone*	*Windward Coast*	*Gold Coast*	*Bight of Benin*	*Bight of Biafra*	*West Central Africa and Saint Helena*	*Southeast Africa and Indian Ocean islands*	*Totals*
1581–90	25,448	237	0	0	0	0	31,206	0	56,891
1591–1600	5,370	0	2,482	0	0	2,346	70,368	0	80,566
1601–10	9,991	0	0	0	0	0	81,936	0	91,926
1611–20	8,541	0	0	68	1,873	1,142	137,308	0	148,932
1621–30	6,652	0	0	0	1,655	2,247	172,595	345	183,494
1631–40	4,562	0	0	0	1,988	1,630	112,020	0	120,199
1641–50	24,476	1,372	0	2,429	4,092	31,442	59,530	0	123,342
1651–60	17,723	752	351	1,437	12,163	24,791	95,382	3,088	155,687
1661–70	6,407	154	0	19,193	29,926	37,668	126,758	9,432	229,539
1671–80	13,267	0	0	28,835	29,813	34,394	108,966	7,116	222,391
1681–90	21,927	1,894	0	16,274	79,890	21,709	109,373	9,497	260,564
1691–1700	22,558	2,671	999	40,443	108,412	31,299	130,939	2,237	339,557
Totals	166,922	7,080	3,832	108,679	269,812	188,668	1,236,380	31,715	2,013,088

Source: Trans-Atlantic Slave Trade Database.

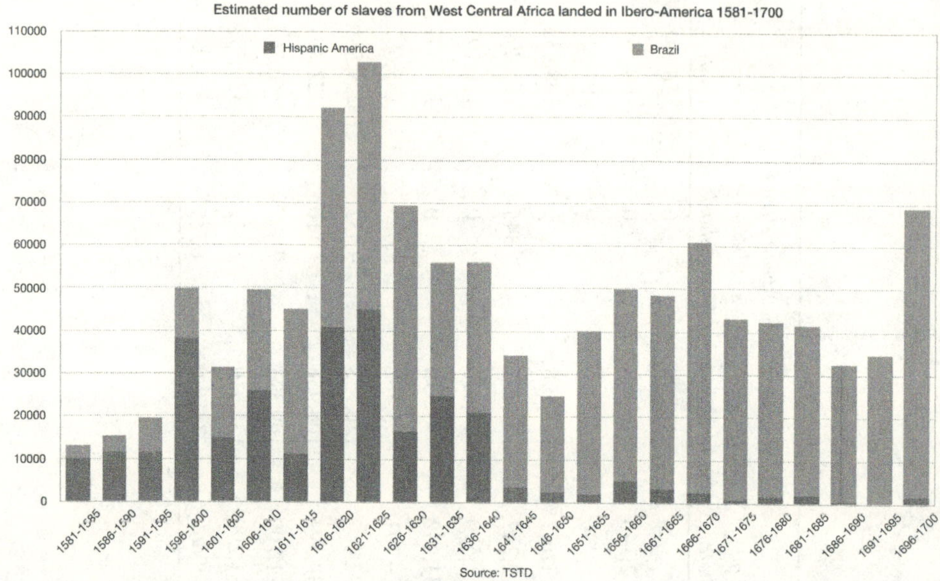

Figure 1. Estimated number of slaves from West Central Africa landed in Ibero-America, 1581–1700. Source: Trans-Atlantic Slave Trade Database.

with the political decline of Enrique de Guzman, the second Count of Olivares in Spain, who had protected the new Christian merchants and bankers, the tribunals of the Inquisition that had been set up in Lima in 1570, Mexico in 1571, and Cartagena in 1610 began to target the community of converted Portuguese merchants (*conversos*). In Cartagena in particular, the punishments increased during the 1630s, further disturbing the *asentista* network and transcontinental Portuguese trade (Cross 1978; Studnicki-Gizbert 2005).

Disruption of the Atlantic trade with Africa and Europe had particular consequences for Brazil. The Dutch seizure of Bahia (1624–25) and Pernambuco (1630–54), along with the deployment of Iberian and local troops to fight those invaders, created demand for all types of supplies. As a result, raids targeting Indian communities in the south of Brazil were conducted to supply São Paulo, whose colonial economy still depended largely upon indigenous slave labor. These raids, which were carried out between 1627 and 1640 in the areas of Guayra (in the modern state of Paraná) and Tapes (in Rio Grande do Sul), appear to be the biggest slaving expeditions in the Americas during the seventeenth century. In São Paulo, and to a lesser extent in Rio de Janeiro, Indian slaves were employed in farming and food production, raising livestock, land transport, as well as the construction of ships and other equipment to supply Bahia and reinforce regional defenses in the south. As John Monteiro has shown, it was during this period that São Paulo, using native slave labor, became a center of wheat production for the Brazilian market (1994, 76–79).

However, with the retaking of Luanda in 1648, the Angolan trade restarted and was increasingly directed toward Brazil. With an eye to displacing the great *asentista* commerce in Spanish America, Portuguese maritime supply chains and the Angolan slave trading networks were reoriented toward the ports of Brazil. Indeed, the number of slaves (70,000) who were transported from West Central Africa, almost entirely from Angola, between 1651 and 1660 rivals the total number of slaves (69,500) who were transported form the region to Spanish American ports between 1631 and 1640, the last decade that the Portuguese held the *Asiento*. This leads us to the seemingly paradoxical observation that the fallout from the Iberian Union that had the greatest impact on Brazil took place outside of the New World, on the Angolan side of the South Atlantic network. Although thousands of indigenous Americans were enslaved in the period, the Portuguese Restoration transformed the character of the Brazilian labor market. Sooner or later, the increasing demand for labor in colonial Brazil would be met by the huge number of African slaves supplied by *asentista* agents between 1595 and 1640. In other words, the story of the displacement of indigenous captives by African slave labor in Brazil was written in the tides of the South Atlantic, and not along the tracks of the Brazilian forest.

All these facts, and others that I have examined elsewhere (de Alencastro 2006; 2015), show that beyond the disciplinary divisions that divide African specialists from scholars of the Americas, beyond even the unified history of South America pursued under the outdated rubric of "Latin America," a proper history of the South Atlantic itself is needed.

Translated by Joseph R. Slaughter

NOTES

This chapter is a slightly modified version of a contribution that was first published as "La traité des noirs et la construction de l'Atlantique ibérique," in Dartois (2014).

1. Among the many sources on this topic, see Lipschutz (1966, 779–814); Frank (1968); Stavenhagen (1973, 10–16, 74–94); and Romano and Stein (1984, 121–134). On the debates over the historiography of the region in the United States, see Feres Júnior (2010).

2. I should note that Jérôme Baschet (2011, 2013) does not make any reference to sub-Saharan Africa. More specifically, in his debate with Brazilian historians, he affirms that his research is based mostly on New Spain and Hispanic modes of colonization. In this discussion, Baschet and his interlocutors, Ana Carolina Lima Almeida, Clinio de Oliveira Amaral, and Marcelo Santiago Berriel (2013), specialists in medieval history at the Universidade Federal Rural de Rio de Janeiro—Rio having been the biggest slave trading port in the New World—discuss colonization in the Americas without once mentioning the African slave trade.

3. I want to thank Serge Gruzinski for bringing Las Casas's commentaries on the Canaries to my attention.

4. Parts of this section are drawn from fuller historical analysis that I have elaborated elsewhere (de Alencastro 2000, 2013).

5. As the Benedictine Charles Martial de Witte (1958, 455) and A.C. de C. M. Saunders (1982, 36–37) have shown, Rome endorsed the justifications for the African slave trade offered by the Portuguese king.

6. *Disputationes* 32–40 concern slavery, while 34–36 deal directly with the African slave trade. For Hespanha (2001), who has studied the *disputatio* closely, this might be a working document that Molina used in his courses at Coimbra and Évora.

7. For a detailed discussion of Molina's arguments, see García Añoveros (2000).

8. Bishop Arrais, a doctor of theology at the University of Coimbra, was both against the slave trade and anti-Semitic, to the point of accusing Jews of creating Islam in order to weaken Christianity. In favor of expelling the Jews from the kingdom, he was against the forced conversions favored by the Iberian kings. See Arrais ([1589] 1974, 112–115).

9. Here is one of the main differences between the Catholic missions of the first and second periods of European expansion. Whereas the Jesuits, Capuchins, and Dominicans sent missionaries to the four corners of the earth in the sixteenth and seventeenth centuries, during the second period of European expansion, in the nineteenth century, missionary orders tended to concentrate on specific cultural areas of the globe. For example, the Congregation of the Holy Ghost was recreated in 1848 as a postabolitionist order charged with heading missions in Haiti, Martinique, and sub-Saharan Africa. The *Pères Blancs* were founded in 1868 by the Archbishop of Algiers in order to serve Muslim North Africa, and the Societas Verbi Divini, founded by the German priest, Arnold Janssen, in 1875 was primarily active in China. The cultural and regional specialization of nineteenth-century missions deprived them of the global multicultural approach pursued by the missionaries during the first

European expansion. This needs to be kept in mind when studying the writings of the two periods.

10. There is debate among Vieira specialists about the proper edition and chronology of his sermons. See Cantel (1959); Smulders (1997); Castro (1997); Muhana (1997); Marques (1997).

11. Vieira came to Bahia and Minas Gerais during the period when gold was discovered, which transformed Brazil and attracted many Portuguese colonists.

12. Boxer's biography of Salvador de Sá (1952) and Frédéric Mauro's *le Portugal et L'Atlantique* (1960) could be considered the founding books of the historiography of the South Atlantic. See the review by Huguette and Pierre Chaunu (1954, 44–54); see also Chaunu (1961). On the global conjuncture in this period, see the book by one of Chaunu's brilliant disciples, Serge Gruzinski (2004, 249–278).

13. "West Central Africa" is one of the eight major continental zones identified by Philip Curtin (1969), which the curators of the Trans-Atlantic Slave Trade Database have also adopted.

A World Girded

Saint-Simonian Space and Race in the Nineteenth-Century Latin Transatlantic

Jaime Hanneken

In 1833, Prosper Enfantin wrote a letter from Paris to his friend Emile Barrault, who was traveling through Egypt looking to initiate an infrastructural project that would facilitate commercial traffic across the Suez Peninsula. Enfantin encouraged him in this endeavor, writing: "It is up to us to make between ancient Egypt and old Judea one of the new routes to India and China. . . . We will thus place one foot on the Nile, the other on Jerusalem. Our right hand will stretch out towards Mecca, our left arm will cover Rome and will still be resting on Paris. Suez is the center of our work life. There we will commit the act that the world is waiting for" (Régnier 1991, 283). At the end of the letter, in what appears to be a non-sequitur, he added: "Later, you will leave for the New World, touching its South and its North; and, waving hello, in passing . . . to the island where the Blacks have liberated themselves; then, circling around, you will wait for me . . . at Panama" (284).

The description of Enfantin, also known as le Père, the leader and quasi-messiah of the Saint-Simonian movement during the 1830s, bears all the markings of a signature vision of capital on the cusp of the precipitous industrial advancements of the nineteenth century. This vision, which had enduring influence over notions of credit, trade, labor, and infrastructure, is that of a shrunken globe draped in flexible networks, where everything appears at arm's length. Indeed, the mystical brand of socialism expounded by Enfantin and his followers—derived from the postrevolutionary utopian philosophy of Henri de Saint-Simon—is best known for its lasting impact on the abstract and material structures of capitalist development. The greatest feat of the Saint-Simonian generation, as Enfantin stated near the end of his life, was to "have girded the globe in our networks of iron, money, steam and electricity" (quoted in Picon 2002, 244).

My first objective here is to outline the spatial features of Saint-Simonian capital, showing in particular how the various distortions of scale they exercise help to establish a unified space of transatlantic commerce, where, as one critic writes, "through the piercing of the two isthmuses of Suez and Panama, the world would be just one body, traversed by an uninterrupted circulation of men and merchandise" (Régnier 1989, xxx). These same coordinates, however, also plot an area shaped by overlapping narratives of race and imperialism during the long nineteenth century. In fact, Suez and Panama could be seen as the limit points of what I am calling the Latin Transatlantic, a sphere of "Latin" influence stretching from the Eastern Mediterranean to South America roughly between 1830 and 1930. The Latin Transatlantic consists of discourses of race, genealogy, and civilization that evolve to match shifting hegemonic configurations and to fix racial stratifications at local, regional, and continental levels. The trope of the oversized male who lumbers across the globe, "waving hello" to Haiti as he crosses the Western Hemisphere, also underwrites the fundamental narrative of Latin racial identity, suggesting how space and race are mutually constituted in the transatlantic age of industrial imperialism.

The notion of the Latin race promoted by French and Latin American intellectuals starting in the 1850s has traditionally been understood as an ideological repurposing of classical Roman heritage to justify France's economic and political interventions in the Americas, as well as the acculturation of indigenous and African populations under official Spanish American national identities. Because its mobilization of race appeals more to lofty affinities of religion, language, and spirit than to scientific racism, *Latinité* is often dismissed as an elitist fiction with little connection to race-based practices of exclusion and domination. In examining its imbrication with Saint-Simonian space, my aim is to show that, far from being merely an effete fantasy, *Latinité* in fact helps to solidify neocolonial exploitation under global commerce; in other words, it discursively and spatially prepares for the material production of race as an effect of power. *Latinité*, I argue, translates the Saint-Simonians' collapse of global and corporeal space to the principal labor formats of expansionist capital: the centrifugal production scheme of the agricultural commune, on one hand, and the centripetal primary export model employed by imperial trade, on the other. In doing so, it mirrors the overlapping technologies of discipline and security Michel Foucault tracks in the evolution of "race war" discourse, tapping an abstract and infinite source of laboring life that is nonetheless "embodied" as Latin.

If Saint-Simonianism has a spatial brand, it involves a conceptual adaptation of the radical space-time compression that rail travel, steam power, and engineering feats like the Suez Canal itself were to bring about in the next decades. Life in the industrial age, in Richard Wittman's words, was characterized by "overlapping spatio temporalities: the inescapable primary space-time of the body inevitably remained primary, but a multiplying number of facets of daily life . . . now sensibly involved the individual in spatiotemporal frameworks that were constituted by forms of disembodied communication and were not susceptible to phenomenal experience" (Wittman 2010, 26). The result of the Saint-Simonian globe, he says, is to "extend the immediacy of embodied spatial experience . . . to the geopolitical scale, with no concession to differences between the two" (36). The utopian tableaux of early Saint-Simonianism prefigure the spatial conceits of popular nineteenth-century spectacles like the panorama and the universal exposition, which also aimed to draw viewers' bodies into relation with a miniaturized display of the world. Panoramas and dioramas, mass attractions that placed spectators before giant, 360-degree illustrations of modern metropolises and historic events, not only presented participants with far-off spaces on a larger-than-life scale but invited them to complete the picture with their own bodies: their fundamental effect, as François Robichon explains, was created "by a deficit in the mechanism that the spectator must supplement with an imaginary that adheres to the spatialization of his body" (1985, 83). As in world exhibitions, which offered working-class audiences grandiose displays of the latest commercial and industrial marvels, panoramas trained viewers in new arrangements of production and consumption. In the world exhibition, Walter Benjamin writes, "the worker occupies the foreground, as customer" (1999, 7), learning to admire but not touch the commodities he is employed to produce; in the same way, the panorama provides "a esthetic ordering of geopolitical space with an eye to its consumption" (Robichon 1985, 83). Thus the spatial manipulation commonly found in nineteenth-century global imaginaries not only anticipated visually the "annihilation of space" achieved by ever-faster circuits of trade and transportation but also simultaneously reinforced the distribution of social roles in the order of capitalist expansion.

The Saint-Simonians' own theories about labor exemplify the power of bodily metaphor to shape the rising ethos of bourgeois hegemony. Their guiding notion of "universal association"—in essence, the total union of social actors under which each finds his or her place in an ideal hierarchy of production and reproduction—draws directly on physiological principles.[1] Saint-Simon himself understood social order in the manner of biological diversity, so that societies, like organisms, could be ranked according to the complexity and specialization of the organs and circulatory systems they contained. Just as in the natural world of the biologist, as John Tresch describes, for Saint-Simon "a higher rank [of society] meant a greater division of labor, as well as more, more varied, and more harmoniously disposed 'vessels' for the circulation among its parts. Thus the highest stage would be a society that constantly developed its channels and networks for the movement of goods, people, ideas and credit" (Tresch 2012, 197). Universal association is often credited with developing key mechanisms of worker alienation because of the way it requires all subjects to identify with their exploitation. The Saint-Simonians were the first to define exploitation exclusively as the exploitation of nature; for them, work did not involve the alienation of some men's labor by other men, but the collective effort to reap full benefit of the earth, each according to his abilities.[2] Much less remarked upon, however, is the way the same organicist perspective that presages European economic structures during the nineteenth century underwrites the colonial endeavors that would support them. The harmonized social body that fetishizes the immediacy and speed of modern life in European capitals also figures more expansively the proximity of raw materials flowing in from colonial satellites, the accessibility of African, American, and Asian labor, and mystical notions of racial mixing that would have a lasting, if subterranean, impact on assimilationist policies under France's Second Empire.

These connections are already vividly laid out in the early poems of Michel Chevalier, a key disciple of Enfantin: in one, titled "Les Colonies, en avant!" (1833), he surveys the three continents given as a dowry in humanity's "new nuptials" as they sprawl out across the globe. America, a "svelt red-skin" stretches his limbs from one pole to another, his spine "the longest chain of mountains," while Africa, a "vigorous worker," reclines his head on the Cape of Good Hope, propping one foot on Gibraltar and the other on the Nile as he watches European ships go by (Régnier

1991, 258–259). Another poem, "Géographie et physiologie," catalogs the biological and topographic components of the globe, first listing "three races distinguished by skin": "the life of the white skin" it says, "is in the nerves"; "the life of the black skin is in the muscles", and the red skin in lymph fluid and blood. Next are listed three "new lands," America, Oceania, and Africa, flanked by the two "sacred routes" of Suez and Panama (249–250). The image of France's projected imperial hinterlands arrayed as so many corporeal essences enclosed within the isthmuses of Suez and Panama, or as continental masses come to life in giant laborers, not only captures universal association's articulation of body and capital; it also attests that the industrialist's dream of global integration demanded the interpellation and hierarchical ordering of non-European populations. Decades after he wrote these poems in the first heady days of the Saint-Simonian movement, Chevalier served as top political advisor to Napoleon III, spearheading the intervention in Mexico (1861–67) and drafting the seminal proposals for the French campaign to build the Panama Canal (1880–89). His mentor Enfantin was also instrumental to the Second Empire; in 1833 he sponsored a mission of some eighty Saint-Simonian disciples to Egypt to secure what they referred to as a reunion of Orient and Occident, spiritually through the hunt for a female messiah to wed the prophet le Père, and materially through initial negotiations to dig the Suez Canal. Both projects ended in failure and ridicule, but when Enfantin was chosen to lead the official expedition to examine the prospect of French expansion into Algeria, the same spirit of ethnic and industrial association would inform his blueprint for colonial integration.[3]

In a way, the histories of the building of the Suez and Panama canals act as geographic and chronological bookends to a cohesive epoch of relations in the Southern Atlantic, one characterized by a certain way of thinking about global space and racial identity. This mode of thought, represented by *Latinité*, is of course in the first instance intimately related to France's imperial ambitions. After the loss of almost all its American territories following the Louisiana Purchase and the Haitian Revolution, France sought to strengthen its claims to the Western Hemisphere and to secure access to Asia across the Pacific. The fantasy of a globe enclosed in networks, as Antoine Picon notes, also drives home "the reality of the finitude of Saint-Simonian space [making it] an object of conflict among the peoples and races that vie for its possession" (Picon 2002, 225). Suddenly finite, the earth appeared to be carved into blocs of massified "races" defined by religious, historic, and civilizational ties. The argument for "Latin" union bolstered France's cultural tutelage in the nascent Spanish American republics against the encroachment of "Anglo" America, at the same time that it propelled the colonization of North Africa, and later Western Africa, in the service of the French "*mission civilisatrice*."

It is with these eventualities in mind that Chevalier, in what by many accounts is the first manifesto of *Latinité*, sums up the geopolitical state of the world as a mortal contest among Germanics, Slavs, and Latins: France, he declares, "is the custodian of the destinies of all the nations of the Latin group on both continents. Only she can prevent this entire family of peoples from being buried by the double inundation of the Germans or Saxons and the Slavs" (Chevalier 1853, 8). France's role as the keeper of the Latin race, Chevalier observes, obliges her to guide and protect the less developed members of her family, "to awaken them from the lethargy in which they are submerged on both hemispheres": She is called to become the patron of the new republics of South America, "which do not yet find themselves in a condition to maintain themselves," as well as to "favor the development of the vitality that seems to revive itself among the Arabs" (8). Chevalier thus characterizes as a sacred racial duty the imperial interests that would fuel France's adventures in North Africa and Latin America over the next century.

The same tropes of ethnic alliance and embodied space that dominate France's overtures to the Southern Atlantic world appear in discourses of Latin American sovereignty and solidarity circulated by the region's elites starting in the 1850s. In one of the first treatises articulating Iberian America's "Latin" unity, written in the aftermath of racial conflicts produced by the completion of the Panama railroad by US firms in 1855 and the flood of North American Forty-Niners traveling through Central America to reach California's goldfields, the Chilean intellectual Francisco Bilbao describes Latin America as a titan extended across the Andes, reaching his two arms to the North and South poles (Bilbao 1941, 142).[4] He envisions Panama, the modern "pillars of Hercules," as a "future colossus that, looking at both Oceans, will raise higher than his volcanoes not only the lighthouse of the traveler but the splendor of justice" (154). Writing amid the pan-Hispanic fervor of the early twentieth century, following the Spanish American war and Panama's US-sponsored secession from Colombia, the Argentine Manuel Ugarte similarly imagines Latin America as a giant man in which "each republic is a limb, a joint. . . . Argentina is a hand, Central America is a foot" (Ugarte 1978, 11), and from which he watches Colombia "agitating its mutilated arm" (26). How, he asks, can this organism survive the "amputation" perpetrated by Anglo-America, "if they cut off the man's other foot, if they snuff out his eyes, . . . if they reduce him to a poor trunk dragging itself along?" (11). And Peruvian diplomat Francisco García Calderón, weighing the future outlook of the Latin race on the brink of World War I, likens world events to a clash of amalgamated races, "vast unions of scattered peoples . . . springing into formation" like enormous warriors: "Slavs, Saxons, Latins, and Mongols are contending for the possession of the world . . . above the quarrels of precarious nations are rising the profound antagonisms of millennial races" (García Calderón 1913, 396). He positions Latin America on this global scene as the promising auxiliary in which "the exhausted Latin world may renew itself" (394) and Panama as the "gate of civilization to Eastern Asia and Western America, as Suez is to Central Asia, Eastern Africa, and Oceania." Providing rapid access to the burgeoning markets of the Pacific and ethnic vigor to its European affiliates, García Calderón suggests, Panama is to become the future center of a new, fully integrated globe, making the Atlantic "the ocean of the Old World" (388).

The tropological patterns that emerge from all the texts examined thus far suggest that race comes into play in Saint-Simonian space as a magnified embodiment of geopolitical processes. But what impact, if any, does this optic have on the material practices of social control and racial imaginaries that take hold in different locales of the Latin Atlantic? In other words, is there a meaningful relationship between the spatial logic I have described and the discriminatory ordering of groups under the aegis of *Latinité*, such that this discourse would not amount merely to an indulgent ideology of Latin American and French elites but also reflect the way local populations are situated in wider industrial circuits? Insofar as such a relationship can be pinpointed, I want to argue, it obtains in the paradox between centripetal and centrifugal forces, a vortex of fusion that is also flung outward toward the world. In short, it mimics the dynamic of a Fourierist commune. As Benjamin observed, the phalanstery—the pastoral commune first imagined by Charles Fourier in the early nineteenth century—forms the utopian counterpoint to Saint-Simonian networks: while one predicts the endless expansion of the global economy, the other recedes into a nostalgic concentration of labor and capital (Benjamin 1999, 627). In its folksy refashioning of modern production as diminutive, specialized agricultural plots, the phalanstery forces capitalism onto a human scale, where the minute distribution of tasks acquires the aura of village life.

Not surprisingly, Latin America and North Africa, precisely the lands said to guarantee the rebirth of Latin civilization, attracted dozens of documented Fourierist experiments in the mid-nineteenth century.[5] The 1860 proposal of Athénase Airiau to build a canal and European settlement on the isthmus of Darién, near the site of the present-day Panama Canal, visually captures the tension between Saint-Simonian and Fourierist conceptions of space. His logistical and topographic study of the projected colony is accompanied by intricate maps of an agricultural city traversed by a flat canal and divided octagonally into farms for the cultivation of tobacco, cotton, cacao, indigo, nopal, and dairy and poultry products. The city radiates outward from an ornamental pool straddling the canal, which he envisions crowned by "an octagonal lighthouse telling the hour on its eight faces, mounted by a pedestal that displays an emblem of France protecting New Grenada" (Airiau 1860, 114). This elaborate founding monument, he adds, is supported by a giant archway under which "the tallest masts" will pass unobstructed from the Atlantic to the Pacific. Names of New Granadian departments and leaders mingle with those of French cities and European capitals along the avenues, quays and ports that connect the city. The design for Airiau's colony conceives of a bantam city that is simultaneously a world panorama, quite literally a gateway for global industry. By symbolically fusing Latin American and French place names, it also predicts the way the spatial intimacy of the agricultural colonial model is meant to bring about cultural assimilation.

Indeed, although Airiau's gestures toward a French-Latin American union remain vague and ornamental, for many pioneers of colonial ventures the new spatial ordering of communal industry is directly linked to the ethnic melding of native and European populations. The authors of the charter of the Union Agricole d'Afrique, requesting authorization in 1846 to establish the phalanstery of Sig, near Oran (which the Argentine statesman Domingo Sarmiento would visit and later praise in his *Viajes por Europa, Africa y América*), signal the civilizing benefit of attracting Arab workers to their commune and imbuing them through proximity and habit with European norms of work and property. The document reproduces the mandate of association spelled out by Enfantin's early teachings, to "assign a special role to each people [and] distribute the functions that these different organs of the social body must accomplish" (Enfantin 1868, 207). The authors stress that the principle of association, grafted onto the property systems of tribal communities, "offers the genuine and the only method of linkage and union of races on African land" (L'union agricole d'Afrique 1846, 6). Their conviction echoes the general approach to colonial consolidation following the first turbulent decades of French occupation. In the face of vigorous rebellion in Kabyle and Arab strongholds on one hand and the growing resentment of European settlers on the other, the question of the very survival of the colony centered on whether and how indigenous traditions of land tenure and civic hierarchy could be absorbed into a modern economy based on private property and proletarianized labor. The radical solution of autonomous "Arab Kingdoms" implemented by Napoleon III in 1860 adopts Saint-Simonian association as official doctrine, proposing to convert all of Algeria into a "reduced traditional, pastoral, and artisanal native reserve, encircled and enframed by European culture and industry" (Abi-Mershed 2010, 163).[6] In the de facto founding statement of the Arab Kingdoms, Enfantin's protégé Thomas Urbain underscores the ethnic assimilation likely to result from such arrangements: the Algerian population, working in tandem and with the discipline of a peaceful army—the indigenous as laboring soldiers, the French as supervising officers—would forget its antagonisms once "the association of interests lead[s] to the fusion of families" (Voisin 1861, 158).[7]

Associationist ideas about economic and ethnic management were by no means limited to the Algerian administration. Not only, as in Airiau's plan, did they color various French attempts at the more or less formal subjugation of Latin America during the nineteenth century, they also resonated forcefully with many local intellectuals' theories about their own societies' progress and its place on the global scene. Thus, the New Grenadian (Colombian) luminary José María Torres Caicedo, composing an inventory of the world's races in 1859, prefaced his comments by noting approvingly that "the press, the missions, commerce, aided by steam, the intimate connection of industrial interests in varied latitudes, the fertile spirit of association, all this is preparing the fusion of races and the harmony of humanity" (Torres Caicedo 1875, 170). The following year, when his compatriot José María Samper published a promotional overview of New Grenada and its people, his attention was similarly centered on the commercial and racial confluence of its citizens. The country's population, parceled out vertically along different altitudes of three giant mountain chains, forms a veritable topographic commune. Samper explains that the demographic diffusion created by Spanish colonization—creole whites and Indians in the *altiplano*, mestizos in the middle altitudes, and African slaves in the tropical valleys—obliged the colonizers' European influence to assume "a double movement of descent and ascent": while civilization flows down to the mountainsides and valleys, barbarity rises up to the plateaus, resulting in a "marvelous work of mixing of races and civilizations that had to give birth to . . . a race of republicans representing at the same time Europe, Africa, and America" (Samper 1860b, 122–123). Even more impressive for Samper is the varied and abundant flow of commodities circulated among the New Grenadians. In Europe, he notes, all agricultural sectors produce the same crops according to the season, resulting in a limited and staggered variety of offerings; the climactic diversity of New Grenada, in contrast, allows tropical products like rice, sugar, bananas, coffee and tobacco to travel up from the lowlands as potatoes, corn, wool and valuable woods travel down from the mountains. Unlike anywhere in the world, here "the population can count simultaneously on all of the globe's products, but classified by the type of climate at different altitudes, [making] an incessant movement of interior commerce on an immense scale" (Samper 1860c, 255).

Samper's New Grenada is an exemplar of dual fusion: The racial synthesis of American, African, and European elements corresponds to the instantaneity and abundance of commercial exchange, in a relationship that appears to connect local populations symbiotically to their economic practices. His article, written in French and published in the *Revue Orientale et Américaine*, appeals to a European public steeped in Saint-Simonian expansionism, in effect inserting New Grenada onto a new world map inflected by the ethos of universal association. The 1859 inaugural issue of the *Revue* describes a mission driven by the desire "that progress spread simultaneously from Orient to Occident, from North to South," giving "all an equal part of debit and credit in the extensive endeavor of progress" (Rosny 1859, 1–2). The journal's focus on "America" and "Orient," explored in ethnographic and commercial surveys of South and Central America, Africa, and the Near East, claims to adhere to a broader initiative of expansion patterned after the endeavors of Christopher Columbus: the modern era's "gigantic feats" in engineering and infrastructure, it asserts, will finally "open through the New World the most direct route to reach the last limits of the Orient" (2). The editor's rhetoric exemplifies the way the nineteenth-century French imperial vision—abetted by regional elites like Samper—often viewed Latin America and North Africa as parallel components of a single trajectory of westward development.

In 1857, the small newspaper *El Panameño* featured a series of articles penned by a French author under the pseudonym Jules de France dedicated to promoting a French-led transformation of the isthmus in the mold of Algeria. "Our intention," he writes, "is to establish a point of comparison between the fertility of our beautiful colony in Africa and that which it would be so easy to obtain from the soil of the Isthmus of Panama" (France 1857a, 3). For Jules de France, it is precisely the spatial invigoration of Algeria under French rule that has succeeded in bringing it into the fold of civilization: what once was only a "nest of pirates" living precariously off their plunder, in a "shapeless heap of low, dark, and humid constructions, piled one on top of the other and separated by squalid alleyways" (France 1857b, 3), through French colonization has undergone a seemingly instantaneous metamorphosis: "the streets were cleared out and widened, the houses rose multiple stories, plazas with monuments, fountains, etc came to beautify and sanitize the city, the suburbs were sprinkled with flowers and verdant farmhouses"; and the surrounding plains, once fallow, were regenerated into the present-day "breadbasket of France" (3). The vivid memory of this transformation, reflects Jules de France, must be "the source of the emotions the sad aspect of degenerate Panama gives rise to in me" (3).

Jules de France's portrait assumes subtle but telling racial associations. It first references the urban renewal of colonial Algiers, a de facto campaign of racial cleansing that, sweeping away the Turkish and Arab features of the city and replacing them with French place names, architecture, and spatial distribution, would by extension dictate the circulation and interaction of native and European inhabitants; in the same way, Panamanian bids for foreign investment from the early nineteenth century on intended at bottom to attract an infusion of European blood that would homogenize the motley Afro-Panamanian, West Indian, and mestizo populations that formed the majority of Isthmians. According to Panama's tiny white merchant-class oligarchy, the economic stagnation of the isthmus was inseparable from its biological disarray, and its development into a cosmopolitan point of commerce could only bring with it the salutary effect of a much-needed demographic order (an order, it should be noted, that ultimately would be achieved by US-imposed segregation after 1903).[8] Travel narratives by European and North American visitors from the 1850s second this sentiment, expressing particular dismay at the miserable state of the shantytowns that surrounded the coastal cities, where black and mestizo peddlers and dockworkers hawked their goods and services to arriving throngs of travelers.[9] Doubtless the "degenerate aspect" of Panama that saddens Jules de France comprises its racial as well as spatial disorder: his proposed duplication of Algeria on the isthmus imagines a more appropriate alignment of its ethnic components, much in the same way that the renovation of Algiers—where, as he adds, one formerly found only "Turks, Moors, and Jews"—modeled the city around European settlers.[10]

From the foregoing examples we have seen that the spatial imaginary of the nineteenth-century Latin transatlantic, caught between the centripetal model of the phalanstery and the centrifugal explosion of Saint-Simonian networks, inserts nonwhite populations into global schemes of labor and trade. To attempt a more cohesive theorization of this troping of space and of its determinate relationship to shifting techniques of social control during the nineteenth century, I want to revisit some of the main points of Michel Foucault's meditations on race discourse and biopower in his lectures at the Collège de France. Foucault's analysis tracks the evolution of modern race-thinking to the resuscitation of "race war" discourse by eighteenth-century French noblemen: what is originally invoked as a "counter-history" to the triumphalist mythology of the absolute monarchy, a narrative of ancient enmity among warring peoples, is appropriated and reinterpreted by the French revolution as class warfare; later, race discourse is incorporated into the liberal bourgeois state as the struggle against an internal Other that threatens the national body. "State racism," writes Foucault, "takes over and reconverts the form and function of the discourse on race struggle, but it distorts them and it will be characterized by the fact that the theme of historical war—with its battles, its invasions, its lootings, its victories, its defeats—will be replaced by the post-evolutionist theme of the struggle for existence" (Foucault 1997, 80). What is so significant about Foucault's theory is the way the changing idea of race keeps pace with the emergence of new technologies of social control. The transition of race from an ethnic divide between opposed but equal civilizations into a marker of biological unfitness also expresses the consolidation of state sovereignty through the overlapping regimes of discipline and security. In the first, power regiments the movement of society as individual bodies, while in the second, power addresses its subjects no longer properly as bodies or a "people" but, in a "massifying" move, as species and population; likewise, security's strategy, rather than the atomized surveillance of persons, aims at the calculation and neutralization of risk, the generalized "homeostasis" of the life of the species through "forecasts, statistical estimates, and overall measures" (1997, 246).

Numerous critics have noted that Foucault's treatment of race is stunted by its overwhelming focus on European histories of state-led exclusion, and by the fact that it has little to say about imperialism: resituating his points within the historical particulars of racial domination in different colonial contexts, as well as in their reciprocal impact on methods of controlling metropolitan subjects, we can perceive more concretely how the fluidity among sovereign, disciplinary, and security modes of power shapes the racialization of imperial subjects.[11] Under imperialism, as Ann Laura Stoler has shown with the social policies of the Dutch Indies, "both the notions of a 'population' and a 'people' often were being crafted by administrators cum ethnographers at the same time. As populations were being enumerated, classified, and fixed, 'peoples' were being regrouped and reconfigured according to somatic, cultural, and psychological criteria that would make such administrative interventions necessary and credible" (Stoler 1995, 133). This same slippage is detectable in texts of *Latinité*; in Samper's overview of New Grenada, for example, ethnographic depictions of different regions and customs are interspersed with the statistical breakdown of black, indigenous, white, and mixed-race populations, as well as with encomiums to the self-consciously "Latin" character of its inhabitants. New Grenadians might be backward vis-à-vis Europe, Samper concedes, "but they are also a courageous, hardy, hospitable, generous people, full of the sense of honor and of consciousness of their role in *Latin* America" (Samper 1860a, 161). These subjects are recommended as a healthy addition to the species—as we saw before, Samper praises their economic vitality and the "marvelous" mixing of their biological types—but their health stems in part from conscious moral qualities, in short their active embrace of "Latin" ideals. *Latinité*, then, oscillates between the sense of race as a people, a unified agent in politics as war (as Chevalier's original formulation shows, Latin identity discourse is often couched in narratives of a millennial clash of civilizations), and concern with the survival and security of a population. When García Calderón, predicting the onset of World War I, speaks of giant masses of Latins, Anglos, and Slavs "springing into formation, in the name of . . . a common origin," or when Ugarte describes Latin America as a colossus "amputated" by US imperialism, their images refer simultaneously to the sovereign body of the people and to the struggle for existence; the rise of Japan, the aggression of Germany, and the rapacious incursions of the United States imperil Latin populations' access to resources and markets, a threat that ultimately involves not just war but total extinction.

If it is true that *Latinité*, following Foucault's ideas, is tied to a power whose function is to make live, to populate and to secure a species of man, it nonetheless expresses this power through the fetishized embodiment of immediacy and access. I have traced this paradox to the Saint-Simonian rhetoric of industrial expansion, but it also corresponds to the spatial distinction Foucault makes between discipline and security: On the one hand, discipline "isolates, concentrates" (Foucault 2007, 67), as in the phalanstery (not coincidentally, one of his prime examples of discipline), where "the very layout of the estate articulated . . . the disciplinary mechanisms that controlled the body" (Foucault 1997, 251); on the other, "apparatuses of security . . . have the constant tendency to expand; they are centrifugal [and involve] organizing, or anyway allowing, the development of ever-wider circuits" (Foucault 2007, 67). While the racial fusion and localized harmony of *Latinité*, we may say, orders bodies through the discipline of the commune, its body is also "massified" as the personification of infinite circulation and endless expansion. In order to understand more fully how this leap in scale between territory and circuit is achieved, we must add to Foucault's paradigm the dimension of imperialism that he overlooks: If there is in fact common ground between *Latinité*'s imperialist agenda and its use of biopower, it has to do with what Hannah Arendt calls the "political emancipation of the bourgeoisie." In *The Origins of Totalitarianism*, Arendt locates the roots of the insatiable "scramble" of high imperialism starting in the 1880s in the generation of excess capital in European markets, and its overflow into schemes of foreign investment (of which the Suez and Panama Canals were preeminent examples), which "threatened to transform large strata of society into gamblers, [and] to change the whole capitalist economy from a system of production into a system of financial speculation" (Arendt 1958, 135). The crucial outcome of this radical liberalization of capital, coupled with the growing political clout of the bourgeoisie, was the conversion of the political edifice of government into an economic machine, and the resulting conversion of imperialism into a national duty. A correlative effect, as Arendt illustrates in the rise of pan-German and pan-Slav movements, is the obligatory turning of "race war" discourse toward the task of suturing national populations, in a pseudo-political mandate, to an ever greater and more diverse array of "peoples."

Arendt fills in the imperialist link between sovereignty and biopower that Foucault elides: The two studies put together suggest that imperialist capitalism's usurpation of national governance and biopower's usurpation of old technologies of sovereignty are synchronous and kindred processes. Saint-Simonian space, I am suggesting, emblematizes both of them. Not only is the Saint-Simonian model of politics, based in the authority of public banks and the guarantee of unlimited public credit for the maximum circulation of value, a transparent avatar of the imperialist mantra that "expansion [is] a permanent and supreme aim of politics" (Arendt 1958, 135). As Ludovic Frobert puts it, the movement's political vision quite literally "culminates in the hope of replacing the 'government of men' with 'the administration of things,' meaning the economy absorbs politics" (Frobert 2011, 733). But more important for considerations of race is the way the shift in scope from political territory to economic circuit, and from national population to global species, fundamentally *abstracts* the people it controls. In Marx's words, the "annihilation of space with time" precipitated by the Saint-Simonians' own railways and canals automatically, as Foucault puts it, "massifies" laboring bodies: it regards labor "not as the working day of the individual worker, but as the indefinite working day of an indefinite number of workers," making "the basic doctrines of population" as integral a principle of capitalist relations as profit and credit (Marx 1973, 240). The translation of political subjects into "indefinite," or infinite, labor carried out by capitalist speculation and its imperial aegis helps to explain *Latinité*'s instrumentalization of race for overseas expansion. In it, the generalized and finally abstract terrain of labor, resources, and credit captured by industrial networks is supplemented, in essence given a "body," by race war discourse. It does not just exemplify the way the "strategic polyvalence" (Foucault 1997, 76) of race allows it to co-opt and combine different modes of social control, making, for example, the sovereign body of ancient peoples into a vehicle for biopolitical technology; it also highlights the hand imperialist capitalism has in legitimizing such translations and in securing the paradigms of power they give rise to.

Latinité's symbiosis of abstract and embodied race—a mostly diffuse, if salient, feature of nineteenth-century political discourse—comes increasingly to shape official definitions of nation and empire with the intensification of pan-Hispanism and the recrudescence of French colonialist agendas after 1900. Onésime Reclus's *Le Partage du monde* (The Division of the World, 1906) boldly illustrates the concomitant sharpening of its spatial hallmarks. Reclus was a French geographer and author of several treatises from the 1880s that argued aggressively to extend France's empire into sub-Saharan Africa; in *Le Partage du monde*, he gives a painstaking inventory of the Anglo, Slav, and Latin races, narrating the historic rise of each group, describing the terrain, climate, and inhabitants of their member nations, and evaluating their chances for world domination. Reclus addends his geographic accounts with a series of tables that tally the total acreage and population accrued to each race's "share" of the globe. Calculating the figure of 2,179,000 acres and 72,880,000 Latin and "neo-Latin" subjects represented by French Canada and Latin America, for example, he proudly summarizes: "That is more than 56% of the total American territory, and 48% of its population . . . in a region of which one can say that it truly has infinite resources" (Reclus 1906, 225). Reclus's image of the earth, then, is composed at once of "peoples" and "populations," who may fight each other to the death as they may also extinguish one another's existence by usurping their biological stock or blocking their uninhibited movement in world markets. Gauging the Yankee threat to Latin populations of Central America, he weighs the latter's advantages against US incursions both in the terms of biopower and through personified allegory. The Latins, he reasons, "will perish soon if Brother Jonathan soon opens his mouth with its long yellow teeth; they will be saved if he delays too much, for the neo-Latin nations double every thirty years. . . . Even if they are swallowed whole, they will shortly come back out undigested . . . one does not denature 18 million Latins just like that, or one risks throwing them back in a sudden fit of vomiting" (207). The picture of Brother Jonathan (Uncle Sam) as a giant ogre waiting to gobble up the Central American isthmus plays upon the importance size and ethnic identity alike have for political survival. The neo-Latins are protected by their sheer numbers and prolificness—so many souls, Reclus suggests, could not physically be devoured by their enemy. But this demographic edge is complemented by the indelible quality of race, which makes them naturally impervious or "undigestible" to cultural annihilation.

Through images like these, Reclus reproduces the spatial imagination of the Saint-Simonians nearly a century later to draw a world map of future Latin dominance at once endless and cut to human measure. So complete is this duality of scale in *Le Partage du monde* that in a single paragraph Reclus can instruct his readers, first, that "to think about taking hold of the world in one grip, you [must] first know that it is very small and graspable," only then to remind them that "the citizen of the world has naturally measured his gaze, his ambitions, his efforts by the growing magnitude of his horizon" (279). His rather strabismic perspective, which conceives a world in constant growth that is also at one's fingertips, reflects the tendency of official imperial discourse after 1870 to view colonial dominions as an extension or appendage of the nation. Reclus's generation was the first to talk about the French empire as "La plus grande France," a vast nation whose imperial satellites joined their capital across thousands of miles of shipping routes, railroads, and telegraph lines, converting a massive, disjointed territory into a graspable corner of the world. His visual summary of the Latin Transatlantic hinges on this contrast, painting the immense distances separating its European, African, and American reaches as an area of man-sized proportions: thanks to the colonization of French West Africa, he avers, "we can say without violating the truth that we . . . touch [South America]" (267). From the "French Pernambuco" of Dakar to the Brazilian Pernambuco, "the ships have only 700 leagues to cross"—"not even half the distance between Brest and New York" (267). In sum, Reclus's Latin world covers a territory descending south from Europe through the strait of Gibraltar—which, he notes, is "so slender that we have conceived the project of traversing it by tunnel"—over the Sahara to Dakar, crossing the Atlantic to Pernambuco, and terminating at the fjords of Tierra del Fuego. "Our special world, belonging to us natural or adopted sons of the Latium, extends like a floating scarf from the Northeast to the Southwest, from the 51st northern latitude to the 56th southern, without any more interruption than a nearly enclosed sea and an ocean open between the New and Old Worlds: in short, it is compact" (268).

Recognizing that even fantastical constructs like Reclus's Latium attach themselves to biopolitical fictions forces us to see *Latinité*, well beyond the usual philological investigations into its development, as a supremely malleable vector of race relations in the Southern Atlantic. Such a view is not simply a tool for understanding localized contexts but, more important, one for identifying the ways otherwise unrelated groups, responding to a variety of impulses, milieus, and phenomena, are hailed into a single grid of intelligibility of modern race thinking. It can help to explain, for example, how *mestizaje* and *francophonie*, the major discourses descended from *Latinité* in twentieth-century Spanish America and West Africa, respectively, have much less to do with managing real practices of cultural or racial mixing than with capturing laboring subjects for liberal and neoliberal production circuits.[12] If, as Walter Mignolo writes, "the history of 'Latin' America . . . is the variegated history of the local elite . . . embracing 'modernity' while indigenous, Afro, and poor Mestizo/a peoples get poorer and more marginalized," the "homogenizing discourse of official francophonie" (Mignolo 2005, 57), in Patrick Corcoran's characterization "is . . . part of the process of creating and sustaining a myth that serves to mask [the reality] of the asymmetrical nature of power relations between centre and periphery" (Corcoran 2007, 9). Quietly bringing together histories like these, *Latinité* remains a powerful but untapped foundation of the global South Atlantic.

NOTES

Unless otherwise indicated by the bibliographic information, all translations from original French or Spanish texts are my own.

1. Political organicism, of course, does not begin with Saint-Simon's theories. The notion of the state as a sovereign "body" is central to Hobbes's *Leviathan*, as well as to medieval political theology, as Ernst Kantorowicz showed in *The King's Two Bodies* (1997). However, its Saint-Simonian formulations are unique insofar as these are meant to mobilize global circuits of trade and labor beyond national borders.

2. Benjamin, for example, famously commented in "Paris, Capital of the Nineteenth Century" that the Saint-Simonians, "despite their participation in industrial and commercial enterprises around the middle of the century, were

helpless on all questions concerning the proletariat" (1999, 18). For an exposition of the Saint-Simonian concept of exploitation, see Cunliffe and Reeve (1996).

3. The spiritual or "religious" moments of Saint-Simonianism, like the 1833 "mission des compagnons de la femme," have commonly led to the movement's reputation for eccentricity, and were roundly disavowed by the followers, like Chevalier, who reinvented themselves as political economists under Napoleon III. For the influence of the mission to Egypt on the colonization of Algeria, see Picon (2002), chapter 4.

4. As Aims McGuinness (2003) demonstrates, the influx of US Forty-Niners attempting to reach California through Panama during the gold rush—in particular the resulting racial conflicts between US travelers accustomed to slavery and Afro-Panamanians, who under Colombian law enjoyed the full rights of citizenship—was instrumental to the emergence of the title and notion of "Latin" America from 1856 on.

5. For an overview of the most prominent Fourierist and Owenist experiments in Latin America, see Abramson. Algeria was also the site of numerous imagined and attempted communes; besides the Sig phalanstery discussed later, an ambitious plan was put forth by colonial official Léon Christophe Louis Jouchault de Lamoricière to finance fourteen communes directly inspired by Enfantin (Abi-Mershed 2010, 114).

6. Both Abi-Mershed (chapter 6) and Lorcin (chapter 8) provide thorough analyses of the conflicts that roiled Algeria's colonial administration until 1870. Each points out that the opposing doctrines of "assimilation"—the overt incorporation of Algeria and its institutions into national jurisdiction, and the conversion of indigenous Algerians into French citizens—and "association," which aimed at looser governance over autonomous indigenous groups, were never applied one to the exclusion of the other. The Arab Kingdoms, although a purportedly associationist initiative, nevertheless clearly sought the assimilation of Arab populations.

7. George Voisin was Urbain's nom de plume. Urbain, born in French Guyana to a white French father and a black slave mother, was often held up as a living example of universal association, both because of his mixed heritage and because, inspired by his experiences during the Saint-Simonian mission in Egypt, he converted to Islam and dedicated his career as an imperial translator and official to the "arabophile" cause. For a discussion of Urbain's relationship to Islam, see Levallois.

8. As Peter Szok explains, both the movement for independence from Colombia and the campaigns to build a canal through foreign investment, for elites were tied to the opportunity to bolster the white population of the isthmus against Afro-Panamanian, and later West Indian, efforts to gain greater recognition in national politics. See Szok (2012), chapter 1.

9. McGuinness (2007) gives examples of 1850s travel accounts of Panama and an analysis of the economic development of the isthmus during the nineteenth century; see Chapter 2.

10. For an analysis of the colonial agenda behind the rebuilding of Algiers after 1830, see Clancy Smith (2009).

11. In addition to Stoler (1995), both Venn (2009) and Rasmussen (2011) attempt to supplement Foucault's thinking on race with histories of imperialism.

12. The most famous architect of *mestizaje*, the Mexican José Vasconcelos, as well as the father of *francophonie*, Senegalese president Léopold Sédar Senghor, were both champions of *Latinité*. See, as signature documents of their thought, Vasconcelos's *La raza cósmica* (1948) and Senghor's "Eloge de la Latinité" (1961).

Scheherazade in Chains

Arab-Islamic Genealogies of African Diasporic Literature

Jason Frydman

Focusing on foundational texts by figures such as Olaudah Equiano, Mary Prince, and Frederick Douglass, scholars have traditionally viewed the New World slave narrative as a literary genre genealogically linked to Protestant spiritual autobiography and the picaresque novel. While over the past decades interdisciplinary Africana studies have increasingly excavated the presence of African Muslims within the archive of slave narratives,[1] less has been done to think through the specifically literary implications of Muslim slave narratives.[2] This material, penned by slaves or their amanuenses in Arabic, English, French, and Portuguese, and distributed quite evenly around the Americas, appearing in Canada, the United States, Panama, Jamaica, Trinidad, and Brazil, lays out a Global South Atlantic field of literary production whose formal and philosophical influences radically reorient the foundational genres and geographies of New World Black literature.

In particular, Arabic sources such as *The Thousand and One Nights*, the eleventh-century *Maqamat* of al-Hariri, fifteenth-and sixteenth-century Maghrebi epistles of captivity, and the classical Arabic *sira* or exemplary life story, in conjunction with Orientalist textual, ethnographic, and mercantile mediations, fashion a literary formation that displaces Protestant spiritual autobiography and the Spanish picaresque novel as privileged origin, while asserting greater centrality to the Caribbean basin and the Senegambia region as formal and philosophical engines of the African diasporic literary tradition. Furthermore, the narratives of Job ben Solomon/Ayuba Suleiman Ibrahima Diallo, Prince/Ibrahima Abd al-Rahman Jallo, and Abu Bakr al-Siddiq foreground a liminal time and space constituted by the experience of administrative detention, of the expired visa, of deportation, and of repatriation.

These *avant la lettre* experiences proffer Muslim slave narratives as generative forebears of transnational, multicultural literature in both England and the United States—anticipating Global South Atlantic literary crossings with multiple diasporic and postcolonial traditions—yet forebears consistently marked in their own time and subsequently by an aggressively racist dialectic of amnesia and surprise. We can also detect in their enduring oscillation between obscurity and legibility, and in our own efforts to assemble the dispersed traces these Global South Atlantic forebears left behind in Brazilian, Canadian, English, Jamaican, Panamanian, Trinidadian, and US newspapers, letters, ledgers, and legal documents, a strategic archival reticence that vexes even as it structures the archive of the Global South Atlantic. The transoceanic subjects who deposited their traces in this archive rendered tangible, against multiple forces of erasure, shared networks of language, trade, education, religion, and discursive self-fashioning; and they also defiantly withdrew, at long last, into an opacity that delimits our own archival task.

The Muslim slave has made scattered appearances in Anglophone fiction. A small selection of nineteenth-century novels explore the figure of the Muslim slave in the United States, from Harriet Beecher Stowe's *Dred, A Tale of the Great Dismal Swamp* (1856) to Joel Chandler Harris's *The Story of Aaron, So Named, the Son of Ben Ali* (1896). Alex Haley's *Roots* (1976) and Toni Morrison's *Song of Solomon* (1977) famously stage the recovery of Muslim ancestry for twentieth-century readers. Whereas the former texts rely on an exotic Orientalism that dissociates African Muslims from the mainstream of the African American population, the latter texts attempt to weave Islam into a common, if often reticent and obscured, ancestral fabric. Yet despite their concern with figures genealogically linked to the Arab-Islamic culture of West Africa, neither set of texts formally appropriate Arab-Islamic literature as an intertextual influence.

The punning title of Guadeloupean writer Daniel Maximin's 1995 novel *L'île et une nuit*, on the other hand, anticipates a suspenseful night of vernacular storytelling formally linked to *Les milles et une nuit*. As a hurricane approaches Guadeloupe, the narrator-protagonist Marie-Gabriele braces herself for the anticipated storm at dawn by recounting in tale, in song, and on the phone, the story of her life, her island, and her spiritual universe. Maximin figures *creolité* under the sign of Scheherazade, whose "nocturnal poetics" of survival highlight the discursive and material subordination of this *française d'outre-mer* (Ghazoul 1996). In narrating New World creolization through Scheherazade, Maximin taps a long-lived imperial incitement to make the African diasporic subject speak, to narrate, to offer a story for a life.

A story for a life: The shadow of Scheherazade's macabre transaction hangs over enslaved Muslim textuality, in particular, as it intersects with European Orientalist possession of and enthrallment to *The Thousand and One Nights*. This intersection emerges irresistibly in the story of Job ben Solomon, or Ayuba Suleiman Ibrahima Diallo. Son of a "High Priest" of Bundu, north of the Gambia River, Job belonged to a class of "Muslim clerics with mercantile interests" (Curtin 1967, 37). Sent by his father in 1730 to trade with an English vessel recently docked on the Gambia, specifically to sell two slaves and to buy paper, Job could not come to terms with one Captain Pike and continued on to the other side of the river. After selling his two slaves, he was himself abducted by a band of Mande and sold to the very same Captain Pike he had originally failed to reach terms with. Captain Pike gave Job leave to send to his father for ransom, but as the return trip of the letter-bearing messenger took longer than the ship was to remain in port, Job endured the Middle Passage.

Arriving in Maryland, he was set to work on Alexander Tolsey's tobacco plantation. Unused to physical labor, mocked during his devotions, and "grown in some measure desperate," his contemporaneous biographer Thomas Bluett writes, Job "resolved to travel at a venture; thinking he might possibly be taken up by some master, who would use him better, or otherwise meet with some lucky accident, to divert or abate his grief, he travelled through the woods, till he came to the County of Kent" (Bluett, in Curtin 1967, 42). Job's contemporary biographer Douglas Grant notes the particular literary mediation Bluett subjects Job's broken English tale to; he "introduces Job's escape as though it was the beginning of a picaresque adventure" that obscures the terror of an unknown wilderness patrolled by bounty-hunting Native Americans and English settlers (Grant 1968, 82). As a curiosity brought out of his jail cell to entertain the county gentlemen in their cups after a day of court, Job wrote and recited lines of Arabic, the lingua franca of West Africa. When he "pronounced the words Allah and Muhammad; by which, and his refusing a glass of wine we offered him, we perceived he was a Mahometan, but could not imagine of what country he was, or how he got thither; for by his affable carriage, and the easy composure of his countenance, we could perceive he was no common slave" (Bluett, in Curtin 1967, 42).

Here we see one of the first appearances of that dialectic of amnesia and surprise that will mark the histories of African Muslims, in North America in particular, from the eighteenth century to the present. Reading newspaper advertisements for runaway slaves, Michael Gomez argues that throughout the eighteenth century and well into the nineteenth, European colonists and their descendants were intimately familiar with the physiological and cultural diversity of African ethnicities (Gomez 1998, 5). Yet in Bluett's retelling, the gentlemen in Maryland "could not imagine of what country he was, or how he got thither." Judging by the fact that this group shortly procured the translation services of a Wolof-speaker among the local enslaved population, such information was not so hard to come by. Instead, the repetition of this pattern of ignorance and surprise across centuries suggests that there is some cultural-cognitive block refusing the recognition of African Muslims in the Americas, perhaps rooted in the disjuncture between the status of Islam as a "civilization" and the alleged barbarity of Africans, but to be explored more fully later.

Through the aforementioned Wolof-speaking intermediary, Job revealed the name of his owner, with whom he shortly negotiated better terms on the plantation. Furthermore, by communicating his high station in his native land, he enticed Tolsey and this gathered body of gentlemen to allow him to write once more to his father: "he therefore wrote a letter in Arabick to his father, acquainting him with his misfortunes, hoping he might yet find means to redeem him" (Bluett, in Curtin 1967, 43).

The circulation of this purloined letter would imbricate Job in Orientalist networks of power and pleasure, knowledge and finance. For while addressed to his father in Bundu by care of Captain Pike, the captain's itineraries consistently failed to line up with the itinerary of the letter, which ended up reaching the deputy governor of the Royal African Company, noted prison-reformer and "philanthropist" James Oglethorpe. Oglethorpe "was so struck by its curiosity and unusual history" that he sent it to John Gagnier, who held Oxford's Laudian Chair of Arabic. "Oglethorpe," Grant writes, "was so deeply moved by it and impressed by the sense of its author's character that he decided without hesitation that such a person could not be left in slavery and must be redeemed . . . In June 1732, Oglethorpe gave his bond for the payment of 45BPS—Job's purchase price—upon Job being delivered to him in London" (Grant 1968, 85). For

Henry Louis Gates, the story ends here: "Job Ben Solomon literally wrote his way out of slavery; his literacy, translated into forty-five pounds, was the commodity with which he earned his escape price" (Gates 1989, 13).

Actually, however, as Job recognized at the time, he remained a slave and had merely exchanged Tolsey's ownership for Oglethorpe's. The next installment of Job's narrative turns on reiterated Scheherazadian storytelling performances that would prolong his relative liberty until such time as he could achieve true freedom, a freedom that would be partially enacted by retreating from the prolixity that singled him out among contemporaries and in the archive as "no common slave."

Bluett, a cleric with the Society for the Propagation of the Gospel, traveled with Job from Maryland to England, teaching him English and observing his Muslim practices. He saw him installed in lodgings arranged by Oglethorpe's factor Henry Hunt, and after a brief trip on his own business he returned to a "very sorrowful" friend: "Mr. Hunt had been applied to by some persons to sell him, who pretended they would send him home; but he feared they would sell him again as a slave, or if they sent him home would expect an unreasonable ransom for him" (Bluett, in Curtin 1967, 44). Job's tale-bearing prompted Bluett to remove him from these lodgings and to circulate him in the rich merchant circles of Cheshunt, the Orientalist societies of London, and the royal court. In Cheshunt, Job "had the Honour to be sent for by most of the Gentry of that Place, who were mightily pleased with his company, and concerned for his misfortunes" (Bluett, in Curtin 1967, 45). Job's presence in London, anticipated by the circulation among Orientalists of his Arabic letter to his father, presaged his incorporation into the Gentleman's Society of Spalding, a preeminent group of intellectuals, antiquarians, and Orientalists including George Sale, translator of the Koran, Sir Hans Sloane, collector of rarities, and the poet Alexander Pope.

Yet even this seemingly advantageous development concealed grave risks for Job's liberty. Sloane and the others believed that as his owner, the Royal African Company would "behave honourably" toward Job and that "he was, in fact, more secure by being their responsibility" than he would be were he free, and they therefore exerted pressure against efforts to release him from his bond (Grant 1968, 103). Aware of his precarious position, outside of his meetings with scholars and Orientalists, Job tirelessly sent himself out into a world of influential merchants, bankers, and aristocrats who took an interest in the African trade. It is important to remember that Job himself was a merchant, and he played the English desire to gain position over the French in the Senegambian gold and Arabic gum trades to his advantage (Curtin 1967, 22). Of such social encounters, Bluett records: "In Conversation he was commonly very pleasant; and would every now and then divert the Company with some witty Turn, or pretty Story" (Bluett, in Curtin 1967, 48–49). And in a strange presaging of the fate of Sudan's lost boys on the fundraising circuit in the West, Grant notes: "He often introduced lions into his conversation, especially when he saw how much they were appreciated" (Grant 1968, 93).[3] Through these narrative seductions, Job soon raised enough funds for the subscription started to purchase his complete freedom from the Royal African Company, with contributors including the Duke of Montague and the Bey of Tunis, reimbursing the Company not only for Job's purchase price but, outrageously enough, the costs of his upkeep during nearly two years of not-quite-liberty in England.

Both Philip Curtin and Douglas Grant, Job's preeminent modern biographers, read eighteenth-century interest in Job through the lens of the period's fascination with the noble savage, especially as embodied in Aphra Behn and Thomas Southerne's Oroonoko. But whereas Oroonoko militantly sacrifices himself and his beloved in keeping with a tragic code of honor and chastity, Job sustains his relative liberty through acts of refinement, wit, and narrative seduction strongly articulated through Arabic and Islamic traditions (while in England he transcribed from memory three Qur'ans), as well as a keen sense of mercantilism. So while Oroonoko offers one sympathetic European paradigm for the enslaved African in the first half of the eighteenth century, we should remember that at the same moment England was positively stuck on Scheherazade, emblem of a story-cycle trafficked by merchants from East Asia to West Africa, embodying the carnivalesque wisdom literature of the marketplace.

Translations of Antoine Galland's enormously popular French *Les milles et une nuit* began to appear in 1706 as *The Arabian Nights Entertainment*, after which Grub Street editions were continuously republished, and the Orientalist class would certainly have been aware of the on-going French production of Oriental tales including exiled English author Anthony Hamilton's 1730 *Les quatre facardins*. It was precisely the Orientalist circles surrounding the Gentleman's Society of Spalding that pushed hardest to keep Job at hand as a native informant, a Scheherazade harem-ed in Bloomsbury, "to read some of Sir Han'ses stones with [Arabick] characters" and "translating several manuscripts and inscriptions upon medals" (Grant 1968, 100–1; Bluett, in Curtin 1967, 55). On the other hand, with an experienced merchant's wiles, he lured traders and bankers with promised connections to the interior African trade. He enticed evangelicals and philanthropists with visions of heathens uplifted by means of Western technology—"a rich gold watch from Her Majesty" and "tools" from the Duke of Montague (Bluett, in Curtin 1967, 57). Job at least persuaded them to allow him to continue serving as a native informant back in his native land, working as a factor for the Royal African Company, and not a very well treated one at that, according to a contentious record in the company's archives, nickel-and-diming Job once more (Austin 1984, 107). After 1744, no archival trace remains of his connection with the Company, which bankrupt and anachronistic lost its charter in 1750, or with his friends and contacts in England, who by "some witty Turn, or pretty Story . . . were mightily pleased with his company, and concerned for his misfortunes."

Maximin, we recall, figures black Antillean speech as the speech of Scheherazade, imposed upon and incited by imperial decree, yet seductively turned toward self-preservation. Calling into being a field of Global South Atlantic narrative production before retreating definitively from the network of connections that would have ensured him a more extensive inscription in the archive, Job ben Solomon's native education, his itinerant occupation, and Orientalist encounters in bondage insinuate Scheherazadian narrative strategies into the repertoire of New World Black literature, to be perused and appropriated by future narrators, enframers, and creole storytellers such as Maximin and Marie-Gabriele.

Another Caribbean intellectual, Edward Blyden, would elect another protagonist out of the Arabic tradition as a figure of transatlantic diasporic speech, al-Hariri's Abu Zayd. Originally hailing from Charlotte Amelie, in the Danish West Indian holding of St. Thomas, Blyden took an early interest in things Semitic, studying Hebrew as a teenager with members of the island's Sephardic community. After impressing a local Methodist mission with his intelligence, and after being denied the opportunity to pursue divinity studies in the United States, he was sent to Liberia to complete his education at Liberia College, where he was soon ordained and took a professorship in classics. Blyden expanded into Orientalist studies, partly out of a desire to refute racist interpretations of the Bible, and partly out of his encounter with the Arab-Islamic culture of West African Muslims.

The eleventh-century *Maqamat* of al-Hariri (1054–1122) emerges as the most important nonsacred work in the portrait of West African letters offered by Blyden in his many writings.[4] These *Maqamat*, along with those of al-Hamadhani, represent the foundational texts of the *maqama* tradition in Arabic, and subsequently also in Hebrew, Persian, and Syriac. Written in rhymed, rhythmic prose (*saj*ʿ), *maqamat* (often translated as "assemblies" or "settings," "*séances*" in French) episodically recount the travels of rhetorically gifted, roguish trickster figures through the social geography of the Islamic world. Blyden's fondness for the *Maqamat*, as well as for the West African Muslim culture he gained familiarity with in Liberia, prompted him to incorporate al-Hariri into the Anglophone curriculum of Liberia College, thereby bringing it in line with the Arabic curriculum of the Sahel. During senior exams in 1870, Blyden invited "a learned Muslim from Kankan" to sit in as the students read from the Qur'an and the English translation of the French Orientalist Silvestre de Sacy's edition of the *Maqamat* of al-Hariri:

> Our Mohammedan visitor happened to have with him the whole of the fifty Makamat in elegant manuscript. He followed the students as they read, repeating after them in an undertone. Of course he could not judge of the translation, as he understood not a word of English. I communicated with him in Arabic. After the students had read I requested him to read the same portion, that they might hear his pronunciation. He read in the musical cantilating manner of the East, and the listener who had travelled in these countries might have fancied himself on the banks of the Nile, or on Mount Lebanon. (Blyden 1871, 69–70)

Blyden's retelling of the learned Muslim from Kankan's visit to his classroom allows him to double and redouble the figure of the ambulant, cosmopolitan Muslim that so captured his imagination: from al-Hariri's hero Abu Zayd traveling throughout the Islamic world; to those "African Moslems" who, Blyden observes, "are continually crossing the continent to Egypt, Arabia, and Syria;" and finally to Blyden's own repetition of those itineraries, alluded to here but documented more fully in his 1873 travelogue *From West Africa to Palestine* (Blyden 1871, 96). West African participation in the *umma*, or world Islamic community, fosters for Blyden a vision of mobility and intellectualism whose ancient legacy refutes racist erasures of African historicity and cosmopolitanism. It also fueled his own efforts to reconvene scattered Atlantic trajectories in a contemporary West African cosmopolitanism comprising indigenous elements, emigrants to Liberia and Sierra Leone, and the "liberated Africans or returned exiles from Cuba and Brazil" that made up one quarter of the population of Lagos during the years that Blyden shuttled between that city, Freetown, and Monrovia (Lynch 1970, 220).

Additionally, Al-Hariri and his hero Abu Zayd provide Arab-Islamic letters with a figure of piercing social analysis and verbal performativity carried forth to the New World in the memories of enslaved Muslims. An 1871 volume, *The People of Africa*, brought Blyden's revisionist studies of biblical and classical antiquity, and his early writings on Islam in West Africa, together with Theodore Dwight's "Condition and Character of Negroes in Africa," a survey of enslaved Muslims in the United States originally published in 1864. An antislavery activist and founding member of the American Ethnological Society, Dwight's work with "Omar-ben-Sayeed, long living in Fayetteville, N.C." helps us expand Blyden's constellation of al-Hariri with this field of Global South Atlantic literary production (Dwight 1871, 60). Omar ibn Sa'id (1770–1864), a Fulbe from Futa Toro, would gain significant attention when his "autobiography," composed in Arabic, circulated widely in the 1830s, '40s, and '50s. Interest spiked again when this text appeared in translation in the *American Historical Review* in 1925.

Ibn Sa'id had received extensive education in Arabic before being captured and sold into New World slavery. His letter of 1819 reproduces from memory extensive selections from the Qur'an and the *oeuvre* of al-Hariri (Hunwick 2003–4, 63–65). His autobiographical letter of 1831 also employs numerous tropes from the epistolary captivity narrative genre prevalent in the Maghreb in the sixteenth and seventeenth centuries, which as Nabil Matar shows in *Europe through Arab Eyes*, draws extensively on al-Hariri's *maqamat* (Matar 2009, 245). Like those captives, ibn Sa'id fashions himself as "someone who went every year to the holy war against the infidels" and who remains "in the Christian land . . . by reason of great necessity" (Hunwick 2003–4, 63). Furthermore, ibn Sa'id's flight from "a small, weak, and wicked man called Johnson, a complete infidel, who had no fear of God at all;" his subsequent arrest and time "in the great house (which, in the Christian language, they called jail);" and his ultimate deliverance into the hands of Jim Owen, "who never beats me, nor scolds me," uncannily echoes that of the *pícaro* Lazarillo de Tormes, whose itinerary took him from the house of a very un-Christian priest to the jail cell from which he offered his life story in an appeal for legal clemency (Dwight 1871, 60–61). As mentioned earlier, scholars have long read the slave narrative as an heir of the picaresque novel, a genealogy accounted for by the place of such texts as *Pilgrim's Progress* in Anglo-American, Protestant literacy as well as the problematic narrative frames imposed by white amanuenses such as Thomas Bluett. However, the West African context of ibn Sa'id's education directs us to the well-documented descent of the picaresque from Arabic *maqamat*. Ismail el-Outmani for example charts how the "roguish wanderings [*apicaradas andanzas*]" of the *maqamat* in al-Andalus "fostered the subversiveness of the picaresque," a subversiveness accreted in ibn Sa'id's employment of choice Qur'anic *suras* to subtly denounce slavery and demand liberation (El-Outmani 1994, 106). Ala Alryyes, for example, suggests that ibn Sa'id's recitation of Surat al-Mulk in the opening of his 1831 narrative denies the legitimacy of slavery: "The *sura* contends that it is God who is the owner of all and everything" (Alryyes 2011, 18).

Dwight and the American Colonization Society were eager to recruit Africans with knowledge of the interior for the success of their mission in Liberia. Yet despite their intervention, and the national renown ibn Sa'id achieved through his Arabic writings, the Owen family refused to manumit him. In this, James Owen resembles Thomas Foster, the owner of another West African Muslim in bondage who achieved national fame in the early nineteenth-century United States, Ibrahima Abd al-Rahman Jallo, also called Prince. In fact, Alryyes wonders whether the same *Surat al-Mulk* with which ibn Sa'id opened his 1831 autobiographical letter might not have worked its way into one of the foundational tracts of African American letters through Abd al-Rahman. Echoing the *sura*, David Walker's 1828 *Appeal*, a millennial denunciation of slavery, claims that "God Almighty is the sole proprietor" (Alryyes 2011, 18). Alryyes speculates about possible conversations the two men may have had when Walker served as Second Marshal at the Boston gala in honor of Abd al-Rahman, recently released from three decades of bondage in Natchez, Mississippi and en route, as we will see, back to Africa.

Abd al-Rahman's story, bringing him from the royal house of Futa Jallon to servitude in Natchez, Mississippi, then back to the shores of Africa after a year-long tour of the northern US states, will offer once more a network of Orientalist desires and misrecognitions that allow "Prince" to spin Scheherazadian seductions into the fact of liberation and repatriation. If in the case of Job ben Solomon, the debate over his status *qua* liberty and self-ownership while awaiting repatriation in England raged in small quarters, the heated political context of a nation headed toward civil war raised the stakes of Abd al-Rahman's status in the interim period between his release from bondage in Natchez and his transport to Liberia. Through the lens of his denunciation in the Southern press as a violator of the contractual terms of his "right of passage," we can see African Muslims as archival figures presaging the suspect foreigner working on an expired visa, the lifelong undocumented resident trying to salvage the unity of his multigenerational family while under the sword of imminent deportation.

In 1788, a twenty-six-year-old Abd al-Rahman led a military expedition to protect the borders of Futa Jallon, the emergent state ruled by his father, Sori. After an initial victory, he and his men were captured in a surprise attack and sold into slavery. After transport to Dominica, he ended up on the plantation of the aforementioned Thomas Foster. Abd al-Rahman maintained a strict Muslim dietary code, refraining from pork and alcohol, and also became known for his ethical comportment and leadership. With much of the plantation labor under Abd al-Rahman's direction, Foster's plantation flourished and he became one of the leading men of Natchez. Then in 1807, nearly twenty-years since his capture, something extraordinary happened in the streets of Natchez. Abd al-Rahman spotted a one-eyed Irishman, Dr. John Coates Cox, a ship's surgeon who had fallen ill while hunting on the West African shore in 1781. He was taken in by the aforementioned Sori, king of Futa Jallon. For six months, Dr. Cox convalesced, befriended the royal family, and even took a local wife, before he desired to return to his family in Ireland. Upon seeing Abd al-Rahman in the streets of Natchez, he immediately pressed Thomas Foster to sell him, yet according to Thomas Gallaudet, one of Abd al-Rahman's friends, benefactors, and biographers, "His master doubted whether his freedom would increase his happiness" (Gallaudet, quoted in Alford 2007, 104). His twentieth-century biographer Terry Alford counters that perhaps it was Foster's happiness that was at issue, for through Abd al-Rahman's leadership, the plantation was thriving: "Ibrahima," he concludes, "had made himself invaluable" (Alford 2007, 71).

Nearly twenty years later, Abd al-Rahman would push for his freedom once again through his friendship with Colonel Andrew Marschalk, publisher of the *Mississippi State Gazette*. Marschalk sent an appeal to the Mississippi senator Thomas Reed on behalf of Abd al-Rahman, mistakenly claiming that he belonged to "the royal family of Morocco," and he enclosed a letter in Arabic written by Abd al-Rahman to his family (Austin 1984, 198). Reed forwarded Marschalk and Abd al-Rahman's letters to the State Department, which forwarded them to Thomas Mullowny, the United States consul in Tangier. In order to maintain good diplomatic relations with the King of Morocco, Mullowny recommended to Secretary of State Henry Clay that Abd al-Rahman be purchased and sent home, to which he as well as President John Quincy Adams consented. Thomas Foster subsequently agreed to manumit Abd al-Rahman, under the condition, as Henry Clay writes, "that Prince shall not be permitted to enjoy his liberty in this country, but be sent to his own free from expense to Mr. Foster" (Austin 1984, 198–199). Yet, bailing on his wife, his five children, and his eight grandchildren was not exactly what Abd al-Rahman had in mind. As Gallaudet would write, "Cheering as his situation was, his delight was mingled with the deepest anguish. What was personal freedom when such social ties prevented his enjoying it? His very freedom was almost a curse" (Gallaudet quoted in Alford 2007, 108–109).

Abd al-Rahman explained, in person, to Secretary Clay and President Adams that he was not Moroccan, but Fulbe, and that he requested passage to Liberia, only three hundred miles from Futa Jallon's capital city of Timbo. The statesmen acceded and authorized a passport for him and his wife Isabella. The government of the United States had previously agreed to the expense of returning Prince to Africa, authorizing Cyrus Griffin, who succeeded Marschalk as Abd al-Rahman's tireless advocate and amanuensis, "to defray the expenses of decently, but plainly clothing him . . . and those incident to his voyage and journey to this place . . . to draw upon [Secretary Clay], at sight, for a sum not exceeding two hundred dollars" (Austin 1984, 196–197). With their new knowledge of his origins, they would not make any further provisions for his transatlantic journey, or for the liberation of his American family. Thus begins Abd al-Rahman's campaign to raise the $8,500 the American Colonization Society thought it would take to purchase from Foster his entire family and equip themselves for their resettlement in Liberia. With the funds approved by Secretary Clay, Griffin had acquired for Abd al-Rahman a colorful Moorish outfit for the steamer ride to Cincinnati, and thence on to Washington, D.C. This outfit would only be the most visible misrecognition of Abd al-Rahman. As he plotted the liberation of his family and their return to Africa, this "Unfortunate Moor" and "King of Timbuctoo" would ply many of the same strategies as Job ben Solomon (Alford 2007, 115). From the satisfaction of Orientalist desires to the fulfillment of Christian evangelism, Abd al-Rahman would reflect back to audiences their exotic fantasies and religious certainties.

Gathered audiences, affected by the wondrous and sentimental tale of Abd al-Rahman's life, would fill subscription books with their pledges, emoting in newspaper accounts of this "romantic and extraordinary case" (Alford 2007, 115). Similarly, major players in the American Colonization Society such as the wealthy merchant Arthur Tappan saw in Abd al-Rahman's royal connections the potential to broker a political engagement between Liberia and Futa Jallon, the development of commercial relations that would surely ensue, and ultimately the extensive conversions to Christianity that such commerce would foster. "It is more than probable," he wrote of the opportunity that Abd al-Rahman presented, "that within two years, we should hear of a thriving commerce with the whole of that vast interior . . . and what is of more weight still with the Christian and Philanthropist, a way would be opened for the entrance of Charity and the Christian Religion" (Austin 1984, 178). Abd al-Rahman, as he gained knowledge of the ideology of the American Colonization Society, tailored his message to convince them that their investment of time, ink, and money would pay off. In an outrageous falsehood matched only by the ignorance it was expected to meet, he writes in an open letter, "When I left my country almost all the young people followed the Christian religion. Whether they continue to follow it, I know not. When I take home the two books [you have given me], the Arabic Testament [Bible] and [an Arabic tract on the truth of Christianity], I think they will follow the Christians. I hope when I go home to tell them the Christian way, and that they will go by it" (Austin 1984, 157). While Abd al-Rahman regularly recounted tales of his youth in the royal court, and his Islamic education in Timbo and Timbuktu, he fashioned his experience of slavery, for white audiences especially, as one that led to an earnest desire to raise the banner of Commerce and Christianity.

Often, though, the tenor of the gatherings on the fundraising circuit differed significantly between white and Black audiences. As the right-wing Andrew Jackson's presidential ambitions gained traction in the South, reports of Abd al-Rahman's speaking engagements in African American communities, purportedly sponsored by President Adams and Secretary Clay, led to a firestorm in the Southern press. "Read the toasts drank at the dinner given to this said negro in the city of Boston! Read them, Frenchmen of Louisiana, and remember St. Domingo! Read them Americans of Louisiana, and remember the Frenchmen of Hayti!" screamed one New Orleans editorial (Austin 1984, 215). "This slave of Mr. Foster is travelling through the United States, with the passport of Mr. Clay in his pocket, the stipulations of the contract with the slave's master to the contrary notwithstanding" (Austin 1984, 218). While this latter editorialist perhaps speaks to the letter of the agreement brokered between Thomas Foster and the US government by Marschalk and Griffin, he clearly has no interest in the motivation behind Abd al-Rahman's travels, namely to raise money for the liberation and African journey of his entire family. The hysteria in the southern press over Abd al-Rahman's abuse of his "right of passage," resonates particularly strongly from the vantage-point of a twenty-first century moment when the US government is deporting record numbers of undocumented, foreign-born residents after decades in the country and despite their extensive multigenerational family ties (Human Rights Watch 2009; Ercolani 2013).

As a slave, Abd al-Rahman had "earned by faithfulness and residence the right for his children never to be ironed and dragged away" (Alford 2007, 97). And yet now these southern Jacksonians demand that the price of his freedom, "his contract" and his "passport" back to Africa, should be precisely this earned right to keep his family together. In this reaction to the specter of Abd al-Rahman's free passage around the United States, we can sense an early archival appearance of the arbitrary, asymmetrical enforcement of immigration and visa laws, exacting a price from second-class "citizens" even as they are escorted to the door.

Nonetheless, things worked out for Abd al-Rahman's family. Enough money was raised to purchase them from the Foster family, and Ibrahima and Isabella's children and grandchildren followed their parents' ship the *Harriet* to Liberia in 1829 aboard the *Carolinian*. Sadly, Abd al-Rahman died in Liberia before reaching Timbo. However, from the moment his ship "hove in sight of Cape Mesurado . . . Ibrahima recommenced the practice of Islam. His friends in the United States were surprised and irritated" (Alford 2007, 183). That Abd al-Rahman's commitments fell aside once near the shores of Africa serves to index the unevenness structuring his negotiations with US power, from the terms of his "contract" to the expectations of the American Colonization Society. Similarly, Job ben Solomon had also enticed his Anglo-American listeners with promises of uplift and the interior trade, only to slip discretely back into Fulbe life after a brief, contentious tenure with the Royal African Company. Lest we bemoan these Scheherazadian betrayals, we will remember that Job ben Solomon shortly disappeared from the records of the Royal African Company, the Gentleman's Society of Spalding (aside from a death notice in 1773), and the Society for the Propagation of the Gospel; and Austin points out that "Abdul Rahahman was not long remembered, even in the American Colonization Society Reports. A review of the year included mention of the Carolinian's cargo in general, its long voyage, and its 'unusual mortality'—but nothing on Rahahman's descendants" (Austin 1984, 239–40). These African Muslims, *causes célèbres* in their day, shortly disappeared from the mainstream of collective Anglo-American memory. In this, they hew to that pattern of amnesia and surprise structuring the discourse on African Muslims in New World slavery. Not only were first-hand witnesses to their lives struck with amazement that these bearers of Arab-Islamic knowledge and literacy be Black, but latter-day audiences as well revert to the same tenor of doubt and surprise. Allan Austin cites James Michener's amnesiac, politically motivated criticism of *Roots* that Kunta Kinte's religious affiliation "is an unjustified sop to contemporary developments rather than true reflection of the past" (Austin 1984, 4). Perhaps out of misconceptions like these, Moustafa Bayoumi, prefacing his investigation of the Panamanian manuscript of Sheikh Sana See, can still write, "New World African Arabic has barely received its due scholarly scrutiny" (Bayoumi 2003, 61). Bayoumi is particularly interested in how to archivally process, against historiographical forces that render African Islamic script and scribes invisible or outside the purview of modernity, this finely rendered excerpt from a meditative text of the West African Qadiriyya Brotherhood that languished in a Virginia attic for nearly 140 years. The disappearance of this manuscript symbolically echoes the rerouted and purloined letters of Job ben Solomon, Abd al-Rahman, and Omar ibn Sa'id. This reiterated experience of rerouted and purloined textuality, however, suggests a supplemental, angular approach to the dialectic of amnesia and surprise critically outlined thus far.

Rather than cast African Muslims in the roles of overlooked and written-over players on the historical stage, perhaps we may cast them as agents of archival reticence who figure the dispersed, resistant, and decentered archive of the Global South Atlantic. We will thus end this speculative genealogical excavation into the Arab-Islamic and Orientalist sources of African diasporic literature with a somewhat uncanny repetition out of the archive of Abu Bakr al-Siddiq of Timbuktu, Jamaica, and, perhaps, Timbuktu once more. Like Job ben Solomon one hundred years before him, penning his own narrative in Arabic, Abu Bakr enticed the Special Magistrate Richard Madden, resident in Jamaica during the "apprenticeship" interlude before Emancipation, into repatriating him as a guide and factor, this time in John Davidson's expedition to Timbuktu. Beginning with his paternal grandfather's generation, Abu Bakr narrates a sweeping drama of filial devotion, rivalry, and reconciliation, drawing upon tropes from the classical Arabic *sira*, or exemplary life story, to establish his own prestige in the land to which the expedition is destined (cf. Alryyes 2011, 26, 36). Like Job ben Solomon, though, Abu Bakr al-Siddiq soon vanished from the archive. His greatest advocate, Sir Richard Madden, "newly appointed Commissioner of Inquiry on the state of British forts on the Gold Coast, distributed leaflets for circulation into the interior, offering one hundred dollars reward for information about Abu Bakr's whereabouts." Eventually, "The British vice-consul at Mogadore received word from a man recently returned by caravan from Timbuktu that since Abu Bakr as-Siddiq reached Jenne nothing further had been heard of him" (Curtin 1967, 156).

These unanswered British leaflets, casting about West Africa for Abu Bakr al-Siddiq, reconfigure the near erasure of his enslaved coreligionists. For while, like Scheherazade, power incited and imposed upon their speech, once free, they were at liberty to purloin themselves, to steal away and disappear into the interior, to refuse to be interpellated. So beyond amnesia-and-surprise constituting only an act of racist and historiographical aggression, perhaps it is also a beleaguered reaction to the power of the verbal, textual, and archival reticence of these African Muslims, a reticence that carries with it a sigh of relief and discursive release. And perhaps we, dispersed archivists of the Global South Atlantic, must heed this sigh, by insisting that our own efforts to recover and reconstruct this oceanic overlay pause at the opaque silences of sea and Sahel to which these subjects retreated.

NOTES

1. Key historical texts on African Muslims in the era of New World slavery include two relatively early collections, both pioneering and invaluable: Curtin (1967) and Austin (1984). More recent crucial studies include Diouf (1998) and Gomez (2005).
2. One notable exception is Judy (1993), which reads Anglophone slave narratives alongside the *Bilali Muhammad Document*, also known as *Ben Ali's Diary*, an Islamic legal treatise written in Arabic and Pulaar on Sapelo Island, Georgia, in order to critique the Romantic paradigm of disciplinary literary knowledge and its universalist, humanist foundations. For the role of Muslims and Islam in US literature and culture, without a particular focus on Arabic language and literature, see Marr (2006).
3. For lions and Sudanese lost boys, see Eggers (2006, xiii).
4. This discussion of Blyden's encounter with Arabic in Liberia overlaps with, but also explores different aspects of, my book *Sounding the Break: African American and Caribbean Routes of World Literature* (Frydman 2014, 1–7).

Southern by Degrees

Islands and Empires in the South Atlantic, the Indian Ocean, and the Subantarctic World

Isabel Hofmeyr

There are few narratives of "southern-going ships," to use Joseph Conrad's phrase (1897a, 20), that do not include a storm-wracked passage around the Cape. From Camões (1572) onward, these stories pivot on a tempestuous transition from one ocean to another. At times invoking Camões's Adamastor, the exiled titan and vengeful gatekeeper of the Cape, these accounts reprise the entry (and exit) of Europeans into (and out of) a non-European world. South African poet Roy Campbell, in "Rounding the Cape," figures Adamastor as the slumbering giant of African nationalism taking shape in response to settler violence, a world "hated and adored" by the speaker in the poem who is leaving the Cape for Europe (1930). While less indebted to Adamastor, Conrad's "round the Cape" stories, like *Nigger of the "Narcissus"* (1897a) and "A Smile of Fortune" (1897b) follow a similar pattern of ambiguity and loss. Going eastward around the Cape represents loss (in "A Smile of Fortune," the chief mate is washed overboard) and an entry into the addictions of a master/slave world and its creole ambiguities. Going westward (in *Nigger of the "Narcissus"*) represents an escape from the thralldom and manipulation of this world.

This colonial troping of the oceans has come, of course, under question. Writers such as Amitav Ghosh have refigured the Cape crossing by setting it on a Southern latitude. Rather than thinking of the passage between oceans on a North/South grid, this work creates plot lines that configure colonized and unfree groups from across "the South," a theme in part prefigured in *Moby Dick* (1851) with its cosmopolitan crew and its own "Cape Tormentoso" set piece. In *Sea of Poppies* (2008), Ghosh's subaltern ocean epic, a ship, the *Ibis*, used in the Atlantic slave trade has been repurposed for the transportation of indentured labor in the Indian Ocean. The ship sails from Baltimore to Cape Town, where the white crew desert to be replaced by lascars, sailors from South Asia and other Indian Ocean regions, under the second mateship of an African American, Zachariah Reid, the son of a freedwoman. This rounding of the Cape presages gain as much as loss as a "Southern" cast of characters takes shape on the ship as it collects indentured workers from Calcutta to transport them to Mauritius.

The novel constitutes a geopoetic recalibration between the Atlantic Ocean and the Indian Ocean and invokes broader debates on the two as world systems. In the Anglophone domain, such comparisons draw our attention to the North Atlantic as the hub of slave-created modernity. But what of the South Atlantic, the lesser known arena, "South" in more ways than one? In both the older traditions of rounding the Cape and the more recent ones, the South Atlantic features as something of a narrative blank: on the eastward journey, a prefatory space leading up to the losses (or gains) of the Cape of Storms and from there, the Indian Ocean world more generally; on the westward passage, a fast-forward space as the ship hurries home to the metropole.

One notable exception to this narrative erasure is Yvette Christiansë, whose corpus takes shape around two islands of the South Atlantic: Saint Helena and Robben Island. Using these two points, she weaves a series of ambitious themes that relativize the territorialized historiographies of South Africa. Her novel *Unconfessed* (2007) tells the story of Sila, a slave from the Mozambique region who is imprisoned on Robben Island for killing her son. The novel moves between the plantation/farm and the prison island, thereby recontextualizing one of the major tropes of southern African literature, the farm novel, by linking it to narratives of slavery and the sea. Her poetry collections *Castaway* (1999) and *Imprendehora* (2009) focus on Saint Helena, an island with a history of penal exile, slavery, as well as indenture (the fate of many slaves "freed" by the British who took to patrolling Indian Ocean waters after they had abolished their own slave trade in 1807). In examining these intersections, her work explores the articulation of unfree labor systems across the Indian Ocean and South Atlantic worlds. The work looks both to the North Atlantic and engages with the historiographies of Atlantic slavery and to the Indian Ocean world with its carceral archipelagos of which Saint Helena forms an extension.

Today Saint Helena is a British overseas territory comprising three island clusters: Saint Helena itself, Ascension Island, and Tristan da Cunha. While the former two islands are subtropical, Tristan da Cunha stands on the cusp of the Antarctic world, on the outer edge of a fringe of subantarctic islands that ring the south polar region. In this configuration, Saint Helena looks not only to the Indian Ocean islands but also to the insular world of the subantarctic.

These two island systems (the carceral archipelago of the Indian Ocean/South Atlantic and the subantarctic islands) are generally not bracketed together. Tropical as opposed to semipolar, inhabited (if in some cases through slavery and indenture) as opposed to uninhabited, the two systems are analytically discrete and occupy different academic domains. Yet, there are good reasons to draw them together since both functioned as strategic steppingstones in the larger story of global resource colonialism. As a substantial body of work on Antarctic history argues, this region was not a remote wilderness waiting be "discovered" during the late nineteenth and early twentieth century "heroic age of Antarctic exploration" (Dodds 2012). As Andres Zarankin and María Ximena Senator (2005) indicate, whaling and sealing had long drawn the region into a world economy. Exploration and the "scramble for the Antarctic" formed a further chapter in this longer story of global imperialism.

As with broader arcs of European imperial rule, islands were central proxies in the Antarctic story—markers of exploration and discovery, strategic staging posts, sites of experiments in sovereignty and science, and nodes of invisible labor to sustain these prestige projects of what became the "Antarctic Club" of nations and whose Antarctic involvement marked them as "white" (Collis 2007; Collis and Stevens 2007; Van der Watt 2012).[1] The imagination that informed these developments was not that different from the ideologics dominating the penal assemblages of the Indian Ocean carceral archipelagos: possession, conquest of nature, environmental colonialism, racialization through geography (to be penally transported to the tropics made one "black" whereas transportation to temperate domains made one "white") (Anderson 2000, 2012; Gupta 2010; Perera 2009; Sivasundaram 2014). To adapt a phrase from David Vine's discussion of Diego Garcia, the Indian Ocean atoll that formed part of the British empire and was then ceded to the United States, forcibly cleared of people, and used as a base and torture center in the "war on terror," these islands made up an "empire of bases," rather like the contemporary US empire with its string of military depots across the world, many of them islands or islandlike enclaves (2009, 42).

While much of this island stockpiling was driven by European nations, one striking feature of the Antarctic story is the involvement of regional powers as subimperial forces. Argentina, Chile, Australia, New Zealand, and to a lesser extent South Africa all constructed themselves as key players with historical and strategic rights to the southern polar world, a story in which islands played an important role. Antarctic politics enabled the emergence of a "southern hemispheric empire," a commonwealth of science in which the legatees of British and Spanish imperial authorities found common cause (Van der Watt 2012; Dodds 1994).

This chapter begins by outlining this story of the "southern" scramble for the Antarctic islands. We then change gear and examine two very different literary representations of these islands. The first dissects H. Rider Haggard's novel *Mary of Marion Isle* (1929), a subantarctic Robinsonade (or Swiss Family Robinsonade) whose plot deposits the leading characters on the insular cluster of Marion Island and Prince Edward Island about 1,350 miles (2,177 km) southeast of Cape Town in the Indian Ocean.[2] The second addresses Yvette Christiansë's *Imprendehora*, a collection of poems largely focused on Saint Helena.[3] A concluding section touches on Mojisola Adebayo's play *Moj of the Antarctic: An African Odyssey*.

The Southern Scramble for the Antarctic Islands

Early in January 1948, South Africans discovered that their national borders had shifted and that the country had acquired the subantarctic Prince Edward Islands (Hanekom 2014, 82–87; Van der Watt 2012, 70–83). In what was called "Operation Snoektown" (an affectionate but slightly parodic name for Cape Town), a contingent of troops had set off from the port in late December aboard the whaler SAS *Transvaal*. Arriving at Marion Island, the men made their way to land by rubber dinghy and waded thigh-deep through the kelp to the shore. Here they raised the South African flag, read out a proclamation of sovereignty that was then signed, placed in a brass cylinder, and buried in a disused penguin burrow. On January 4, 1948, the same ceremony was reenacted on Prince Edward Island. In both cases, the event was filmed and photographed.

The annexation had been in the pipeline for some time driven by Britain's desire to beef up its polar presence as a counter to Argentinian claims, especially in the Falkland Islands Dependency but in the subantarctic belt more generally. The Prince Edward Islands were nominally British but had never been properly claimed. Worried about possible Soviet interest, keen to establish a relay of islands that could enable air routes and gather meteorological data, the British Foreign Office had approached the South African government to assume responsibility for the islands in 1945. Lacking the expertise and infrastructure to take on such a task and already committed to meteorological stations on Tristan da Cunha and its close neighbor Gough Island, the South African state demurred. Two years later, the request was again made and this time the South African state agreed, citing both military concerns (that the island could be used as a base to attack the country) and civilian themes of science and meteorology (Van der Watt 2012, 70–83).

As part of the same broader objectives, the Foreign Office had also approached the Australian state with a view to their taking over the subantarctic Heard and MacDonald Islands, whose sovereignty was likewise uncertain. The Australians agreed and so at the same time as Operation Snoektown, similar claimant ceremonies were undertaken on Heard and MacDonald. As the *Rand Daily Mail* informed Johannesburg readers on January 3, 1948, there was now a "long chain of southern defence islands stretching around the world." An accompanying map with a shaded band showed the British and Commonwealth-owned subantarctic islands between Argentina and New Zealand (with a few French ones thrown in). The London *Times* noted that "the chain of islands between 35 and 55 degrees south encircling the Antarctic are now all in the possession of the Western Powers." Another London paper, the *News Review* produced a map captioned "The strategic islands which bar the way to the Antarctic" (Van der Watt 2012, 79; "Polar Air Bases" 1948).

Unlike Australia and New Zealand, South Africa was a relatively late entrant into the Antarctic race, as Lize Marié (Susanna) van der Watt's exemplary work (2012) has demonstrated. As part of consolidating its Antarctic claims of 1908 and 1917, Britain was keen to bring Antarctica under imperial rule. Or, as the Foreign Office indicated "the Empire should have no neighbours at all in the Antarctic or in its adjacent islands" (State President's Archive 1928). Australia and New Zealand took up the baton, enthusiastically exploring and "occupying" their respective "sectors" of Antarctica by building bases. Lacking any coherent policy or lobby group, South Africa showed little interest and in 1929 rather absentmindedly agreed to cede its sector to Norway with whom Britain shared strong whaling interests (Van der Watt 2012, 52).

In the post–Second World War and Cold War context, South Africa began to take a stronger interest in the Antarctic as a way of positioning itself as a Western nation. From the late 1950s South African expeditions began going to Antarctica itself (as opposed to the islands) and two bases were acquired from the Norwegians. As apartheid increasingly made the country a pariah state and after its exit from the Commonwealth in 1960, South Africa used its Antarctic connections to define a role for itself as a Western ally. Through the channels of Antarctic science, the South African state via its scientists cooperated with countries like Norway even as the latter pursued a high profile anti-apartheid agenda. South Africa also forged close relations with Argentina and Chile turning the South Atlantic into something of an anticommunist zone (Dodds 1994). Being part of the "Antarctic Club" was an important token of prestige and one counter to the country's increasing isolation (Van der Watt 2012, Chapter 4).

Relations in the club were far from smooth, however, as member countries elbowed each other to consolidate their presence in the Antarctic. Seven countries (Britain, France, Norway, Australia, New Zealand, Argentina, and Chile) had territorial claims; the United States and the Soviet Union, while having a strong presence, did not have formal claims but reserved their right to make these. The territorial disputes between Britain, Argentina, and Chile were especially acute.

Yet, these quarrelling factions began to lay aside some of their differences when in 1956 India raised the Antarctic Question in the United Nations General Assembly. Speaking in the idioms of Bandung (held the previous year), the Indian delegation felt that the scramble for the Antarctic perpetuated European imperialism and that the sovereignty disputes could spread the reach of the Cold War. A real concern was that nuclear tests could destroy the global weather system and obliterate the monsoon (Howkins 2008).

The motion was however not successful, largely because it could not enlist the support of Latin American delegates who backed Argentinian and Chilean claims and thwarted the anti-imperial spirit of the initiative. The Indian proposal did produce a strategic and uneasy alliance within the Antarctic Club, however, as members strove for common objectives, their differences notwithstanding. The International Geophysical Year of 1957–58 (an international earth sciences project with a strong polar focus involving sixty-seven nations) consolidated this spirit of strategic cooperation and paved the way for the Antarctic Treaty System of 1959, which established the current governance of the region. The Treaty recognizes but suspends existing claims while serving as a holding pattern for earlier imperial claims (Dodds 2012; Scott 2011).

H. Rider Haggard's Mary of Marion Isle

In her magisterial account of fictional portrayals of Antarctica, Elizabeth Leane (2012) demonstrates, that despite the idea of the poles being unwritable blanks, beyond representation, they have in fact supported long and variegated traditions of literature. Much of this fiction has been in a frontier tradition, where life beyond the boundary is decisively and often threateningly different. In Leane's words, Antarctica emerges as a "weird, hellish region that produces monsters and lures unsuspecting sailors and explorers to unspeakable fates. This Antarctic acts as the world's subconscious, harbouring our deepest fears." The region represents "an instability at the margins of the subject and the margins of the world" (Leane 2012, 18 and 79).

Like all frontier literatures of exploration, the idea of the island has been central to this fiction. As Leane indicates, the island informed the self-imagination of the Antarctic explorers who "tended to see themselves as metaphorically inhabiting island space, whether or not they were literally doing so." They frequently cast themselves as polar Crusoes, even if they weren't literally on an island, an uncertainty endemic to the landscape with its ambiguous geography of water, ice, land (Leane 2007, 67).

H. Rider Haggard's subantarctic novel *Mary of Marion Isle* can usefully be bracketed into these categories: an imperial romance of islanding and a subantarctic Robinsonade that uses its island setting to promote ideas of reinvigorating the imperial race.

The novel was first conceptualized in 1916 as Haggard undertook a trip on behalf of the Royal Colonial Institute, visiting South Africa, Australia and Canada to promote settlement schemes for white ex-soldiers in the dominions. In South Africa, he succeeded in getting the immigration regulations "modified so that any white soldier or sailor throughout the Empire, whatever his state of health or pocket, [could] now enter [South Africa] unquestioned." The Chartered Board of the British South Africa Company promised 500,000 acres in Rhodesia for approved settlers (Pocock 1993, 204; Higgins 1981, 225–226).

On the journey from South Africa to Australia, Haggard began working on a book *The Empire and Its Land*. He also began conceptualizing a novel as he spent time watching the ever-present albatrosses: "I have evolved the plot of a new story to be called *The Fatal Albatross* of which the scene would be laid in some of the desolate islands we are passing, the Marion group perhaps. Or it might be called *Mary of Marion Isle*" (Higgins 1991, 225–226; Pocock 1993, 204).[4]

Haggard arrived in Tasmania on April 3, 1916, and began propagating his schemes in speeches and interviews. A piece by Haggard in the Hobart *Mercury* read:

> Now, what is our Empire? It covers fully one-fourth of the globe and it is held by about 60,000,000 white people of whom 40,000,000 dwell in the United Kingdom. It is just all that we can do to hold the Empire with the population . . . Now is the opportunity for the Empire to try and secure for that land . . . the finest settlers in the world. (Pocock 1993, 204)

For Haggard, the future of empire lay in its white dominions, which needed to be secured by vigorously settling and extending an imperial race. The novel shares these concerns and explores them through a series of romance and marriage plots, which by a process of elimination define the form most suited to maintain the imperial family.

The first part of the novel unfolds in London where we are presented with an exhausted society collapsing under the weight of its overrefined and regulated civility. This malaise is illustrated through a series of misaligned families and marriages. The protagonist, Andrew West, is an orphan who has been raised by his aristocratic uncle Lord Atterton. Clara Maunsell, his cousin and also an orphan, has been brought up in the same household and the two are initially presented rather like brother and sister. Lord Atterton's only son, Algernon, is wracked by consumption and dissolute living. Andrew, a medical doctor with socialist views, is on bad terms with his uncle, whose aristocratic privilege he regards with suspicion. Andrew lives and works in the East End, boarding with Mrs. Josky and her daughter, Laurie, whose life he has saved. Andrew initially works in a charitable hospital run by Dr. Watson before taking up a job on Harley Street working with a fashionable general practitioner, Dr. Black. Andrew falls in love with Dr. Watson's mercenary daughter, Rose, who suggests a secret engagement even while pursuing a dalliance with Dr. Black. While Andrew is in Egypt, having taken Algernon on a trip to try and improve his consumption, Rose marries Dr. Black. His daughter Arabella marries Dr. Watson.

On his return from Egypt (where Algernon has died), Andrew discovers that Lord Atterton has also passed on, bequeathing his money to Clara and his title to Andrew. Clara lures Andrew into marriage and engineers an upwardly mobile career for him, first as an MP, then Under-secretary for Colonies and then an appointment as Governor General of Oceania. On the trip out to take up the position, in the subantarctic regions of the Indian Ocean, the ship hits an iceberg. Everyone makes it to safety except Andrew and his secretary, who are trapped behind the watertight doors and are presumed dead. They have managed to escape, however, and find a lifeboat. In a Titanic-meets-the-Ancient-Mariner escape story, an albatross leads them to Marion Island. The secretary dies, but Andrew survives living like a "polar crusoe" (198). While exploring the island he discovers Mary, a castaway who has been living on the island for fifteen years. As a young infant, she had been dispatched by her mother in London to her father in Sydney. The sailor, Old Tom, into whose care she had been assigned, saves her from the shipwreck, and the two of them make it safely to the island. Tom has died, but Mary survives subsisting on fish, penguin eggs, and oats that she has planted.

She has largely forgotten her English but soon learns from Andrew, although throughout her speech is slightly ungrammatical. A "little savage" (244), she is eventually taught and "tamed" by Andrew, who instructs her from the only two books they have on the island: *Whitaker's Almanac* and the Anglican Prayer Book. Initially a daughter/pupil under tutelage, she graduates to become a wife and in due course, a mother.

The albatross that had initially lead Andrew to the island is tame, having been hand-reared by Mary, and one day they decide to tie a small tin plaque to its neck giving details of their location. The albatross dies on the West Coast of Australia, but a prospector spots the tin message among the bones. A search party, which includes Clara, sets off to find the castaways. Clara is determined to make Andrew return to London and to get rid of Mary and the baby. Matters are resolved when a storm comes up, the boat that is ferrying her to the shore capsizes, and she is drowned. Andrew, Mary, and the baby, Janet, remain on the island.

The opening sections of the novel sketch a range of misaligned families, where questions of gender and age are askew. The first problem appears to be women who are too scheming or bossy: Clara, Rose, and Arabella are all judged wanting. Mrs. Josky is more favorably portrayed but threatens to engulf Andrew with what the book portrays as her Jewish maternal excess. The men are equally wanting: Lord Atterton is too aristocratic, his son too physically and psychologically weak. Dr. Watson is under the whip of the strict Arabella and Dr. Black at the mercy of the grasping Rose. These various family forms threaten to sap the energy of empire at its very center. Blighted by aristocratic lassitude, Andrew's middle-class vigor cannot find its proper expression, distorted on the one end by socialist ideas and on the other by "bossy" women. Relations of age, generation and gender are topsy-turvy: "Brother" marries "sister," fathers swap daughters. A monstrous regiment of women brings the basis of patriarchal authority into question.

The island setting and castaway story offer the necessary blank page on which a new beginning for empire can be imagined. Fortuitously uninhabited, the island offers a site for experimenting with the ideal family form: the island we are told has "germless air" (195). On the trip out, Andrew stops off in Cape Town and does some sightseeing, including a trip to Robben Island (169) to see the leper asylum, which was established in the latter half of the nineteenth century. In contrast to this dumping ground for the sick and polluted, Marion island is pure and has on it only healthy white bodies. A further contrast is established with the tropical zones. On his trip to Egypt, Dr. Black warns Andrew: "Good luck, and don't fall in love with tropical blooms which this climate never suits" (96). The racial purity of England can be assured in the uninhabited, subantarctic colony/island where a new "island race" can take root—Marion Isle, a miniature and purified version of the British Isles.

In this novel, the island plays its accustomed role in the geopolitical imagination of imperial power. Part utopia, miniature and ideal colony (Andrew sees himself as Governor General of the seals; 189), site of experiments whether with sovereignty or racial science, the island becomes the site for reordering imperial relations through the family.

In this eugenically safe space, a new white heterosexual family form emerges: the vigorous and nonaristocratic "father"/husband/metropolis can tutor the "daughter"/wife/colony in an imperial union. Here the "natural" order of age, race and gender is restored rather than the inverted arrangements of the metropolis. Yet, any such romance plot where father becomes husband must collapse on its own incestuous contradictions. Written in 1916 and published in 1929, a year after Haggard's death, the novel can be regarded as a late imperial paroxysm, an attempt to regenerate empire even as it went into decline. The incestuous impossibility of its plot speaks powerfully to the contradictions of British imperialism itself. As Tom Pocock points out, Haggard, famed for his depictions of lost empires, was in fact deeply concerned with the future of the British Empire. In this, one of his final novels, as the British Empire itself was becoming lost, Haggard sought to save it through projecting his story into the subantarctic world, the space par excellence of late European imperialism.

Yvette Christiansë's Imprendehora

To move from Haggard to Christiansë is to move from island to anti-island, from Crusoe to anti-Crusoe (one section of the volume, *Imprendehora* deals with Fernão Lopez [b. 1545], mutilated and then exiled by the Portuguese to Saint Helena for seditious activity in Goa and known in the popular literature as "the Crusoe of the South Atlantic") (Brooke 1824, 49–50). The volume resists any idea of the island as a bounded entity instead depicting it as a node in a sprawling oceanic assemblage that turns people into property. As the paratextual apparatus tells us, the title of the volume *Imprendehora* (Enterprise) comes from a slave ship, seized by British patrols in the Indian Ocean with those on board being declared "liberated Africans" before being delivered to Saint Helena as indentured labor. The volume is hence not only about slavery but also about the articulation of unfree labor systems across two oceans.

The structure of the collection, divided into two sections "Atlantic" and "Indian" reiterates these concerns. This architecture points outward to a range of historiographical traditions that are brought into conversation. The first relates to the intersections between the Atlantic and Indian Oceans, an important analytical move designed to relativize the Atlantic, which has long dominated understandings of slavery and has obscured the Indian Ocean slave trade and its dynamics (briefly these include the latter having more women than men and more household than plantation slaves; the boundaries between slave and free being more porous and the institution of slavery being less racialized than the Atlantic system) (Campbell 2004). Yet, as other scholars and indeed Christiansë's volume illustrates, the two systems are not entirely discrete but interpenetrate—plantation slavery, for example, being present in the Indian Ocean world (Allen 2008).

This concern with intersecting historiographies of slavery extends to an engagement with Caribbean intellectual traditions on the ocean and slavery ("tidalectics" adapted to a South Atlantic context) as well as US debates on slavery, with Christiansë being at pains to resist any simple notion of agency or voice. The collection also engages with South African scholarship, where for a long time slavery was sidelined by the antiapartheid narrative, which was national, territorialized, and focused on the struggle of "native" and "settler." Discussions of seventeenth- and eighteenth-century slavery at the Cape, which sucked in captives from South and Southeast Asia, were sidelined while the idiom of "slavery" was absorbed metaphorically into the antiapartheid struggle, South African history often being referred to as three hundred years of slavery. Postapartheid, the study of slavery in its own right has become more prominent as a way of widening and understanding South Africa's multiple inheritances. This project has involved an oceanic turn as scholars relativize the territorial and nationalist emphases of the antiapartheid struggle (Baderoon 2009; Gqola 2010). An important figure in this new turn, Christiansë reinserts the missing ocean, a project signaled quite literally by the section titles ("Atlantic" and "Indian," with the word "ocean" not appended).

The opening section comprises a series of lyrical expressions in a range of anonymous voices. The themes of these poems could apply to most situations of enslavement and forced labor and much of the poetry plays out in a logic of compression and broken bits, as people are squashed and pounded in an attempt to make them into objects. One recurring image is of stones in a wall, each trying to free itself by pressing down on those below, or of impossible tasks, like spiders trying to move stone.

Under this unbearable pressure people are broken into bits, "scraps" in the title of one subsection of "Atlantic"—"Atlantic scraps," if one runs them together. The people taken into captivity are made into scraps—scraps from the Indian Ocean slave trade, effectively reenslaved a second time, denuded of everything, trying to survive with remaindered bits of themselves. They are dumped on an Atlantic island scrap (or scrap island), an outcrop of rock battered like the slave body itself, as Karen Press (2009) points out.

The volume itself adopts a method of scraps; the poems are rather like scraps of flotsam on the water, cohering and separating, creating a microtidalectics. As one reads down the titles in the table of contents, they configure into brief moments of sense and then disperse again. The currency of the poems is drawn from everyday scraps: spider, tree, stone, cricket, bird, ship, water, wave, horizon, moon, wind, fire, smoke, fish, stars.

These hyperconstrained circumstances of pressure and brokenness leave almost no room for maneuver. Any tiny nook or cranny that can be claimed entails its own enormous cost, as the theme of chosen death in the poems illustrates. The collection opens, in fact, with two poems on this subject, one about a suicide, the other about seven men who try and escape by boat but drown.

These themes and aesthetic strategies could of course be read as applying to any situation of slavery. The comparative orientation of the volume invites such a reading even as it inserts paratextual and epigraphical reminders that the setting is Saint Helena, although the lightness of this apparatus does not insist or impose such a reading. Yet, as the volume proceeds, this Southern setting becomes more marked. After the compressed anonymity of the first section, we move on to two lyrical portraits of historical characters: the first is a women of slave/indenture descent who has become an ardent Christian tramping across the island so as not to miss a sermon and is named in the poem as Sister Thomas. She espouses a homemade theology of the sea, continuing the tradition of creative survival inherited from her ancestors. Yet, postslavery, her life remains constrained, her black female body a source of sin and chastisement.

The second historical character is Fernão Lopez, the Portuguese dissident. In a series of first-person poems, we hear him recalling his previous life in Portugal and Goa in the midst of his denuded existence on the island. He is no Crusoe come to turn the island into property. Instead, like other forced exiles, he explores the minimal art of creative survival, in this case as a gardener.

Both figures are shaped in the intellectual and religious circuits of the South. Sister Thomas creates a theology out of the scraps of the island. She in fact is the real missionary on the island spreading Christianity on foot and in terms comprehensible to her community, forging a "Southern" Christianity shaped by its foot soldiers rather than its European missionaries. Yet, even these European missionary networks are not straightforwardly on a North/South axis. The epigraph to the section on Sister Thomas, drawn from a mission biography, *St. Helena and the Cape of Good Hope: Incidents in the Missionary Life of the Rev. James McGregor* reminds us of the subimperial networks of the South: Christian activity on the island falls under the authority of a South African diocese, just as Saint Helena in general functioned as an informal colony of South Africa. Fernão Lopez who sided with Rasul Khan in Goa against his countrymen, probably converted to Islam. His biography unfolds on Southern axes: Portuguese Goa, Indian Ocean Islam, and Saint Helena.

This southerly drift of the volume continues as we enter the final section entitled "Indian." This is followed by the heading "Katembe" and then a long poem "Ship's Register." Read together, these three titles (plus internal clues in the poem) suggest a Portuguese Mozambique region in which people have been taken captive (whether by Portuguese or "Arabs" is not clear) and have then been "liberated" by British patrols. Now turned into indentured labor, they are being taken on board another ship where their details are entered in English into the ship's register. The poem is made up of thirty such entries describing each "liberated" person ("343 Male Russel. Age 1 year/Child of Rosamuna 342"; "344 Female Sarah. Age 12. Stature 4–8/ Mother's name Koollewah"; "345 Male Samuel. Age 4. Stature 3–3/Mother's name Neammhoo? Neammorhoo?" and so on

[2009, 83]) interspersed with an imagined voice (or voices) of one (or several) slaves (possibly a child or children) both on the ship and off, as she/he/they enter a world of forced labor.

The poem gains its momentum from the jarring contrast between the register and the voices. The rhythm of the register is like the insistent hammering of a labor regime attempting to create modular units of property—the entry itself being a proclamation of property, or in this instance translating people from one form of property (slave) to another (indentured laborer). The slave voices speak in the additive style of much southern African oral poetry which seeks to enumerate the identity of a person or thing though heaping up attributes of that the person or object. The form is open-ended and creates the impression that it could continue indefinitely since to have a neat ending would imply that identity was not infinite. This additive form runs alongside the ship's register, which appears to have its own infinity; it runs from 343 to 372 and one assumes it will continue in the relentless logic of private property, of turning people into identical units of labor, one interchangeable with another. In the face of this abstraction, the voices insist on lineage and memory, and of the impossibility of making people into things. While this is not a collection that believes in any consoling form of redemption, the utterances of the slave voices do become longer and more insistent, rendering the ship's register entries as increasingly isolated fragments—although any sense of optimism this rising tide may represent is undercut by the knowledge that the end of the book loops us back to the beginning, slavery becomes indenture, one form of unfree labor issues onto another.

This configuration may, of course, not sound particularly Southern: another narrative of capital and labor, North and South. Yet embedded in the poem are signs of Southern latitudes in which Portuguese settlers have become indigenized chieftains (*prazeiros*) and slaves are headed for destinations in the Indian Ocean. The languages present in the poem (English, Makhuwa, French, Portuguese) also attest to the complexities of Indian Ocean intersections and creolizations.

This theme of enforced and compressed creolizations constitutes an important preoccupation in Indian Ocean studies. As part of the mass migrations precipitated by European imperialism, the Indian Ocean world witnessed extensive extrusions of people on a forced or semivoluntary basis. Jumbled together, these colonized groups had to forge new forms of association and interaction. These "lateral" colony-to-colony linkages are increasingly being recognized as a prehistory of the Global South. By extending an investigation of these questions into the South Atlantic,

Imprendehora becomes an important text for thinking about the Global South more generally.

Sailing Farther South

Mojisola Adebayo's play *Moj of the Antarctic: An African Odyssey* (2012) tells the story of an African American women disguised as a sailor who goes to Antarctica, "the deep deepest south of the earth." The play is loosely inspired by the story of Ellen Craft an African American slave woman who cross-dressed as a white man to escape slavery.

Seeing her first albatross, Moj, the protagonist says:

> The spirits of drowned sailors
> Jumping bravely
> Into the ocean waves
> Ascend into the albatross
> Which soars the sky
> In the shape of a cross! (2012, location 635/4433)

Moj's albatross provides a useful route into drawing together our two texts and moving toward a conclusion. Apart from a Northern Pacific presence, the albatross inhabits a southern band from 30 to 50 degrees south, roughly the area of the subantarctic islands. By linking this zone to slavery, the play reminds us of the broader articulations of global resource imperialism that worked as much through tropical insular systems as the subantarctic islands. Haggard's novel deploys a subantarctic setting to disavow this link, using the idea of the uninhabited island as a way of imagining imperialism without the slavery and forced labor that enabled it. Read alongside Adebayo's play, Haggard's albatross comes to represent the political unconscious of the novel, its tin plaque reminiscent of a colonial worker's identification tag.

Christiansë's collection teems with birds, one or two of which could in theory be an albatross which is found on Saint Helena despite its being at 16 degrees south. These birds dive and swoop through the poems, now cackling cruelly ("The laughter of birds can break a knuckle" [2009, 23]) now representing an impossible freedom ("Should I dance, it would be/ along those wings above waves, / I would gull and dive" [21]), now mocking that freedom ("songs/that escape like birds from graveyards" [71]). At times, people become birds, their spirit flying away. In "Abundance," the poem about seven men escaping by boat, one stanza reads: "One man calls, wind to shore / One man waves, a crane's wing" (15).

In both Adebayo's text, the spirits of drowned slaves and sailors, are martyred and sacrificed (as the cross implies). The albatross comes to stand for a confederacy of slaves and the oceanic working class of the South (or at least the Atlantic South). While Christiansë works in less epic idioms, the birds in her text embody fleeting memories that flicker across the subaltern seas.

A second symbol in Adebayo's play is Gondwana (the ur-continent comprising what is now South America, Antarctica, Africa, South Asia, and Australia). A griot figure in the play says:

> Once,
> Gondwana,
> Africa and Antarctica
> Antarctica and Africa
> One content Continent. (2012, location 613/4433)

This idea becomes a way of claiming Antarctica for Africa and seeing the black volcanic rock in Antarctica as an African giantess.

This use of Gondwana as a metaphor for the South is of course not unusual. In a very different context, South African Prime Minister Jan Smuts said in 1925 that "the round table of meteorology should become the meeting place and reunion of the scattered members of the ancient mother continent of Gondwana land" (Van der Watt 2012, 38).

However different, the visions of Adebayo, Smuts, Haggard, and Christiansë point to the idea of a Southern domain. Whether a subempire of science, a renewed and racialized Southern commonwealth, or a tenuous oceanic space of shared memory among slaves and workers, the subantarctic has enabled a rich range of Southern hemispheric imaginings. That the subject of this volume, the South Atlantic occupies the area where much of Gondwana lay seems appropriate.

NOTES

1. See Van der Watt's discussion on the "Black Antarctic" examining the labor that sustains polar bases (2012, 227–230).
2. I became aware of this novel through Rousset (2012).
3. This collection has been chosen here for its conscious focus on both the Atlantic and Indian Ocean rather than her collection of poems *Castaway* (1999) which has a more Saint Helena focus, although there are Indian Ocean dimensions to the collection.
4. Higgins speaks of "Marion group" and "Maori group."

PART II

South Atlantic Cold War Modernities

Beyond the Color Curtain
The Metonymic Color Politics of the Tricontinental and the (New) Global South

Anne Garland Mahler

Contemporary capitalist globalization has created the conditions for a new era in solidarity politics where the immediacy of global communication and the increased movement of materials and peoples across geopolitical borders allow grassroots movements to create alliances beyond the confines of the nation-state. The networked character of politics today challenges the models with which critics engage politically resistant cultural production, leading to a divergence in the last fifteen years from the rubrics of postcolonial and ethnic studies to what might be characterized as horizontalist approaches to cultural criticism. These approaches—such as the increasingly circulating concept of the "Global South"—view power as unmoored from territorial boundaries and emphasize lateral dialogue and mutual identification among oppressed groups in terms transcendent of a shared experience of European colonization or of national, ethnic, and linguistic affinities.[1] They aim to devise a "thick" globalization theory that provides an alternative to the discourse of neoliberalism by viewing the transnational experience of global capitalism from below.

These new horizontalist critical categories are valuable for engaging our contemporary political imagination. However, their newness risks eliding the historical context from which contemporary solidarity politics emerge and thus reproducing the atemporal "end of history" narrative of globalization. In the following essay, thus, I trace the roots of the contemporary notion of the Global South to the ideology of a profoundly influential but largely forgotten Cold War alliance of liberation movements from Africa, Asia, and Latin America called the Tricontinental. I argue that tricontinentalism—the ideology disseminated among the international radical Left through the Tricontinental's expansive cultural production—revised a specifically black Atlantic resistant subjectivity into a global vision of subaltern resistance that is resurfacing in contemporary horizontalist approaches to cultural criticism, such as the Global South. In this way, I propose the Global South Atlantic as a particularly useful conceptual apparatus that not only inherently recognizes the black Atlantic foundations of the Global South but also calls contemporary solidarity politics into accountability to these intellectual roots.

The term "Global South" originally came into use in the late 1970s to refer to economically disadvantaged nation-states and as a replacement for the term "Third World," thus shifting the East-West framework of European colonialism and Cold War decolonization to a Gramscian North-South vision of power relations in which multidirectional capital flows mostly benefit the geographic North.[2] However, in the last ten years and in such fields as cultural studies, history, and sociology, the concept of the Global South has diverged from a mere regional designation used to describe an economic divide between a geographical North and South. Rather, it is now used to address spaces and peoples negatively impacted by globalization including within the borders of wealthier countries, such that there are economic Souths in the geographic North and Norths in the geographic South.[3] Moreover, the Global South has come to refer to a mutual recognition among the world's poor of their shared condition at the margins of global capitalism and an emergent political imagination that undergirds contemporary social movements.[4]

If we understand that postcolonial theory developed out of the exchange between Cold War radical leftism and poststructuralism (Young 2004), the Global South then would be characterized as its post–Cold War counterpart. As a concept, the Global South speaks to the farce of the supposed triumph and inevitability of neoliberalism that was ushered in with the collapse of Soviet communism. It suggests that we have not indeed witnessed the end of mankind's ideological evolution, as Francis Fukuyama argued, but rather are seeing the formation of a resistant political community created from within the contemporary economic structure. This resistance from within is, in fact, the central paradox of the Global South: the deregulation and international integration that are the hallmarks of neoliberalism are also the very avenues through which transnational movements of opposition to that system are formed.

However, despite the general association of Global South theory with the post-Soviet period, I suggest that the Global South also has its origins in Cold War political thought and actually represents an attempt to recover an ideology that has been all but completely elided in postcolonial studies.[5] That ideological legacy is located in the Tricontinental, an alliance of delegates from the liberation movements of eighty-two nations in Africa, Asia, and Latin America that came together in January 1966 at the Tricontinental Conference in Havana, Cuba, against imperialism. Through the artistically innovative and politically radical films, posters, and magazines that the Tricontinental published in English, Spanish, French, and sometimes Arabic and distributed globally, it had a profound impact on international political radicalism and radicalist cultural production around the world. Its vision of global resistance was shaped by its foundations in black Atlantic thought and by the close involvement of African American and Afro-Latino activists.

According to the Tricontinental's International Preparatory Committee, the Tricontinental originated in the well-known 1955 Afro-Asian Bandung Conference, in which twenty-nine nascent postcolonial nations allied under the principles of state sovereignty, cooperation, and against interference from the heavyweight Cold War powers (International Preparatory Committee 1965, 3).[6] While the reality was in fact more complicated, in general, Bandung—often viewed as the political cognate for what would eventually become academic postcolonial theory—and the Tricontinental might be taken as two major cornerstones of Cold War anticolonialism, separated by an ocean and a decade.[7] It is a key contention of this essay that as tricontinentalism represented a shift from a Bandung-era solidarity, based around postcolonial nation-states and a former experience of European colonialism, to a more fluid notion of power and resistance, tricontinentalism largely anticipates a transition currently taking place in related theoretical approaches to transnational politics, such as the shift from postcolonial theory to the Global South.

Specifically, what I find significant about the Tricontinental is that as the Afro-Asian solidarity begun at Bandung expanded into the Americas, this alliance explicitly began to reach out to African Americans. In its copious materials, the Tricontinental theorizes imperialism as a global system of power affecting peoples not only in occupied territories or in regions suffering from foreign economic exploitation but also those oppressed peoples located inside the geopolitical boundaries of imperial centers. This particularly applies to African Americans. According to tricontinentalist thought, racial inequalities in the United States represent a microcosm of a transnational experience of imperialism such that the African American freedom movement is chiefly representative of the Tricontinental's global struggle.[8]

Through privileging the African American freedom movement, Tricontinental materials consistently employ the racial categories "white" and "colored," using white policemen to signify global imperial oppression and an African American identity to stand in for what Che Guevara in his 1967 "Message to the Tricontinental" calls "we, the exploited people of the world."[9] This is what I call the Tricontinental's *metonymic color politics*, in which the Jim Crow categories of "white" and "colored" are employed not as indicators of phenotypic difference per se but as metonyms for ideological positions in a global struggle. The Tricontinental forges its transnational, transethnic, and translinguistic solidarity through a discursive coloring of resistant peoples such that phenotypically white people who share its views are sometimes described as "colored." With this transformation of color into a political signifier, the Tricontinental articulates its critique of a global system of imperialism through a condemnation of racial inequality but simultaneously takes a radically inclusive stance that attempts to destabilize racial essentialisms. It is this global concept of power, lateral solidarity among liberation struggles, and destabilization of trait-based claims to belonging that makes the Tricontinental a model that anticipates and is intrinsically relevant to the contemporary Global South imaginary.

In devising its political signifier of color, the Tricontinental attempts to revise a specifically black Atlantic anti-imperialist tradition that circulated through the transatlantic exchange between *négritude*, *negrismo*, and the Harlem Renaissance.[10] While it is well known that black Atlantic intellectuals like W. E. B. Du Bois, Aimé Césaire, and Richard Wright among others, were integrally involved in anticolonial coalition building, I maintain that tricontinentalism does not simply reflect an engagement with a black Atlantic tradition or the participation of a transatlantic black intelligentsia. Rather, in its focus on the African American freedom movement, it aims to respond to a specific dilemma within black Atlantic anti-imperialist thought. Tricontinentalism responded to prior framings of anti-imperialism in the American hemisphere, and specifically to a formulation of blackness in the *négritude/negrismo*/New Negro movements of the

1920s–40s as the emblem of both a transnational experience of imperialist exploitation and an anti-imperialist resistance to that exploitation. The political signifier of blackness conceived in these movements would travel—so to speak—with Richard Wright from Paris, where he was living and collaborating with *négritude* writers, to the 1955 Bandung Conference. Wright would use his notion of the "color curtain," from his memoir *The Color Curtain: A Report on the Bandung Conference* (1956), to expand this use of blackness as a political signifier to include people of non-African ancestry. However, his presentation of the "color curtain" would continue to maintain the racial determinism and essentialism for which the *négritude/negrismo*/New Negro movements were often criticized.

Tricontinentalism, I suggest, would respond less to the actual realities of the Bandung moment and more to the meanings ascribed to Bandung within black internationalist networks in the American hemisphere. In this sense, the Tricontinental, in its self-described expansion of the Bandung moment into the Americas, would attempt to push *beyond the color curtain*, meaning that the Tricontinental would transform the category of color into a political signifier that does not denote a racially deterministic signified.

In what follows, I track the Tricontinental's attempted revision of black Atlantic anti-imperialism into its vision of a global and broadly inclusive resistant subjectivity. This shift, I argue, is foundational to contemporary horizontalist theoretical approaches, such as the Global South. Through this tracing, I aim to shore up the use-value of the Global South Atlantic as a conceptual apparatus that calls much needed attention to the Global South's inherent roots in a black Atlantic intellectual tradition. In following this black Atlantic thread that sustains the Global South, I intend to lay the groundwork for a better critical engagement with contemporary theories and praxes of transnational subaltern solidarity politics.

Black Atlantic Anti-Imperialism and Dixie's Travels in the Caribbean

While the Tricontinental's worldview has deep and varied roots, here I limit my focus to black internationalism of the 1920s–40s, such as that found in the Harlem Renaissance, *negrismo*, *négritude*, *afrocubanismo*, *afroantillanismo*, and Haitian *indigénisme*, because of the way the Tricontinental positions itself within this legacy. Richard Jackson has described the Francophone and Hispanic Caribbean manifestations of this larger transatlantic outpouring of black internationalist writing as the *afrocriollo* movement.

Within the dialogue between the *afrocriollo* movement and the Harlem Renaissance, I argue, there emerges a specific formulation of blackness as a symbol of anti-imperialist resistance. This black anti-imperialism, and a transnational black resistant subjectivity that emerges from it, will influence anti-imperialist discourse in the Americas and largely inform the ideology of tricontinentalism a few decades later.

The *afrocriollo* movement, which includes *negrismo* in the Hispanophone Caribbean and *négritude* in Francophone African and Caribbean countries, was a transnational cultural and artistic movement that, while highly heterogeneous, can generally be characterized by a pan-Africanist cultural vision, an engagement with cubism, surrealism and Harlem Renaissance writings, and a political stance of anti-imperialism. In the Hispanophone Caribbean, the backdrop for the emergence of these movements was the massive unemployment and political instability caused by the collapse of the sugar industry following the 1920 sugar crash and subsequent Wall Street Crash of 1929. The instability in the sugar industry greatly contributed to the eruption of workers' strikes in Puerto Rico and Cuba and led to the overthrow of the dictatorship of Gerardo Machado in Cuba. In this context, *afrocriollo* writings in the Hispanophone Caribbean generally reflect strong resentment toward the United States, which, in its efforts to expand the sugar industry, forced the rapid proletarianization of farmers in the countryside as well as the mass importation of immigrant workers into sugar-producing regions, exacerbating the economic crisis for many domestic workers (Ayala 1999).

It bears noting that the cultural and artistic movements mentioned before are internally heterogeneous and served diverse functions in their respective geographical and linguistic contexts. For example, many *negrista* writers, artists, and composers, in contrast to their *négritude* counterparts, were not of African descent. Whereas *négritude* implies the radicalist indictment of French colonialism and the antiracist assertiveness of black writers like Aimé Césaire, Léopold Sédar Senghor, or Léon-Gontran Damas, *negrismo* is often associated with the gesture of European primitivism through which white writers such as Emilio Ballagas, Alejo Carpentier, and Luis Palés Matos and composers such as Ernesto Lecuona and Gonzalo Roig ventriloquized blackness for nationalistic purposes (Jackson 1988, 26). While it is important to keep these differences in mind, *afrocriollo* writings share some important similarities.

First, *afrocriollo* writings generally tend to uphold blackness as both the emblem of a transnational experience of imperialist exploitation, beginning with slavery and European colonialism and continuing into twentieth-century US expansionism, as well as the symbol of anti-imperialist resistance to that exploitation. This general tendency arose contemporaneously with the US military occupation of multiple Caribbean islands in the years during and immediately preceding the rise of the *afrocriollo* movement: Haiti from 1915 to 1934, the Dominican Republic from 1916 to 1924, and Cuba from 1917 to 1922. Leading up to these back-to-back military campaigns, US expansionism was already inspiring a growing solidarity between Afro-descendant peoples within the United States and in the Caribbean. In *The Strange Career of Jim Crow* (1955), Comer Vann Woodward discusses how although Jim Crow laws existed in the US South since the end of Reconstruction (1877), with the US expansion of the Spanish-American War (1898), this undemocratic doctrine of white supremacy would come to define US foreign policy toward former Spanish colonies such as Puerto Rico and Cuba. As Jim Crow gained footing abroad, the possibility of challenging its inequalities on the domestic front would appear even further out of reach.

While Jim Crow became more entrenched in the US South with the Spanish-American War, it "took flight," according to Glenda Gilmore, with the US occupation of Haiti in 1915 (2008, 22). The occupation of the only black republic in the Western hemisphere would serve as proof for many that US imperialism and Jim Crow were mutually imbricated and inextricable such that Haitian dissidents, like writer Jacques Roumain, reached out to black political groups in the United States, and African American activists, like NAACP Secretary James Weldon Johnson, protested against the occupation (2008, 22–24). The transnational system of racial oppression fueled by US expansion, which Gilmore simply calls "Dixie," would foment the development of a black internationalist anti-imperialism that circulated among Antillean and US writers alike. This is not to diminish the legacy of slavery and European colonialism behind racial oppression within the domestic spheres of Caribbean islands, but the series of US occupations would lead to the common recognition of a transnational racial hegemony that superseded national and linguistic contexts.

For many *afrocriollo* writers, whether a black person was living in Cuba, Puerto Rico, Haiti, Harlem, the US South, in Martinique under French colonial rule, in the French, Portuguese, or British colonies in Africa, or in a country where slavery was abolished as early as 1791 or as late as 1880, the presence of an imperial power and the experience of racial oppression appeared to go hand in hand. This is the awareness that sparked Aimé Césaire, in his *Notebook of a Return to the Native Land* (1939), to trace a pan-African geography of oppression, referencing the Caribbean countries of Guadeloupe and Haiti and the Southern US states of Florida, Alabama, Tennessee, Georgia, and Virginia. This is also the conceptual basis from which Fernando Ortiz in *Cuban Counterpoint: Tobacco and Sugar* (1940) presented his Caribbeanist argument for the similarities of plantation-based economies throughout the Antilles, claiming that the plantation has led to "foreign ownership, corporate control and imperialism" (1995, 51). Phenotypic blackness, pan-Africanist symbology, and the experience of slavery and exploitation suffered by black people were, for *afrocriollo* writers, the platform for resistance against the history and continued presence of white/imperial oppression. For Ortiz, this oppression was embodied in the US-owned sugar plantation; for Césaire, it was French colonialism that starved "the hungry Antilles" (1995, 1). Conversely, Palés Matos presented the shaking of the *mulata*'s hips as a provocation against Uncle Sam, and for Alejo Carpentier, the bongo in his *Ecué-Yamba-Ó* (1933) served as the mode of resistance to the pervasive Yankee invasion.[11] This *afrocriollo* use of blackness to signify anti-imperialist resistance will profoundly influence tricontinentalism.

The second major tendency in *afrocriollo* writing that is relevant to tricontinentalism is its general tendency toward essentialist representations. Some critics have argued that while the Francophone *négritude* movement sought to challenge racism, *negrismo* did little to dismantle negative stereotypes and often heralded colonialist caricatures of blackness like the cannibal figure and associations with myth and lasciviousness (Branche 2006; Jackson 1988). However, both *negrista* and *négritude* writers have been criticized, to varying degrees, for engaging what Stuart Hall has called "inferential racism," or the unquestioning inscription of racist premises into apparently naturalized representations of black subjects (1995, 20).[12]

This is precisely the well-known critique that Frantz Fanon would launch in his *Black Skin, White Masks* (1952) against both Aimé Césaire and Léopold Senghor's *négritude* as well as the writings of Langston Hughes. While Fanon recognizes the importance and value of *négritude* for black self-definition, he argues that it touts an essentializing representation of black culture and that the identity it fashions is antithetically dependent on a relationship to whiteness. He quotes Jean-Paul Sartre's *Black Orpheus* (1948), saying:

> Negritude appears as the weak stage of a dialectical progression: the theoretical and practical affirmation of white supremacy is the thesis; the position of Negritude as antithetical value is the moment of negativity. But this negative moment is not sufficient in itself and the

> Blacks who employ it well know it; they know that it serves to pave the way for the synthesis or the realization of the human society without race. (Fanon 2008, 112)

Fanon sees Sartre's intervention as grounded in a paternalistic view that reduces *négritude* to merely a stage. However, he does in fact agree with Sartre's critique of the antithetical value of these writings in which *négritude* is proposed in response to, but never achieves transcendence of, a colonial construction of whiteness.[13] For Fanon then, *négritude* represents a step toward but not the ultimate end goal of what Sartre calls an eventual "realization of the human society without race" (2008, 112). Fanon concludes his *Black Skin, White Masks* with an appeal for a synthesis to this dialectic in which people move away from the "the inhuman voices of their respective ancestors so that a genuine communication can be born" (2008, 206). While I do not claim that tricontinentalism actually delivers this neat synthesis, I will argue that the crux of Fanon's critique plays an important role in shaping the Tricontinental project.

From the Black Atlantic to the Color Curtain

Three years following the publication of *Black Skin, White Masks*, the black anti-imperialism of the *afrocriollo* movement traveled to the 1955 Bandung Conference with Richard Wright. In his memoir, *The Color Curtain: A Report on the Bandung Conference* (1956), Wright would document his experience traveling to and participating in this meeting of newly decolonized African and Asian nation-states that aimed to foster lateral cooperation and to oppose intervention from the United States or the Soviet Union. Wright traveled to Bandung from Paris where he was living at the time and where he collaborated with Césaire on the literary review *Présence Africaine* (1947–). The following year, in September 1956, Wright participated in the First Congress of Black Writers and Artists in Paris, which was frequently described by the participants as a follow-up to Bandung and in which Césaire, Fanon, Senghor, and James Baldwin were present. According to Baldwin, who published the essay "Princes and Powers" (1957) about his participation at the conference, one of the central questions for the writers present was: "Is it possible to describe as a culture what may simply be, after all, a history of oppression?" (1985, 7). The myriad responses to this question dealt with how transnational black intellectuals might articulate a common subjectivity and position that does not present itself either as a mythic return to a precolonial origin or as an antithesis to a colonialist notion of whiteness.

Considering Wright's participation at this conference and the Afro-Antillean dialogues in which he found himself in Paris, Wright perhaps could have proposed Bandung—the movement of solidarity among decolonized peoples of diverse ethnicities and nationalities—in his *The Color Curtain* as a step toward articulating the synthesis outlined by Fanon and later discussed in Paris. In other words, Wright could have viewed Bandung as providing an outlet for destabilizing prior framings of both blackness and anti-imperialist resistance as being antithetical to whiteness. With his notion of the "color curtain"—much like W. E. B. Du Bois's use of the "color-line" to reference "the relation of the darker to the lighter races of men in Asia and Africa, in America and the islands of the sea"—Wright uses the term "color" to refer to all racialized peoples, not just those of African descent (1997, 45). In other words, Wright's "color curtain" broadens an *afrocriollo* pan-Africanist political subjectivity to include the Asian peoples represented at Bandung. However, despite this expansion from a black resistant subjectivity to a color curtain, he continues to maintain the antithetical discourse that was the subject of Fanon's critique.

Throughout *The Color Curtain*, which is composed of Wright's own reflections as well as interviews with conference delegates, Wright remarks that all of "these people were ex-colonial subjects, people whom the white West called 'colored' peoples" (1995, 11). According to Wright, this shared "colored" identity allows him and his interviewees to speak frankly with one another. While one of his interviewees claims that "the West calls some nations 'colored' in order to impose a separation between the dominator and the dominated," "colored" for Wright clearly implies not just the experience of domination or an anti-West sentiment but, throughout the text, is directly tied to skin color (1995, 68). Wright views the colonial experience of exploitation, as well as the anti-imperialist resistance that Bandung embodies, as incorporating people of non-African descent. However, "color" as a physical attribute is still central for Wright to defining who is included within the "color curtain."

In addition to the emphasis he places on the physical traits of the people included within this alliance, Wright associates the African and Asian people with whom he comes into contact with religious fanaticism and irrationalism. He ends the book with a call for the African and Asian elite, whom he claims have all been educated in the West, to take the lead or else the "Asian-African secular, rational attitudes will become flooded, drowned in irrational tides of racial and religious passions" (1995, 219). Wright's embrace of rationalism and portrayal of the nonelite in Africa and Asia, about which Henry Louis Gates Jr. has written a biting critique, uncritically represents racialized peoples through the very tropes that have been used in their oppression and thus falls into the same trap that Fanon describes (Gates 2008). With his representation of Bandung, Wright expands the *afrocriollo* black anti-imperialist resistance, including some of its essentializing representations, into a "color curtain." In this sense, although Wright uses "color curtain" to refer to the Afro-Asian solidarity of the Bandung Conference, we can submit the term to a deeper analysis by considering it as a metaphor for a general tendency toward a flattening racial essentialism within some black Atlantic anti-imperialist thought. The color curtain, as a concept, encapsulates a political resistance of "color" that, like the iron curtain from which Wright takes its name, is overdetermined and constitutive of binary oppositions.

Tricontinentalism, I argue, represents an attempt to push *beyond the color curtain* or an attempt to move toward the synthesis for which Fanon calls. By this I do not mean that the Tricontinental responds specifically to Wright's memoir about his experience at Bandung. Also, I do not intend to collapse Wright's notion of the color curtain with the ideas expressed in the speeches and debates of the conference itself. Indeed, although Indonesian President Ahmed Sukarno's opening address at Bandung referred to the meeting as "the first intercontinental conference of coloured peoples in the history of mankind" and many of the speeches and the Final Communiqué condemn racism, not everyone at the conference felt that what united the delegates was a race-based community (Kahin 1956, 39). As political scientist Robert Vitalis writes, "Color was a fact for some, not for others, but for no one was it what united them. To the contrary, many rejected the idea that color mattered. They called it racialism and warned against appealing to it as a dangerous and retrograde step. Nehru, for one, detested such talk" (2013, 270). Similarly, the Turkish delegates at Bandung objected to Sukarno's framing of the conference since they did not necessarily characterize themselves as colored, and many Indonesians, who had only recently been occupied by the Japanese military, viewed Sukarno's vision of a communion of colored peoples with much skepticism (Roberts and Foulcher 2016, 70–83).

After reading Wright's article, "Indonesian Notebook," which later became part of *The Color Curtain*, Wright's host in Indonesia—the novelist and newspaper editor Mochtar Lubis—wrote that Wright had seen Indonesia "through 'coloured glasses,' and he had sought behind every attitude he met colour and racial feelings" (10). Indonesian writer Beb Vuyk later repeated this impression in "A Weekend with Richard Wright," in which she relates several conversations with Wright that she regards as evidence for her description of him as "color crazy" (187). In other words, Wright's representation of the Bandung Conference in *The Color Curtain* provides a window into the perspective of a prominent black American writer—and perhaps even of other writers within Wright's black internationalist circles—on the Bandung moment, but it certainly should not be collapsed with the conference itself.

In contrast to Wright's vision, the so-called spirit of Bandung that would foster the formation of the Non-Aligned Movement has been described by Christopher Lee as a *communitas* based on political feeling and precisely not on essentialist notions of "locality or blood" (2010, 26). Although the Tricontinental movement would diverge from Bandung's nonviolence, its position of neutralism, and its primary association with heads of postcolonial nation-states, it is that communitas—that political solidarity that is transcendent of ethnic or territorial affiliations—that the Tricontinental will uphold and extend into the Americas. By claiming that the Tricontinental aims to push *beyond the color curtain*, thus, I am not intending to confuse Wright's vision of Bandung with the actual conference nor am I arguing that the Tricontinental directly addresses Wright's text per se, but rather I suggest that the Tricontinental responds to the essentializing tendencies within some black Atlantic thought that Wright's text embodies. The Tricontinental's expansive cultural production attempts to destabilize the black Atlantic-cum-color curtain anti-imperialism by intentionally avoiding colonialist stereotypes of people of color and by expressing a broader revolutionary subjectivity that is inclusive of all resistant oppressed peoples, regardless of skin color, ethnicity, or locality.

The Tricontinental's expanded resistant subjectivity, however, does not empty this prior black Atlantic anti-imperialism of its critique of racism. Rather, tricontinentalism articulates its global vision of power and resistance precisely through the language of racial inequality and racial violence. Yet the language of racial inequality in Tricontinental materials takes on a unique form since racial categories are sometimes used not to refer to perceived embodied difference but rather as metonyms for the global political positions that inform the Tricontinental project. This is what I call the Tricontinental's *metonymic color politics*: Whiteness is used metonymically to refer to global empire and color functions as a metonym for a transethnic resistant subjectivity that does not exclude phenotypically white people. In other words—in contrast to the overdetermined category of the color curtain—within the tricontinentalist political signifier of color, color remains an umbrella for a politics of anti-imperialism but does not necessarily denote the skin color of the peoples included under that umbrella.

From the Color Curtain to the Tricontinental

While the Tricontinental helped to usher the communitas of Bandung into the American continent, there were pivotal shifts that took place in the eleven years between these two events. Although, for many years prior to the Tricontinental, pan-Africanism created political solidarities across the Atlantic, generally at the time of Bandung there were "two analogous but separate spheres of subaltern struggle": one in Asia and Africa and the other in Latin America (Young 2005, 17). The US military intervention in Vietnam and the recognition of Cuba and Vietnam as participating in a joint struggle would bring these realms together at the Tricontinental (Young 2005). Like Afro-Asianism, the Tricontinental remained interested in preventing foreign military occupation and encouraging economic alliances to allow for more advantageous trade agreements with the North. However, Bandung was largely made up of heads of state and had a rhetoric that Dipesh Chakrabarty has characterized as "an uncritical emphasis on modernization" and a development model posed as "catching-up-with-the West" (2010, 53–54). The Tricontinental's delegations included heads of state as well as representatives of liberation movements, shifting the focus away from the development rhetoric and principles of nonviolence associated with Bandung and toward a discourse of militant resistance. More important, the Tricontinental would explicitly state its unity with struggles within imperial centers, such as African Americans in the United States, thus necessitating a more flexible concept of imperial power and subjugation.

From its inception, the Tricontinental (a.k.a. the Organization of Solidarity with the Peoples of Africa, Asia, and Latin America or OSPAAAL) produced a plethora of propaganda that it distributed around the world. This included *Tricontinental Bulletin* (1966–88, 1995–), published monthly in English, Spanish, French, and occasionally in Arabic; the bimonthly *Tricontinental* magazine (1967–90, 1995–), published in English, Spanish, French, and Italian; posters that were folded up inside of the magazine that were each devoted to solidarity with a different liberation struggle; books and pamphlets; radio programs; and the ICAIC Latin American Newsreel, short films made by the Cuban Film Institute and headed up by Cuban filmmaker Santiago Álvarez. Through its publications and films, and through the iconic posters for which it is now recognized, the Tricontinental provided both physical and textual spaces in which diverse political groups came into contact and functioned as an ideological nerve center that simultaneously shaped and was shaped by the perspectives of the various delegations it represented.

Considering Cuba's close relationship with the Soviets as well as the profound influence of Marxism on many of the anticolonial and independence struggles represented at the Tricontinental, one would expect the unity between the diverse movements it represented to be described in these materials as a common commitment to international class struggle. While references to Marxism abound, the socialist camp—especially in the early years of the alliance—is viewed as one force among several "great revolutionary currents, which are repeatedly dashing against the bastion of imperialism" (*Tricontinental Bulletin* 1968, 26).[14] "Imperialism" here is broadly defined, encompassing the forces of exploitation and oppression suffered by all member organizations. It combines the territorial notions of settler colonialism (faced for example by the Palestinian struggle) and exploitation colonialism (such as in the Portuguese colonies in Africa) with a more deterritorialized, Leninist theory of imperialism. The imperialism that Lenin called the "highest stage of capitalism"—a notion profoundly relevant to Latin America's relationship to the United States—refers to the ever-increasing concentration of production and capital by multinational monopolies that, through the complicity of big banks and with backing by military power, come to dominate the entirety of the global market (2010).

Although particularly critical of the United States, the conceptualization of imperial power in Tricontinental materials is not necessarily tied to the actions of any one nation. Tricontinentalism thus envisions a resistance to this deterritorialized empire that will be equally global, a concept summed up aptly by Che Guevara in his 1967 "Message to the Tricontinental" in which he characterizes the delegations as "we, the exploited people of the world."[15] Among these "exploited people of the world," the Tricontinental, especially in its first ten years, consistently privileges African Americans. This includes explicit statements of inclusion of African Americans into the alliance, numerous articles devoted to the African American struggle in its publications, posters that state the Tricontinental's solidarity with African Americans, and several newsreels including the famed six-minute film *Now* (1965) by Santiago Álvarez (Mahler 2015).

Wright claims in *The Color Curtain* that the only mention of African Americans at Bandung came from the US congressman Adam Clayton Powell, who, Wright alleges, was sent by the US government to defend its "bill of racial health" (1995, 175).[16] The shift in focus toward the African American freedom movement in the Tricontinental then seems to be related not only to the increasing radicalization of this movement but also to the extension of this solidarity into the Americas where the legacy of the *afrocriollo* movement was foundational for anti-imperialist thought.

In its bulletin and magazine, the Tricontinental consistently argues that African Americans are fighting in the very "guts of the imperialist monster" (*Tricontinental Bulletin* 1966, 9:5). This position is summed up aptly in a 1971 OSPAAAL poster (published in Spanish, French, English, and Arabic) in which an abstract drawing of an African American man holding a gun appears inside an outline of the map of the United States (Figure 2). The caption beneath it states, "We Will Destroy Imperialism from the Outside. They Will Destroy It from the Inside." Although arguably the use of "we" and "they" undercuts the Tricontinental's explicit inclusion of African Americans into the alliance, the statement of solidarity at the bottom of the poster reinforces the shared cause of African American activists with liberation struggles in the three continents. More important, the poster captures precisely the tension that tricontinentalist subjectivity inhabits in which "they" become a part of "we," and exploited peoples inside the geographic boundaries of imperial centers are viewed as united with those from outside.

This especially representative position attributed to African Americans stems from the view expressed in Tricontinental materials that policies of racial inequality within the United States prop up the maintenance of US power abroad. This is parallel to Gilmore's "Dixie," a racial hierarchy that accompanies and facilitates US expansionism in the early twentieth century, installing Jim Crow policies abroad while further entrenching them within the US South. For the Tricontinental, African Americans do not simply inhabit a geographic inside but a systemic inside. They are on the front lines of a system of racial subjugation that is integral to US power at home and abroad such that their fight is essential to the struggle facing the three continents.

The importance attributed to the African American cause for—as the *Tricontinental Bulletin* claims—"they are striking at U.S. imperialism from inside, while we are dismembering it from outside" is meant to extend as well to other groups struggling from within the United States (1969, 43:15). This includes "the white population . . . and other national minorities—Puerto Ricans, Mexican Americans, and others in the heat of the present process of radicalization" (*Tricontinental Bulletin* 1970, 46:15). The fight being fought by African Americans is one for which other US

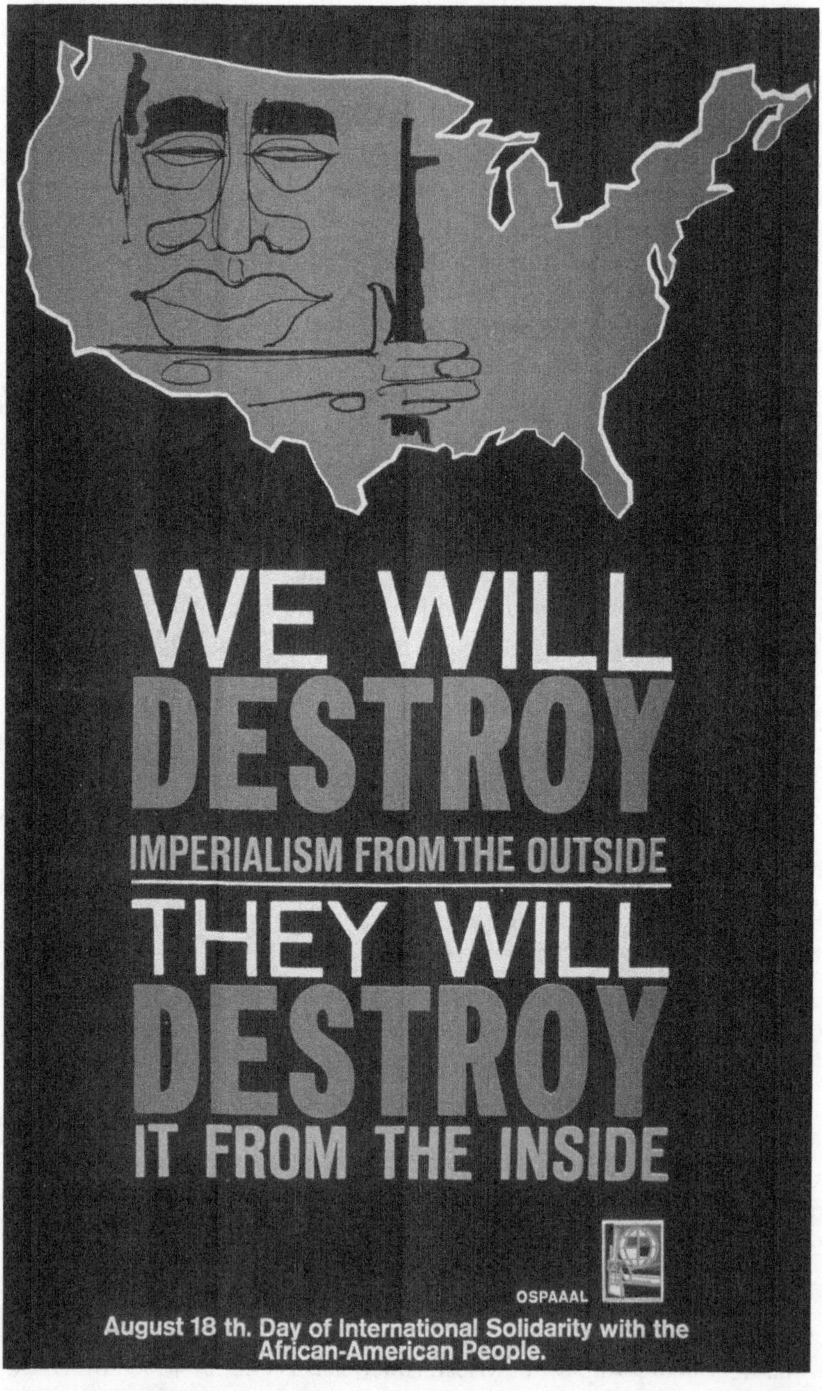

Figure 2. *We Will Destroy/They Will Destroy*. Poster image courtesy Lincoln Cushing/Docs Populi.

radicals, regardless of skin color, are also responsible. In other words, African Americans become emblematic of the Tricontinental's slippage between we-and-they, outside-and-inside, a liminality that also applies to ethnicity and skin color.

The liminal positionality attributed to African Americans is articulated in many other Tricontinental materials, such as the newsreel *El movimiento panteras negras* (*Black Panther Movement*, 1968). This newsreel by filmmaker Santiago Álvarez portrays encounters between black militants and police in the United States. It opens with the sounds of sirens and bongos—a sonic representation of the divide between the white police and the black protestors depicted in the film—while a voiceover reads a quote by Malcolm X: "*El problema afro-norteamericano no es un problema de los negros ni un problema de los norteamericanos sino un problema de la humanidad*" (The African American problem is not a Negro problem or a North American problem but a problem of humanity).[17] With this opening, the film immediately establishes the connection between African Americans' struggle and a larger international community.

The rest of the film alternates between quotes by Martin Luther King Jr. and Black Panther leader Huey Newton coupled with images of police brutality against African Americans and images from a police manual on riot gear with a voiceover that—in a *détournement* that is typical of Tricontinental materials—sarcastically narrates the manual with an invented text that reads like an advertisement. Images from the police manual instructing on the use of military-grade mace are narrated by a man's voice who states with the bravado and rhyming wit of a radio advertisement: "*El mace es un novedoso producto químico para lanzar sobre los ojos de los negros amotinados. Nunca falla. Negro tocado, negro segado. Solicite una muestra gratis. Use mace y ríase de lo que pase*" (Mace is a novel chemical product to spray at rioting blacks' eyes. It never fails. A sprayed black is a down black. Request a free demonstration. Use mace and laugh at what takes place). While the film posits that the tear gas, mace, flame-throwers and tanks in the police manual are designed specifically for use against black militants, the voiceover also boasts that these weapons are "*económicos y eficaces contra obreros, contra estudiantes, contra negros, contra blancos, y contra todos los que perturben la paz y el orden*" (economical and efficient against workers, students, blacks, whites, and against all whom disturb peace and order). By extending the possible victims of police oppression to whites and to the general descriptors of students and workers, the film signals the many images of bloodied black protestors as emblematic of a larger power struggle that goes beyond a simplistic black-white divide.

This point is further emphasized in the last frame of the film, which states over a map of the world that 1968 is the *"año del guerrillero heróico"* (year of the heroic guerrilla fighter). Instead of ending the film with a statement of solidarity with the Black Panthers or African Americans in general, the film explicitly collapses their struggle into a global unity and signals African American militants as representative of all the *guerrilleros* fighting imperialism all over the world. The film is at once a reference to the African American cause and to the struggles of black people everywhere as well as an abstraction of the global struggle with which every Tricontinental member can identify. The white policeman becomes a metonym for global empire and the black protestor stands in for all "the exploited people of the world."

This strategy is often expressed in Tricontinental materials through defining the Tricontinental's global revolutionary subjectivity not through the socialist rhetoric of class struggle but through employing the term "color" (such as in "colored peoples" or "colored leader") to refer not necessarily to skin color but to one's alignment with the Tricontinental's anti-imperialist politics. This was first brought to my attention through the work of Besenia Rodriguez, who noted that Robert F. Williams—the president of the Monroe, North Carolina, chapter of the NAACP who became a political exile in Cuba in 1961 and who attended the 1966 Tricontinental conference in Havana—refers in his writings to Fidel Castro, the son of a Spanish landowner, as a "colored" leader. She calls this a specifically "tricontinentalist" approach, by which she means that it is used "to forge a solidarity based on a common exploitation" (2005, 75). In other words, Williams uses color here to emphasize his and Castro's shared belonging to the global revolutionary subjectivity described by Guevara's "exploited people of the world."

The rhetorical openness of the use of "color" in Williams's writings, which Rodriguez aligns with a tricontinentalist ideology, is also present in Tricontinental materials. The March 1971 issue of *Tricontinental Bulletin*, for example, is devoted to the Young Lords Party, a New York Puerto Rican radicalist group who are described as a "revolutionary party fighting for the liberation" of "all colored and oppressed people" (20). This issue prints the Young Lords Party's thirteen-point platform, in which it states that "Puerto Ricans are of all colors and we resist racism. Millions of poor white people are rising up to demand freedom and we support them. . . . Power to all oppressed people!" (1971, 21). Similar to the way in which Robert F. Williams's description of Castro as "colored" places him among

Guevara's "we, the exploited people of the world," the Young Lords' conception of "colored and oppressed peoples" is not necessarily meant to be a descriptor of physical appearance. "Colored"—here made equivalent to oppressed—becomes a signifier for a transethnic politically resistant subjectivity that includes "poor white people" who are "rising up to demand freedom" (1971, 21). In other words, belonging to the Tricontinental's "colored and oppressed peoples" is predicated on a person's radicalization and ideological adherence to tricontinentalism.

In this sense, Guevara's revolutionary subject arises out of a preexisting discourse, which Richard Wright called "the color curtain," that appropriated the colonial language of color to create a phenotypic label for international resistance. However, while Guevara's "exploited people of the world" may arise from this preexisting discourse of color, the tricontinentalist use of color is an ideological referent that does not necessarily describe the skin color of the tricontinentalist revolutionary but rather the anti-imperialist contours of her politics. Again, I refer to this racial abstraction as the Tricontinental's metonymic color politics. By this, I mean that through the use of racially coded terminology and through the repetition of images of mostly Anglo-American policemen and African American protestors, Tricontinental materials metonymically employ the colonial and Jim Crow categories of "white" and "colored," using white policemen to signify global imperial oppression and an African American identity to stand in for all "the exploited people of the world." In this way, the Jim Crow racial divide of "Dixie" functions as a metonym not for a global color line of phenotypic difference but for a Tricontinental power struggle in which all radicalized, exploited peoples regardless of skin color are implicated and thus discursively colored.

These metonymic color politics are distinct from the colorblindness for which Soviet communism was often criticized in that the Tricontinental does not reduce its project to a class struggle that will resolve racial inequality through the institution of socialism but rather places liberation from racial subjugation at the forefront of its political project.[18] Additionally, it does not engage in what Gayatri Spivak calls "a strategic use of positivist essentialism in a scrupulously visible political interest," or the homogenizing suppression of difference that is often used by marginalized peoples to forge an essentialized group identity for political purposes (1987, 205). Rather, the common ideology that metonymically "colors" and unifies the Tricontinental's delegations creates a chain of equivalences that recognizes various experiences of oppression and exploitation. Diverse ethnic, national, and linguistic groups are linked through a shared tricontinentalist worldview yet maintain their heterogeneity as individual movements with distinct causes and goals.

From the Tricontinental to the Global South

Tricontinentalism takes up a preexisting signifier of black anti-imperialism, which Wright expanded into a color curtain to include people of non-African descent, and attempts to move beyond its relationship to perceived physical difference and essentialist representations and toward an abstract use of color that refers to a shared political ideology. In this way, the Tricontinental provides a framework for imagining a new global revolutionary subjectivity that is increasingly relevant in our contemporary moment.

Although its materials continue to be produced and disseminated to this day, the central contributions of the Tricontinental have been largely forgotten. This erasure is due to a combination of several factors, such as disillusionment with Cuba's repression of intellectual freedoms and the severe weakening of the Left in the Americas in the 1970s and '80s. Equally significant is the way in which Cold War decolonization discourses would become preserved within the academic field of postcolonial studies, a field which has tended to focus on the former African and Asian colonies represented at Bandung and which has had a contentious relationship with Latin Americanism.[19] Moreover, postcoloniality would be based on a historical circumstance of former colonization rather than an ideological stance of anti-imperialism. In contrast, the Tricontinental was focused on global solidarity organized around ideological affinities. While it recognized similarities between experiences of oppression, the basis of its solidarity was not dependent on those similarities nor was it dependent on trait-based characteristics, such as skin color or geographic location.

However, despite this general erasure of the Tricontinental, in 2000, much in the same way that the Tricontinental did over forty years ago, Michael Hardt and Antonio Negri theorized a contemporary Empire facilitated through global capital and founded on the US model of networked, constituent power that expands continuously outward toward the frontier. Hardt and Negri claim that in this age of deterritorialized empire, which is not bound by national borders nor controlled by any single nation-state, "there is no more outside" (2000, 186). In other words, although there are margins and centers, within the empire, everyone becomes interpellated, everyone is on the systemic inside. According to Hardt and Negri, this in fact creates more revolutionary potential since it yields an international "set of all the exploited and the subjugated, a multitude that is directly opposed to Empire" (2000, 393). This concept, radically similar to Guevara's Tricontinental notion of "we, the exploited people of the world," attempts to capture the way in which the networked power of contemporary capitalism creates the conditions for an equally global emancipatory politics that joins together people of diverse nationalities, ethnicities, and languages, and with varying levels of access to the benefits of the neoliberal economy.[20]

Similar to Hardt and Negri's "multitude," new critical categories like the Global South have emerged over the last ten years as attempts to describe the mutual identification and shared worldview of oppressed groups across national boundaries. These new concepts aim to transcend regional and ethnic identities and a narrowly defined historical condition of postcoloniality, and they aim to recognize the negative effects of contemporary globalized capitalism on groups located within the global North. In this sense, the Global South and similar concepts could be viewed as an attempt to describe a contemporary revival of the ideology of tricontinentalism.

Yet, I would argue that this contemporary revival of tricontinentalism is only partial. In recent years in the American continent, for example, we have witnessed widespread protests against neoliberal policies and economic inequality and a burgeoning movement against state brutality toward racially oppressed peoples. Despite the enthusiasm and media frenzy often generated by these so-called Twitter Revolutions, there is a fundamental paradox within social movements in the Americas today. On the one hand, protests against deregulation, integration, and corporate greed within global capitalism tend to reproduce the rhetoric of multiculturalism, generating silences around racial inequities. On the other, movements organized around racial justice tend to frame violence toward racialized populations within a context that is limited to a critique of the state, sidelining a broader consideration of the intersection between racial violence and global capital flows. In this sense, the contemporary revival of tricontinentalism within horizontalist politics is stripped of its most valuable contribution—its metonymic color politics—which allowed for an inclusionary resistant subjectivity but which still kept racism and the image of global capitalism as a racializing apparatus in the spotlight. In contrast to the Tricontinental, the transnational solidarity of anticapitalist political resistance today tends to reproduce the colorblind multiculturalism of neoliberal discourse, producing silences around racial inequalities.

For this reason, the Global South Atlantic emerges as a particularly useful paradigm in that it recognizes the centrality of a black Atlantic intellectual tradition to the phenomenon and theory of the Global South. It calls attention to the fact that the Global South imaginary was always already a Global South (black) Atlantic imaginary. In recognizing the intellectual roots of the Global South, the Global South Atlantic inherently calls transnational solidarity politics into a renewed engagement with black Atlantic thought, foregrounding the fight against racial inequities in general and the fight for justice for peoples of African descent more specifically as a prerequisite to the futurity of Global South political resistance.

NOTES

I am grateful to Lincoln Cushing for permission to use the image here and to Magalí Armillas-Tiseyra, Valérie Loichot, Lanie Millar, Dierdra Reber, Mark A. Sanders, Scott Selisker, and the editors, Kerry Bystrom and Joseph Slaughter, for their comments on previous drafts.

1. Similar terminology includes Arjun Appadurai's "grassroots globalization," Boaventura de Sousa Santos's "subaltern cosmopolitanism" and "counter-hegemonic globalization," Fernando Rosenberg's "cosmopolitismo alternativo, sureño" (alternative, southern cosmopolitanism), and Shu-mei Shih and Francoise Lionnet's "minor transnationalism."

2. For detailed information on the development of the Global South as a geopolitical concept, see Dirlik (2007). I thank Alfred J. López for kindly pointing out to me in such clear terms how Gramsci's North-South vision transforms the East-West worldview of European colonialism.

3. This usage has been largely theorized through the work of New Southern Studies that compares the parallels between the US South and other Souths, such as Latin America. See, for example, Cohn (1999).

4. For example, Alfred J. López, founding editor of the journal *The Global South*, describes it as the "mutual recognition among the world's subalterns of their shared conditions at the margins of the brave new neoliberal world of globalization" (2007, 1). Vijay Prashad defines it similarly but adds an implication of political action provoked by this shared consciousness: "this concatenation of protests against the theft of the commons, against the theft of human dignity and rights, against the undermining of democratic institutions and the promises of modernity. The global South is this: a world of protest, a whirlwind of creative activity" (2012, 9).

5. The work of Robert J. C. Young is an exception to this general elision of the Tricontinental within postcolonial studies (2005). Prashad devotes a chapter of his *The Darker Nations: A People's History of the Third World* (2007) to the Tricontinental, but he treats it as a single event rather than a movement.

6. There has been much debate around the historical significance of the Bandung meeting and whether its apparent success was more myth than

reality. Generally, however, the so-called Bandung Spirit—which some use to refer to a method of international diplomacy and others to a "feeling" of Third World Solidarity—is understood as a forerunner to the Non-Aligned Movement (NAM), which first convened in Belgrade in 1961 (Lee 2010, 17).

7. The Tricontinental (Organization of Solidarity with the Peoples of Africa, Asia, and Latin America, or OSPAAAL) actually represented an extension of the Afro-Asian Peoples' Solidarity Organization (AAPSO) into the Americas. Although the Tricontinental preparatory committee described the AAPSO, an alliance of seventy-five organizations founded in Cairo in 1957, as originating "in 1955 at the meeting of the heads of State in Bandung," the AAPSO is generally considered significantly more communist-aligned than the 1955 Bandung Conference (International Preparatory Committee 1965, 3). See OAS (1966) for details on the shift from the AAPSO to the OSPAAAL.

8. This element of the Tricontinental's ideology is intimately tied to an exchange between the Cuban Revolution and African American intellectuals that began in the early 1960s. Besenia Rodriguez uses the term "tricontinentalism" to refer to the "critique of global capitalism and its exploitation of the world's racialized peoples" expressed in several articles composed by African American activists who traveled to Cuba in the early 1960s through their participation in the Fair Play for Cuba Committee (2005, 63). Additionally, Sarah Seidman has written extensively on the relationship between African Americans and postrevolutionary Cuba, noting a "shared Tricontinental ideology" that connected, for example, Stokely Carmichael to Cuba (2012, 2). For more on African Americans and the Cuban Revolution, see Gosse (1993), Guridy (2010), Joseph (2006), Sawyer (2006), Seidman (2013), Tietchen (2007), and C. Young (2006).

9. By claiming that the Tricontinental privileged the African American freedom movement, I do not mean to imply that other movements do not receive equal attention in Tricontinental materials. Indeed, the expansion of the Afro-Asian alliance of Bandung into the Tricontinental was largely based on the view that Cuba and Vietnam were participating in a joint struggle (Young 2005, 17). Struggles in Vietnam, the Congo, Puerto Rico, and Palestine, for example, are frequently discussed in the early years of *Tricontinental* and *Tricontinental Bulletin*. The African American cause, however, represents a unique case since, as the August–September 1966 issue of *Tricontinental Bulletin* states, "although geographically Afro-Americans do not form part of Latin America, Africa, or Asia, the special circumstances of the oppression which they suffer, to which they are subjected, and the struggle they are waging, merits special consideration and demands that the Tri-Continental organization create the necessary mechanisms so that these brothers in the struggle will, in the future, be able to participate in the great battle being fought by the

peoples of the three continents" (1966, 21). The "special consideration" that the Tricontinental offers to African Americans is, I suggest, integral to its devising of an inclusive, global revolutionary subjectivity that is geographically unbounded and that is foundational to the fluid geography of a contemporary notion like the Global South.

10. While I employ the term "black Atlantic" here, it is important to acknowledge that the geography implied by Paul Gilroy's conceptualization in *The Black Atlantic: Modernity and Double Consciousness* (1993) does not always map on perfectly to these exchanges since many of these intellectuals' networks and travels extend beyond the Atlantic region to the Soviet Union and beyond.

11. For this reading of Carpentier's first novel, see Kutzinski (1993).

12. Here, I am following the lead of Kutzinski, who uses Hall's term to characterize *negrista* writings (1993, 14).

13. Despite Fanon's position, one can find many instances of *négritude* writings that resist this antithetical and essentialist position. Césaire's *Notebook*, for example, draws an equivalence between the experiences of black people and that of "a jew-man . . . a Hindu-man from Calcutta" as well as the more general "famine-man, the insult-man, the torture-man you can grab anytime" (1995, 11–12). These comparisons between diverse experiences of exploitation, which he would later develop more fully in his *Discourse on Colonialism* (1955), undermine the racial determinism and essentialism that Fanon might otherwise attribute to Césaire's text. Similarly, Brent Hayes Edwards discusses how some Francophone radicals in the 1920s broadened "the term nègre into the service of anti-imperialist alliances among what W. E. B. Du Bois called 'the darker peoples of the world'" (2003, 36). These moments, among others, suggest that although tricontinentalism would reject some of the more essentialist representations of *afrocriollo* writings, we can also find the presence of a budding tricontinentalism in these writings, especially in the *négritude* movement.

14. This flexible ideological definition was the result of key disagreements and compromises made in the initial founding of the organization.

15. Young views Guevara's characterization of this nonproletarian revolutionary subjectivity as central to the formation of a postcolonial subjectivity (2001, 212).

16. The US State Department also sent African American journalist Carl Rowan for a similar purpose, and Margaret Cartwright, the first black reporter assigned to the United Nations, and journalist William Worthy were also present. W. E. B. Du Bois and Paul Robeson had hoped to attend the Bandung Conference, but their passports were denied. However, statements by Robeson and Du Bois were read aloud at the conference, and con-

trary to Wright's claim, these statements did in fact mention a relationship to African American struggles (Daulatzai 2012, 27; Rodriguez 2006, 189–190). Since Bandung spoke out against racism in general and, as Sohail Daulatzai writes, "challenged the white world, foregrounding the role of race in both international and domestic affairs," it had profound implications for African Americans and black peoples around the globe (2012, 26). However, overall, the African American struggle, although gaining momentum on the world stage in the mid 1950s, was not on the forefront of issues discussed at Bandung.

17. All translations from Álvarez's film are mine.

18. Domestically, Cuba claimed to have eliminated racial inequality on the island through socialist reforms. Through internationalist forums like the Tricontinental, in which Cuba presented itself to the world as militantly antiracist, the predominantly white Cuban government externalized racial injustice to the imperialist North, denying its continued presence on the island and furthering a domestic myth around the nationalist and socialist achievement of racial harmony. In this sense, it should be noted that tricontinentalist racial discourse—which was the result of a transnational exchange of activists and intellectuals—is not identical to the racial discourse of the Cuban state. Although the Tricontinental platform was often used by the Cuban state to dismiss domestic racial inequities, it should not be characterized as merely a propaganda tool of the Cuban state. This characterization risks flattening the multiplicity of issues and interests to which tricontinentalism responds and eliding the central contribution of black internationalist intellectuals to the discourse and ideology of tricontinentalism. For a discussion of the distance between Cuba's domestic and internationalist racial discourses, see Sawyer (2006).

19. For in-depth discussions of the Latin Americanist debates on postcolonial studies, see Acosta (2014), Coronil (2008), and Lund (2006).

20. For a discussion of "networked power," see Castells (2011).

South Africa, Chile, and the Cold War
Reading the South Atlantic in Mark Behr's *The Smell of Apples*

Kerry Bystrom

For a rather slim novel, Mark Behr's *The Smell of Apples* (1993, 1995) has generated a hefty amount of commentary. Much of it revolves around the confession that accompanied the novel and, some say, secured its success. In 1996, as part of a keynote address at a conference in Cape Town entitled "Fault Lines—Inquiries around Truth and Reconciliation," Behr confessed to having been a spy for the apartheid government while studying at Stellenbosch University. Writing the novel, he claimed, was his way of confronting his own complicity in state-sanctioned terrorism and opening a similar pathway for others: "as an act of creation *The Smell of Apples* represented for me the beginnings of a showdown with myself for my own support of a system like apartheid. . . . If the book's publication has assisted white people in coming to terms with their own culpability for what is wrong in South Africa, then it has been worthwhile" (Behr 1996; quoted in Heyns 2000, 42). Behr here implies that the act of writing inspired a deep acknowledgment of his own guilt, eventually prompting a public confession that asks others to take responsibility for their actions. More skeptical critics suggest a different moral arc. As Sarah Nuttall argues, "the fact that people confess to their crimes does not necessarily imply a compulsion to confess as an escape from a burden of guilt" (1998, 87). One can confess out of "fear of exposure" (Nuttall 1998, 87) or, indeed, to generate that whiff of scandal known to increase sales figures.

Beyond the controversy surrounding Behr's confession—a controversy that foreshadows so many of the debates about sincerity that would arise in the South African Truth and Reconciliation Commission (TRC) proceedings, just beginning at this time, and to which I will return—critical writing on Behr's novel has underscored the novel's deconstruction of cherished myths about Afrikaner Nationalism and the state created on its behalf, as well as the cultural manufacture of support for this state. Michiel Heyns (1996), Rita Barnard (2000), and Cheryl Stobie (2008) all discuss, through different lenses, the text's exposure of the ideological mechanisms of apartheid, including its tensions and contradictions.[1] A bare outline of the plot suffices to show the poison lurking in what Stobie calls "apartheid's Eden" (2008, 84). In the novel, the young Afrikaner Marnus Erasmus narrates two different but defining moments in his life: first, in 1973, when he witnesses the rape of his best friend, Frikkie, by his father, a major general in the South African Defense Force (SADF); and second, in 1988, when he is injured and presumably dies while fighting apartheid's, and thus his father's, proxy war in Angola. If the representation of these two events sheds light on the ways in which young men were "seduced" (Heyns 1996, 82) or coerced into supporting a patriarchal authoritarian state, then it also reveals the rot at the very heart of the white family, building block and prized metaphor for the Afrikaner nation.

While this chapter engages with this body of scholarship, it also takes discussion of Behr's novel in another direction—one that triangulates an emerging interest in new Cold War studies with the South Atlantic frame privileged in this volume. Collections such as *Beyond the Border War: New Perspectives on Southern Africa's Late-Cold War Conflicts* (2008), edited by Gary Baines and Peter Vale, and *Cold War in Southern Africa: White Power, Black Liberation* (2009), edited by Sue Onslow, lay the groundwork for a wide-ranging and multidisciplinary reconsideration of mid- to late twentieth century South African history through the lens of a disaggregated Cold War. These volumes treat the Cold War as "not simply a bipolar contest between the United States and the USSR," but also as a "complicated dynamic of domestic and international rivalries in the aftermath of independence from European colonial powers" in which both white minority regimes and black nationalist groups in Southern Africa drew in and on external assistance—from the United States, Soviet Union, and many other sources—for their own ends (Onslow 2009, 1–2). Focusing mainly on South Africa's links to struggles in Angola, Namibia, Zambia, and Zimbabwe along with the US, Soviet, and Cuban contributions to these same struggles, these volumes ask us to rethink South Africa within a matrix of international exchanges that crystallized in public imagination as the Cold War.[2]

In the realm of literary studies, critic Monica Popescu has done the most to situate South Africa within this global and decentered Cold War context. Her article "Licence for Shooting" (2008), which looks at representations of South Africa's often covert operations in Angola in recent literature including *The Smell of Apples*, uses the figure of Marnus as a soldier to highlight South Africa's involvement in regional and global politics, as well as to underscore the necessity of broadening the frames through which we read South African literature and culture more generally. In her book *South African Literature Beyond the Cold War*, Popescu expands on these ideas with reference to Françoise Lionnet and Shu-mei Shih's concept of "minor transnationalism," echoing these scholars in their call for attention to "the creative interventions that networks of minoritized cultures produce within and across national boundaries" (quoted in 2010, 17). Looking specifically at the deep relationships that grew between Southern Africa and Eastern Europe over the course of the Cold War, Popescu attempts to broaden a "field of study concerned primarily with a North-South Axis of representation, in which the North has almost exclusively meant Western Europe and North America" (2010,171). She examines "how postcolonial writers and scholars forged essential alliances with Eastern Europe during and after the Cold War" and focuses attention on "relations between what used to be called the Second and the Third Worlds" (2010, 17).[3]

In this chapter, I work in a similar vein but focus on a different figure almost invariably commented upon in descriptions of the novel but not as yet closely investigated, and who points toward South Atlantic itineraries overlooked even in scholarship like Popescu's invested in drawing threads between "minor" powers. This is the Chilean general who happens to be visiting Marnus's father when Marnus witnesses the rape of Frikkie. What can a Chilean general mean to Marnus? What is a Chilean general doing in 1970s South Africa, anyway? In other words, what were the real and symbolic relationships developed between apartheid and Latin American dictatorships during the Cold War? I respond to these questions in a perhaps circuitous fashion, by analyzing the forms of mimicry and doubling at play in Behr's novel. This analysis allows me to suggest that the Chilean general serves as an uncanny double whose representation helps to reveal the psychological mechanisms of acknowledgement and repression that underpinned Afrikaner support for apartheid's military regime. I further suggest that Behr's concomitant use of Augusto Pinochet's Chile as an uncanny double for apartheid South Africa points to Cold War anticommunist military and political networks—often routed through the United States but also existing bilaterally among Argentina, Brazil, Chile, Uruguay, Paraguay, and South Africa—that allowed for the circulation of both technologies and cultures of state-sponsored terror, and that later (perhaps ironically) opened into shared modes of democratic transformation. In this manner, I hope not only to deepen our understanding of a novel that remains a rich examination of what Barnard calls the "moral airlessness" of apartheid (2000, 208), but also to add a new dimension to the discussion convened in *The Global South Atlantic* about movements between Africa and Latin America and literary engagement with them.[4]

Let me begin with the General and Marnus. As noted earlier, the novel has a split time scheme. Most of the text is narrated from the point of view of the eleven-year-old Marnus as he begins his summer holiday in Cape Town in December 1973. Interspersed with this narrative, however, are passages written from the point of view of Marnus when he is much older, and serving as an officer in the South Africa Defense Forces (SADF) in Angola. In one of these passages, Marnus thinks back to his childhood:

> Perhaps that summer ultimately determined it. Possibly not even the whole summer, just that week in December. Yet, by now, I know full-well that you cannot satisfactorily understand an event unless you have a picture of everything that accompanies it: the arrival of the visitor cannot be divorced from what preceded his coming. To understand my own choice, I need to muster as much of the detail as possible. (1995, 31)

This passage is somewhat cryptic, not least in its failure to define the "choice" that Marnus is talking about, or to provide any explanation linking "the visitor" to it. Nevertheless, I will argue that this very gap between the General, who is the visitor in question, and Marnus's unspecified decision points not only to the profound influence of the General on the narrator's life, but also to the psychic mechanisms through which this influence plays out.

Key to the General's importance is what the young Marnus perceives to be his similarity to his own father, Johan. As Barnard argues, "the novel is very much concerned with mirrors, as well as doubles, recognition and misrecognition . . . likenesses and differences, originals and copies" (2000, 212–213; see also Stobie 2008, 75, 77). Barnard links these various forms of doubling to the reproduction of apartheid ideology. Extending this insight, I would say that this play between originals and mirror images, with their likenesses and differences, is nowhere more obvious than in the relation between Johan and the General. The General enters the house as Johan's mysterious guest; Marnus and his older sister Ilse are instructed to refer to him as Mr. John Smith, a businessman from New York, but his parents inform them that "Mr. Smith" is actually an officer from Chile in South Africa on a secret mission.[5] The General then, like Johan, is high in the military command of a state that viewed itself as a key bulwark in a war against communist aggression, and the two men share common goals and values. The young Marnus also notes the physical similarities between the General and Johan: "He seems younger than Dad, but they've got almost the same build' (1995, 30). Indeed, all that really differentiates them is the General's slightly darker complexion and a thick scar roping down his back.

Marnus initially views the General with a kind of hero-worship. Over the course of the visit, however, he glimpses in and through him uncomfortable and disturbing things—the increasing restlessness of Ilse with the strictures of Afrikaans culture, the unhappiness of his mother, forced to sacrifice her career and even her relationship with her sister for her husband and her children, and, most dramatically, the predatory nature of his own father. The latter becomes fully apparent on the last night of the General's visit. After hours listening to Johan and the General exchange stories from their battles against "Communist terrorists," Marnus and Frikkie fall asleep on the living room floor. Later, when the General is supposed to have left, Marnus wakes and discovers that Frikkie is missing. Peering through a hole in the spare bedroom, he finds his friend sitting on the bed with a man he takes to be the General, and watches as a series of increasingly terrifying acts occur: "The General puts his arm out towards Frikkie, and it looks like Frikkie is trying to push himself up against the wall. The General puts his other hand on Frikkie's shoulder. Then he bends forward. . . . [His] hand is on Frikkie's John Thomas. Now his face is against Frikkie's and it looks like he's pushing him up against the wall and kissing him" (1995, 175). Finally convinced that "what the General is doing to Frikkie is a sin" (1995, 175), Marnus runs to his parents' bedroom to wake up his father. There, however, he finds his mother asleep alone. The question that arises—"where is Dad?" (1995, 176)—is answered when he leaves his mother asleep in her bedroom and goes again to spy on Frikkie. It is then that he sees "the General" rape Frikkie and also discovers that "the scar is gone from the General's back" (1995, 177). His father is Frikkie's assailant.

As Marnus's evasive narration of his father's crime suggests ("the scar is gone from the General's back"), Marnus recognizes the physical and emotional violence that suffuses his household through the General, but he does so in a way that both represses it and replicates this violence. This dynamic is repeated on the following day. Betraying the extent to which his father and the General have become fused and confused in his mind, Marnus tries to reject his father by rejecting the parting gift that the General has left for him: his epaulettes. This is a highly symbolic gift, standing as the "insignia of militaristic manhood" that dominates his family as well as his country, and into which he has been groomed to step (Stobie 2008, 79). His refusal to accept it provokes a second and symbolic rape scene, one in which Marnus serves as a double for Frikkie, as Johan beats Marnus ferociously across his back and across his buttocks.[6] Forced in this manner to accept the epaulettes, Marnus undergoes a cognate psychological shift—burying his pain, shame and disgust to enthusiastically accept the masculine codes of violence he has witnessed and experienced. As Heyns suggests, this acceptance seals his choice to keep his father's violation of Frikkie a secret, and it prefigures his later choice to become a military officer like his father (1996, 94–95). These, I would argue, are the linked choices to which the meditations from Angola cited above must refer. The gap between the visitor and the choice is then a space in which unspoken memories are kept from surfacing, but where the act of repression prompts a continuing complicity with the very forms of violence Marnus wishes to bury.

Repression is a common technique for dealing with the intense psychological violence perpetrated by militarized regimes of state terror, as Diana Taylor has shown in relation to South America. Speaking of Argentina's "Dirty War," she describes the tendency of "good" Argentine citizens to engage in "percepticide": acts of shutting down one's senses in order not to see, hear, or feel the crimes committed by the state (1997, 119–124). "Percepticide" in the long run, of course, merely allows these crimes to continue. Behr's novel proposes an interesting twist on this dynamic by positioning the General as an uncanny double for Johan in the Freudian sense of the term. For Freud ([1919] 1955), to recall, the uncanny or *das unheimliche* is not the opposite of *heimlich* but a variation of it. According to Freud, "the uncanny is that class of the terrifying which leads back to something largely known to us, once familiar," and which at the same time "ought to have remained hidden and secret, and yet comes to light" (241). The link between these two definitions is the act of repression: "this uncanny is in reality nothing new or foreign, but something familiar and old—established in the mind—that has been estranged only through repression" (242). Marnus sees in the General a reference to monstrous yet intimately familiar aspects of his father, pointing to knowledge about his family, his household and his society that he believes ought not come to light. When it has come to light, it must be repressed yet again, even at the cost of reproducing it *ad infinitum*.

There are ways in which the General differs from Johan, and that might, as Stobie points out, have led the young Marnus to escape the life of masculine militarism (2008, 76–77, 82). Specifically, the General is identified as having mixed Spanish and South American Indian ancestry. Such *mestizaje* aligns him with those people in South Africa categorized as "Coloured"—an apartheid legal category that includes those of biracial or multiracial heritage who could be classified as neither "white" nor "black," and therefore given fewer privileges than whites and more than black Africans under apartheid rule (see Wicomb 1998, 101; Christiansë 2002, 390). If coded as "Coloured," the General would become an example of "playing-white" or "passing," engaged in the subversive doubling of mimicry that threatens the pure white nation Johan is so busy defending. Homi Bhabha argues that the colonial mimic man inspires a profound ambivalence because of his race. If the colonial or racial double is "almost the same but not white," his existence both reflects and disrupts Western power and authority (Bhabha 2004, 128). "Mimicry," for this reason, "is at once resemblance and menace" (Bhabha 2004, 123). The General himself at times underscores this difference, and with it his potential to unsettle structuring binaries. In a scene where Marnus, Ilse, his mother and the General discuss *Moby Dick*, the General poses himself as a Queequeg figure. Ilse, however, insists that both the General and her father are Ahab—Ahab who is pictured on the cover of Ilse's book harpooning the white whale in a manner that resonates with Frikkie's rape (Barnard 2000, 218–219). Confronted with a similar opening later on, when Frikkie indeed tries to label the General as "Coloured," Marnus closes it down by insisting that indigenous South Americans are "not black" and as such remain outside the South African color hierarchy (1995, 166). This refusal to engage in an evident racial double standard allows Marnus to see the General and his father only in terms of similarity, each one standing for an aggressive defense of his own anti-Communist ideology on one side of the South Atlantic—for instance, Johan showing pictures of his torture of black freedom fighters in what was then Rhodesia, and the General boasting about firebombing the Chilean presidential palace in Chile's coup of

September 11, 1973 (1995, 171–173).[7] This doubled vision of aggressive anticommunism is one Marnus himself will further reproduce in Angola as a soldier for the apartheid state.

These speculations have not yet fully addressed the question of why it matters that the General is Chilean, rather than, say Mexican (Mexico as a country is much more widely known than Chile for having a *mestizo* population) or French (unlike Mexico, France did engage in actions that contravened the arms embargo, as pointed out in Behr's novel [1995, 19]). I might first of all say that this detail points to a largely unrecognized web of real military, trade and cultural relations between the Southern Cone of Latin America and South Africa. This web is best understood as part of a wider global network linking countries fighting the "red terror" throughout the Cold War, supported but not necessarily controlled by the United States,[8] and indeed signaled by Behr as a background to the relationship between Johan and the General (1995, 80). This network connected the United States with Latin America, through the School of the Americas, which trained many of the military dictators of Latin America in the 1960s, '70s, and '80s, and Operation Condor, which coordinated national security doctrine among "friendly" regimes in the Southern Cone (Roht-Arriaza 2005, 21–30). These hemispheric efforts were tied to other transnational alliances spawned by the Cold War, like NATO, whose most prominent members, namely the United States, the United Kingdom, West Germany, and France, all carried on economic and military relations with South Africa despite the arms embargo and various sanctions regimes, in addition to visibly supporting other brutal African dictatorships. Also key to this global network was Israel, which coordinated activities with the United States and also built its own partnerships with states such as Chile, Argentina, and South Africa (Polakow-Suransky 2010, 6).

Cutting across these perhaps more familiar security blocs, and bringing South Africa into direct relationships with South America, was concern over the South Atlantic. Beginning in 1966, Pretoria launched an initiative to increase "dialogue" with countries in Latin America like Argentina and Brazil (Hurrell 1983, 180; see also Cockram 1970, 82–88; Fig 1979). From the mid-1970s in particular, however, there was a sharp rise in fears that the South Atlantic was becoming a "Soviet lake" (Hurrell 1983, 181). Such anxiety prompted a resurgence of an older interest in forming a South Atlantic Treaty Organization, to include (in various configurations) the United States, Argentina, Brazil, Chile, South Africa, and Uruguay, and it inspired at least one official international conference, held in Buenos Aires in 1981, dedicated to this end (Hurrell 1983, 178, 182). While Andrew Hurrell, in a 1983 survey of SATO proposals, ultimately dismisses its likely emergence on practical grounds, he points to the "intuitive logic" such a bloc seemed to present to military strategists and to its durability as a concept over time (178, 192).[9] Geographer Klaus-John Dodds further underscores the importance of the *idea* of SATO and the South Atlantic more generally to geopolitics on both sides of the ocean. Looking specifically at Argentina and South Africa in the 1970s and '80s, he poses the South Atlantic Ocean as a "sea of signs" or as a "container" for military thinking in which overlapping visions of an anticommunist regional order could be solidified. Here, an oceanic expanse often considered peripheral on the global stage was strategically constructed and presented by military thinkers as a key site for protecting access to vital minerals and other resources associated with Antarctica, sea routes for trade, and, beyond commerce, a "Western and Christian civilization" itself endangered by Soviet expansionism—a vision that of course justified the unsavory regimes propagating it as it posed defense in the South Atlantic as a global priority (Dodds 1994, esp. 33–38).

While SATO never materialized, the interlaced interests that it reveals were in a manner of speaking more generative. Visits that took place as a result of or in response to the imperatives behind such negotiations between South Africa and Brazil, Argentina, Chile, and Paraguay allowed other kinds of informal and often sinister relationships to develop. South Africa saw increased trade and development grants with various South American countries (Fig 1979, 1983). Paraguay offered land to white South African immigrants afraid of the black African Communist "menace," and even sent its dictator General Alfredo Stroessner on a visit of state in 1974, in what turned out to be a largely futile attempt to manufacture a sense of international legitimacy for the apartheid regime (Fig 1979, 24–25, 30). For its part, Argentina sent top military brass. One General D'Almeida, for instance, participated in a South African security conference leading up to the development of "total strategy" in then-President Botha's 1979 "White Paper on Defense" (Truth and Reconciliation Commission 1998, 2:28; see also Daniel 2009, 44–45). Argentine military delegates also took trips to South Africa to give seminars on techniques of psychological torture. These techniques became known in the security police as the "Argentinean system."[10]

The topic of military exchanges brings us specifically to Chile. While not always included in SATO proposals because of tension between Argentina and Chile and especially their Antarctic claims, Chile and South Africa seemed to have had some sort of special relationship. Anti-apartheid periodicals from the United States denounce the participation of South African weaponry corporation ARMSCOR in military trade fairs in Santiago during the Pinochet era, where it debuted new technology such as the "bounce bomb" meant to immobilize guerilla enemies (Nairn 1986). A report coming out of Cuba from the early 1980s similarly alleges that Botha and Pinochet had close ties; following the 1973 coup, South Africa pledged to supply 40 percent of Chile's military needs, including transferring to Chile weaponry illegally manufactured for South Africa in France, while in 1980 Chile sent approximately five hundred mercenaries to fight for South Africa in its border wars. The same report notes a marked increase in nonmilitary trade between the two countries in the late 1970s and early 1980s (Breto 1984, 189). Ariel Dorfman, noted Chilean author and exiled member of the Allende government, recalls a "friendship" between Pinochet and Botha that included shipping tear gas canisters from one country to the other (2010). The claims are echoed in South African publications like *Paratus* and *Unisa Latin American Report* (Richards 2010).

In an essay written to denounce participation by South African artists in the Valparaíso Biennial of 1987, artist and critic Colin Richards points our attention also to a network of "softer" exchanges between South Africa and Chile (Richards 2010). These include not only Chile's formal invitation to South Africa to exhibit in the Biennial, to which South Africa sent a delegation four times beginning in 1979, but also shows of Chilean painting, ceramics, and crafts in South Africa. Richards further points to eerily fitting publicity exercises like the Chilean decision to send the naval ship Esmeralda—a ship that, he points out, was denounced by Amnesty International for having been the site of illegal detentions while moored off the coast of Chile—to Durban, where it became part of the Republic Day festivities in 1981. One of the visitors to the ship was the wife of Prime Minister P. W. Botha, reported to be "visibly moved" when the crew sang the South African anthem in Afrikaans (Fig 1983, 252). We could add to this list of "cultural diplomacy" initiatives the Chilean pavilion (set up in addition to those of other states such as Israel, Taiwan, and West Germany) at South Africa's annual Rand Easter Show, a cross between a world fair, trade expo and military revue considered the country's "shop window to the world." In 1988, the Chilean pavilion featured on the cover of the program for the event.[11]

Beyond breaking the silence that has settled around such relationships between pariah states, which seems important in and of itself, the General's Chilean nationality in *The Smell of Apples* has two further implications. One is directly indicated in the text and the other is a rich offshoot from it, if not a direct intertextual linkage. Both concern the ways in which Chile functions and circulates as a symbol or figure within the imagination of South Africans, based on various kinds of real exchanges of people and information as well as on fantasies or impressions that may not always correspond to lived experience in this foreign land.[12] They thus, in a sense, take us back to the suggestion made by Dodds that the South Atlantic acts as a "sea of signs" and as a "lake or *mirror*" (italics mine) which could be filled with selected meanings and from the surface of which certain desired "identities" could be reflected back, "read" and "secured" (1994, 33, 38, 48); though I focus not on the South Atlantic Ocean per se, as Dodds does, but on the way countries linked through it can serve as doubles or reflections of each other as writers (in addition to state officials) strive to solidify or challenge a given geopolitical order. These reflections, though "imaginary," may nonetheless have real impacts (Dodds 1994, 34).

First, the choice to make the General Chilean poses Pinochet's dictatorship as a defamiliarizing mirror for apartheid—one in which aspects of South Africa that South Africans might choose to ignore are made visible, even exaggerated. Much like the case of the General and Johan, Pinochet's Chile as a whole can be seen as an uncanny double for apartheid South Africa. In addition to twinning the two generals, Behr also draws attention to the geographical likeness between the two countries—the General comments on the way Table Mountain reminds him of the Andes in Santiago (1995, 116–117). He also has the General note similarities of their cuisine, for instance the parallel between the *braaivleis* and the *pariada* (1995, 37), and the way Johan's family resembles his own. Further, the dates of the two narrative sequences interwoven in the book almost perfectly bookend the Pinochet dictatorship: 1973 is the year of the *golpe de estado*, the coup d'état that brought down Salvador Allende's experiment in the "democratic path to Socialism" and put Pinochet in power (an event in which, to recall, Behr's fictional General was an active participant), and 1988 is the year in which Pinochet lost the public referendum on his continued rule and Chile's democratic transition began.

There is much at stake in this doubling. While Pinochet was a darling of the Right, from the very start of his rule, and even more strongly once news of the thousands of people he "disappeared" leaked out, Pinochet was regarded by the Left in South Africa and beyond as an archetypal figure for unfreedom. This unfreedom was linked to the murder of political activists as well as to censorship; both André Brink (1983, 190–192) and Nadine Gordimer (2010, 393–395), for instance, refer in their nonfictional writings from the late 1970s and early 1980s to the abuses carried out in Chile under Pinochet to describe what Brink calls "writing in a state of siege."[13] Historian Steve Stern further points out that, in addition to the brutalization of the citizenry through tactics of torture, "disappearance," and censorship, Pinochet became a symbol in the radical imagination for the turn to "Washington consensus" or neoliberal capitalism, with its shock austerity and privatization programs, and also served as "an icon of the U.S. government (or Nixon-Kissinger) complicity with evil in the name of anti-Communism" (Stern 2006, xxiv). Chile thus stands as a potent metaphor for South Africa, and directs attention to what were at the time of the writing of Behr's novel insufficiently acknowledged elements of apartheid: the way South African state terrorism intersected with a global "dirty war" against Communism, the perverse methods used and justified by a militarized state to maintain control of internal and external populations, and the social costs of enforcing capitalism. Appearing in the early 1990s when many (white) South Africans still claimed that they "didn't know" the full extent of the abuses carried out by the apartheid regime, and when F. W. de Klerk was still calling for the country to forget about the past, Behr's Chile both estranges the workings of apartheid and asks readers to recognize them in a new way.

World events between 1988, the year in which the later story in the novel is set, and 1993, the year in which the novel first came out in Afrikaans, lead to my second point. If 1988 was the date of Pinochet's failed plebiscite, 1990 was the inauguration of Chile's democratic president Patricio Aylwin, which means that Mandela stepped out of prison almost precisely as Chile welcomed democracy. These same years saw the fall of the Berlin Wall, the collapse of the Soviet Union, and the turn to capitalism throughout Eastern Europe. The countries undergoing the shift from dictatorship to democracy in the wake of these events did not do so alone; immense interest arose in comparative approaches to what came to be known as "democratic transitions" and "transitional justice." International conferences bringing together activists and leaders from countries such as Argentina, Chile, Uruguay, Brazil, Germany, Romania, Poland, Bulgaria, South Africa, and the United States took place from the late 1980s onward.[14] In such events, Chile's National Commission of Truth and Reconciliation (1990–91)—a body that investigated murder and disappearance during the Pinochet era—was a much-studied model, and one that would have a lasting impact on South Africa.

Indeed, only shortly after the initial publication of Behr's novel, in 1994, Alex Boraine at the Institute for Democracy in South Africa organized a conference on the topic of "dealing with the past." Among the attendees was the Chilean activist, legal scholar, and truth commissioner José Zalaquett. His opening presentation stressed the point that, when responding to mass atrocity, "different measures of truth, justice, forgiveness and so on are tools to advance the twin goals of prevention and reparation in a process of moral reconstruction," and that in this process of moral reconstruction, "*all things being equal*, forgiveness and reconciliation are preferable to punishment" (in Boraine, Levy, and Schaffer 1994, 9–11). "Truth" was crucially important however both in the uncovering of hidden knowledge and in the sense of public "acknowledgement" of past abuses, since this allows a country to come together or reconcile on the basis of a united memory (12–13). Such arguments would help to shape the later South African TRC, to which Boraine would be appointed as deputy chair (Lodge 2003, 178). Two years prior to the IDASA conference, in 1992, Dorfman's internationally renowned play on the dilemma of truth versus justice in Chile, *Death and the Maiden*, written almost simultaneously with and critiquing many aspects of the Chilean TRC, was staged in Johannesburg at the Market Theatre. The play's role in stirring political debate can be measured in the fact that Desmond Tutu, in his "Chairperson's foreword" to the 1998 South African TRC Report, refers to one of its characters to explain South Africa's amnesty policy (Truth and Reconciliation Commission 1998, 1:10; see also Bystrom 2014). The report later describes this commission's efforts to build on but improve previous truth commissions held in Latin America (54).

For readers of *The Smell of Apples* in 1990s South Africa, where the image of the new Chilean democracy circulated in these ways, this South American state may have served as a second, less uncanny kind of double or mirror—one opening up possible, but not yet crystallized, paths to the future. If Behr asks readers to see South Africa differently through the lens of Chile under Pinochet, then his novel also offers them the possibility of registering Chile's experiments in democratization and of entering into dialogue with them. While this task is not explicitly signaled within the text (which, to recall, was written prior to the consolidation of the South African TRC paradigm) Behr's stint as a student of the Argentine political scientist Guillermo O'Donnell, the "father" of the field of democratic transitions, suggests that it might have been an underlying concern.[15] The author's controversial participation in debates about the TRC discussed at the beginning of this chapter further opens *The Smell of Apples* to retrospective readings within the democratic transition framework. From this angle, the book can be seen to endorse the kind of truth-telling that Behr models in his "Fault Lines" address and that would become central to the South African TRC, as it raises the question of what might have been averted if only Marnus had been able to voice to others his father's crime. It is, after all, Marnus's silence and his belief that Frikkie will and should also remain silent—he rationalizes, "if he didn't even want to tell me about Dad, then he'll *never* tell anyone. And it's right that way" (1995, 199)—that perpetuates the dynamic of repression and violence at the heart of the text.

These last comments bring us full circle to the questions of confession and truth with which I opened this chapter, though they appear now in a regional and transnational rather than a national frame. I would like to end by focusing on this frame, thinking out from Behr's text to make explicit a series of larger sets of questions and reading strategies opened up by and threading through my analysis of it in the Cold War and the South Atlantic contexts. These strategies and questions resonate with many studies collected in this volume.

The first has to do with uncovering in more detail and depth the variety of concrete—if relatively "minor"—transnational exchanges that took place between South (and Southern) Africa and the countries of the Southern Cone throughout the twentieth century. I have already pointed to an extensive network of military flows between right-wing national security states, be they of personnel, strategies, or actual weapons, that took place from the mid-1960s through the late 1980s, and to moments of artistic cooperation or forms of cultural diplomacy like the Valparaíso Biennial. Such networks run counter to another set of Latin America–Southern Africa ties that developed in roughly the same time period as the dreams of Bandung were displaced by the politics of Tricontinentalism: the links between Cuba after its revolution in 1959, other socialist regimes such as those in Allende's Chile (1970–73) and Sandinista Nicaragua (1979–90), and black African liberation movements in Southern Africa. To take the best-known example, it was Soviet and Cuban support for the Marxist People's Movement for the Liberation of Angola that sparked the interest in SATO proposals described earlier (Dodds 1994, 47)—and the national security states were right to be concerned. Cuban military assistance in Angola, which ultimately leads to Marnus's death in *The Smell of Apples*, also finally led to the New York Accords that secured the independence of Namibia and furthered negotiations on the release of Nelson Mandela. Mandela in fact took one of his very first trips after his release from Robben Island to Cuba, and there credited Cuban internationalism with playing a major role in bringing down the apartheid regime (Mandela 1991,

20). If flows between pariah governments point to sinister alliances whose effects ripple into the present, can excavating histories of socialist internationalism nourish renovated forms of solidarity? A critical "anti-imperial nostalgia" that Jennifer Wenzel theorizes as "a desire not for a past moment in and of itself, but rather for the past's promise of an alternative present: the past's future" (2009, 17)? An understanding of what Lanie Millar, in her analysis of the Cuba-Angola South Atlantic axis in this volume, calls a "poetics of disappointment"?

Second, in conjunction with efforts to trace and explore the implications of such transnational exchanges, we might reread the 1960s, 1970s, and 1980s in South Africa—and particularly the period after 1976, with the development of the "total onslaught" and "total strategy" theories and the States of Emergency—through a comparative lens with work from and about this same time period in Latin America. This would mean being attentive not so much to material exchanges of people and objects but to affinities, echoes, the strange and estranging doubles that I have charted here; and thinking about how such inexact comparisons can alter understandings of the world before us. We have seen already how a Chilean play like *Death and the Maiden* could resonate with South Africans as they faced questions about how to deal with the legacy of apartheid, and how Taylor's theory of "percepticide" sheds light on the forms of self-censorship and the "Emergency mentality" that gripped the Republic of South Africa in the 1980s. Novels such as the Chilean Roberto Bolaño's *Nocturno de Chile* (*By Night in Chile*, 2000) and the Argentine Martín Kohan's *Dos veces junio* (*Two Times June*, 2002), which look back on the "dirty wars" in these countries and formally mimic the structures of psychological repression underlying complicity with them, might also provide—especially in conjunction with similar South African texts like *The Smell of Apples*—key insight into the way a South Africa governed by many of the same doctrines and fantasies as the dictatorships in Latin America enacted its covert psychic violence on citizens. Magalí Armillas-Tisyera, in this volume, does a similar kind of comparative juxtaposition of South Atlantic texts to shed light on dictatorship—in this case, Augusto Roa Bastos's *Yo, el Supremo* (*I, the Supreme*, 1974), Sony Labou Tansi's *La vie et demie* (*Life and a Half*, 1979), and Ngũgĩ wa Thiong'o's *Wizard of the Crow* (2006). What other texts, images, or theories could serve as magic mirrors in this way? What models for this kind of scholarship, such as Barbara Harlow's *Barred* (1992), need to be recovered and engaged with?

Finally, both transnational perspectives and comparative scholarship on democratic transitions in Latin America may be useful to understand South

Africa's own immediate transition to democracy and its continuing process of transformation (or lack thereof).[16] Perhaps mention of Chile's ongoing struggles is relevant here. The limited scope of the Chilean TRC, with its mandate to investigate only the crimes of murder and disappearance and its failure to make public the names of any of the perpetrators, led not to permanent reconciliation but to continuing campaigns on behalf of victims and their families. One result was the establishment of a second truth commission, held from 2003 to 2005, to address those who suffered from torture and political imprisonment. Another—inspired by the 1998 London extradition drama in which a Spanish judge indicted Pinochet for human rights violations while the former dictator was traveling in the United Kingdom, causing British authorities to arrest him, if not ultimately to extradite him (for reasons of Pinochet's poor health)—was the attempt of judges within Chile to overturn Chile's amnesty law and to begin domestic legal proceedings against Pinochet-era officials. These developments highlight the way, as Naomi Roht-Arriaza suggests, the dilemmas of "transition" often extend well beyond that seemingly encapsulated time; historical trauma addressed in part rather than in whole continues to fuel social paroxysm, and desires for retribution or revenge may reemerge with the coming of age of new generations (2005, 220–221). Such a caution is only too relevant in South Africa, where, over twenty years into the "new" nation, and even as its TRC has become a celebrated global model, a sense of failure of the projects of reconciliation and transformation pervades public discourse.[17] If we have not seen a high volume of legal cases against apartheid officials, in part because of the way the South African TRC modified the Chilean model, both the TRC and (more to the point) the ANC's patent failure to date to convincingly address the country's fundamental historical fault-line—by which I mean the economic oppression of people of color that characterized the periods of colonialism, segregation, and apartheid—has suggested to many that South Africa too needs a "second generation" of formal and informal transitional processes.[18] In this circumstance, is there something to be learned from Chile and elsewhere about how to provide a multidimensional justice (legal, social, economic) capable of addressing past injuries and sustaining democracy?

Which brings me back one final time to Behr and *The Smell of Apples*. If a more extensive process of uncovering the secrets of the past and bringing them to public view is integral to creating deep democracy in South Africa, then we may do well to follow the hint in Behr's novel and the example set by his confession that a full reckoning with past crimes must extend beyond the national borders. It should also, I would add, extend beyond the full exposure of Cold War security cooperation to the global political, economic, and ideological networks that allowed the structural violence of apartheid to occur—and, in some respects, to continue to occur. Even here, though perhaps in an unconventional reading of his text, Behr may be helpful. As he puts readers inside the head of a willing accomplice to the violence of apartheid—in what Barnard colorfully describes as "something of an uncomfortable position—with eyes glued, voyeuristically, to the convenient hole that Behr has made for us to peep through" (2000, 210)—he may also, through the imaginative transit and forms of doubling he creates between South Africa and Chile, open up space for revealing and acknowledging much wider forms of complicity inherent in supporting the policies of governments aligned by the struggle against communism during the Cold War and beyond.

NOTES

This chapter is a revised version of an article that first appeared as "Reading the South Atlantic: Chile, South Africa, the Cold War, and Mark Behr's *The Smell of Apples*," *African Studies* 71 (1) (2012): 1–18. It appears here courtesy of Taylor and Francis.

1. Barnard (2000) most explicitly and thoroughly theorizes the question of ideology in the novel, but Heyns (1996) and Stobie (2008) also focus their attention, respectively, on the way the text represents and potentially deconstructs apartheid's techniques of ideological interpellation. Monica Popescu (2008) also reads the novel in relation to questions of the dissemination of apartheid ideology, specifically through attention to the media; I will return to a different aspect of Popescu's work.

2. The interest in South African studies in decentering the Cold War is also seen more widely. See, for instance, Andrew Hammond (2006 and 2012).

3. Given its emphasis on rerouting transnational inquiry, Popescu's project—or, perhaps more precisely, my invocation of it here—also has clear resonance with the paradigm of Indian Ocean studies that scholars such as Isabel Hofmeyr (2007; see also this volume) have built into a vibrant field of scholarship.

4. As Slaughter and Bystrom discuss in the Introduction to this volume, the past decade and a half has seen an emerging interest in the question of movements across the South Atlantic Ocean, though this has often—if not exclusively—tended to focus on the Lusophone world and specifically questions of the slave trade carried out within the Portuguese Empire and (later) by an independent Brazil. For the Lusophone South Atlantic, see, for instance, de Alencastro (2007). For other models bringing together Africa

and Latin America, see, for instance, Pitman and Stafford (2009); Goyal (2014); and Popescu, Tolliver, and Tolliver (2014).

5. The United States plays an important role in the foreign relations of the apartheid regime that is also signaled in Behr's novel. I do not have space to discuss this topic here, beyond pointing out that not only do Johan and his wife, Leonore, meet while in the United States for military and diplomatic purposes, respectively, but Johan and the General also meet in the United States. Their collaboration in US anticommunist maneuvers seems to have inspired military exchanges between South Africa and Chile that did not always require US mediation. I will pick up and develop this point to show how North-South pathways forged during the Cold War morphed into South-South exchanges. Thanks to Max Rayneard for helping me to formulate these points.

6. Along with Frikkie and Marnus, there is another small boy character who suffers from violence that is specifically described as being targeted at the bum: Little-Neville, the son of the Erasmus family's "Coloured" housekeeper, who is beaten, smeared with fat around the buttocks, and then set on fire. This tripling—rather than doubling—brings in the question of race, which is central to the story though repressed in the young Marnus's consciousness; this is a topic I will turn to briefly here. On the question of Little-Neville, see also Barnard (2000, 222–3) and Stobie (2008, 79).

7. See also Stobie's discussion of this scene, where Johan presents to the General a picture of "détente" (2008, 76); a personal photograph, and here Stobie quotes Behr, of "a soldier holding up a black arm with pink meat hanging out of it where it was cut from the body (172)" (2008, 76).

8. As Weschler points out, the idea that "the doctrine of national security was an entirely American export" is a "massive oversimplification" (1990, 119). Rather, the United States tended to set up structures that allowed contact between likeminded regimes to take place, and members of these regimes then influenced each other (Pinochet, Videla, and Noriega all went to the School of the Americas [1990, 119]) as well as impacting US policy. The United States also vied with the French, for instance, for influence over counterinsurgency strategy (Weschler 1990, 119–20).

9. The considerable practical difficulties Hurrell sets out have to do with internal disagreements between each country's foreign policy. Brazil and Argentina, for instance, each wished to control SATO and therefore wanted the other sidelined. And no one wanted to be seen supporting apartheid South Africa (1983, 180–188).

10. Donald Woods reports this in the documentary film *Biko: Breaking the Silence* (dir. Edwina Spicer, New York: Filmmakers Library, 1987). Daniel points out that four infamous torturers from the notorious concentration

camp and torture center called the Naval Mechanics School (ESMA) were sent to South Africa as military attachés to the Argentine embassy in Pretoria in 1980–81 (2009, 52); it may be that these were the torture technicians to which Woods refers, or there may have been others. The South African TRC Final Report also documents travel of this kind between South Africa, Argentina and Chile in 1982, citing a report from *X-Ray* (a British journal) of "growing use of new forms of torture in South Africa, which are known to have been used in Argentina" (vol. 2, 28 [1998]); and notes how Argentine "torture experts" organized "seminars in which South African security police and the Argentines exchanged ideas regarding methods of interrogation" (vol. 2, 196 [1998]).

11. I thank Isabel Hofmeyr, for pointing me to the Chilean presence in the Rand Easter show, and Hannes Venter, who gave me access to the Rand Easter Show archives.

12. I think here of Popescu's description of South African visions of Eastern Europe: "These positive and negative depictions have not always been faithful representations of Eastern Europe; South Africans have created virtual images of this geopolitical area that have more to do with their own passions and fears than the reality in the streets of Moscow or Prague. Nevertheless, they draw attention to cultural alliances previously overlooked" (2010, 4).

13. Roht-Arriaza states the case succinctly when she writes: "Pinochet was, after all, the symbol of the dictatorships that had plagued much of the world during the 1970s and 1980s" (2005, vii).

14. In *A Miracle, A Universe*, Lawrence Weschler describes in some detail a conference he attended with delegates from Latin America and Eastern Europe sponsored by the Aspen Institute in 1988, and where José Zalaquett, to be discussed, was a participant (1990, 3). Alex Boraine describes the influence of Weschler's book on his own attendance at and attention to conferences on similar themes from 1992 onward, and leading up to the influential conference he organized at IDASA in 1994 (1994, ix–xi). For an excellent overview of the conferences in which the "democratic transitions" and "transitional justice" paradigms were jointly formed, see Arthur (2009).

15. Argentine-born and US-based scholar Guillermo O'Donnell was Mark Behr's professor at Notre Dame University for a class on "Transitions to Democracy" in 1993. See O'Donnell's response to Behr's confession (1996). This exchange is also cited in Stobie (2008, 73).

16. This has been emerging as a popular arena for scholarship (though not literary scholarship) crossing the South Atlantic; see for instance Phelps (2004), Hamber and Wilson (2002), and Humphrey and Valverde (2008).

17. Scholars such as Richard A. Wilson (2001) pointed out a number of years back the likely dilemmas that would be produced by the closures of the TRC in South Africa—in Wilson's case also through reference to the experiences of Latin America.

18. Indeed, recognizing this situation, the ANC already in 2012 called for a "second transition" focused not on political but on social and economic transformation (African Nation Congress 2012). Yet, and as Achille Mbembe points out, such official plans failed even to diagnose the underlying problems facing the country (2013). The more recent student movements such as #RhodesMustFall are a powerful symptom of these failures.

Islands in Distress

Making Sense of the Malvinas/Falklands War

Oscar Hemer

The short war in 1982 between Argentina and Great Britain over the Malvinas/Falkland Islands in the South Atlantic was for a long time regarded as an anachronism, as the last war of a bygone colonial era, with little if any reference to the ongoing, late era Cold War.[1] For the outside world the unexpected armed conflict between two formerly friendly western nations seemed truly to be what anglophile Argentinian writer Jorge Luis Borges likened to a pair of bald heads fighting over a comb. Yet, as the British historian Sir Lawrence Freedman notes in the concluding "envoi" of his two-volume *Official History of the Falklands Campaign*, "while in many respects this conflict still stands out as the last war of a past imperial era, in others it can now be recognised as the first of the post cold-war era" (2007). A similar retrospective observation is made by one of the harshest British critics of the campaign, writer and former *New Left Review* editor Anthony Barnett, who wrote *Iron Britannia* in the nationalist frenzy of the military victory. For the thirtieth anniversary of the war, in 2012, the book was republished with a new foreword, and Barnett, having expected to add a brief, ironic introduction of a past polemic for young readers with no recollection of the Falklands War, is instead "appalled at how relevant *Iron*

Britannia has once again become" and ends up writing a new fiery polemic on the devastating legacy of "the Falklands syndrome" (Barnett 2012).[2]

Indeed, the disputed sovereignty over the barren islands in the South Atlantic remains an "unfinished business" (McGuirk 2007), again on the verge of escalating into open conflict, if not war, since massive oil reservoirs have been discovered under the seabed. After having been compromised for decades by its association with the military dictatorship and the preceding "dirty war" against the militant left, Malvinas resurged on the Argentinian political agenda as one of the key rhetorical figures of the former Kirchner government.[3] At the inauguration of the special Museo de Malvinas, in the former precincts of the ESMA, the most famous of the Argentinian concentration camps, now turned into the Museum of Memory, then-president Cristina Kirchner declared the museum to entail "a commitment to put an end to the last residue of Colonialism" and urged her compatriots to continue the historic battle: "We have the reason, the truth, the memory and the will to move on forward" (my translation, quoted in *La Nación*, June 10, 2014). The British gut reactions to the renewed Argentinian claims evoked the martial spirit of 1982, and there is little to suggest that any current British prime minister would be more willing to compromise than Margaret Thatcher was, now that this formerly neglected southernmost British outpost has literally become "Fortress Falklands" (Bound 2012).

I have previously engaged with this intriguing conflict from the Argentinian perspective, as the catalyst for the end of the military dictatorship and return to parliamentary democracy; I was particularly concerned with literature's role in the deconstruction of the national mythology, in which the recovery of Malvinas has always been a key feature (Hemer 2012). Revisiting my own analysis in a comparison with corresponding British reactions and responses (both artistic and academic), I am struck not only by the similarities of the respective symbolic and mythic significations attached to the islands (and the conflict), but even more by the minimal communication between the public spheres of the two countries in processing the war experience. There is an enormous abundance of literature on both sides, from hardcore military porn to sharp-edged cultural critique, and some of the finest literary achievements in contemporary fiction. The fictional aspects of the conflict, and literary fiction's role in revealing state fiction, has been thoroughly analyzed by, among others, Martin Kohan et al. (1993), Lucrecia Escudero (1996), and Beatriz Sarlo (1998) in Argentina, and by their British counterparts David Monaghan (1998) and Kevin Foster (1999). These studies have had either an Argentinian or a

British focus; there have only lately been two major attempts at integrated comparative analyses, by American literary scholar Laura Linford Williams (2005) and British Latin Americanist Bernard McGuirk (2007).

The similarities surprise more than the differences, given the outcome of the war: Margaret Thatcher's resounding victory and the Argentinian junta's humiliating defeat. The British triumph turned, however, in retrospect into a somewhat shameful one. Literary critic Mark Lawson likened the status of the conflict, twenty years afterward, to that of "the mad aunt no one quite mentions: a position that it shares with the Prime Minister of the time" (Lawson 2002). Argentina's defeat was similarly ambiguous, as it put an end to the military dictatorship and paved the way for the transition to restored parliamentary democracy. But whereas the Falklands Campaign brought the far away South Atlantic to the British public's awareness for the first time and, as we shall see, gave the barren islands the very specific meaning of an imagined Arcadian premodern Britain, the austral islands had always formed an essential part of the Argentinian national mythology, as a lost and missing limb of the national body. Hence, while the Falklands campaign's peculiar epitome of imperial nostalgia was soon to vanish again as the nonmediated distant conflict was eclipsed by other events like the culminating Cold War and, eventually, the less victorious crusades to Iraq and Afghanistan, Malvinas has remained but a temporarily suppressed phantom in Argentina's national imaginary, ready to pop up again at its earliest convenience.

The junta had very consciously played the Malvinas card in its attempt to fend off growing popular discontent, and the Kirchner government similarly pushed the sovereignty issue to the top priority of their diplomatic agenda.[4] A pressured David Cameron may have been tempted to play the Falklands card, as Margaret Thatcher arguably did, but even if this option remains available to his successors on Downing Street, it is not very likely that the South Atlantic islands will ever again attain a symbolic meaning comparable to the one they were acquired in the Thatcher era's project of national reconquest. The then long ignored and abandoned sheep farmers who evoked World War II nostalgia and sympathy are now potentially the wealthiest community in the world, protected by what is probably the most costly per capita military defense in the world. Yet, with or without its former mirroring mythical implications, which, I will argue, have been more thoroughly scrutinized in Argentina than in the United Kingdom, the conflict remains unresolved.

Before looking into the actual unfolding of the events, let us consider the archipelago's (potential) role in a wider South Atlantic scenario. Today it is de facto the somewhat misplaced southernmost outpost of NATO. It could, however, under slightly different circumstances, have become one of the main bases of the envisioned counterpart SATO, the South Atlantic Treaty Organization that was more and less seriously launched at different occasions during the Cold War, as Kerry Bystrom discusses elsewhere in this volume. In the 1970s, during the ongoing anticolonial liberation wars in Southern Africa and the less successful revolutionary struggle of the militant left in the Southern Cone (Argentina, Chile, Uruguay), there was serious concern among the military on both sides of the ocean that the area could turn "into a Soviet lake," and SATO was proposed to be "an alliance against world communism" (Hurley 1983, 190). Although this military treaty never materialized,[5] there were de facto important contacts between the military dictatorships in the Southern Cone and the apartheid regime in South Africa (ibid.; see also Bystrom in this volume).

As Hurley notes, Britain had maintained an "extremely low profile" in the South Atlantic before the conflict with Argentina (1983, 191). Its military presence more or less receded with the cancellation of the Simonstown Agreement with South Africa in 1975.[6] Hence, the United Kingdom, unlike the United States, was never involved in the SATO discussions. But in spite of the disinterest at an official policy level, there was a "significant body of opinion" that argued for "both the reestablishment of closer ties with South Africa and for consideration of a wider regional security arrangement which would include Latin American countries" (192). Such arrangement would naturally have given key importance to the scattered island clusters of the South Atlantic, many of which were British overseas territories. Although some of these islands had historically been "strategic stepping stones in the larger story of global resource colonialism" (see Hofmeyer in this volume), the Falklands seemed a distant and disregarded link in the island chain that the British might well have been willing to transfer to Argentina as part of a regional security treaty. At the time of the war, the islands' natural resources were not a main issue. For Argentina, and as it turned out, for the United Kingdom as well, the symbolic value of Malvinas/Falklands overweighed any prospective future economic gain, whereas the newly discovered undersea riches may be the principal motivational force behind the renewed conflict. This also implies a shift in the regional perspective. From being a peripheral outpost in the South Atlantic, the archipelago now appears as a gateway to the Antarctica, the frozen continent that may be up for scramble when the current Antarctic Treaty opens for review in 2048, with overlapping British, Argentinian and Chilean claims.[7] It may even be that the Malvinas/Falklands war will be regarded by future historians not only as the last war of an imperial era, and the first of the post–Cold war, but also, and more significantly, as "a first major conflict over Antarctica," as Russian journalist Sergei Brilev has suggested (quoted in *MercoPress*, May 31, 2010).

The War: Recap

In 1982, after six years of "national reorganization,"[8] growing popular opposition challenged the Argentinian military government. On March 30, a huge mobilization of the Peronist labor movement CGT was brutally dispersed with teargas and beatings at the Plaza de Mayo in Buenos Aires. Three days later, the same square filled with largely the same people manifesting their fervent support for the Malvinas campaign. The surprise disembarking on the islands on April 2 appeared to be a desperate means to divert attention away from the disastrous domestic affairs,[9] and this cynical maneuver was certainly successful in that sense; even the Montoneros,[10] who had barely survived the total defeat in the dirty war, immediately joined sides with their former enemy in this "anti-imperialist" endeavor.

Ever since independence, Malvinas had been one of the symbolic cornerstones of national identification, and the recuperation of this long-lost part of the imagined national territory was one of the foundations of Argentinian nationalism—left and right. Malvinas was hence a last trump card to play, but with an imminent risk of recoil. As historian Federico Lorenz puts it: "From the very beginning, the war over Malvinas transcended its circumstance as an armed conflict and territorial claim: many, apart from those directly involved, saw in the islands lost in June 1982 a chance of regeneration, a way out, a future" (Lorenz 2006, 63). As it turned out, the campaign and its disastrous military defeat were to become the decisive blow to the dictatorship. But the two months between occupation and capitulation was a period of nationalist frenzy that many, if not most, Argentinians remember with embarrassment as "*la vergüenza nacional*."[11] In Great Britain, the unexpected war served a similar nationalist purpose and cemented the position of Prime Minister Margaret Thatcher, whose epithet "the Iron Lady" was largely due to her firm commitment to the Falklands Task Force.[12] The victory was generally received as Thatcher's personal triumph, although the war had in fact been willed by parliament as much as by the government itself, and a key factor in parliament was the role of the Labour front bench (Freedman 1983, 451).[13] As English writer John Fowles put it, in a review of Gabriel García Márquez's novel *Chronicle of a Death Foretold*, which grew into a lucid commentary on the war:

> The junta and Mrs. Thatcher might almost have colluded, so bare were their political cupboards just before the attack. They equally faced growing unpopularity, equally craved a diversion, and equally knew, with the heaven-sent scapegoat in the South Atlantic, that their initial guilt (the flash-fisted aggression, the decades of British *dolce far niente* that provoked it) would be quickly forgiven by their respective nations and their allies . . . provided they won, of course. (Fowles 1982, 723)

The UN Committee on Decolonization had in 1964 put the Falklands/Malvinas on a list of territories in need of decolonization, and a year later, Resolution 2065 of the UN General Assembly urged both sides to work toward a peaceful solution to the dispute, while "taking the interests of the islanders into account."[14] Although the occupation was obviously a violation of international law, Argentina's territorial claim on the islands had wide international support. With the flagrant exception of Chile, who refuted the claims, and Colombia, who abstained from voting, all Latin American governments, including Fidel Castro's Cuba, unanimously backed the junta's bold challenge to the (former) imperial power.

Myths of National Rebirth

The young, aspiring Argentinian nation contesting the old and decaying British Empire was a recurrent theme in the official propaganda that apparently appealed to all sectors of Argentinian society.[15] It was literally true, in the sense that between 60 and 70 per cent of the Argentinian soldiers were conscripts, mainly from the class years of 1962 and 1963; that is, young men—or boys—of the ages eighteen to twenty, who were to fight a generally older, far better equipped and much more experienced enemy.[16] The conscripts were popularly and affectionately called *los chicos* (the boys), and throughout the short war, from the disembarking in April all the way to the defeat in June, their youth was regarded as an asset. In this exalted period of *malvinización*,[17] the islands in the South Atlantic became the great touchstone for an entire nation's aspirations for change and renewal; the boys waiting in the trenches for the arrival of the British troops formed the new nation's avant-garde, and the people united behind them were assured that they would stand the test, "because the enemy is fighting for their past and we are fighting for our future" (quoted in Lorenz 2006, 70). After the war, however, it was precisely their youth and lack of experience that served as the main explanation for the humiliating defeat. The British had been overwhelmingly superior in weapon technology and ammunition power, and they took maximum advantage of this superiority by waging their attacks at night, and by surprise. The death toll of the Argentinians in the actual battles was, subsequently, very high. The boys were not to be blamed, however; instead, they were regarded as innocent victims, not of the superior British troops but of their own officers, who had allegedly used and abused them.[18] In an overnight twist of perception, the soldiers who recently represented the nation's future were, instead, assigned the part of the sacrificed youth who had been sent out to war, not to kill, but to be killed.[19]

The media, which had maintained an almost monolithic silence about the violations of human rights during the Argentinian dictatorship, suddenly started to publish testimonies of the recent state terror, giving room for what was later described as *el show del horror*. As a consequence of this saturation of the public sphere with horrifying victim stories, the Malvinas conflict also inevitably was viewed in a different light: After all, the war and state terrorism had been conducted by the same agent, the armed forces. The discrediting of he military was, of course, a matter of alarm for those sectors of society who had openly or passively supported the dictatorship. The grave concern was that the defeat in the Malvinas war would deprive the armed forces of their preceding victory in the war against domestic "terrorism." And that was precisely what happened. The notorious Navy official Alfredo Astiz is the perfect example of this sudden degradation. After surrendering almost without resistance in the battle of the South Georgia islands, he was not only discredited as a military man; he was moreover disclosed as having been an infiltrator among the Mothers of Plaza de Mayo.[20] The slick Astiz, more than the drunkard General Leopoldo Galtieri or the ascetic Jorge Rafael Videla, came to personify the detested dictatorship in a process that soon evolved into the democratic transition. Tales of bullying and mistreatment of the conscripts on behalf of their officials were added to the ongoing media "horror show" as proof of the continuity in human-rights violations.

The image(s) of young, unskilled and ill-equipped "boys" who were sacrificed for no purpose in an ill-conceived war certainly informed the later conception of (the majority of) the disappeared as politically immature adolescents guided by innocent idealism.[21] Victimization was, hence, one of the principal ways of dealing with the disgraceful past, and a key role in this process was played by the testimonies of returning soldiers. Journalist Daniel Kon's book *Los chicos de la guerra* (1984) disclosed the horrible conditions that the conscripts had to endure, and confirmed all of the allegations of abuse and failing military leadership. The book was the basis for the feature film with the same name, directed by Bebe Kamin, which premiered later that year. In concurrence with a couple of films about the Dictatorship years, of which the Academy award winning *La historia oficial* (1985), written by Kamin and Kon, is the most famous internationally, it was to have a huge impact on the public imaginary in the years of the transition.

In the United Kingdom, the media did not unanimously support the Falklands campaign, although the tabloid press fueled the warrior frenzy from the very moment the task force sailed out on its mission.[22] But the remoteness of the war, which made it impossible for newspapers and television to communicate discouraging images of death and destruction, in combination with the speediness and efficiency of the expedition—and the correspondent failure and incompetence of the Argentinian adversary—raised popular support and gained enormous momentum by the time the campaign reached its triumphant conclusion. In the course of the two months, from April 2 to June 14, Thatcher managed to transform the fight over the Falklands into a myth of national rebirth, which obviously struck a deep chord with the population of a country "apparently locked into an irreversible postcolonial decline" (Monaghan 1998, xii).

In her comparative analysis, Laura Linford Williams points to the mirroring myths of national renewal and their adjoining crusade or romance-quest rescue scenarios.[23] In the Argentinian mythology, the islands are sacred ground because they belong to the Fatherland and embody its lost identity. This sacred ground is said to be occupied by a morally inferior enemy who desecrates it by his very presence (Williams 2005, 96). Only when the islands are reunited with the mainland will the Argentinian national body become whole and complete, physically as well as spiritually. In the abundant Malvinas poetry from before and during the war, the islands themselves are often personified as an abducted victim that yearns to be liberated from its oppressor (Williams 2005, 95–106). The purpose of the British rescue mission is, by contrast, to save "our own people" from the barbarians. Although the Argentinian military regime may be characterized as criminal or barbaric, the British reactions to the crisis had clearly racist implications, as expressed by Sir Bernard Braine in the emergency debate in the House of Commons on April 3: "The very thought that our people, 1800 people of British blood and bone could be left in the hands of such criminals was enough to make any normal Englishman's blood—and the blood of Welshmen and Scotsmen—boil, too" (Morgan 1982: 16). Thatcher repeatedly referred to the Islanders' "British stock" and their common identity as "island people." The hitherto unknown (and neglected)

Falklands were portrayed as an Arcadian premodern Britain, an epitome of the idealized English countryside with its village communities that cut across traditional divides of race, class, and gender, and the rage over the Argentinian seizure of Stanley was "as if the Nazis had taken over Ambridge" (quoted in Foster 1999, 29).[24] This World War II association was not incidental. Thatcher very consciously evoked the legacy of Churchill, the uncompromising dictator-slayer, and assumed the role as his rightful successor.[25] She would "put the Great back into Britain" by reinstating its position as beacon of the free world.

A key to restored greatness, in the making of the myth of national rebirth, was the return to Victorian values. The successful task force became a symbol of the decreed social and economic transformation. It showed the way ahead, and, in Foster's words, "confirmed that the nation's future lay in a return to the past: "The same virtues of leadership, duty and sacrifice that had served the nation so well in subduing large tracts of Africa, Asia and the Caribbean had ensured victory over Argentina, and could now be turned to the reconquest of Britain itself" (Foster 1999, 26).

Demalvinization, Remalvinization

In Argentina, the shame of disillusion and defeat gave way to the celebration of the end of the military regime and the restoration of democracy. But the former combatants of the South Atlantic, who, as anthropologist Rosana Gúber put it, had gone from being boys to veterans without passing maturity, were sadly neglected, as the whole Malvinas complex was deeply suppressed into public unconscious.[26] The transition implied a process of *desmalvinización*, and the oblivion has largely persisted to this day, in spite of the Kirchner government's attempts at stirring up slumbering patriotic emotions. This abandoning of one of the great national priorities was, of course, strongly opposed by the armed forces, whose leaders have eagerly referred to the just and popular cause of Malvinas to whitewash their sullied reputation. But the veterans also contested it when they started to organize themselves politically. In contrast to the image of abused adolescents, which was perpetuated in the public sphere in the mid 1980s, the veterans' organization presented its members as the true patriots and anti-imperialists, inheritors of a progressive military tradition that goes back to "San Martín and his glorious Liberation Army," and comprises "all those who honoured their uniforms by contributing to building a greater Fatherland" (quoted in Lorenz 2006, 210). In one of their publications, with the evocative name *Malvinizar*, they called for "remalvinization" under a new and different banner. In their view, the defeat against "Anglo-Yankee colonialism" was due to the treason of the military leaders and the complicity of the sellout politicians (quoted in Lorenz 2006, 211). This rhetoric, echoing that of the guerrillas of the 1970s, and in a way, in fact, preceding the vindication of the militancy in the so-called memory boom a decade later, had little, if any, resonance in an Argentina of newly reinstated democracy, where the violent past had been effectively sealed by the theory of the two demons.[27] But the anachronistic appeal of the obstinate excombatants—who may not have been representative of the group as a whole—illustrates the confluent, militarist tradition of Argentinian society and points toward the future (current) reinsertion of the islands in the national pantheon.

From the horizon of Buenos Aires, the Malvinas seemed almost as distant as the Falklands from London, and the military campaign had been almost entirely a mediated war, whereas in Patagonia, and especially Tierra del Fuego, it was experienced as a palpable reality. But with the exception of the sparsely inhabited South, a relatively small proportion of the population was directly affected by the conflict. Malvinas was conspicuously absent in the memory boom of the 1990s, yet it has, in the course of the more than three decades that have passed, gradually reinserted itself as a sanctified part of the national history and mythology. Because, as Lorenz demonstrates, it serves the patriotic discourse perfectly well, it is a space where internal conflicts are not at play; it is inhabited by the pure heroes who fought and died for it. These were both military and civilian—the soldier-citizen of the conscript bridging the recurrent Argentinian divide between military state and civil society. In other words, it provides a form of narrating the nation that can serve both conservative and revolutionary purposes.

Postwar (Imagining the Islands)

In Britain, the Falklands War had a huge immediate impact on cultural production. David Monaghan lists some thirty works in the decade after the war, spanning over a broad generic spectrum, from children's books and cartoons, stage plays and novels, to feature films and TV documentaries (Monaghan 1998, xii-xiii). The common denominator of all these productions is that they rework or reframe the official Falklands myth, making it function instead as a metaphor for a neoconservative Britain "where power and wealth are concentrated in the hands of a small, corrupt élite, leaving the rest of the population to seek escape from their unsatisfactory lives in nostalgia or violence" (ibid.).

The main target of critique is Margaret Thatcher herself—Maggot Scratcher, as her grotesque and deliberately offensive caricature is called in Steven Berkoff's stage play *Sink the Belgrano!* (1986), which inverts the myth by systematically turning Thatcher's own reading of the war on its head (Monaghan 1998, 61–69). Most of the works analyzed by Monaghan are also on Laura Linford Williams's list and fall under her second category of "demythologizers." Apart from the bountiful adventure and thriller novels, there is actually only one major "myth perpetuator" among the British samples, Ian Curteis's *The Falklands Play*. This hagiographic story of the negotiations and decisions of Thatcher and her cabinet before and during the war sparked a heated media controversy in 1985, after BBC's cancellation of its production. Curteis accused the BBC of "left-wing bias," a common conservative complaint at the time, and the furor over the alleged censorship forced BBC Director Alasdair Milne to resign.[28] Williams defines *The Falklands Play* as a distorted romance quest, where the role of the questing hero is played not by the task force, but by "England" personified by Margaret Thatcher, in just the same way as Churchill had once been perceived as the embodiment of the national will (Williams 2005, 109). The Argentinian enemy is subsequently demonized as Nazi-like villains, while at the same time ridiculed with a scorn and mockery that comprises all of South America, "all Comic Opera Land", in the words of Deputy Prime Minister Willie Whitelaw (quoted in Williams 2005, 113). The enemy image is thus not reserved for the fascist junta, but includes the Argentinian people themselves. The nationalist Plaza de Mayo demonstrations with waving flags and choral speech are in the stage directions envisioned as "a kind of tribal dance" (ibid., 127); "Words such as *hysterical*, *weeping*, *screaming* and *frenzied* adequately summarize the British attitude toward Argentinian people in general: they are irrational and ignorant, bordering on barbaric, and almost uncontrollable in their passions. Surely such a nation should not, indeed *could* not govern British subjects in the Falklands" (ibid., 117). Even though Curteis's play may be representative of the government position and the dominant popular opinion, its unreserved prowar stance is exceptional in the cultural production. Yet, while most of the British works sharply contest the rationale for the war, few put the conflict in a larger global context, and many, if not most, of them convey a condescending view of the Argentinian side. Even the one novel that might claim the epithet of Falklands novel, *Swansong* by Richard Francis (1986), depicts the fictional South American adversary Costanagua as a banana republic, run by operetta figures, much in accord with the general cliché presented in *The Falklands Play*.

Breaking the Binary Structure

Except for the lofty Malvinas poetry, the austral archipelago has remained largely unexplored by the Argentinian literary imagination. A number of short stories were published in the early 1990s, but they were generally far removed from the actual conflict.[29] Among the exceptions to the rule are two of the most remarkable contemporary Argentinian novels, Rodolfo Enrique Fogwill's *Los pichiciegos: Visiones de una batalla subterránea* (1983; *Malvinas Requiem*, 2007) and Carlos Gamerro's *Las islas* (1998; *The Islands*, 2012). The extraordinary thing about *Los pichiciegos* is that it was written in one week during the height of the war, before any witness reports of the disaster had reached the Argentinian mainland.[30] The *pichiciegos*, or *pichis*—"dillos" in the English translation—are a group of Argentinian deserters who have buried a tunnel and established a subterranean bunker (*la Pichicera*) on the outskirts of the battle zone, on territory that is unmarked on the deficient Argentinian maps.[31] They are obviously the negation of "*los heroes de Malvinas*," cowardly deserters and even collaborators, spying on their countrymen on behalf of the Brits, trading with both sides, unscrupulously plundering the shipwrecked and the dead, denouncing and delivering "useless" members of their own community who do not conform with the rules of the warren's, strictly hierarchical, miniature nonsociety.

To literary critic Beatriz Sarlo, the ephemeral dillo community demonstrates the paradox of the Malvinas war—the dissolution of the very idea of a nation that the campaign intended to re-construct. Everything dissolves in the pure present of *la pichicera*, dictated by the sole principle of staying alive.[32] Yet the struggle for subsistence is to no avail. All dillos but one—Quiquito, who tells their story—eventually suffocate in the subterranean shelter, due to the accidental clogging of their ventilation shaft by British communication cables. Quiquito recapitulates this final lugubrious scene in the same register of rational deduction and minimal emotion. After stepping out of the warren, "if he remembered correctly, he cried a little." The laconic expression of sentiment, which in Sarlo's analysis is all the subjectivity that the war allows, condensates what she does not hesitate to call the *truth* of the novel. This truth revealed by *Los pichiciegos* equally refutes the victorious discourse of *la malvinización*, and the following victimization discourse of the transition, the two grand narratives by which the story of Malvinas is still being told in Argentina. As Maria Elena Molina (2008) notes, it is *literature*, with Fogwill at the head, that breaks and deconstructs this binary structure.

Fogwill's fictional Malvinas is an extreme, yet accurate approximation of what was really happening on the islands, and it appears with hindsight as an even more astonishing anticipation of the postdictatorial Argentina of Carlos Menem.[33] Carlos Gamerro's *Las islas* is the story of that prophecy materialized, a tragicomic hyperbole of the grand illusion of the 1990s. It passed relatively unnoticed by the critics in 1998, but its reputation grew as the small first edition sold out, and the long-awaited reissue in 2007 was preceded by its legend as the unobtainable "great novel about Malvinas" by one who, in contrast to Fogwill, *had been there*. The novel's basic story line reads like a film noir plot. The setting is ten years after the war, in a slightly distorted Buenos Aires, resembling the near-future cityscapes of cyber punk. Like many of his unfortunate peers, the main protagonist and focalizer Felipe Félix finished his war adventure at the psychiatric hospital Borda, recovering from a mortar blast that had burnt part of his helmet into his skull. This metal souvenir has literally become part of his organism, giving him extraordinary computing capability, but also connecting him, in nightmarish flashbacks, with the suppressed memories of both Malvinas and Borda.

Felipe is assigned to hack into the archives of the Secretariat of State Intelligence, SIDE, to track a possible conspiracy. As a former combatant, Felipe is the perfect agent for this mission impossible. The new SIDE office is swarming with Malvinas veterans, and he uncovers one fantastic plan after the other for reconquering the islands: one is to kidnap Prince Charles and Lady Diana and request one island as ransom for each royal; another is to form an unholy alliance with the IRA, and a third is to challenge England to an all-or-nothing "friendly" football match. The nationalist prospects are nurtured by even more fantastic fantasies: legends of the lost treasury of the last Spanish viceroy, which allegedly was brought to Malvinas during the English invasions of the late nineteenth century; allegories of the national body with the islands representing the hands, like the cut-off hands of Perón; or less amiable theories of a millenarian Anglo-Zionist conspiracy.[34]

Gamerro's surreal hyperbole is a satirical tour de force, exuberant, hallucinatory, mercilessly self-ironic. For example, Felipe makes a videogame of the Malvinas war by putting together a concoction of previous and later conflicts, in which Iraqi soldiers of Desert Storm play the Argentinian conscripts.[35] But *Las islas* is just as much an elegy over the recent and recurrent tragedy, resonant with clarified anger and sorrow, and Gamerro's great accomplishment is, in my view, the consistent dialectic between these two narrative registers. The actual combat—the long-awaited battle of Mt.

Longdon—is narrated like an instant, incomprehensible inferno, and in the end it is somehow the darker undercurrent that stays with the reader. Felipe, the sole survivor of his company, carrying the burden of the others' deaths, finds Gloria, another survivor, from the Garage Olimpo concentration camp, and their emerging, unromantic love represents a gleam of clarified beauty and hope at the heart of the tragic-comedy.

Late in Translation

Completely different as they are, both *Los pichiciegos* and *Las islas* have already become touchstones of Argentinian fiction. Both are, in a sense, the opposite of witness literature. They work on what Martín Kohan calls *the void of experience* (Hemer 2012, 476). Gamerro, born in 1962, was supposed to be one of *los chicos de la guerra*, and he writes the novel as if he were one of the veterans, as if that actually had been his fate, a parallel fictional life. "When someone asks me if my fiction is autobiographical, I say, yes, it's a negative autobiography. It's what could have happened to me but didn't. Yes, I should have gone to the Malvinas. So it's as though my life divided itself into a real life and a ghostly life that somehow accompanies me" (Hemer 2012, 383). Personal, rather than geographic, proximity is an important factor in explaining why the conflict was represented so differently on the respective sides. In Argentina, the Malvinas disaster remains a national trauma, intrinsically interwoven with the preceding decade of armed struggle and military repression. For Britain, the faraway Falklands did not become the Vietnam that some of the critics had envisioned. Even for Thatcher herself, the victory was soon eclipsed by other events. In British literature, the Falklands are, according to Mark Lawson, "lost and regained between chapters" (Lawson 2002). In spite of the immediate impact on cultural production, as analyzed by Monaghan, no British self-examination of national (and imperial) mythologies is equivalent to the one undertaken in the Malvinas novels. When the war does appear in contemporary cultural production, as in Shane Meadows's film *This Is England* (2006) or David Mitchell's fine childhood novel *Black Swan Green* (2006), it is mainly as a time marker and symbolic backdrop to the era of Thatcherism; the actual conflict remains as distant and abstract as when it happened.

The Argentinian side of the story remained moreover largely unknown to English readers, in spite of the fact that there is an English-language work, strangely disregarded in the British overviews, which, as McGuirk suggests, may be judged as "the literary sense-maker not of the War but of the process of conflict that was and is—and will it be?—Argentina of the last three decades or more" (McGuirk 2007, 351). Colm Tóibín's *The Story of The Night* (1996) tells the tale of Argentina's transition through the eyes of Richard/Ricardo Garay, son of an English mother and Argentinian father, as a remarkable journey into the night, where darkness connotes both dictatorship, postdictatorship neoliberal nihilism, and the shadow of AIDS. Tóibín's novel was translated into Spanish as *Crónica de la noche* (Emecé) in 1997, a year after its English publication. By contrast, it took twenty-four years before *Los pichiciegos* was translated into English, for the twenty-fifth anniversary of the war, as *Malvinas Requiem* (2007),[36] and English readers had to wait another five years—the thirtieth anniversary—for *The Islands*.[37]

Fortress Falklands: Epilogue

In literature, the Malvinas/Falklands War has been treated rather as a farce than as a tragedy, although in reality there was of course not much comedy to the drama. But what if history repeats itself? The question pops up as I read Falkland islander Graham Bound's insidious reportage about "life under siege in Britain's last outpost" (Bound 2012). The islander perception of the lingering conflict and persistent Argentinian aggression echoes Thatcher's wartime rhetoric. Bound talks condescendingly about Argentina's obsession with the islands and depicts the Kirchner couple, and especially Cristina, as if they were Ferdinand and Imelda Marcos of the Philippines (whereas Menem is saluted for his laissez-faire pragmatism). The islanders' attitude toward Argentina, and Latin America in general, remains patronizing, at best, when not openly racist. Defying the Argentinian blockade and diplomatic isolation from the rest of the continent, they hope to set up direct air links with Miami, and count on continued British military protection. Yet, in Bound's account, they do not want to return to the bosom of the mother country as an overseas British territory—like Saint Helena, Ascension, and Tristan da Cunha—but remain in the governmental gray zone as an autonomous "homeland," with indisputable ownership to the natural riches of the surrounding seas.[38] With a population of less than three thousand, the Falklands hence aspire to become the richest community per capita in the world. In this "Dallas of the South Atlantic," the perceived threat of an (unlikely) imminent Argentinian invasion is now giving way to worries about how wealth and prosperity may endanger the "islander spirit." Will they end up like the Gulf States, living on luxury benefits while guest laborers, presumably from the continent, perform all menial work?

It seems impossible to imagine a replay of the armed British-Argentinian confrontation. A surprise attack on the fortified Falklands would be a suicide mission, to begin with. No British "rescue mission" would be required. But, given that such an attempt is not imagined even in the wildest Argentinian fantasy, it will in the long run be increasingly difficult for any British government to mobilize domestic support for maintaining the costly military defense of this "last outpost." On the other hand, it seems as unlikely that NATO would ever give up control over what has become its Southern stronghold. From a NATO perspective, Argentina and Latin America would be regarded as allies, and at least not as military contenders, especially not in the light of the newly initiated normalization process between the United States and Cuba, which however may be jeopardized by Barack Obama's successor in the White House. But alliances can shift in a volatile multipolar world, where Brazil may want to assert its position as regional power and "the Soviet specter" possibly reappears in the guise of Russian claims on the Antarctica. The Malvinas/Falklands deadlock remains regardless, and the Anglo-Argentinian dispute over the islands will most likely not be resolved in another generation. Yet, the often-made parallel to the Anglo-Spanish disagreement over Gibraltar makes an interesting comparison. In the EU referendum of 2016, 96 percent of Gibraltar's population voted to remain, and immediately after the Brexit vote, Spain renewed calls for joint Spanish/British control over the peninsula. A joint Argentinian/British administration of the Malvinas/Falklands seems indeed as impossible as an imminent new war. But, in fact, even Graham Bound ends on a somewhat ambivalent note, reluctantly realizing that, in the end, the Falklands may not be able to escape a South American destiny (2012, 224).

NOTES

1. Argentina's claim on the islands in the South Atlantic goes back to the time of Spanish colonialism, when Spain, in alliance with France, gained sovereignty over the desolate territory from the British, who never actually renounced their claim. Independent Argentina saw itself as Spain's inheritor and established a colony on the islands in 1829. This small settlement was destroyed by the American sloop USS *Lexington* in 1831. Two years later the British returned to the Falklands and have retained control ever since.

2. The Falklands Syndrome is defined as the entitlement to demonstrate military superiority whenever possible ("being bold, adventurous even," as Tony Blair put it in his "Chicago Doctrine" to motivate the need

for intervention in Iraq). Moreover, any defeat or setback only vindicates the need for the Falklands Syndrome (Barnett 2012).

3. The late former president Nelson Kirchner and his widow, Cristina, both have a background in the Peronist militant left. It was the first Kirchner administration that broke the indemnity policies of the Menem regime and reopened the trials against the human rights violators of the dictatorship. The coincidence of the renewed judicial process against the military perpetrators and the renewed claims on Malvinas with adjoining diplomatic campaigns at regional and international level may not be incidental.

4. Malvinas obviously remains a prioritized issue for the current Argentinian administration as well. At a recent meeting with EU leaders in Brussels, president Mauricio Macri stated that "Brexit or not, our Malvinas claim will never change" (*MercoPress. South Atlantic News Agency*, July 5, 2016).

5. The main reason, besides Brazil's reluctance to be associated with apartheid South Africa, was rivalry and conflict between the prospective American member states. Brazil and Argentina were historical regional competitors, and Chile and Argentina were in the late 1970s at the brink of war over some islands in the Beagle Channel in Tierra del Fuego, which connects the South Atlantic with the South Pacific. In the conflict over Malvinas, Chile was the only Latin American country that refuted Argentina's territorial claims. Colombia abstained from supporting Argentina and was nicknamed "British Colombia," but it did not actively side with the British, as Chile did. Interestingly enough, in the confrontation with Chile, the Argentinian junta was backed by the Soviet Union. In the conflict with Britain, however, Moscow, like Washington, took an outwardly neutral stance. Recently revealed documents in the US National Security Archives and investigations by Russian journalist Sergei Brilev have, however, pointed to the (potential) Cold War dimension to the conflict (*MercoPress*, May 31, 2010). For a thorough discussion of the economic and political relations between Argentina and the USSR, see, for example, Vacs (1984).

6. This naval cooperation agreement was signed in 1955, when the Royal Navy gave up its base at Simon's Town and transferred it to the South African government in return for continued access to the base. Ironically, the termination of the agreement impeded the British Navy from using the base during the war with Argentina.

7. In 2012, the UK provoked not only Argentina by naming the hitherto unnamed southern part of its claim Queen Elizabeth Land, as a tribute to the Queen's Diamond Jubilee, which also happened to be the thirtieth anniversary of the war.

8. *Proceso de reorganización nacional* was the military junta's official term for the war on the militant left, more commonly known as "the dirty war."

The systematic extermination of some 15,000 alleged terrorists was most intensive in the dictatorship's first three years, 1976–78.

9. There is consensus among historians on the connection between these events. See for example Novaro and Palermo (2003) and Lorenz (2006). In Stockholm, a demonstration had been organized outside the Argentinian embassy on April 2, in response to the violent suppression of the March 30 demonstration in Buenos Aires. But when news about the disembarking in Malvinas reached the protesters, some of the organizers insisted on immediately calling it off, and the demonstration dissolved in confusion.

10. The Montoneros were left-wing Peronist guerrillas who appeared on the political scene in 1970 with the abduction and assassination of the former general Aramburu, who had toppled the first Peronist regime in a military coup in 1955.

11. The "national shame" (*la vergüenza nacional*) was a recurring exclamation in my interviews with Argentinian intellectuals during my fieldwork in 2008 (Hemer 2012). An interesting "unashamed" depiction of this time of exaltation is given in Tóibín (1996).

12. The nickname was coined by the Soviet newspaper *Kraznaya Zvezda* already in 1976. In 1980, Thatcher's neoliberal policies were questioned by a large contingent of her own conservative party, who requested a policy U-turn. At the 1980 Tory conference, Thatcher answered her critics in a speech written by the playwright Ronald Millar: "You turn if you want to. The lady's not for turning." After the Falklands war the Iron Lady caught on as her standing epithet.

13. In his discussion of "the Falklands Syndrome," Barnett points out that "the martial spirit inspired New Labour even more than it inspired the Tories" (Barnett 2012).

14. The talks that followed yielded little result, and in 1968 Britain unilaterally changed the conditions for negotiation by declaring the wishes of the Islanders to be paramount, as opposed to merely their *interests* (Williams 2005, 7).

15. Stigmatizing the British enemy was a delicate task, since British culture was commonly regarded with high esteem in Argentina. One solution was to depict the British as torn between their great cultural tradition and their ugly imperialist vocation. In an article headlined "Las Malvinas, Macbeth y los bárbaros modernos," philosopher Santiago Kovadloff urged the progressive sectors of the British people to rid their country of the yoke of modern primitivism that colonialism constitutes (quoted in Lorenz 2006, 74).

16. Some 12,400 Argentinians were engaged in the military operations. The vast majority (nearly ten thousand) belonged to the army, two thousand to the navy, and the remaining four hundred to the air force. In the army, the

conscripts constituted between 60 and 70 percent, and the navy had a similar general percentage of nonprofessionals, but on the cruiser ARA *General Belgrano*, which was sunk by the British, the number of conscripts was only 37 percent. In the air force, the percentage was less than 30. The great majority of the conscripts were born in 1962. Around one-fifth were born in 1963 and had only two months of military training (Lorenz 2006, 88).

17. Analyzing the information during the war, Lucrecia Escudero launched the notion of a "malvinization" of almost all the print media, and especially the journals (Escudero 1996, quoted in Lorenz 2006, 69).

18. The view of the soldiers as victims, not primarily of the British enemy, but of their own superiors, was largely shared by the relatives of the fallen, wounded and disappeared excombatants—*los padres de las Malvinas* (the parents of Malvinas), as they were named in an influential book in the immediate aftermath of the defeat (Bustos 1982), with obvious allusion to *las madres de Plaza de Mayo*. Isaías Jiménez, one of the founders of the relatives' organization, asked the democratic government of Alfonsín "if the parents of the heroes of Malvinas would also have to put on white turbans and walk around the pyramid of Plaza de Mayo in order to be heard" (Lorenz 2006, 125–126). He found it unacceptable that the politicians were more interested in the disappeared of the guerrilla war than in the disappeared of Malvinas.

19. The notion of (Christian) martyrdom was also a strong element in the Montonero imaginary and political practice (Hemer 2012, 312–316).

20. Under the alias Gustavo Niño, he had traced an unknown number of abducted human rights activists to the ESMA, where he simultaneously served as one of the high-ranking commanders. His clandestine activities became publicly known only after the war (Lorenz 2006, 166).

21. That is how the Comisión Nacional sobre la Desaparición de Personas (CONADEP) described the "boys": "They are not mature yet, but they are not kids anymore. They have not taken the key decisions of life, but they are beginning to trace their paths. They do not know much about the complexities of politics and they have not completed their cultural education. They are guided by their sensitivity. They do not resign themselves to the imperfections of the world they have inherited from their elders" (quoted in Lorenz 2006, 148).

22. After the controversial sinking of the *Belgrano*, which implied the irreversible escalation of the war and ruled out any peaceful solution to the conflict, the front page of the *Sun* was covered by the exclamation Gotcha! That is also the title of Harris (1985).

23. She distinguishes between three categories of texts: *myth perpetuators*, *demythologizers*, and *countermythologizers*. The apologetic texts are quite easily identified on both sides, whereas the distinction between the second two cate-

gories is somewhat blurry. Countermythologizers are defined as "texts that not only question or deconstruct official myths, but deploy myths of their own that work to subvert, and thus replace selected myths" (Williams 2005, 190).

24. Ambridge is the fictitious village of *The Archers*, the BBC Radio soap opera that has been broadcast daily on Radio 4 since 1951.

25. Barnett coined the term *churchillism* to describe this feature in British postwar politics, but he accused Thatcher of betraying the inclusionist part of Churchill's legacy.

26. Many of the former heroes suffer from mental disorders, and suicides are extremely prevalent. Twenty-five years after the war, 460 excombatants had killed themselves, according to Centro de Ex-Combatientes Islas Malvinas (CECIM, Center for Malvinas Veterans), as compared to the 655 who died in battle (*The Observer*, January 21, 2007). Among British Falkland Veterans, the number of suicides is also higher than the 255 killed in action, but allegedly not higher than the suicide rate among the general population (*The Guardian*, May 14, 2013).

27. The contested theory of the two demons stated that Argentina in the 1970s was subject to two equally alien ills: the terror inflicted by left-wing guerrilla groups and the counterterror by the military and right-wing militias. The "birds of a feather" explanation was accused of diminishing the implications of the state terror, but it appealed to the public by absolving civil society from any complicity in the dirty war (Hemer 2012, 279–280).

28. The play was eventually produced for the twentieth anniversary of the war in 2002, on radio and television, with a reception that was sharply divided along political lines (Williams 2005, 107).

29. See, for example "La soberanía nacional" and "El aprendiz de brujo" in Rodrigo Fresán's collection *Historia argentina* (1991), "Memorándum Almazán" by Juan Forn (in *Nadar de noche* 1992), and "El amor de Inglaterra" by Daniel Guebel (1992), which takes place in an imaginary time and space. Osvaldo Soriano's allegorical novel *A sus plantas rendido un león* (1986) was also set in a fictional (African) country.

30. The first edition was published in December 1983. But fourteen copies of the manuscript had circulated in Brazil immediately after its completion, before the war had even ended. A second edition was published in 1994, and a third one in 2006.

31. *Pichiciego* is a species of armadillo, a small, armor-coated, burrowing animal that is active only at night. The identification with animals has a curious, yet crucial dimension. When hunted, the armadillos often freeze halfway down the burrow, paralyzed by fear. The hunter then simply grabs one by the tail and sticks a finger up its anus, whereby it immediately gives up all resistance. The pichis, likewise, expect to be literally sodomized any moment, by

either the Brits or the Argies. The recurrent sodomy metaphor may be seen as an overly explicit symbol of the Argentinian state violence and abuse. With the victorious Brits, the real or imagined submission is more ambiguous, as in the homoerotic relation between one in the group and an infiltrating British soldier. In her overview of Argentinian fiction on Malvinas, Maria Elena Molina notes that the image of the British hardly appears at all, and certainly not as the enemy. The antagonist is clearly the Argentinian military dictatorship (Molina 2008).

32. In Sarlo's rereading of the book twelve years after its conception, she compares it to French filmmaker Claude Lanzmann's *Shoah* (1985), with its time and motion study of every step in the death machinery of the Holocaust (Sarlo 1994).

33. *Menemism*, the happy-go-lucky sell-out savage capitalism of the 1990s, would ironically be the closest Argentinian correspondent to Thatcherism.

34. The border between myth and history, true and false, is consistently blurred. Florentino Ameghino, author of *El origen del hombre en el Plata* (The Origin of Man in the River Plate) may, for example, seem like a Borgesian fiction, but refers to a historical paleontologist and anthropologist, although the title and thesis of his principal work have been distorted to a theory of River Plate as the cradle of mankind, from which the progenitors sailed north across the sea and lost their natural brown color due to the harsh weather conditions.

35. From a British perspective, the parallel to Saddam Hussein's equally disastrous surprise occupation of Kuwait may seem perfectly natural. The arguments for actively participating in the two Iraqi wars appealed to "the Falklands spirit," which in turn connoted "the Dunkirk spirit" of World War II. But for an Argentinian to identify, albeit ironically, with Saddam Hussein's miserable troops is truly exceptional.

36. The publisher's decision not to translate the original title as "The Armadillos" enraged Fogwill, who saw it as lending a sanctimonious touch to what he wanted to be a condemnation of all ideologies in favor of the dreadful demands made of terrified youngsters on both sides of the war, whose only wish was to survive and get home safely (Nick Caistor, the translator, in the obituary over Fogwill in *The Guardian*, August 27, 2010).

37. Both books received critical acclaim, but whereas Fogwill's short novel passed relatively unnoticed, Gamerro got instant media attention, being compared to Thomas Pynchon and Roberto Bolaño along with the inevitable comparison to Joseph Heller's *Catch-22*.

38. In a referendum in 2013, the year after the publication of Bound's book, 99.8 percent voted in favor of retaining political status as a British overseas territory.

Orientalism and the Narration of Violence in the Mediterranean Atlantic

Gabriel García Márquez and Elias Khoury

Christina E. Civantos

Since the late 1970s, when the works of the renowned Colombian author Gabriel García Márquez (1927–2014) were first translated into Arabic, they have taken the Arabic-reading audience by storm.[1] This essay focuses on one of his works in particular, the 1981 novella *Crónica de una muerte anunciada* (*Chronicle of a Death Foretold*), and analyzes its relationship with the 1994 novel *Majma' al-Asrar* (The Collection of Secrets) by the prominent Lebanese writer Elias Khoury (Ilyas Khuri; b. 1948). By focusing on García Márquez's novella and the parallel text by Khoury, I examine how the Arab migration routes spanning the southern Atlantic have generated a literary dialogue that points to the limits and possibilities of representing the Other.[2] In *Majma' al-Asrar*, Khoury, while commenting on Orientalist tensions, also looks beyond them to use *Crónica*, and a narrative style understood to pertain to Third World—or Global South—realities, to attempt to understand violence and the narrative act in South Atlantic contexts.[3] The multiple forms of violence with which Khoury's novel grapples are a constellation of interrelated exertions of power, ranging from types of discursive violence (e.g., Orientalism) to physical force in the context of political, religious, and ethnic conflict, as well as the criminal justice system and intimate relationships. In the process, Khoury exemplifies a strategy for addressing the challenges faced by literature of the Global South to which he has referred elsewhere. Through a variety of narrative strategies associated with modernity and postmodernity—most notably metafictionality, intertextuality, and shifts in perspective—Khoury narrates violence while circumventing the violence of authoritative, logic-driven, essentialist modes of representation.

The debates that arise from the confluence of comparative literature and postcolonial studies provide the framework for this essay. In the late 1990s and early 2000s, scholarly works on the concept of world literature raised questions about the power dynamics involved in transnational, transregional literary contact. The works of Moretti (2000), Damrosch (2003), and Casanova (2004) focused attention on the diffusion of literary models and themes on a global scale often using the terminology of economics and world-systems theory. In the wake of these works, questions regarding power dynamics and networks of contact arose. In addition to Emily Apter's (2013) problematization of the assumption of translatability that underlies the concept of world literature, critics began to consider what occurs when there is more direct contact across the Global South, contact that is not strongly rooted in a triangulation whereby authors and works from the "periphery" meet in the Euro-American center.[4] Gayatri Chakravorty Spivak, in *Death of a Discipline* (2003), called for an end to a Euro-American model of comparative literature and the reconfiguration of the discipline as one that includes the Global South not as an object but as an agent in the production of knowledge. Françoise Lionnet and Shu-mei Shih, in their edited volume *Minor Transnationalism* (2005), moved away from the models of transnationalism dominated by Euro-America through a focus on horizontal relations between North and South as well as within the Global South itself.

Several of the essays in Lionnet and Shih's volume correctly recognize that colonial and neocolonial power relations are still present even in South-South interactions. This suggests that truly direct contact between literatures from different points in the Global South is, more often than not, an illusion. In this essay, I assess the hazards and gains that arise in a specific type of South-South contact. Through this analysis I propose that when one of the sites of production is located in what has been classified as "the Orient" and the other is a culture resulting from European settler colonialism, the challenges of negotiating European discourses are particularly salient.

Through a focus on two works that straddle the southern Atlantic, linked by migration, Orientalism, the representation of violence, and narrative technique, I consider how the texts interact and how this interaction redefines "Third World" or "Global South" literature. This essay looks at the relationship between the Arab Mediterranean and Latin America, within which migration moves from the Southern Mediterranean to the Atlantic, cultural products about or by Arabs flow back toward the Mediterranean, and, as witnessed in the Lebanese novel studied here, occasionally are reworked and disseminated anew. As noted earlier, it would be hard to come by a case of "pure" (unmediated) cultural contact between countries in different regions of the Global South, and perhaps especially when one of these locales has traditionally been viewed through the essentialist conceptions of Orientalism. Thus, when Khoury builds upon and transforms a work by the Nobel Prize–winning García Márquez, Khoury must negotiate with the Orientalism in García Márquez's text. Eurocentric colonial discourses still inhere in work from the Global South and their psychological and resulting physical violence is in fact integral to the definition of literature from the Global South.

Migration

When Levantine Arabs passionately root for the Brazilian World Cup soccer team, they are part of a network of connections that was generated by nineteenth- and twentieth-century emigration from the Arab Mediterranean to Latin America and by subsequent return migration. From the mid–nineteenth century until the beginning of World War I, a wave of Arabic-speaking immigrants began to arrive in the Americas from the Province of Syria (present-day Syria, Lebanon, Israel, Palestine, and parts of Jordan) under Ottoman rule. This Levantine immigration movement arose out of a combination of political, economic, religious, and cultural factors, many of them linked to the crisis that arose in the Ottoman Empire in the mid-1800s and culminated in its dissolution. Many historians cite the 1860 massacre of Christians in Damascus and reports of widespread Ottoman persecution of Christians. Others also point to the Ottoman policy of forced military service, changes in land tenancy, a crisis in the local silk industry, and the rise in population in Lebanon. Karpat estimates that between 1860 and 1914, among the more than a million émigrés that left the Ottoman Empire for the Americas, there were roughly 600,000 Arabic speakers from the Levant (1985, 185).

The majority of these emigrants were Christians of various sects, though some were also Muslims of different denominations and Jews. However, since these immigrants arrived with Ottoman travel documents and were viewed through a homogenizing Orientalist lens, in the eyes of many Latin Americans these immigrants and their offspring are *turcos* (Turks) and as such are associated with Islam. Within Latin America, the greatest numbers of so-called *turcos* settled in Brazil and Argentina, and, in roughly decreasing numbers, in Chile, Mexico, Colombia, Central America, Venezuela, the islands of the Caribbean, and other areas. These turn-of-the-nineteenth century immigrants usually started out as peddlers and then set up shops. With time, some moved from being itinerant merchants and small business owners to being major figures in business, entertainment, and regional politics. After the turn-of-the-century immigration wave, additional, smaller waves of displaced Palestinians were produced by the 1948 establishment of the state of Israel and the 1967 Arab-Israeli war. Similarly, a small new wave of Lebanese emigrants resulted from the prolonged Lebanese civil war (1975–90).

In Colombia, the two areas in which García Márquez was raised, Aracataca (in the Department of Magdalena) and Sucre (in the Department of Sucre) on the Caribbean coast are known for their high concentration of Levantine Arab immigrants who began to arrive in the mid- to late nineteenth century (García Usta 1997, 123–124). The Arabic-speaking immigrants of this region were part of García Márquez's personal life: He married the daughter of an Egyptian immigrant, and during his adolescence he socialized with various Levantine immigrant families (ibid., 137 n. 1). Arab immigrants appear in a variety of García Márquez's writings as part of the Colombian Caribbean world. In García Márquez's most famous work, *Cien años de soledad* (*One Hundred Years of Solitude*, 1967), Arab immigrants are an integral part of the mythical town of Macondo: They are among the town's first inhabitants and they become symbols of the town's survival and regeneration when they withstand the flooding caused by a storm and stalwartly rebuild the area (García Usta 1997, 135–136).

In García Márquez's 1981 novella *Crónica*, the victim-protagonist Santiago Nasar is a descendent of Arab immigrants. In this text García Márquez uses the story of an actual murder to comment upon prejudice, class, gender roles, and group culpability. *Crónica* centers on an honor killing that is announced beforehand in many ways, but still comes to pass with the violent murder of Santiago Nasar, a wealthy member of the Levantine Arab immigrant community in a small Colombian town. When a local woman from a poor family, Ángela Vicario, marries an extremely rich man from the Caribbean who has recently arrived in town, her new husband discovers that she is not a virgin and returns her to her family. Angela's mother beats her, and her brothers, Pedro and Pablo, ask her for the name of the person who took her honor. Ángela immediately names Santiago Nasar, and, though nobody believes that he took her virginity, her brothers set out to avenge her honor. Although Pedro and Pablo Vicario do everything possible to be stopped by their fellow townspeople, somehow the murder of Santiago still occurs. This story is presented in a spiral fashion, with the narrator, named García Márquez, returning years later to his hometown to ask friends, family, and neighbors about the event. Each person's version adds another layer of often contradictory details and motives. In this way, *Crónica* uses multiple perspectives in a mix of investigative journalism and fiction (including some elements of magical realism) to try to address the secrets surrounding the murder.

In addition to its reiterative, multiperspectival narrative structure, *Crónica* displays an ambiguous relationship with people and things from "The Orient." García Márquez seems to draw from his personal relationships with Arab immigrants in Colombia in the depiction of this community in the novella, so much so that he gives the Arab community a more prominent role in his fictional version of the actual murder that took place in Sucre in 1951. In *Crónica*, García Márquez changes various elements of that historical incident. One of these in particular stands out since it becomes one of the proposed explanations for the murder: García Márquez changed the victim's ethnic background. In the novella, the victim-protagonist, Santiago Nasar, is part of the Arab immigrant community; however, the murder victim in the historical incident was not an Arab, but rather a European immigrant. In the 1951 crime, the victim was part of an Italian immigrant family, though his girlfriend was part of the Arab community.[5] Thus, García Márquez chose to cast the victim as an Arab. The protagonist's "different" background was a choice that has ramifications for the text's system of signification: it brings the link between violence and perceived difference into the text. García Márquez's decision to make the protagonist-victim part of the Arabic-speaking immigrant community heightens this character's difference from the townspeople, who did not intervene to save his life. This particular role for the Levantine community, as well as other references to the Middle East found in the novella, ultimately results in essentialist representations.

Orientalism

García Márquez, drawing from the Hispanic literary tradition that was initially built on Christian Iberian/North African Muslim contact, but from the distance of a former New World colony, is able to critique many forms of essentialism surrounding the Levantine immigrant community that he depicts, yet some types of essentialism remain. Arguably, most, if not all, of the canonical texts of the Spanish medieval and early modern periods grapple in some way with the centuries of Jewish and Arabo-Berber Muslim presence on the Iberian Peninsula and what that prolonged presence means regarding Spanish identity. Although many of these works are likely to have been part of García Márquez's education in Hispanic letters, he is known to have had an intense, and perhaps intensely conflicted, relationship with one text in particular, the text considered to be the foundational novel of Hispanic and even "World" literature: Cervantes's *Don Quijote*. The roles of Moorish culture and the Moorish subject in *Don Quijote* have been the subject of a plethora of critical studies, ranging from those that argue that it treats the *moriscos*[6] as Others, ridiculing them and/or presenting them as deceitful,[7] to those that argue that the novel subtly constructs an ironic, doubled system of signification that critiques the ethnocentrism of the nascent modern Spanish nation-state and defends the oppressed *moriscos.*[8] From my vantage point, outside of specialized Cervantes studies and even the broader field of Early Modern Studies, this debate demonstrates that, while the question "What is the place of the Moor in Peninsular culture?" is central to the fabric of the *Quijote*, there is a great deal of ambivalence, or at least slipperiness, regarding how the text responds to the Moorish question. Ultimately, what prevails in the *Quijote* is an awareness of this identity issue as a source of tension and instability.

Interestingly, García Márquez had a similarly conflicted relationship with the *Quijote* itself, and arguably with the Arab presence in Colombia. Broadly speaking, *Don Quijote*, as *the* Spanish masterpiece, has had a significant influence on Spanish-American novelists, whether as a model to emulate or a work to push against. Tom Holland describes the confluence of Cervantes's playful questioning of truth and close contact with Muslims, and its legacy in Spanish America:

> Islam, the religion of the Moors of Spain, and of the corsairs who had kept Cervantes a slave for five years in Algiers, serves him as yet one more mirror in the great hall of mirrors that is *Don Quixote*. The effect of this on Spanish, and particularly on Latin American, literature has been considerable. . . . The influence of Cervantes results in fantasies that often possess a decidedly Muslim tinge. Islam, in magical realism, is not something merely exotic, but an integral part of the inheritance derived from Spain's greatest writer. (2012, n.p.)

Indeed, various scholars have carried out comparisons between *Don Quijote* and *Cien años de soledad*.[9] However, in addition to noting parallels between the texts, they identify moments in which the twentieth-century Colombian masterpiece parodies the seventeenth-century Spanish masterpiece (Puccini 1989, 738 n. 5).

In García Márquez's 2002 memoir *Vivir para contarla* (*Living to Tell the Tale*), the Colombian author recounts his ambivalent relationship with the *Quijote*. García Márquez first read the canonical work as a young man upon the recommendation of a teacher, but he hated it. Years later, a friend recommended that he read the *Quijote* in the bathroom. García Márquez followed up on that suggestion and found such a deep appreciation for the Spanish text that he became a habitual reader of it. Matías Barchino points to García Márquez's conflicted relationship with the *Quijote* describing it as the need to create "a complicated distancing mechanism" by scatological means: "This scatological acceptance of Cervantes' work, demonstrates the way in which some Hispano-American writers have had to first free themselves from the influence of a *Quijote* that is too serious and academic using precisely the same ammunition as Cervantes—parody, critical excess, anti-dogmatism, and even scatology" (Barchino 2007, 125). This "strategic rejection," or contingent acceptance, of the text that is hailed worldwide as a Spanish masterpiece, arises from the general desire for literary originality and also the heightened need for originality that is part of postcolonial power dynamics.

The Colombian drive to establish political, economic, and cultural autonomy, as a former settler colony of the Spanish Crown, is intertwined with the relationship to the Arabo-Muslim world that is part of the imperial cultural legacy. On the one hand, Spanish, and more broadly all Hispanophone, writers have a relationship with the Arab world and Islam that is rooted in centuries of quotidian contact, participation in a Muslim-led cultural zenith, and the ensuing subjugation and expulsion of Muslims and Jews by Christian forces. As I have argued elsewhere, this legacy creates a Hispanic relationship with the Arabo-Islamic world that is distinct from that of other parts of Europe and North America, where the differentiation between self and other can appear much clearer and neater.[10]

How does New World Hispanic Orientalism manifest itself in García Márquez's *Crónica*? The violence that the story narrates is linked on a figurative level to both the historical contexts surrounding it and the physical and discursive violence of Orientalism. The novella presents a narrator looking back at events that took place parallel to a period of intense political bloodshed. This period of 1948–58, known as *la Violencia*

("The Violence"), consisted of a civil war between the Colombian Conservative Party and the Colombian Liberal Party in which political conflicts and struggles for the control of agricultural land were played out in battles in the countryside.[11] In addition, García Márquez completed and published *Crónica* during the period of conflict between the Colombian government, guerrilla groups, and paramilitaries in the late 1970s to 1990s. Thus, *Crónica* can be read as a commentary on the workings of violence both on the scale of small town neighbor relations and on the broader national scale. Indeed, Carmenza Kline, in a work that argues that violence is the central theme in García Márquez's oeuvre, suggests that the story presented in *Crónica* is an allegory for a Colombia that is a closed, heretofore inescapable realm of violence in which the inhabitants are victims of themselves, that is, of their own social codes (2002, 120).

On the level of neighbor relations as they are depicted in the novella, there are three intersecting axes of difference that cut across the town: patriarchal gender relations, socioeconomic class, and race and ethnicity. This last axis includes tensions between (wealthy, male) whites and (disenfranchised, female) blacks, as well as between *criollos* (those of Spanish, indigenous, and/or African descent whose families have been in the region since the colonial period) and immigrants from the Arab world. It is here that the identity of the protagonist Santiago Nasar is at once privileged and rejected: In the text he is perceived by blacks as white, but by *criollos* at large as a *turco*. And this *turco* identification, via his Arab immigrant father, persists even though he was born in Colombia and his mother is a *criolla*.

As Ottmar Ette points out, most scholarly work on *Crónica* leaves aside Santiago's *turco* identity and other references to the Orient as purely incidental (2006, 215–260). Together with Ette and Heba El Attar, I would like to argue for the centrality of the murder victim's Arab background, as well as connected references to those origins, to the text's system of signification. Moreover, I contend that the attitude toward the Arab world that emerges in *Crónica*, growing as it does out of a history that layers *convivencia* (coexistence and cohabitation) and power struggles both on the Iberian Peninsula and in sites of migration in Latin America, is one of ambivalence. As in the case of *Don Quijote*, certain passages in *Crónica* are evident criticism of prejudice and essentialism, but there are also instances in which, at least, there is ambiguity, and more likely a slippage, a reproduction of the critiqued perspective. El Attar (2008, 917, 923) interprets *Crónica* as a deconstruction of "turcophobia" that is carried out by a mocking of the Orientalist imagery, culminating in the absurdity of Santiago's murder and facilitated by the author's postmodern outlook. However, as Ette suggests, there are certain unresolved tensions that limit the novella's social critique of anti-*turco* sentiment.

Crónica's narrator, named Gabriel García Márquez and representing the author upon his return to his hometown, displays a critical awareness of the townspeople's prejudices against Arab immigrants. The narrator notes that some of the townspeople feared an act of revenge for the murder of Santiago Nasar on the part of the Arab community, although curiously none feared Santiago's mother's *criollo* Colombian family, who were known to be prone to fights and violence. The narrator then defends the Arab community by describing them as peaceful and hardworking people from whom there was no reason to fear revenge (García Márquez 2003, 78–80).

In a similar process, early on in the novella the narrator ponders how it was that Santiago Nasar had become involved in this situation and targeted for death, since there was no reason to believe that he had indeed taken the virginity of the bride in question (García Márquez 2003, 87–88). The narrator presents the most common theory held in the town: that the bride named Santiago as the person who had taken her virginity because he was wealthy and she thought her brothers would never dare to touch him (88). Yet, the narrator later adds a subtle twist to this common version of the crime. He reports that one of the townspeople interpreted Santiago's calm demeanor on the morning after the wedding not as innocence but rather as smugness—the certainty that his wealth made him untouchable. This townsperson's wife then chimes in "*Como todos los turcos*" (99)—"Like all the Turks." This disparaging, resentful reference to the Levantine immigrants from the Ottoman Empire, reveals an underlying animosity on the part of the townspeople toward those still seen as "foreign" even though they had arrived a few generations back.

Other passages, while not uncovering animosity, show how the townspeople perceive Santiago through a lens formed by Orientalist discourses. For instance, a woman in the town reports to the narrator that she saw Santiago when he had already had his guts cut open by the bride's brothers and was walking moribund to the back door of his house. The woman states that at that moment Santiago's "*rostro de sarraceno*" (García Márquez 2003, 117) or "Saracen face," was more beautiful than ever.[12] Ette astutely notes that in this passage Santiago "is transformed by his public execution . . . into a Saracen, an Arab. In fractions of a second, so it seems, sociocultural demarcations are activated, along with their associated mechanisms of exclusion and inclusion, which have not changed in any significant way even in the third generation, despite all of the Arab immigrants' attempts to conform" (2006, 239). Ette and El Attar identify this and other textual details in *Crónica* that mark Santiago Nasar and people and objects associated with him as different, in an Oriental way. It is important to note, though, the points of view of these details. Many of these references appear as the statements of other characters. In this way, these Orientalist details in *Crónica* are used to identify the ways that the so-called *turcos* are marked as different by the townspeople and to subtly criticize this dynamic.

Nonetheless, the critique of Orientalist discourses is undercut by two other descriptive details. While the passages examined above represent the points of view of other characters, at other moments the Orient-flavored references come via the voice of the narrator. This narrator, given that he is not only called García Márquez, but, like the author, grew up in the town in which the murder took place and was friends with the victim, carries an authoritative voice within the text. The narrator, who returns decades later to research the murder by interviewing the townspeople, tells us that when he visits Santiago's mother he can see Santiago in the memory of the deceased man's mother and then proceeds to describe Santiago as he was before the murder. Within this description of Santiago's physical appearance, we find that "he had the Arab eyelids and curly hair of his father" (García Márquez 2003, 7). In this passage, to which I will return, within what the narrator imagines to be Santiago's mother's memory of Santiago, the narrator attributes a noticeable physical difference to Santiago. He marks Santiago as visibly biologically different. In racializing Santiago, the narrator establishes his own perspective as a non-Arab and draws a line of difference between them.

In another passage, after Santiago's funeral the narrator tries to forget the tragedy by going to see the town madam, with whom Santiago had had a close relationship. The narrator finds the madam mourning by gorging herself from a "*platón babilónico de cosas de comer*" (a Babylonian platter of things to eat), while sitting naked on her bed "*a la turca*" (García Márquez 2003, 75)—in the Turkish style, which is often known in English as "Indian style" or cross-legged. Here the image of Oriental debauchery and excess in the form of the large Babylonian plate heaped with food comes together with a suggestion of the closely related image of the odalisque. By presenting the prostitute who was Santiago's true passion as a harem odalisque who mourns through Eastern excess, *Crónica*, in spite of itself, invokes and reiterates essentialist understandings of West Asian and North African cultures.

Other elements of García Márquez's novella are easily read as irony, but even then they seem to slip out of the author's control. An example of this is the name "Santiago" itself. Ette alludes to the symbolic significance of "Santiago" as the patron saint of the Christian *Reconquista* of Spain.[13] This mythical figure is understood to be the Apostle Saint James who, legend has it, arrived in Iberia in the 800s to help the Christians battle the Moors. The famous figure, prevalent in medieval Iberian Christian art, is commonly known as "Santiago Matamoros" or "Saint James the Moor-Slayer." The choice of this name for the victim-protagonist of the novella wraps Santiago Nasar in self-referential irony: The zealous drive to kill Moors (Arabic-speaking Muslims) is directed at a Christian Arab who, by association, is perceived as a *turco* and a Saracen. Yet, the figure of Santiago Matamoros was also adapted for use in the Spanish American context. Iconography of Santiago, depicted as a *conquistador* and renamed "Santiago Mataindios" (the Indian-Slayer), was employed in the Spanish colonization of the Americas and featured in seventeenth-century Spanish imperial art. This repurposed Santiago functioned as a source of divine justification and inspiration in the subjugation of the indigenous population. Apparitions of Santiago Mataindios, intervening in specific battles, were recorded in Mexico, Peru, Chile, and also, in 1536, in Cartagena, in the Caribbean coast region of Colombia.[14] In this way, the figure of Santiago Nasar becomes troublesome as he is connected to a colonial era conqueror and thus associated with the power of the Spanish crown. In another interpretative layer, the conquest can be associated with the conquering immigrant who threatens to displace the local population.

Given the narrator's racialization of Santiago Nasar, the novella's reiteration of the figure of the odalisque, and the polyvalent resonances of the name "Santiago" itself, the critique of anti-Arab prejudice becomes clouded and even conflicted. García Márquez's popularity among readers in the Arab world has led to the opportunity to see what one Arabic-language writer makes of *Crónica*.[15] The renowned Lebanese author Elias Khoury builds on the connections created by transatlantic migration by taking up the figure of Santiago Nasar and creating the intertwined story of his cousin, Ibrahim Nasar (Nassar).[16] The 1994 novel *Majma' al-Asrar* comments upon García Márquez's novella by invoking, reworking, and expanding it in a novel about Lebanese characters in Lebanon.[17] Khoury's text, by taking up some of the characters, themes, and narrative structures found in García Márquez's text, constitutes a riff on the Colombian novella and a response to it. Khoury's text clearly demonstrates admiration for García Márquez's work; yet, at the same time, it subtly criticizes García Márquez's treatment of difference.

The Violence of Representation and the Representation of Violence

In *Majma' al-Asrar*, Khoury makes intertextual references to various European and Middle Eastern texts, both classical and contemporary, but engages most deeply with the Latin America text *Crónica de una muerte anunciada.* Supported by various references to the title and author of the Colombian text, as well as extensive quotes from the Arabic translation of that text, Khoury's novel builds on various of *Crónica*'s themes as it recounts the experiences in Beirut of Ibrahim Nasar, a cousin of Santiago Nasar imagined by Khoury. In *Majma' al-Asrar*, Khoury creates a broader picture of the Nasar family and its origins and, through a letter that he has the Colombian branch of the family write to the branch that stayed in Lebanon, he has the fate of one cousin affect that of the other.[18]

Majma' al-Asrar begins and ends in an eight-day period in 1976 during which Ibrahim mysteriously dies. Yet the text includes Ibrahim's experiences as a child from 1946 to 1948 and at times reaches back to the mid-nineteenth century, and even before, as it recounts the dubious history of the family. Before Ibrahim's death he searches for the letter his family had received when he was a child, the letter from relatives in Colombia that brought the news of Santiago's murder and changed the lives of Ibrahim and his family by convincing them not to emigrate. This is but one of the many episodes in which the narrator leads us, in vain, on a quest to uncover the secrets that underlie the relationships at the center of the novel: the love triangle between Ibrahim—who dies before fulfilling his promise to marry Norma; Norma—who lost her virginity to either Ibrahim or his friend Hanna; and Hanna—an old friend of Ibrahim who continues his relationship with Norma after marrying another woman and survives a mistaken murder accusation and police torture. The historical periods that Khoury depicts are ones of sociopolitical tension and devastating violence: the mid-nineteenth century conflicts between the Druze, Maronites, and Ottoman forces, the end of the French Mandate in the 1940s, the 1958 political crisis and attempted coup, and the outbreak of the Lebanese civil war in 1975. The novel consists of several interwoven stories presenting different perspectives on the events in order to explore violence and group dynamics, Otherness, the multiple nature of truth, and South-South relations.

Through intertextual references to French Algerian Albert Camus's *L'Étranger* (*The Stranger*, 1942), extended engagement with García Márquez's novella, and a storyline that includes political strife, police brutality, violent sexual relationships, and social oppression, Khoury's novel moves beyond the small-town frame of the Colombian text and explores how private, everyday violence as well as large-scale group violence come about. Intrinsic to this is the attention to Otherness, such that Khoury's narrator ponders why difference often meets with a violent response and what exactly constitutes difference, or the status as "stranger." These reflections are enabled and enhanced by taking into account multiple perspectives. The various versions of reality that emerge point to the contingent, plural, and even fictional nature of truth.

South-South relations are integral to all of these avenues of exploration found in *Majma' al-Asrar*: As discussed earlier, ascribed violence as well as actual violence are part of the conditions of the Global South, similarly, the imposition of Otherness and the experience of being Othered (not to the exclusion of Othering) are defining characteristics of the South. Furthermore, by working with García Márquez's text and the Lebanese novel's own characters, Khoury's text brings together perspectives from different points in the Global South, thereby highlighting divergences, as well as points of contact, within the South.

On various levels and in various ways, *Majma' al-Asrar* demonstrates how historical and fictional events in distinct "Third World" locales affect each other. Khoury's narrator notes similarities between the two cousins, Santiago and Ibrahim Nasar, and, referring to both as ghosts, he quotes an Arabic translation of García Márquez's description of Santiago: "he was thin and pale and had the Arab eyebrows and curly hair of his father" ([1993] 1996, 37).[19] The narrator then states: "That ghost resembles our ghost; for Ibrahim Nasar, as Norma described him to her friends at school, was thin and pale, had curly hair and thick, bushy eyebrows. Norma did not say that they were Arab eyebrows, because she is an Arab" (37). Here Khoury notes one of those moments in which traces of an Orientalist outlook arise in García Márquez's text and pushes against it by highlighting Norma's perspective. Elsewhere in Khoury's novel, in support of the idea that Santiago's alienation or strangeness did not come from being an immigrant, but rather from the surreal nature of his death, the narrator says about Santiago: "Everyone who met him thought he was Hispanic, or thought he carried mixed blood, like millions of South America's inhabitants" (44). In this way, Khoury's text asserts that if there were any physical feature that marked Santiago as Arab, it would only be interpreted as such by non-Arabs and then goes on to reject that such a feature exists. Indeed, rather than uphold any ability to mark Santiago as different, Khoury highlights Santiago's similarity to the *mestizo* and *mulato* inhabitants of Latin America. I propose that *Majma' al-Asrar*, by emphasizing points of contact between the Arab world and Latin America, is at once a corrective commentary on the forms of Orientalism that linger in *Crónica* and an homage to García Márquez's narrative techniques that is part of Khoury's broader concern with the defining characteristics of the literature of the Global South. By crafting this novel as he does, Khoury rejects forms of representation that generate discursive and/or physical violence by establishing fixed truths (e.g., Orientalism as well as Occidentalism), and he focuses instead on creative strategies for representing violence.

In one sense, the two texts at hand are separated by the discursive violence of Orientalism, yet in another sense violence is what brings them together. Within the story lines of the two works, Santiago's murder is sometimes ascribed to his ethnic origins, and in Khoury's text this creates the fear that leads Ibrahim's family to forgo emigration. Ironically, identity-based violence finds them at home, through the outbreak of the Lebanese civil war. And here lies one of the common denominators of Colombian and Lebanese cultures at large: both are associated with violence by being part of the "underdeveloped" world and they have also both experienced a great deal of armed violence.

On the one hand, as Anton Blok indicates, violence is typically viewed "as the antithesis of 'civilization'" (2000 23). There is certainly plenty of violence globally—North and South—but often in more industrialized and/or politically stable states it is masked by its manifestation in more subtle or naturalized disciplinary and state-sponsored forms. In contrast, violence is associated with the Global South not only because of armed internecine conflicts and more noticeable corruption and income disparity, but because the imperialist vision of Latin America, Africa, and South and West Asia includes the figure of the violent primitive who lives in a state of chaos—the barbarian who is quick to physical violence and slow to rational thought. For instance, Orientalism as a discourse has promoted the view of the Arab as vengeful and volatile.

On the other hand, while local sources of conflict should not be downplayed, the global economic system has a vested interest in maintaining and even propagating violence in the Global South. As Pablo Mukherjee puts it: "the achievements of Western 'universal civilization,' colonial and post-colonial, depend on ensuring conditions of material/cultural poverty and endemic conflict in the countries of the Global South" (2007, 221). Similarly, Catherine Besteman, in *Violence: A Reader*, states: "Many scholars agree that the economic restructuring of the past several decades (toward globalization and flexible capital) has produced global and local instabilities that characterize a new world order—or disorder" (2002, 306). Besteman then cites the work of Lutz and Nonini that suggests that "the economic restructuring of the global capitalist system has produced a well-protected 'global urban archipelago of wealth' and a global periphery characterized by 'brigandage, mafia-domination, and marauding private ethnic armies'" (ibid., 306). While certain discourses of Otherness create an intrinsic association between "Third World" and violence, geopolitical and economic factors lead to further violence in the Global South.

In addition to essentialist characterizations of the Orient and the "Third World," an imbricated form of discursive violence consists of trying to impose a certain understanding of reality as ordered and linear—and as easily classifiable into East/West, *turco*/Colombian, and so on. The self-conscious examination of reality and fiction for which *Don Quijote* is famous, that is, the questioning of truth via metafictionality alluded to above, is also found in *Crónica* and *Majma' al-Asrar*, with additional innovative narrative techniques. In *Majma' al-Asrar* these include a nonlinear plot, multiple perspectives, a fragmentary style, and intertextuality. All of these are utilized in the treatment of historical events, often of great violence. Indeed, a leitmotif within the novel is that the single-minded search for truth—e.g., through a forced confession of guilt, the naming of the perpetrator of a crime, the identification of ethnically marking physical characteristics, or the establishment of the official version of historical events—only generates more violence.[20] Using metafictionality, perspectivism, and intertextuality, *Majma' al-Asrar* criticizes excesses—both discursive and physical—committed in the name of establishing absolute truths. In this way, Khoury's novel criticizes the role of Arabness in García Márquez's text. Yet at the same time, *Majma' al-Asrar*'s narrative techniques are inspired, at least in part, by the work of García Márquez and respond to Khoury's concerns about "Third World" literature.

Challenges Faced by Literature of the Global South

One year before publishing *Majma' al-Asrar*, Khoury published another novel, *Mamlakat al-Ghuraba'* (*The Kingdom of Strangers*, 1993) that directly addresses the concept of "Third World" literature. *Mamlakat al-Ghuraba'*, in an essayistic style, centers on the act of storytelling through Lebanese legends and intertwined anecdotes. At one point the narrator interrupts a narrative segment to recount a related conversation between himself and Salman Rushdie. This gives way to the following reminiscence: "I remember Salman Rushdie gave me a copy of his *Satanic Verses* manuscript that day. We were discussing his novel *Shame* and I was telling him what scared me about Third World literature was its peculiar tendency to turn into a page out of history and become classified in the West under the category of 'oddities whose problems have no logical solutions'" (1996, 79).[21] Elsewhere Khoury rejects the peculiarity and particularity ascribed to "Third World literature" by seeking recourse in universalism: "My stylistic innovations are simply attempts to express the present, to express what people are living now. What the people in Beirut are living is not particular to Beirut. It can be found anywhere. It is a universal experience. This is true of most Third World literature" (Meyer 2001, 117). It seems that in trying to evade limiting, imposed classifications, Khoury resorts to the particularly limiting idea of so-called universals. However, Khoury's comment, when considered in conjunction with other statements that he has made, can be understood to establish a new type of universality: the common predicament of authors in Third World locales.

In relation to perceptions of Third World literature, Khoury once said: "My basic fear has always been that my works would be translated as social documents, as is the case for most examples of Arabic literature in translation, including those of Naguib Mahfouz. I am not interested in presenting a social document because literature is only partially a social document" (quoted in Haydar 1996, viii). Yet, in the novel studied here, as well as most of his other works, there is a clear concern with reflecting historical experience and perhaps refracting common conceptions of it. Khoury explains this urge to write about the conflicts of the past and the present in a 1993 interview in which he comments on orality and being a Lebanese writer:

> My fear has been that our present and our past were subject to destruction.
>
> . . . I discovered that [Lebanese] society had erased its history, as if it carried along with it a big fat eraser with which it blotted out its own history. So we have a situation where there is no written text about the war of 1860 and nothing about the revolution of 1920 or the revolution of 1958. What terrified me was that I was living a war [the Lebanese Civil War] whose fate might well be similar to the fate of the wars that preceded it and so I had to write it myself." (quoted in Haydar 1996, v)

Thus, much as Khoury may balk at the imposition of a social documentary agenda for literature from the Global South, he does feel a strong need to document the violent conflicts of his country and his region. But how he goes about recording these events is the crux of the matter. On the one hand, Khoury decries being forced into a category of radical difference, of unknowability and irrationality—a showcase of "unsolvable oddities." But, on the other hand, although he is aware of the need to leave a written register of wars and conflicts to avoid further violence in the future, he doesn't want his works to be read as "social documents." This leads to a tension that Khoury resolves creatively in works such as *Majma' al-Asrar*.

The process of documentation, or even trying to make sense of violence via narrative, can be tantamount to the figurative violence of imposing logic or a single truth. In contrast, Khoury creates a type of document with contingent meaning through innovative narrative techniques. *Majma' al-Asrar*, like *Crónica*, is a more playful attempt at narrating violence: rather than reveal one truth, the texts revel in the ambiguity of contradictory, coexisting perspectives. Rather than succumb to the North's imposition of a state of irrationality on the Other, Khoury reaches out to García Márquez to contest the nature of truth and find ways to represent violence, and thus stave off renewed violence, without opposing it with a fixed truth.

Majma' al-Asrar depicts various violent conflicts in Lebanese history, and Khoury wrote it while Lebanon was recuperating from—and trying to make sense of—civil war. Similarly, in these periods Colombia experienced *la Violencia* followed by the rise of guerrilla groups and drug cartels. Yet these are also periods of creative renewal in Arabic and Spanish American narrative. In the 1950s and '60s Arab writers began bringing existentialist introspection, a self-consciousness about artistic technique, and greater political engagement to their work. The 1960s and '70s saw the experimental works known as "the Boom" in Latin American fiction, works which were then disseminated widely outside of Latin America. Khoury's novel creates a textual dialogue that highlights the connections between these literary traditions.

Majma' al-Asrar revises the concept of the Orient that the Colombian text presents yet it does so through a narratological homage to the Colombian text. The Lebanese novel uses a version of the multiperspectival technique for which *Crónica* is so famous to dismantle the essentialist conceptions of difference in the Colombian text and thus addresses a challenge faced by literature of the Global South. This pair of texts presents a strategy for responding to this challenge: connect with other writers from the postcolonial/developing world and use postmodern narrative techniques to denounce violence without reproducing it discursively.

Dialoguing Beyond the Text

Through the intertextual relationship with *Crónica*, Khoury creates a connection with an analogous contemporary text. Unlike the relationship with an ancient classic of a different genre, such as the Bible or pre-Islamic poetry, or with a modern novel from half a century before, such as Camus's *L'Étranger*—all of which are invoked in the novel—the connection with *Crónica* entails a text of the same genre that was published only thirteen years before *Majmaʿ al-Asrar*. This contemporaneity and comparableness create a sense of immediacy and actual dialogue between the two texts. Although this Global South Atlantic dialogue that stretches all the way to West Asia, via a South Atlantic–Southern Mediterranean corridor, is not always triangulated through Europe or North America in terms of the circulation of texts, the European discourse of Orientalism certainly runs through the encounter.

In the process of building and dismantling the concept of world literature, various critics have stressed that the world literary system (or set of systems) is built on inequalities. Casanova in particular addresses the process whereby writers from peripheral locales achieve the status of "world literature" via their consumption and promotion in the European and North American center. However, the case of the two novels studied here demonstrates that more direct South-South literary contact can and does occur. Although certainly García Márquez became a global figure through the mediation of Spanish publishing houses and European organizations such as the Nobel Committee, translation activity from Spanish to Arabic has a crucial role to play in the creation of his Arab readership and *Crónica* is just one of various Hispano-American works by different authors that Salih ʿAlmani has translated. Yet, previous to this, Arabic classics such as *The 1001 Nights*, filtered through European Orientalist translations, had become part of the literary archives of Latin American writers.[22] Together these different translation routes allow for the circulation of ideas, regarding both conceptualizations of literature and power dynamics, across the South Atlantic–Southern Mediterranean corridor.[23] This is one example of the multilayered networks of production and circulation of literature, and cultural products in general, within the Global South Atlantic—and how Eurocentric discourses (Orientalism) still intervene.

The literary interaction between García Márquez and Khoury parallels, and works in tandem with, new South-South economic and political connections such as the meetings of the Summit of South American and Arab Countries (known by its Portuguese and Spanish acronym ASPA), which commenced in 2005 with the goal of increasing economic, environmental, technological, and cultural collaboration between the two regions, and those of the Abu Dhabi Arab-Latin American Forum, which started in 2012 with the purpose of developing a shared strategic vision on economic, political, and social issues, having grown out of forums on Middle East

Peace held a few years earlier in the Dominican Republic, Costa Rica, and Colombia sponsored by the nonprofit organization FUNGLODE. However, just as Khoury and García Márquez's textual encounter demonstrates, economic and political contact across the South Atlantic–Southern Mediterranean corridor must attend to the vestiges of imperialist and neocolonial dynamics in order to avoid the reproduction of various forms of violence.

NOTES

I thank Eman Morsi and her colleagues, who participated in my invited talk at the Graduate Student Colloquium on Comparative Approaches to Middle Eastern Literatures, Department of Middle Eastern and Islamic Studies, New York University, in October 2010, as well as Ramón Stern and Elena Grau Lleverı́a, for providing fruitful comments on early versions of this essay. Likewise, I thank Kerry Bystrom and Joey Slaughter, as well as the anonymous readers of Fordham University Press, for their very helpful feedback on the more recent incarnation of this essay.

1. Mona Eltahaway (2000) reports that, according to Cairo's premier bookshop, Madbouli's, works by García Márquez are among the longstanding favorites of Egyptian readers. See also Rabia (1981). The esteem in which García Marquez is held in the Arab world can also be registered in the responses to his death and the existence of an Arabic-language Facebook page dedicated to him (https://www.facebook.com/GabrialMarquez.ar/timeline). Among responses to the Colombian author's death, see Butalia (2014) and "Rahil Ghabriyil Gharsiyya Marqiz . . ." (2014).

2. To describe the status of Khoury's text vis-à-vis that of García Márquez, Ette uses the term "*alografía*" (allograph) (2010, 228). However, a literary allograph would be a continuation of a text penned by another author. In the case of these two works, as should soon be apparent, the second text to be published is not so much a continuation as it is a parallel text. Khoury's text covers similar years as García Marquez's (the late 1940s to the early 1950s and the late 1970s), but it centers on a cousin of the main character of García Márquez's text in a separate locale.

3. While the terms "Third World" and "Global South" are not completely interchangeable and certainly reflect different historical periods, I use them largely indistinctly here because the authors whom I study wrote at a time in which the preferred term for economically developing countries, or countries in the process of decolonization, was "Third World." At least one of the authors uses this term in his statements about his own sociocultural location. For more on the history, and future, of these two terms, see Dirlik (2007).

4. Apter specifically discusses Moretti (2013, 45–56), Casanova (2013, 6–7), and Damrosch (2013, 325–326 and 329).

5. In 1951, in Sucre, Colombia, Cayetano Gentile Chimento was killed by the brothers of Margarita Chica Salas, when, soon after her wedding, she was returned home by her husband, Miguel Reyes Palencia, who had discovered that she was not a virgin. In addition to the fact that Cayetano was of Italian rather than Arab descent, Reyes Palencia was not an extremely wealthy stranger from another part of the region (as is the case with García Márquez's character Bayardo San Román), but the son of a local family who worked as an itinerant salesman. Pelayo indicates that Gentile Chimento was a childhood friend of García Márquez (2001, 111), and Hart notes that Gentile Chimento's girlfriend was named Lydia Nasar (2005, 37).

6. *Moriscos* is the Spanish term used for Muslims in late medieval and early modern Iberia who converted to Christianity, usually under duress. Starting in the early 1500s Muslims were forced to convert in order to avoid death or expulsion. The term was also used pejoratively to refer to those suspected of being nominal Catholics who secretly practiced Islam. In the early 1600s those known to be *moriscos* were expelled from Spain.

7. See, for instance, Mancing (1981), Corbalán (2005), and Bolaños (2008).

8. See, for instance, Johnson (2009), Childers's review article on Johnson's posthumous book as well as other works within *morisco* studies (2012), Graf (2007), Quinn (2013, 101–132), and De Armas (2011).

9. See, for instance, García Ramos (2007, 335–342), Fleming Figueroa (2007, 281–290), and Joset (1992, 737–744; 1991, 105–117).

10. On how this manifests in the Argentine context see, Civantos (2006, especially 3–5, 25–26, and 58–59). With regard to twentieth- and twenty-first-century Spanish and Argentine narratives that invoke Muslim Iberia, see Civantos (2017).

11. El Attar considers the possible implications of *la Violencia* for the Arab immigrant community in particular (2008, 923).

12. Other such references include when the judge, preparing a report on the case, describes one of the knives used to kill Santiago as "*un alfanje en miniatura*" (57), a miniature scimitar. At another moment, a character addresses Santiago as "*turco*" (112).

13. Ette asks "*¿No fue acaso el Apóstol Santiago, el Jacobo de todas las leyendas de peregrinaje en una peninsula Ibérica dominada por los árabes, el patrono de los españoles en la guerra de reconquista contra los sarracenos?*" (2010, 220) (Wasn't it in fact the Apostle Saint James, the Jacob of all the pilgrimage legends in an Iberian Peninsula dominated by the Arabs, who was the patron saint of the Spaniards in the war of reconquest against the Saracens?).

14. See Ballan (2014), Domínguez García, *Memorias del futuro* (2008), and Domínguez García, *De Apóstol Matamoros a Yllapa Mataindios* (2008). On the apparitions, see Hernández Lefranc (2006, 73; 2011).

15. See note 1 on García Márquez's popularity in the Arab world.

16. In García Márquez's novella, the Arabic surname, which is more accurately transliterated as "Naṣṣār," is spelled "Nasar." I use "Nasar" here for both novels to make it clear that it is the same fictional family, created by García Márquez and expanded upon by Khoury. For ease of reading, aside from this note I only include full diacritics for transliterations in the Works Cited, using the *IJMES* transliteration system.

17. Some of the passages in Khoury's novel closely echo certain passages from *Crónica*. For instance, the parallels between Santiago and Hanna are highlighted by the opening of one of the chapters of *Majma' al-Asrar*, which follows closely the opening passage of *Crónica*: Hanna wakes up early on a rainy morning, with a strange sensation on his tongue after a night of heavy drinking, remembering a disturbing dream in which the sky rained mud. See Khoury (1994, 13).

18. For an analysis of questions of origins and diaspora and *Majma' al-Asrar* as part of migration literature, see Civantos (2015).

19. García Márquez refers to Arab eyelids (*párpados*, 2003, 7), but Khoury, quoting from one of the Arabic translations of *Crónica*, uses "eyebrows" (*hajiban*) in place of "eyelids." Khoury does not indicate the translation or publication information for his citations, but there are three published translations of *Crónica* into Arabic: (1) translated from the Spanish by 'Almani as *Qissat Mawt Mu'lan* (1981), (2) translated most probably from another language by Salim as *Sard Ahdath Mawt Mu'lan* (1989), and (3) translated from the French translation by 'Amiri as *Waqa'i' Mawt Mu'lan* (1990). I have been able to confirm that both 'Almani (1981, 10) and 'Amiri (1990, 9) used "eyebrows" instead of "eyelids" in their translations. The ease with which *eyelids* is substituted by *eyebrows* underscores the arbitrariness of the racialization process.

20. This leitmotif is also seen in Khoury's more recent novel *Yalu* (*Yalo*, 2002).

21. Taken from Paula Haydar's translation of the novel *The Kingdom of Strangers* (Khoury 1996, 79). The reference can be found in the original Arabic text at Khoury (1994, 98).

22. On how García Márquez and Jorge Luis Borges drew from *The 1001 Nights* in their development of magical realism, see 'Abd al-Nasir (2011).

23. On the role of translation between metropolitan and "peripheral" languages within conceptualizations of "World Literature," see Damrosch (2003) and Apter (2013).

Marvelous Autocrats
Disrupted Realisms in the Dictator Novel of the South Atlantic

Magalí Armillas-Tiseyra

In the opening scene of Sony Labou Tansi's *La vie et demie* (*Life and a Half*, 1979) the dictator of the fictional country of Katamalanasia slits the throat of, disembowels, and cannibalizes the opposition leader, Martial. But Martial refuses to die. His voice emanates from his remains until the Providential Guide, as the dictator is called, tears them apart. Martial then haunts the Providential Guide; when he takes Martial's daughter as a mistress, Martial prevents him from consummating the affair. Yet, as the novel progresses, Martial himself becomes overbearing and violent, attempting to dictate the actions of his daughter and granddaughter, even raping the former. His descendants, too, engage in acts of extreme violence. Figuratively, Martial's ghost represents the afterlives of dictatorial oppression and the reproduction of destructive hierarchies of power in opposition to dictatorship. As a concrete presence in the text, however, his specter pushes the novel into the realm of the supernatural or fantastic, suggesting the limits of realism as a narrative mode for the depiction and critique of dictatorship.

This essay takes as its subject this and other such departures from the conventions of realism in the dictator novel, a genre that spans the South Atlantic and, in a wider frame, the Global South. At stake are questions of classification as well as method; specifically, of how to read comparatively across Latin American and African literatures without subordinating one to the other. Taking into account the practical need for at least provisional categories for the work of literary criticism, I offer the methodological model of a constellated comparison of novels about dictators in the South Atlantic. "Constellation" here serves as a figure both for the relationship of individual texts or textual features to each other (a loose configuration or grouping) and for a mode of comparison that proceeds by juxtaposition and collage rather than more rigid hierarchical systematization. It is particularly apt for this case because, drawing on its function as both noun and transitive verb, a constellation simultaneously exists in and of itself and only exists in so far as its individual components can be drawn together into some configuration. Constellation as a figure, therefore, allows me to approach and grapple with the difficult relationship between critique and narrative form.

Dictator novels rely on reference to an empirical reality that lies beyond the text. This is the history of dictatorial regimes (and individual dictators) from which details are drawn and against which these novels are targeted.[1] Yet, if realism is the narrative mode most intimately concerned with the representation of a recognizable empirical reality and the production of what Ian Watt called "an authentic account of the actual experiences of individuals" (2001, 27); and if, following from this, the capacity for exposition or disclosure is what grants realism its critical heft, raising consciousness and thereby fostering political action (Sartre 1988, 65–66); then, how should we read deviations from the precepts of realism such as those in Labou Tansi's *Life and a Half*? Or, for that matter, those in Gabriel García Márquez's *El otoño del patriarca* (*The Autumn of the Patriarch*, 1975), Augusto Roa Bastos's *Yo el Supremo* (*I the Supreme*, 1974), Ahmadou Kourouma's *En attendant le vote des bêtes sauvages* (*Waiting for the Vote of the Wild Animals*, 1998), or Ngũgĩ wa Thiong'o's *Mũrogi wa Kagogo* (*Wizard of the Crow*, 2006)?

Despite the close association of realism with the culture and writing of resistance—as per, for instance, Jean-Paul Sartre's theorization of *littérature engagée*—recourse to the fantastic or departures from a recognizable empirical reality governed by familiar physical laws are a recurrent feature in novels about dictators and dictatorship in the South Atlantic.[2] These departures serve a critical function. In *Autumn of the Patriarch*, for example, the dictator is forced to sell the Caribbean to the United States; the sea is packed up and moved to Arizona. This is an expression of the dictator's subservience to the foreign powers that sustain his regime. In *I the Supreme*, the dictator sends his men to "capture" a meteor that has fallen from the sky. The meteor resists but is subdued, and the dictator keeps it chained to his chair as a memento of his power (1986, 98–99). In *Waiting for the Vote of the Wild Animals*, the dictator is also in possession of a magic meteor, identified as the fetish that assures his hold on power. The novel's dismantling of this fetish object parallels its critique of authoritarian power.[3] Finally, in *Wizard of the Crow*, facing difficulty in securing funds abroad and mockery at home, the dictator swells with rage, becomes buoyant, and must be tethered so as not to float away. This comically physical manifestation of the dictator's vanity also points to his dependence on foreign support and foreign capital.

The literary critical shorthand for the combination of the demystifying and critical functions of realism with the fantastic, the supernatural, or the nonmimetic is "magical realism." The term is most strongly associated with Latin American literature and the novels of its international "boom" in the 1960s, although it has circulated widely since then. In its broadest sense, "magical realism" refers to the coexistence of the natural and unnatural (or, ordinary and extraordinary) and its defamiliarizing effects (Siskind 2014, 62; Zamora and Faris 1995, 5–6; Warnes 2009, 16). It combines and therefore confounds the hierarchies between the real and the fantastic, positing equivalence between the two domains (Quayson 2006, 728). Like realism, magical realism is an example of what Jameson calls a "hybrid concept" in which an epistemological—or even ontological and often ideologically inflected—claim is presented as an aesthetic ideal (2013, 5–6). It is also, as the wide-ranging body of critical literature suggests, a diffuse and slippery term that oscillates between the status of genre and mode.

The designation of these dictator novels as "magical realism," however, would fail to grasp the specific nature of their departures from realism; nor would it account for the implications of this departure within each individual text. Instead, I argue that the deviations from realism in these novels point to a constitutive problem of the dictator novel; that is: to the difficulty of representing the dictator, as a *literary* figure, as well as to the complicated relationship between literature and history encapsulated by this figure. To grasp this is both to better understand the nature of the dictator novel as a genre and to perceive the limits of literary category as such.

In lieu of rigid classification, and following interventions in genre theory by Jacques Derrida and Wai Chee Dimock, I offer here the more flexible critical category of the "constellation." This is a collection of textual practices associated with the representation of the dictator in the dictator novel of the South Atlantic. It is a purposefully open-ended system to which features may be added or subtracted. I call this constellation "disrupted realisms," and it is within these larger constellations of association that the critical force of the dictator novel becomes clear. My argument unfolds in three parts; first, I outline definitions of my key terms; second, I summarize the history of magical realism and its relationship to Latin American and African literatures; finally, I return to the constellation of disrupted realisms in the dictator novel, laying out the principal coordinates of this assemblage.

The Dictator Novel in the South Atlantic

Already in *The Wretched of the Earth* (*Les damnés de la terre*, 1961) Frantz Fanon warned against the danger of newly independent nations in Africa descending into dictatorship, invoking the "shortsighted fascism that has triumphed for half a century in Latin America" as a cautionary example (2004, 117). Fanon's warning proved prescient. Dictatorships flourished on both sides of the Atlantic during the Cold War, in which Latin America and Africa were interrelated "theaters."[4] The political phenomenon of dictatorship occasioned a literary response: works of resistance and denunciation that aimed to uncover and dislodge the practices of authority on which dictators relied. In brief, the dictator novel is a tool for critique of the dictator.[5] It is distinguished from the larger category of novels about dictatorship by its inclusion of the dictator as a character in the text, up to and including focalization from the dictator's perspective. In its occupation of the dictator's perspective, the dictator novel becomes an analytic endeavor. It is concerned less with the enumeration of the dictator's crimes, although this is a component, than with the critical dissection of the dictator himself (Rama 1976, 10).

Fanon's observations open a comparative itinerary for reading the dictator novel across the South Atlantic. More generally, the history of Cold War dictatorships offers possibilities for comparison across the Global South. A constitutive feature of novels about dictators in the Global South is their attention to the role of foreign powers in instituting and maintaining dictatorships before, during, and after the Cold War. Yet the iconic figure of the so-called Third World dictator—captured in films such as *Bananas* (1971), *The Last King of Scotland* (2006), and *The Dictator* (2012)—is most deeply rooted in the history of dictatorship in Latin America and Africa. While several of the observations I make here may be generalized to the Global South, the specificity of my engagement with the South Atlantic has to do, first, with the particularities of Latin American and

African political and literary history, and, second, with the difficulties of comparison as they pertain to the constitution of the South Atlantic as a framework for thinking about literature.

The term "South Atlantic" presents conceptual challenges, as outlined in the introduction to this volume. It is at once a geographic designation (referring, first, to the ocean and, more broadly, encompassing the Caribbean, Latin America, and Africa), a historical formation (as Luiz Felipe de Alencastro describes in his contribution to this volume), and a conceptual category. To use the term "South Atlantic" is to recall the frameworks of Atlantic studies and the Black Atlantic, which extend over much of the same geographical and historical space. These take as their starting point material relations of circulation and exchange. The South Atlantic shares this history—here the dominant imperial powers were Spain and Portugal—although it has received comparatively little attention. However, the material and conceptual connections (historical analogy; political, cultural, and critical exchange; and shared reading practices) between Latin America and Africa make it a vital space for comparative analysis in the present.

The South Atlantic, further, shares with the term "Global South" a tension between apparent locational clarity and acknowledgement of ideological and political inflections in its definition. In both, the term "South" carries implications of delayed modernization and underdevelopment. Even as its resuscitation in the phrase "Global South" emphasizes South-South cooperation, these connotations remain (Dirlik 2007, 12–15). For literary and cultural critics, what defines the Global South is the recognition of the failures of globalization as a master narrative (López 2007, 3). It is, in this sense, best understood as a political consciousness, and therefore a successor to the Third World as an ideology and project (Mahler 2015, 95–96; Prashad 2012). The same is true of the South Atlantic, in the sense put forward in this volume. As signaled by Fanon and sustained in the present, there is increasing recognition of analogous historical trajectories as well as of continuing material and ideological interconnections, particularly when it comes to issues such as dictatorship, economic marginalization, human rights and postconflict resolution, and the mechanics of international debt. The South Atlantic is an essentially comparative space, and one in which the practice of comparison itself can be submitted to analysis.

Comparison, as method and praxis, has recently been the subject of critical debate for its imbrication with colonialism or Eurocentrism, as well as its tendency to institute hierarchies amongst objects compared.[6] Against hierarchy, models of comparison as relation, equivalence, or juxtaposition have emerged. Because of its historical interconnections, the South Atlantic is an ideal space for what Shu-mei Shih terms "comparison as relation," which approaches texts as part of a network connected by historical intersections or isomorphism (2013, 96). This requires a broader and more properly global conception of history and textual production, one that links the histories of dictatorship and its literary representation in Latin America and Africa. As my intent is to redirect critical attention to the narrative strategies undertaken in the texts themselves, I find Susan Stanford Friedman's notion of "collage" as a juxtapositional comparative methodology particularly useful. Collage here serves as an analogue for "constellation," in its function as a transitive verb; both are compositions. As Friedman explains, collage "maintains the particularity of each [text], refuses hierarchy and instrumentalism, and fosters identification of new generalities based on what texts share" (2011, 759). Rather than assimilate texts to each other (using one to measure the other) via insistence on homology, it reads texts together in their incommensurability, using this to generate new theoretical frameworks.[7] It is from here that my own analysis of the dictator novel in the South Atlantic begins.

The Dictator as Literary Subject and the Problem of Magical Realism

On both sides of the Atlantic, the dictator seems to defy literary representation. To paraphrase Carlos Fuentes, how can the (fiction) writer compete with history? (1993, 92). Along similar lines, Ngũgĩ asks: "How does a novelist capture and hold the interest of the reader when the reality confronting the reader is stranger and more captivating than fiction?" (1986, 78). Another version of this problem is what Achille Mbembe has called the "aesthetics of vulgarity." In *On the Postcolony* (2001), Mbembe describes the ways in which authoritarian rulers make use of the obscene or grotesque as part of the aesthetics and practice of power (2001, 103, 133). To simply point to the dictator's vulgarity or excesses does not suffice as critique; in fact, it misses the ways in which the dictator's subjects, too, find purchase and participate in this system of signs and symbols.

In the larger framework of the dictator novel in Latin America and Africa, there are many works that remain rooted in realism as the vehicle for critique. However, the term "realism" refers less to the narrative mode itself than to the mandate to represent the underlying "truth" of a situation. See, for instance, Josaphat Kubayanda's call for a "new realism" in the introduction to a special issue of *Research in African Literatures* on dictatorship and literature (1990). Yet, following Ngũgĩ, it is not enough to list the dictator's crimes: the task of the writer is to render these in a new light. Here, the use of nonmimetic narrative techniques has less to do with descriptive capacity than with critical potential. It is most often in the ostensibly unrealistic, dreamlike, and outright fantastic moments that these narratives gain meaningful traction. See, for instance, the use of stream-of-consciousness narration and the shifts in narrative perspective to show the many dimensions of life under dictatorship in Miguel Ángel Asturias's *El señor presidente* (*The President*, 1946). The way forward, then, lies through the imaginative and critical capacities of form.

Disorientation and defamiliarization are key strategies for grappling with the dictator as a literary subject. Writing to Mario Vargas Llosa about *Autumn of the Patriarch*, García Márquez declared: "I want to see up to what point it is possible to convert into a poetic narrative the infinite cruelty, the delirious arbitrariness and the immense solitude of that exemplary barbarian of Latin American mythology" (March 20, 1967; my translation). This act of conversion is expressed in the novel's formal complexity. It includes sudden shifts between the dictator's perspective and that of a collective "we," which stands for the dictator's subjects; sudden alternations in narrative time, as the dictator's reign stretches over more than a century; and the use of long, grammatically unwieldy sentences with very few paragraph breaks. The novel, in short, refuses to systematize (simplify) its historical or even political narrative. The resulting disorientation and defamiliarization are part of its "magical" effect.

I the Supreme, meanwhile, is a radically postmodernist text. It mixes real and fictional archival materials, many filled with marginalia of unknown provenance, with the notes of a fictional and mysterious "Compiler," who functions as a stand-in for both the writer and reader. It is not simply that the identity of the narrator or the terms that structure the narrative are purposefully unclear, this novel puts into question the very validity or efficacy of writing as a recording technology. While not "magical" in the same way as García Márquez's novel (indeed, Roa Bastos often seems to be ironizing the tropes of magical realism), it shares with its contemporary the desire to push the limits of narrative form.

Writers also make recourse to alternate cultural sources as means for broaching the dictator. As Ngũgĩ explains, his solution to the representative impasse outlined above was to turn to the Gikuyu oral tradition familiar to his intended audience. He chose the figure of the ogre (*marimũ*)—man-eating creatures that live off the labor of others—as a central metaphor (1986, 81). The ogre plays a key role in *Wizard of the Crow*, as well as Ngũgĩ's first Gikuyu-language novel, *Caitaani Mũtharaba-*

Inĩ (*Devil on the Cross*, 1980).[8] In "The Language of African Fiction," Ngũgĩ describes this as a central development of his "fiction language"; that is: "fiction itself taken as a form of language, with which to effectively communicate with one's targeted audience" (1986, 75).[9] For Ngũgĩ, language choice, form, and content are the three key aspects of a socially relevant critical text (1986, 78).

In the case of *Wizard of the Crow*, the object of critique is not just the dictator, but the long economic, political, cultural, and psychological afterlives of colonization. It is against these forces that Ngũgĩ marshals Gikuyu language and culture. Ngũgĩ's "fiction language," then, draws on the aesthetic principles associated with orality in order to rethink (or "convert") the formal parameters of the novel. The resulting defamiliarization produced by these juxtapositions, along with the incorporation of "unnatural" events, are part of what makes *Wizard of the Crow* "magical." But the quick application of the label "magical realism" to this dictator novel and those like it is debatable.

Following an observation made by Lydie Moudileno in a discussion of Labou Tansi's *Life and a Half*, magical realism tends to function as "a privileged modality for the expression of syncretism, paradox, and other such dualities that characterize contemporary postcolonial societies" (2006, 31). Since its international dissemination with the Latin American literary "boom" of the 1960s, there has been a tendency toward expansive use of the term. Gayatri Spivak, for example, noted its rise to prominence in the criticism of the 1980s, citing a reference to García Márquez as a "paradigmatic case of Third World literary production" (1993, 63). At about the same time, Homi Bhabha declared in the introduction to *Nation and Narration* that magical realism had become, "the literary language of the emergent post-colonial world" (1990, 7).[10] But, as Moudileno argues, such declarations (effectively comparisons) have been a problem for African literature, which tends to be read into the dominant paradigms of non-Western literature rather than on its own terms. In this case, it is magical realism, as identified with a particular moment in the history of the Latin American novel and specifically García Márquez's *Cien años de soledad* (*One Hundred Years of Solitude*, 1967), which, to paraphrase Mariano Siskind, has functioned as the archetypal text of magical realism in its global circulations (2014, 85–95).

The concept of (or, group of ideas associated with) magical realism has a long and piecemeal history.[11] The Cuban writer Alejo Carpentier first theorized the core principles of what he called the Latin American *real maravilloso* (marvelous real) in the prologue to his novel about the Haitian revolution, *El reino de este mundo* (*The Kingdom of this World*, 1949). For Carpentier, the European encounter with the Americas, its natural phenomena, and its people is the constitutive moment of the marvelous real, and it is sustained in the present by the cultural syncretism that has defined the region. Carpentier's formulation was not entirely new. Two decades earlier, the German art critic Franz Roh used the phrase "magic realism" in describing post-expressionist painting, also called New Objectivism.[12] And the marvelous real was not the only precursor for the magical realism of *One Hundred Years of Solitude*. Literary historians have long emphasized the influence of modernist writers—James Joyce and William Faulkner, for example—on the development of the literary aesthetic that would become Latin American magical realism (Martin 1989, 127).

These contending genealogies put pressure on the locational specificity that undergirds Carpentier's notion of the marvelous real. They also make visible the origins of magical realism in the tension between a Latin American investment in cultural autochthony (oriented toward the past, primitivism, and the anthropological turn) and engagement with international modernist or avant-garde movements (oriented toward the future, modernity, and technological development) in the early twentieth century (Rosenberg 2006). Tensions existed not just between Latin America and Europe, but also within Latin American societies. As Alberto Moreiras points out, in Latin America in the 1930s and 1940s there was in the intellectual public sphere a confrontation between "the centripetal forces of regionalism/nationalism and the centrifugal forces of the artistic avant-garde" (2001, 184).

There is a fourth term in the series: *réalisme merveilleux* (marvelous realism). Formulated by the Haitian writer Jacques Stéphen Alexis, marvelous realism helps to bridge questions of ontology (the nature of Latin American reality) and narrative form (its literary expression). Alexis was in explicit dialogue with Carpentier as well as the Haitian *indigéniste* movement, which arose in response to the American occupation of Haiti (1915–34). Like Carpentier, Alexis gestures to European arrival in the Americas as a starting point (1956, 252). But, unlike Carpentier, who speaks of indigenous and African cultures only as resources or archives, Alexis emphasizes their continued evolution and ongoing influence (1956, 250–251; Dash 1998, 95).

Moreover, Alexis frames his discussion in clearly political terms. At stake here, once again, is the content of the term "realism" as it pertains to audience and the question of politically committed literature:

> [R]ealism for Haitian artists means beginning to speak in the same language as their people. Haitian Marvelous Realism [the marvelous realism of the Haitians] is therefore an integral part of Social Realism, in its Haitian form it follows the same concerns. The wealth of tales, legends, the symbolic systems of music, choreography, and of the visual arts [*plastique*], all the forms of Haitian popular art [can] aid the nation in resolving the problems and in accomplishing the goals that lie before it. (1956, 268; my translation)

Many writers identified as "magical realists," including García Márquez and Ben Okri, insist that they are in fact social realists (Gaylard 2005, 38; Zamora and Faris 1995, 4). To take such statements at face value, however, would be to ratify an ethnographic understanding of magical realism, effectively treating it as a form of "marginal realism" (Takolander 2007). Alexis does not claim that Haitian reality is itself "marvelous" or "magical." The drive of marvelous realism is not toward representative (mimetic) fidelity to an external reality, but instead toward effective communication (critique) in order to bring about political change. Here, Alexis recalls the conclusions Ngũgĩ reaches in "The Language of African Fiction." Like Alexis, Ngũgĩ's aim is to speak to the people about their present political reality in a familiar (literal and figurative) "language." This approach shares the critical, demystifying function of realism, but disrupts the particular textual features associated with that narrative mode.

I have in the preceding paragraphs moved from the question of ontological specificity and cultural autochthony to the disruption of inherited or borrowed cultural forms with the aim of crafting a locally specific representation of lived experience. Yet these articulations of magical realism in its various permutations remain unclear on the subject of formal prescriptions. It is an umbrella term, at best. In the face of this ambiguity, critics argue that magical realism retains explanatory power, that it can be a "decolonizing agent," and that it represents both an appealing disruptive force and an articulation of the "politics of the possible" (Cooper 1998, 15; Faris 2004, 1; Slemon 1995, 408; Sangari 1987, 157). With this in mind, it is possible to reread Bhabha's declaration that magical realism is the literary language of the postcolonial world as an appeal to the possible utility of the label "magical realism" as a bridging mechanism for reading together geographically and historically far-flung texts; facilitating, for example, comparative work in the South Atlantic.

But such readings risk overdetermination. The celebration of magical realism as a disruptive force always also risks reifying difference, and, by extension, making all forms of difference equivalent. It similarly threatens to flatten the internal cultural dynamics that supply that "disruptive" material (Morieras 2001, 145; Franco 2002, 159). The most pressing risk, for my purposes, is the extent to which magical realism has become the default mode in which texts from Latin America—as well as the South Atlantic and Global South—are read. In this sense, the problem of magical realism resembles the problem of genre's double function as classificatory and exclusionary apparatus (Derrida 1980; Dimock 2006).

In order to illustrate this problem, I return to Labou Tansi's *Life and a Half*, which narrates the reign of the Providential Guides, a line of dictators "supplied" by an unnamed European power. As the novel progresses, characters and generations proliferate and repeat at a dizzying pace. In the final third, a portion of the original country secedes, sparking a highly technological arms race and, later, open warfare. Both countries are reduced to radioactive ash and, at the end of the novel, one character (Jean Calcium) emerges from an underground shelter to find a new political order in which people have "chosen reality" and refuse to speak of the past. The novel has been compared to *One Hundred Years of Solitude* and treated as an example of magical realism transported—or, translated—to Africa.[13] There are similarities, but the vision of technology expressed in the final third of the novel is a far cry from, for instance, the encounter of the villagers in Macondo with the various technological wonders that the gypsies bring on their annual visits.

This critical slippage is the target of Moudileno's essay "Magical Realism: 'Arme miraculeuse' for the African Novel?" in which she argues that the latter sections of *Life and a Half* should be read not as magical realism but as science fiction, privileging its concern with technology and orientation toward the future (2006, 34–35). Here, magical realism and science fiction are taken to be mutually exclusive. If the fantastic (including magic and the mythical) is the defining trait of magical realism, for science fiction it is the incorporation of future-oriented technological speculations, which keeps it grounded in rationalism (Jameson 2005, 63). But in practice these are not hard and fast distinctions; as Eric Smith observes, both magical realism and science fiction serve the dialectical function of yoking together incommensurable realities (2012, 4). Moreover, in recent years there has been a postcolonial reclaiming of science fiction in a critical gesture that has upturned the conventions of the genre (Langer 2011, 9).

With this in mind, Moudileno's emphasis on the turn to science fiction in *Life and a Half* proposes to shift the ways in which "Africa" is read, challenging the foundational oppositions that have historically coded the continent as the space of ahistorical "magic," as well as violence and barbarism (2006, 35–36). Moudileno's fruitful analysis of *Life and a Half* can be pushed further. At its end, the novel reinscribes its nuclear apocalypse into a myth of origin. Immediately after describing the scene of nuclear destruction, the narrator adds: "Rain fell on Felix-Ville for two months after Jean Calcium had stopped sending his murderous vibrations. This is how the Nile, that witnessed the births of all the pharaohs, was born, along with the Nyassa, the Victoria, and the lake region" (2011, 131). Time, already distended, becomes cyclical and the narrative is reframed as a prehistoric myth in which we might read the codes that govern the present. This gesture recalls the conclusion of *One Hundred Years of Solitude*, in which the last member of the Buendía family deciphers the prophesy of their history as Macondo is destroyed by the wind. The turn to the cyclical temporality of myth, moreover, accords with Labou Tansi's assertion in the opening warning (*Avertissement*) that the novel should be read as a fable.

At the end of *Life and a Half*, then, the reader is left with a series of overlapping possible registers in which to read the novel: fable, magical realism, science fiction, and myth. It would be a mistake to privilege any of these to the exclusion of the others. The novel's narrative polymodality is in fact a feature and not a bug of the dictator novel, produced by the challenge of representing the dictator as a literary figure. *Life and a Half* is best understood as a collage or constellation of narrative registers, each of which is mobilized in the service of narrating as literature (fiction) the particular history of dictatorship with which it is concerned. In a wider frame, this novel as a dictator novel is part of a constellation of textual practices that cannot be reduced to the category of "magical realism."

Disrupted Realisms in the Dictator Novel

At the beginning of this essay I referred to a constellation of aesthetic practices associated with political critique in the dictator novel. I used the word "constellation" to name a set of features, one or several of which may be present in a given text and, conversely, none of which is definitive. My thinking follows recent moves toward more open critical frameworks better suited to accounting for nuances or deviations from the established norm, such as Ato Quayson's identification of four "issue clusters" in magical realism in the essay "Fecundities of the Unexpected."[14] This turn has been motivated by the expansion of literary fields, as in the case of the new World Literature or the emergence of "global" Modernism, and consequent challenges to established taxonomy, terminology, or methodology.[15] In each case, as in my own juxtapositional collage of dictator novels across the South Atlantic, the goal is a critical apparatus that will allow further-flung comparisons, accommodating new texts, features, and questions as the network expands. I am here at once describing and performing a mode of reading. In what follows, I use a selection (collage) of dictator novels to identify a constellation of aesthetic practices that both deviate from the norms of realism and exceed the category of magical realism. I gather these under the general title of "disrupted realisms."

My use of the plural "realisms" aligns with a question raised by Carpentier in a 1966 interview on the topic of politically committed writing: why "realism" in the singular (1985, 141)? Carpentier here points to the limitations of a totalizing and transcendent model for realism, as a singular notion of realism does not allow for variations of the concept across time and space. With this, as well as Alexis and Ngũgĩ's theorization of locally oriented aesthetic practices in mind, realism must be treated as a pliable or open-ended category to which elements may be added or subtracted. These additions or subtractions, which I term "disruptions," produce differing versions of realism, necessitating the plural. In what follows, I outline some principal coordinates (these are the "clusters") in the taxonomic constellation of disrupted realisms in the dictator novel of the South Atlantic. This map highlights key elements, with much overlap between individual clusters. It is, in this sense, a preliminary sketch.

The first and most common cluster concerns the resistance to, skepticism toward, or exhaustion of the critical potential of (strictly defined) realism as a narrative mode. This attitude is expressed in the recourse to alternate generic formulae or modes, including the fantastic or supernatural, romance, myth, fable, and even science fiction. The shift is occasionally explicitly announced, as in the opening warning of *Life and the Half*. More often, however, this critical stance is signaled by the purposeful departure, however brief, from the formal conventions of realism as well as in self-reflexive, metafictional, or postmodernist destabilizations of the narrative. *I the Supreme*, *Autumn of the Patriarch*, *Waiting for the Vote of the Wild Animals*, and *Wizard of the Crow* are all examples.

The second cluster, closely related to the first, concerns the incorporation of popular, vernacular, oral, and autochthonous modes of representation, tropes, or figures. Recalling Ngũgĩ and Alexis, this is not just a means for reflecting local reality, but a heuristic device intended to help the audience interpret that reality. In *Waiting for the Vote of the Wild Animals*, for instance, Kourouma structures the narrative around the performance of a *donsomana* (a Malinké praise poem recited for members of the hunter clan) for the recently ousted dictator, Koyaga. The *donsomana* is a ritual of purification and its completion will allow Koyaga to reclaim power. In order to effectively purify, however, the *donsomana* must also double as a denunciation of the dictator's crimes.

Importantly, these interpolations at once refer to their source and activate new networks of critical and textual interconnection. Ngũgĩ provides a useful example: in *Devil on the Cross*, the ogre functions as a figure for the rapacious national bourgeoisie. When the ogre reappears in *Wizard of the Crow*, however, it is both a reference to Gikuyu orature and an intertextual reference to Ngũgĩ's earlier work; this is emphasized by the many references to *Devil on the Cross* in *Wizard of the Crow*. The ogre also becomes the vector along which Ngũgĩ makes transnational literary allusions, as when a character compares her situation to that of a woman kidnaped by an "ogre" in Amos Tutuola's *The Palm-Wine Drinkard* (2006, 202). The reference itself is imprecise, but the point is the gesture rather than specific content of the allusion.[16] These interpolations are not simply references back to autochthonous cultural formations; they function as literary, intertextual, and intercultural points of contact, activating new and wide-ranging networks of association.

The third cluster comprises the purposeful disorientation or defamiliarization of the reader. This is achieved by the dislocation of the narrative in time or space, as well as on the level of language itself, as in the use of rhetorical strategies intended to unsettle the reader's sense of the real in the world of the text. Examples include the proliferation of characters with very similar names in Labou Tansi's *Life and a Half*. Repetition here not only disorients, it signals the circularity of violence, anticipating the status of primordial myth conferred on the narrative at the novel's conclusion. Along slightly different lines, the continual disorientation of the reader can serve an instructive function. The sudden shifts in narrative focalization in *Autumn of the Patriarch*, for instance, serve to activate the reader as a critical presence in the text. As Ángel Rama has pointed out, the absence of a positive moral force (that is, of a character who stands in opposition to the dictator) in the novel requires the reader to assume that position (1976, 53).

Estrangement, disorientation, and uncertainty also work at the thematic level. The narrator of *Wizard of the Crow*, for instance, repeatedly puts the truth of events reported into question. At the beginning of a section in which the Ruler visits the United States, the narrator appeals to the audience for help in recalling the story, as no one can be in two places at once (2006, 273). This gesture incorporates the reader into the production of the narrative, implicitly aligning her with the narrator's (antidictator) project and invoking the critical function of collective memory and even rumor in opposition to the "official" record. It is, once again, a call to critical (skeptical) thinking on the part of the reader. Similarly, the interweaving of real and fictive historical documents in *I the Supreme* functions as what Linda Hutcheon has called "historiographic metafiction." Here, the past is not an "it" in the sense of objectified reality, but something that can only be grasped through its narration in—and within the interests of—the present (1988, 57). The uncertainty resulting from this is a source of anxiety for the dictator, since he desires total control over not only the nation but also the historical record. The impossibility of this desire folds outward and comes to define the role of the Compiler in the text.

As in previous points of the constellation, this third cluster is a broad grouping that shares elements with other categorical and period designations, including magical realism, modernism, and postmodernism. This is what is meant by reading texts in their incommensurability, and it is here that the model of a constellation most clearly pushes against more rigid organizing frameworks. In refusing to separate *Wizard of the Crow* (for the fantastic swelling and buoyancy of the ruler) from *I the Supreme* (for its metafictional play with the conventions of historiography) according to period, literary tradition, or continent, I am able to highlight the points of convergence between these two rather different dictator novels without pushing either into a categorical designation into which it does not fully fit.

The final cluster in this constellation includes narrative or thematic attention to the global distribution of power, questions of economy (including the function of markets, the fetish nature of the commodity, and large-scale inequalities), and a concern with technology and the potential outcomes of technological innovation that bends toward science fiction. Dictatorship in the South Atlantic, and the Global South more generally, is necessarily embedded within larger global networks of political and economic power. Accordingly, dictator novels of the South Atlantic are crowded with foreign actors, whether they be the "foreign country that supplies the Guides" in *Life and a Half* or the US Marines in *Autumn of the Patriarch*, whose presence links local events to a global network of political and economic interests.

Technology, in both its existing forms and its speculative inventions, frequently serves as the medium for the expression of these concerns. For instance, while *Life and a Half* opens with that scene in which the Providential Guide cannibalizes Martial, a few generations later the practice is transformed. Instead of eating a dissident journalist, the (current) Guide has his European doctor transplant the journalist's major organs into his own body (2011, 113–115). In *Wizard of the Crow*, meanwhile, transplants, cosmetic surgery, and genetic engineering offer the promise of physical and thereby social transformation. At the start of the novel, three of the dictator's henchmen undergo surgeries abroad to enlarge their eyes, ears, and tongue (respectively) in order to secure better positions in his cabinet, offering themselves as the dictator's enhanced eyes, ears, and mouthpiece.

Ngũgĩ further interweaves the transformative function of cosmetic surgery with the vernacular figure of the ogre. During a visit to the United States, a government functionary (Tajirika) is handed an advertisement for a mysterious company called "Genetica, Inc.," which promises complete physical transformation. Tajirika enthusiastically begins the process of transforming himself into a white man. But the company is shut down, leaving him only partially changed. Although Tajirika tries to keep his condition secret, his daughter spots him one day and believes that ogres have taken over her father's body, as they do in stories (2006, 741–743). In tracing Tajirika's transformation to Genetica, Inc., Ngũgĩ rewrites the vernacular figure of the ogre as the kind of monstrous hybrid that is the stuff of science fiction; as Ian P. MacDonald has observed, Tajirika here is not an ogre, but a "cybogre" (2016, 72). This *generic* transformation facilitates the observation that the most "magical" of things come from the progressions of science itself. In doing so, much like Labou Tansi, Ngũgĩ locates his novel firmly within the future-oriented (technological) progress of history.

The clusters I have laid out here are, once again, intended as a preliminary outline to which further examples, specifications, and even clusters may be appended. To paraphrase Wai Chee Dimock on genre, the disrupted realisms I describe constitute a provisional set that will always be bent, pulled, and stretched by its many subsets (2006, 86). Bending, pulling, and stretching are inevitable, because this is a volatile and necessarily incomplete body of material. The purpose of the term "disrupted realisms," therefore, is to point to the multiplicity of engagements with the problem of realism in the dictator novel of the South Atlantic and thereby serve as the starting point for a more careful analysis of individual texts.

In closing, while critical realism would seem to be the narrative mode most suited to the denunciation of the dictator in the dictator novel, the variety of examples I have discussed demonstrate the limitations of that premise. The term "realism" itself names a diffuse and wide-ranging set of textual practices and interpretative imperatives (Jameson 2013, 2–3). Magical realism, a frequently applied substitute, presents many of the same difficulties. More importantly, use of the label "magical realism" also invokes a series of literary associations (particularly with Latin American literature in the 1960s) that risks foreclosing careful analysis of the text at hand, collapsing categorization into interpretation. The more flexible and mobile assemblage (the constellation) I have outlined in this essay is intended to counteract these analytical problems, while acknowledging that some provisional sense of association or category is necessary for discussion to take place.

The problem of genre as an interpretative category weaves throughout this essay. Even as I have insisted on the particularity of the dictator novel as a narrative type and the specificity of the dictator novel of the South Atlantic, I use the term "genre" with hesitation. The dictator novel of the South Atlantic exists at the place of overlap of content (the South Atlantic dictator as literary figure) and literary form (the disruptions or bending of the representative imperatives of realism as a narrative mode for the purposes of political critique). The term "genre" is a useful name for this overlap, but its use should not overdetermine the analysis of individual texts.

Having come to this endpoint through the piecemeal work of comparative collage, which allowed me to identify new generalities based on what these texts share, I return to Ngũgĩ's deceptively simple phrase, "fiction language." This is the proposition that fiction itself functions as a literal and figurative language with which the writer communicates with an audience. The term not only incorporates the question of audience, as do discussions of *littérature engagée*, it also allows for a much wider conception of the features, ranging between content and form, which define particular texts or groupings of texts. To speak of political critique as part of "fiction language," therefore, is to acknowledge the centrality of ideology often buried in discussions of terms such as "realism" and "magical realism." The political critique of the dictator novel of the South Atlantic, then, is directed not just at the problem of dictatorship (and the global forces that sustain it) but also at reading practices that would reduce their strategic disruptions of realism to the confirmation of existing stereotype.

NOTES

I am grateful to Anne Garland Mahler, Lanie Millar, and Tara Mendola for their comments and edits. Thanks also to John Patrick Walsh for his discussion of Alexis as well as to the participants in the Humanities Center Colloquium at the University of Pittsburgh, where I presented an early draft.

1. Examples include José Mármol's *Amalia* (1855), Juana Manso's *Los misterios del Plata* (1855), Miguel Ángel Asturias's *El señor presidente* (1946), Alejo Carpentier's *El recurso del método* (1974), Ousmane Sembène's *Le dernier de l'Empire* (1981), Henri Lopès's *Le pleurer-rire* (1982), and Chinua Achebe's *Anthills of the Savannah* (1987).

2. Rita Barnard observes a similar phenomenon in South Africa's post-apartheid literature of transition. Referring to Zakes Mda's *Ways of Dying* (1995), she notes that it "decisively breaches the generic constraints that the culture of resistance, with its demand for realist immediacy, had for years placed on the black writer" (2004, 280).

3. I have analyzed the critical function of fetish objects in dictator novels at length elsewhere; see Armillas-Tiseyra (2014).

4. The attempts to found a South Atlantic Treaty Organization (SATO) described in the introduction to this volume were an expression of that interconnection.

5. In Latin America, the dictator novel precedes the Cold War and has its roots in the political unrest (the rise of dictatorships) that followed independence in the nineteenth century. In Anglophone and Francophone African literatures, meanwhile, the dictator novel emerged as a subset of the larger category of the novels of political disillusionment, which followed the nationalist literature of the late-colonial and independence periods.

6. For an outline of these debates, see the volume *Comparison: Theories, Approaches, Uses* (2013), which collects essays from *New Literary History* 40 (3) (2009) and *PMLA* 126 (3) (2011) and 128 (3) (2013).

7. As Friedman acknowledges, there are risks to this more open and flexible structure: "The danger of juxtapositional comparison is the license it might provide to juxtapose willy-nilly, for the sake of conjunction without assurance of productive comparison. (Sometimes, juxtaposition is just juxtaposition, not comparison)" (2011, 758). In practical terms, this requires that the critic herself sustain the validity or soundness of a comparison, rather than presume its justification emanates from the texts themselves.

8. For more on Ngũgĩ's advocacy for writing in African languages, see Ngũgĩ (1986).

9. Ngũgĩ's concept of "fiction language" is intimately bound with questions of orality. In his more recent criticism, Ngũgĩ presents the oral tradition not just as a source of tropes or figures, but also as a set of aesthetic principles. Specifically, orality recognizes the interconnections of art forms as a reflection of the interconnectedness of reality (2012, 73–75). Ngũgĩ himself connects orality to magical realism, via a discussion of Kamau Brathwaite's

use of the term (2012, 75). This rests on their shared capacity to confound existing critical categories.

10. The trend continues: a recent issue of *ARIEL* (47.3, 2016) featured a cluster of essays on magical realism, including discussions of Karen Tei Yamashita's *Through the Arc of the Rain Forest* (1990), Junot Díaz's *The Brief and Wondrous Life of Oscar Wao* (2007), and Alexis Wright's *The Swan Book* (2013).

11. For a discussion of the circulations of magical realism as a "world literary discourse" see the chapter "The Global Life of Genres and the Material Travels of Magical Realism" in Siskind (2014).

12. Roh's essay was published in 1925; a Spanish translation appeared *Revista de Occidente* in 1927. Carpentier discusses Roh in a later piece, "The Baroque and the Marvelous Real" (1975), where magic realism is assimilated to surrealism. See Guenther (1995) for a contextual overview of Roh's "magic realism."

13. Moudileno quotes the publisher of Éditions du Seuil describing Labou Tansi's novel as an "echo of other literatures, especially Latin American literature" (2006, 36). She, in turn, pointedly avoids reference to Latin America in defining "magical realism," citing instead a definition from M. H. Abrams's *Glossary of Literary Terms* (2006, 30).

14. Quayson's four clusters or "narrative problems" within magical realism are: (1) generic blurring and the status of the real; (2) metaphorical-literality chains; (3) magical realism and the representation of space, time, and space-time; and (4) magical realism and the philosophy of history.

15. For instance, in reconsidering genre as one possible vector along which to remake the organizational logic of the discipline, Dimock proposes a "broader constellation," which would make visible the coevolution and cross-fertilization of literary forms (2006, 91). Jessica Berman, meanwhile, in reframing modernism as a global phenomenon proposes it be seen as "a constellation of rhetorical actions, attitudes, or aesthetic occasions" (2012, 7).

16. The reference in *Wizard of the Crow* is to the episode of the "complete" (or, "full-bodied") gentleman in *Palm-Wine Drinkard.* This is the story of a Skull who rents body parts to impress and kidnap the daughter of a village head, who in turn enlists the Drinkard to rescue his daughter (1984, 200–213). Both the Skull and the ogre represent magical and malicious forces that operate through trickery or deception, which is the basis for the allusion.

PART III

Global South Atlantic Futures

Postwar Politics in *O Herói* and *Kangamba*

Lanie Millar

Recent analyses of cultural texts about Cuban participation (1975–91) in the Angolan civil war (1975–2002) assert that through Cuba's African interventions, Cuba and Angola solidified their independent revolutionary agendas around notions of African-diasporic solidarity.[1] The ideological framework of Cuba and Angola's alliance exerted a profound effect on the cultural landscapes of both countries. In both locales, literary and cinematic production were conceived of as a fundamental realm of revolutionary action and internationalist collaboration; documentaries, fiction films, poetry, and narrative celebrating the war effort marked the early years of the military collaboration between Cuba and the ruling MPLA (Movimento Popular para a Libertação de Angola/Popular Movement for the Liberation of Angola) in Angola, and were framed as examples of a broader project of international cooperation and examples of transatlantic solidarity that opposed colonial and imperialist incursions into the Global South. However, the postwar period has sparked an ongoing cultural debate about the legacy of these solidarities and the styles in which they were articulated. This essay will explore how two early twenty-first century films, *O herói* (*The Hero*, Angola, 2004) and *Kangamba* (Cuba, 2008) cite documentary cinematic styles and the rhetoric of revolutionary collaboration and friendship from the 1960s and '70s but give them new meaning in the post–Cold War period.

Each of the two films refers to the revolutionary impulse of the early war years in the context of the post–Cold War confrontation with the global circulation of cultural and economic capital. *Kangamba* serves as an example of what historian Rafael Rojas identifies as a post–Cold War restorative impulse that remembers the early years of Cuban revolutionary orthodoxy as stable and purposeful (Rojas 2009, 55 and 120–121) in its depiction of the military and humanitarian collaboration between Cubans and Angolans during a battle in the Angolan civil war. A more critical take on the legacy of the war, *O herói* tells the story of an Angolan ex-soldier struggling to reintegrate into civilian society and the relationships he builds with a former prostitute and a presumed orphan. Considering the two films together will expose how both films assert the importance of understanding the relationship between past politics of South-South solidarity and postwar paradigms of neoliberal development, in which notions of ideological solidarity are blunted, made less visible, or disappear altogether. While *Kangamba* implies a continuity between the 1960s–80s internationalist projects and Cuba's updated international collaboration in "human" capital rather than material investment (Huish and Blue 2013, 8) and opposition to exploitive neocolonial relations between North and South, *O herói*'s ironic allusions to past politics of solidarity point to their failures to realize the social and political changes their architects imagined. Thus *O herói* complicates the notion that histories of South-South relations are, in and of themselves, a sufficient basis for an ongoing politics and poetics of liberation. Taken together, the two films suggest different strategies of how to update histories of internationalist, anticolonial, and anti-imperial collaboration.

Kangamba *and Cuban Revolutionary Cinema*

Kangamba represents a seven-day battle that took place in the village of Cangamba, Angola, in 1983, eight years after official Angolan independence was achieved in 1975—a year that also saw Cuban military troops' arrival in Angola and the transition from colonial war to civil war between the major battling political factions within the country. Between 1975 and 1989, Cuba provided major material support via its relationship with the Soviet Union, as well as strategic support for the leftist MPLA and its armed division, FAPLA (Forças Armadas Para a Libertação de Angola/

Armed Forces for the Liberation of Angola; see Gleijeses 1996–67, 12–13). By 1983 the MPLA's major domestic rival, UNITA (União para a Independência Total de Angola/Union for the Total Independence of Angola), was sustained primarily by the South African proapartheid regime, and covertly by the United States (Gleijeses 2002, 353–358). In the battle depicted in *Kangamba*, an outmanned allied contingency of Cuban and FAPLA forces successfully holds off a much stronger and better-equipped UNITA and South African coalition. The film's director, Rogelio París, has noted in interviews that he intends to present not a testimonial view but rather a (re)creative one, a fact he deliberately highlights in the spelling change from Cangamba the town to the film's title of *Kangamba* (París 2010). The film inserts itself into the decades-long official Cuban narrative of African siblinghood and third-world solidarity through which the island nation's postrevolutionary internationalist missions are narrated. París's resulting film, which references both Cuba's postrevolutionary cinematic innovation and its documentary tradition, draws its viewers into a melodramatic narrative, where the members of UNITA are cast as the puppets of a manipulative, racist, and greedy South African leadership and the Cuban soldiers as friends and defenders of Angolan freedom and national integrity, creating for its assumedly sympathetic viewership "a sort of homage to those lives that weren't given in vain" in Angola (París 2010).[2] Notions of self-recognition and siblinghood among the Cuban and Angolan soldiers are established through the personal relationships the Cuban and Angolan soldiers develop, interlingual practices mixing Spanish and Portuguese in conversation, and a common concern for protecting the civilian communities from wartime suffering.

Both technically and thematically, *Kangamba* alludes to a narrative and an aesthetic in line with a revolutionary style developed through the 1960s and 1970s, and it follows a number of fiction and documentary films about the Angolan experience from the 1970s–90s. It is París's second film about the war, following 1990's *Caravana* (*Caravan*), and is the first in a trilogy of reconsiderations of the war named for three decisive battles, including *Sumbe* (2011) and a third film, expected to be titled *Cuito Cuanavale* (Izquierdo 2011).[3] *Kangamba* offers a nostalgic portrayal of the battle at Cangamba as the height of internationalist collaboration, and thus rearticulates the place for utopian Cuban internationalism in the post–Cold War dissolution of binary global alliances. Consistent with a 1960s–70s revolutionary narrative of trans–Third World solidarity, *Kangamba* insists on the necessity of characterizing Cuban and Angolan alliances as anticolonial, antiracist brotherhoods. The twenty-first-century context in which these revolutionary discourses are resurrected, however, points to a new neoliberal enemy-symbolized in the South African invading forces in Cangamba—who stands in for the imperialist capitalist world alliance. As Huish and Blue signal, Cuba's ongoing internationalist projects can be "understood as a rejection of the sort of foreign relations that entail hegemonic processes of dependency and neo-colonialism" (Huish and Blue 2013, 8). Thus, *Kangamba* might be read as drawing upon Cuba's unique history of internationalist collaboration to argue for an enduring difference in the post–Cold War era between the Global North's shift to neoliberal market-based assistance to the Global South and Cuba's collaborative approach to international solidarity and development.

Cuban film after the establishment of the ICAIC (Instituto Cubano de Artes e Industrias Cinematográficas/Cuban Institute of Cinematic Arts and Industries), the first cultural institution founded after the revolution, took revolutionary action in Cuba and elsewhere in the world as a primary subject of both documentary and fiction films.[4] The subject matter of these films is intimately related to the broader prerogative articulated by Cuban filmmaker Juan García Espinosa in his seminal essay "Por un cine imperfecto" (For an Imperfect Cinema, 1967). Imperfect cinema would erase the division between artist and viewer, making the production and reception of the artistic product part of the same revolutionary action; the function of the filmmaker or individual protagonist is suppressed in favor of a collective, allegorical protagonism. According to Michael Chanan, imperfect cinema fits into broader movements for "cultural decolonization" (Chanan 2004, 306) called for across the Global South, by articulating a new cinematic poetics driven by the new revolutionary context. This poetics would be characterized by a film's explicit attempt to demystify the filmmaking process by making its collaborative nature visible, rather than relying on the myth of the single *auteur* filmmaker; by reflecting the values held by the broader social collective, rather than the vision of a director or producers alone; and would conceptualize film as provoking a response from its audience, including them in its "action" (Burton 1997, 128–129; Chanan 1997, 377). Imperfect cinema has much in common, therefore, with other contemporaneous theorizations of Latin American cinema, such as Fernando Solanas and Octavio Getino's "Hacia un tercer cine" (Toward a Third Cinema, 1969) which recasts the vocabulary of the "three worlds" in circulation during the mid- to late twentieth century.[5] Third Cinema, as a project of cultural decolonization, calls for a participatory aesthetic that mobilizes and politicizes its viewers (Solanas and Getino 1969, 44).

Narratively and cinematically, *Kangamba* reflects the participatory artistic practice theorized in Espinosa's and in Solanas and Getino's essays. The film draws on a number of techniques to portray the Cuban Revolution's refrain of resistance to imperial powers and solidarity with African-descended peoples through a rhetoric of anti-imperial resistance, friendship across the Third World, and racial solidarity among colonized and formerly colonized areas of the globe (Castro 1975; Gleijeses 2006, 103).[6] Technically, the film reflects this discourse in a lack of differentiation between FAPLA and Cuban operatives in the film: the Cuban and FAPLA soldiers speak to each other in a fluid mix of mutually comprehensible Spanish and Portuguese (although the Portuguese is subtitled) and wear similar fatigues, deemphasizing differences among them and allowing the Cuban viewers to see themselves as assistants in world decolonization projects. One of the film's primary characters, the Cuban Captain Mayito, develops a friendship with the Angolan medic João, as well as a romantic relationship with João's schoolteacher sister, Maria. Mayito and João's conversations, during which each character speaks his native language without confusion, contrast with the scenes in which the black UNITA commanders communicate with their white South African benefactors, who use Afrikaans for conversations to which the Angolans do not have access, and who demand English as a mutual language of domination.

The names of the two Angolan characters, João and Maria, are common to the point of generic, and therefore they stand in for the larger Angolan community in the style of the anonymous testimonials common in Cuban documentaries of the 1960s–1970s. In these films, individuals' testimonies about a given social or political situation are meant to serve as allegorical representations of the experiences of the broader public, and thus appear with minimal or no biographical information. As protagonists, Mayito, João, and Maria represent three of the areas of development that have been the focus of Cuba's internationalist missions through the latter half of the twentieth century, including its aid to Angola: military assistance, education, and medicine. The three characters' intersecting collaboration in these areas reinforces the allegorical nature of their functions in the film.

The strategies of mutual identification and allegorical representation of the conflict as part of a global fight against colonialism and oppression appear in very similar form in Cuba's previous films about the Angolan war. By 1976, the first two documentaries about the Angolan intervention had appeared: *Angola, vitória da esperança* (*Angola, victory of hope*, 1976) directed by José Massip, which narrates the history of Portuguese colonialism that led to the war for independence, and *La guerra en Angola* (*The war in Angola*, 1976) directed by Miguel Fleitas. The two films were produced during a period of a flowering of documentary activity focused on internationalist solidarity around the world, and employed techniques that had come to mark Cuban cinema during the 1960s and 1970s. For example, in *La guerra en Angola*, Fleitas employs anonymous interview subjects accompanied by explanatory voiceover to establish a similarly allegorical function for the interviewees' testimonies. In one example, a young man identified as a FAPLA sergeant and former prisoner of UNITA testifies to having witnessed a number of Americans collaborating with UNITA, implicating the opposition parties in a larger project of global imperialism. He bolsters his observation by calling upon the townspeople to corroborate his identification of the foreigners. In a later scene, a woman testifies to witnessing UNITA's slaughter of a number of villagers, including the interviewee's father, for suspected collaboration with the MPLA.[7] In each of these cases, the scenes begin with close-ups of the interviewees' faces as they begin to speak, and as their testimony continues, the camera slowly pans out to include the interviewer and the filmmaking apparatus such as microphones, cameras and camera operators. The documentary stages not only the testimony of the witnesses speaking as representatives of larger populations, but also the act of capturing the interview on film itself. In making the process of filming visible within the documentary, the focus remains on the collaborative process rather than the finished product.

Other strategies that Fleitas's documentary employs place the Cuban collaborators as part of a larger international collective that includes the Angolan people. Alongside Angolan witnesses, the filmmaker includes interviews with Cuban soldiers and doctors about their missions in Angola, as well as newsreels, shots of headlines, and speeches from both Fidel Castro and Angolan president Agostinho Neto. While the majority of the Portuguese in the film is translated into Spanish in subtitles, several scenes are left in Portuguese, including an Angolan news segment reporting on the MPLA's capture of South African prisoners as proof of South Africa's meddling in internal Angolan affairs, reported to a cadre of international journalists through the Minister of Information and a FAPLA commander. The visual footage that accompanies the report depicts news conferences and journalists taking down reports from MPLA officials. The scene thus manifests the revolution's mandate to document and expose worldwide struggles against oppression, but also, in its reliance on visual footage and Portuguese without subtitles, points to documentary film's unique legibility to Cuban and international audiences. The scene is presented as intelligible both in the visual presentation and in the language of reporting, reinforcing the notion both of a shared language of oppression and of resistance across the South Atlantic.

A photographer and documentarian character included among the Cuban contingency as part of the narrative structure of *Kangamba* represents this important area of the internationalist missions, whose images and footage are incorporated into *Kangamba*'s diegetic world. Although mostly shot in color, the film inserts black and white documentary-style footage to signal various key points of collaboration among the FAPLA and Cuban soldiers: Cuban instructors teach FAPLA soldiers to use their weapons, soldiers construct a bread oven and water crops, and scouts discover grenades and signs that announce the borders of UNITA's territory. In each case, the presentation of seemingly rough footage, the whirring sound of the camera, and the vacillation between the documentarian's point of view and the extradiegetic perspective clearly reference the styles of imperfect cinema that dominate Cuban filmmakers' interpretations of domestic and international issues. It underlines París's stated objective of using the fiction film medium to represent the real experiences of "men and women in war," where the men and women are not far-off others but part of a collective that includes the films' viewers (París 2010).

The film's incorporation of these "documentary" shots, concentrated in the first quarter of the film, augments a message of verisimilitude and reminds its viewers that the history of the Angolan intervention has played a fundamental role in the course of the political and social trajectory of the Cuban Revolution. In one scene that cuts back and forth between the documentary style and the fictional world depicted in the film, schoolchildren perform a patriotic play on a stage flanked by twin Angolan and Cuban flags. The documentarian's lens intercuts point of view shots of the performers and then the Cubans and Angolans in the audience watching the play. The technique enhances the impression of *Kangamba* as a celebratory patriotic war memorial to the veterans of the conflict, but it also suggests in the multiple points of view where different groups are alternately shown as the viewers and the subjects of performances that the Cuban and Angolan soldiers' resistance to global imperialism can be reproduced in a recognizable form by different actors and in different locations. The technique of a play-within-a-documentary-within-a-film allows each subject—the schoolchildren performers, the soldiers viewing the play, the documentarian, and implicitly, the directors and the viewers of *Kangamba*—to serve as both protagonist and audience. This double impression reveals the allegorical nature of the conflict. In positing this parallel among the three performances, *Kangamba* insists on the consistency of its message of horizontal solidarities across the Global South as an effective organization for military and ideological resistance to whatever external threat the larger geopolitical context may present. By suggesting the replication of resistance among different generations of participants, the scene also expands the relevancy of this message to the early twenty-first-century moment of its production.

By contrast, in the scenes that depict interactions between the South African and UNITA leaders, visual and linguistic distinctions among the supposed allies create multiple modes of separation between the South Africans and UNITA soldiers. The South African officials and the UNITA general wear different colors of uniforms; while they rely on English as a common language of communication, the South Africans speak to one another in Afrikaans. The linguistic division reveals a power division as well. The South Africans use Afrikaans to discuss their concern over UNITA's failure to take Cangamba, but when the UNITA general asks them to return to English, their discussion ends and they order UNITA to take the city within forty-eight hours. The order, rather than the collaboration portrayed between Cuba and the MPLA, further establishes the separate realms in which South Africa and UNITA operate, as the film never portrays South African soldiers actively engaged in battle.[8] The exchange points to the fundamental incompatibility of an Angolan party born of the anticolonial struggle with the interests of the apartheid regime, coded in the film as a bridge between colonial and imperialist policies in Africa. The different military uniforms, the lack of mutually comprehensible languages, and uneven distribution of resources among UNITA and the South African commanders place the two camps on clearly opposing sides of the world ideological stage of the late Cold War. While Cuba is cast as a primary actor that draws other national and international communities in to revolutionary action through a mutual self-recognition with those it helps, UNITA's leadership reproduces old colonial relations and points to a new era in which the groundwork for neocolonial exploitation has already been established.

The communitarian aesthetic that marks the interactions between Cuban and FAPLA forces culminates in a melodramatic scene in which the exhausted soldiers receive a handwritten letter from the Comandante (Fidel Castro) encouraging them to endure in their fight for the freedom of the Angolan people and the "*libertad y dignidad de África*" (liberty and dignity of Africa). João's question in Portuguese about the letter evokes the same wording in the affirmative answer in Spanish from Mayito—"*para todos*" (for everyone)—pointing once again to the politics of participation that arrives even at the highest levels of national and international leadership. As the letter ends with the Cuban Revolution's rallying cry of "*Patria o muerte, ¡venceremos!*" (Fatherland or death, we will triumph!), the scene reiterates a mutual recognition among the national and international communities contained under the banner of its collective first person, and the thesis that the defense of the "liberty and dignity of Africa" includes Cuba as an "Afro-Latino" nation (Castro 1976). For Christine Hatzky, by insisting on the common African roots of Cubans and Angolans, Fidel Castro "invented a tradition in the sense of Eric Hobsbawm, in establishing a continuity with a suitable historical past as well as symbolizing the membership of a real or artificial community, and, in spatial terms, a 'Black Atlantic'—*avant la lettre*—at the same time" (Hatzky 2015, 11).

Paulo Antonio Paranaguá notes that post–Cold War Cuban cinema has increasingly expressed internal social critiques of enforced conformity, labyrinthine bureaucracy, race- and gender-based social exclusion, and economic hardship. However, he notes that París's codirected 1990 Angolan war film *Caravana* embodies a "wait-and-see conservatism which simply advocates resistance against external threats and against the Wind from the East . . . even if that means supporting the corrupt rather than the cowardly, as the film does" (Paranaguá 1997, 188). A similar notion undergirds *Kangamba*. Its references to the revolutionary film techniques that marked a new era in Latin American cinema are subsumed in the latter part of the film by a cinematic and political conservatism that returns to a traditional narrative structure guided by a voiceover narrator who reads the letter, cuts in clichéd images of African fauna, and wraps up neatly with a definitive victory for the heroes and Mayito's tragic death on the battlefield. Although the film insists on a distinct contrast to the exchanges from the South African leaders and their UNITA beneficiaries, the film's homage to the central role of the national patriarch in guiding the actions of the soldiers reveals a clear parallel between the two sides of the conflict.

International observers frequently expected the Cuban Revolution to collapse during or after the economic crisis precipitated by the fall of the Soviet Union, Cuba's largest trading partner and close political ally. However, as Esther Whitfield (2008) and others demonstrate, the crisis also sparked a period of increasing adaptation to a new economic and cultural climate where Cuba's anti-imperial politics turned not on the divides of the Cold War but on a message of resistance to the dominance of market-based interactions with its neighbors in the Global South. Even as Cuba has shifted to a tourism-based economy with increased privatization and internationalist workers are now often contracted and paid by foreign governments, these workers continue to be seen in official discourse as building solidarity between Cuba and their destinations in Africa, Latin America, and South Asia (Blue 2013, 42). In the context of the 2000s, the film insinuates that although Cuba sells its citizens' labor overseas, its human investment in South-South alliances continue to represent a model of engagement that resists market-driven exploitation and monetary and material investment. Still, the film repeats a message of Third World solidarity that made sense in the midst of global Cold War politics just as it references avant-garde documentary styles, without translating their radical nature in the twenty-first century context. Both the anticolonial messaging and the citation of early revolutionary film serve as historical points of reference rather than proposing a new or even updated politics of engagement across the Global South. The film leaves uninterrogated an implied easy equivalence between the colonialists of the 1970s–80s and a generalized global economic imperialism of the 2000s.

The Hero After the War

The postwar period appears in a very different form in the Angolan film *O herói* (*The Hero*, 2004), the first full-length fiction film directed by Angolan filmmaker Zézé Gamboa. Rather than suggesting military and political victory as constitutive of the revolutionary decolonizing process, the film focuses on the gap between the official processes of the transition from colonialism to independence as well as from war to peace, and the lack of material change that such processes bring to the lives of the characters. *O herói* takes place just after the end of the civil phase of the war in 2002, following the period of renewed and brutal violence that broke out after Angola's first multiparty elections in 1992 and continued until UNITA leader Jonas Savimbi's death in 2002. *O herói* presents the story of the veteran Vitório, who returns to Luanda after losing his leg in a mine explosion at the end of his twenty years as a FAPLA soldier. Rather than grandiose narratives of global solidarity, *O herói* represents the disappointment and exhaustion with wartime factions and ideological divides that have dominated the postindependence era. Through Vitório—whose name, perhaps ironically, means "victory"—Gamboa's film indirectly alludes to both the euphoria and the purpose of the early postindependence period, and it suggests that the prolonged violence and loss have resulted in a national present very different from the one imagined in the early revolutionary years.

Vitório's struggle to find employment and reintegrate into civilian society indicates not only the trauma of a youth lived entirely in the context of armed conflict, but also the problems of extensive unemployment, fractured families, crippled national infrastructure and dependence on foreign investment that characterize early twenty-first-century Angola. Even after he obtains a prosthesis that allows him to walk, Vitório finds that his exemplary service to his country, his patriotic capital, does not help him secure a job or reintegrate into civil society. His prosthesis, representing the promise of reintegration and healing, belies his difficulties in contributing to a transitioning Angolan society that Vitório is unable to anticipate.

The film offers itself to a seemingly straightforward reading of Vitório's struggles on a thorny path to reconstituting a national family broken apart by wartime violence. Vitório eventually forms a familial community of outcasts. He develops a relationship with the prostitute Maria Bárbara, who has lost her son; with Manu, a presumed orphan whose father has disappeared in the war and who now lives in a *musseque* (shantytown) with his grandmother; and with Joana, Manu's teacher who befriends Vitório and helps him eventually secure employment through her well-connected boyfriend. After Vitório's prosthesis is stolen as he sleeps on the street, he tells his story to Joana, who arranges for him to appear on the radio for an interview about his experience with a government minister. Manu, who has exchanged stolen goods for the prosthetic leg at a junk shop, hears the story, and returns the leg to Vitório. The film thus symbolically links the prosthesis to Vitório's recomposed surrogate family; it ends by showing Vitório working in a new job as a chauffeur who takes Manu for a ride, suggesting a paternal relationship with the boy as the two literally and figuratively move forward in the car. Each of the characters in *O herói* stands in for the lost relative of another, and are thus able to reestablish a community despite the familial disintegration evidenced throughout the film.

However, unlike the brotherly relationships suggested among the soldiers in *Kangamba*, the family unit created by Vitório, Manu, Maria Bárbara, and Joana is not a symbolic extension of international and national solidarities, but rather a community that forms in the cracks of a semi-functional and undependable Angolan state. The solution to Vitório's unemployment—finding work as a driver for a government minister—is so localized that it provides no metonymic suggestion of systematic social change, and yet at the same time is the result of the webs of personal connections and mutual favors that, in the film, characterizes postwar notions of solidarity. As Mark Sabine astutely notes in his analysis of the film, *O herói* undermines the straightforward thesis of an optimistic future symbolized in the reconstituted national family. For Sabine, the film comprises a subversive political allegory that both critiques the concentration of power in the hands of a ruling few and the lack of a collective spirit of mutual assistance among the populace, and calls for a return to the independence-era politics of solidarity. Sabine argues that this allegory is constructed around a number of hidden tropes that ironically refer to the ideals of independence-era revolutionary ideology. These tropes include the socialist New Man, ironically evoked in Vitório's broken body, the derailed national development project and the "prosthetic family"; the stalled and decaying construction projects that pervade the shots of the city as ironic evocations of national social construction; and the symbol of transport, privatized and unavailable to the vast majority of the public, signaling limited economic and social mobility for all but the political elite (Sabine 2011, 209–212). Taken as a whole, the effect of these strategies is ambiguous:

> while in *The Hero*'s political allegory, Vitório may end up using his prosthesis to depress the accelerator pedal of the state-owned machine, the viewer cannot be certain whether the leg has come to represent an integral part of the organic body of the nation, or whether, conversely, it is the symbolic agent of Vitório's incorporation into the clientist and kleptocratic body of the state, which props up the hegemony of global capitalism. (215)

If, in fact, the film is advocating for a return to independence-era notions of solidarity, *O herói*'s ambiguity arises in part through the question of whether this solidarity operates horizontally as well as vertically—between the populace and the leadership—or whether a new, postwar solidarity serves as a mechanism of collective opposition to the "clientist and kleptocratic state" that the former anticolonial leadership now represents. As in the case of *Kangamba*, the Angolan film's carefully constructed relationship with prior eras' cinematic and political grammar organizes its relationship to its contemporary postwar environment, and provides support for this second interpretation of postwar solidarity.

Gamboa's 1998 war documentary *Dissidence*, for example, traces an eclectic group of Angolan intellectuals formerly allied to diverse political movements in the independence and postindependence era, each ousted for failing to comply with increasing measures of orthodoxy. Through its imprisoned, executed and/or exiled subjects, the film draws disturbing parallels between the practices of Portuguese colonial control and Angola's postcolonial governance, their parallel neglect of public institutions such as schools and universities, and the atmosphere of fear and violence that pervaded pre- and post-1975 Angola. While similar theses have been thoroughly theorized in canonical postcolonial works from Fanon's *The Wretched of the Earth* (1961) to Mbembe's *On the Postcolony* (2000), Gamboa's treatment of the colonial transition in *Dissidence*—in which Gamboa suggests that Angola's independence has only been partially achieved—can nonetheless shed light on how *O herói* redeploys this critique in the context of the first treacherous postwar years.

Early in *O herói*, the doctor who finally secures Vitório's prosthesis after months of waiting warns him that he will have to learn to walk again, "*como uma criança*" (like a child). Vitório's incredulous response—"*Eu, uma criança?*" (I, a child?)—points to Vitório's and his generation's childhood lost to war and violence; Vitório reveals that he had been conscripted into the armed forces at fifteen years of age. *O herói* presents us with several child doubles of Vitório. Later in the film, as Vitório waits outside the hospital for help after he has lost his prosthesis, Joana and her boyfriend Pedro arrive with a street child whom Pedro has hit with his car. Pedro has attended college abroad on a government scholarship and returned home to a guaranteed job working for his uncle, a government minister, while Joana, an elementary school teacher, is frustrated by the necessity for teacher strikes that close the school in protest of nonpayment of salaries and the lack of resources for education in general. To Pedro, they have done their duty by delivering the child to the hospital, but Joana decides to stay and make sure that he sees the doctor. Joana and Pedro pass Vitório multiple times as they go in and out of the hospital without taking notice of him. For Pedro and those of his elite class, Vitório is a grown-up version of the street child, an uncomfortable part of the landscape that must be dealt with only when it physically (though also metaphorically) lands on the hood of his luxury car. For Joana, however, who strikes up a conversation with Vitório and organizes the radio interview with Pedro's uncle that leads to the return of his leg, Vitório represents a small outlet for her frustrated efforts at assisting others. Manu, another possible child double or inheritor of Vitório's youth, is an ironic reflection of the veteran's sacrifice. He is shown playing in the decaying carcass of a bullet-riddled fighter plane, for example, a scene in which the camera shows us Manu's face only as it pans through the bullet holes of the plane's windshield. Manu and his generation are only visible through the frame of the war's destruction. In another allegorical microcosm of the social divisions that guided the war, rather than dedicating himself to his studies and assisting his struggling grandmother, Manu engages in petty theft and falls on the wrong side of a more powerful bully and leader of an opposing gang. If Vitório, and Manu as his double, can be taken here as representatives of the larger Angolan national body, the film may also be pointing to Angola's inexperience and difficulty moving beyond a violent, thwarted adolescence, despite its nearly thirty years of independence at the time of the film's production.

While micronarratives of everyday existence and frustrated national development dominate the film, *O herói*, like *Kangamba*, takes on the history of international intervention in Angola, though focusing on the international collaboration in the neoliberal turn of Angola's economic development in the twenty-first century. The film demonstrates this dynamic in a scene in which Vitório searches for work, passing a large painted sign proclaiming "*Não há vagas*" (No jobs). Insisting at a construction site that he is fit for labor despite his prosthetic leg, Vitório confronts the foreman's unexpected resistance to hiring him in recognition of his patriotic sacrifice; the supervisor insists he needs "*homens normais*" (normal men) rather than "heroes" for the physical demands of the job. The film's cynical commentary on the value of Vitório's sacrifice extends to the mechanism of national reconstruction. When Vitório mistakes the foreman for the building's owner, the camera cuts to a shot of the Portuguese man looking down through a second-story opening, maintaining the point of view of the two Angolans. The foreman corrects Vitório: "*Eu o patrão? Eu sou só o encargado. O patrão é português. Vais ver aquele gajo ali acima*" (Me the boss? I'm just the supervisor. The boss is Portuguese. Go see that guy up there). This scene presents the ironic reality of the value of Vitório's service to his country; despite his years of sacrifice, the flow of Angolan capital to the pockets of the Portuguese investor suggests that a new era of globalized economic development has done little to interrupt the model of colonial dependency in place prior to 1975.

The government minister who eventually interviews Vitório and secures him a job as a car driver, however, is little better. As the minister pulls away from the radio station, a quiet group of veterans waits outside the gates. The minister, promising to help them, closes his window as he instructs his driver to push carefully through the group; within the film, however, we only see that help coming to Vitório. Similarly to Pedro's interaction with the street child, the film presents the minister as both neglectful and willfully blind to the dire situation in which the rest of the characters live, until political opportunism forces him to act in a limited way. Both Kenneth Harrow's and Connor Ryan's readings of *O herói* focus on the exchange value of the physical and figurative detritus of the protracted period of war and subsequent postcolonial transition in the construction of a new economic and political order. As Harrow signals, the very unavoidability of trash throughout the film reveals its value: "The prevalence of trash on all levels prevents us from evaluating the people and the objects as being permanently worthless because the motility of trash lies in its being ensconced in systems where objects lose value over time and at the same time enter into differing regimes of value" (Harrow 2013, 217). As living incarnations of this debris, the veterans prove to provide passing political capital to the minister: Pedro convinces him to do the radio interview with the promise that it will help him come reelection time. The human casualties of the war who remain outside the world of *O herói*, however, are even more significant. The film depicts the lines of people who come out to speak on the weekly television program *Ponto de Reencontro*, where Angolans announce their missing family members, sometimes with photos and other identifying information. As Ryan suggests, there is little hope for systemic change for Angola without both reckoning with and incorporating the war's living debris into a new transformed order (Ryan 2013, 66).

In the first years following independence in Angola, as in Cuba after the revolution, film was an integral area for cultural development and an important medium for the dissemination of revolutionary ideals. Marissa Moorman's comprehensive study of Angolan cinema summarizes its place in the anticolonial and postindependence cultural order:

> During the [anticolonial] struggle, film was used as a means of propaganda, of mobilizing political support for an exiled nationalist leadership and the guerrilla war they were waging in the country. In the postindependence period, film was taken up by the state as part of the project of forging the nation and national unity through the documentation of local events and endowed with national significance and diffused, primarily, through television. (Moorman 2001, 119)

While Cuba developed a cinema at the vanguard of both theorization and practice in the Global South, engaged in multiple transnational coproductions as well as domestic films throughout the twentieth century, and trained generations of international filmmakers through the ICAIC, Angola's promising beginnings of a national cinema were stymied by reduced state support as the war dragged on, and only reemerged on the international scene with the three fictional films released in 2004 (Ferreira 2011, 222–223; Gamboa 2005; Moorman 2001, 112). Thus the respective conditions of production of *Kangamba* and *O herói* offer an additional commentary on their place in negotiating postwar memorializations of the internationalist collaboration and the legacies of civil conflict.

While París's 1990 film *Caravana* was coproduced with the Angolan state entity Laboratório Nacional do Cinema and employed Angolan actors alongside Cubans, *Kangamba* is a national collaboration between the

ICAIC and MINFAR, Cuba's Ministry of the Revolutionary Armed Forces, and was filmed in Camagüey (de la Hoz 2008) with Cuban actors playing Angolans. Cuba's internationalist support largely limited to humanitarian assistance and programs of paid, limited-term, highly skilled employment under the auspices of foreign government sponsorship have replaced the era of military intervention. By contrast, Gamboa has expressed frustration with the Angolan state or private entities' lack of investment in cinematic production (Gamboa 2013, 233–234), and discussed how his own productions are dependent upon, for example, European investors, particularly from France (Gamboa 2005). Sabine highlights this situation as analogous to the neocolonial development critiqued within the film (Sabine 2011, 215). Ferreira has analyzed the complications that coproductions with former colonial powers can introduce, calling transnational productions "ambivalent" (Ferreira, 2011, 225) for their neocolonizing potential, but they also offer a vital platform for both national and international distribution. Gamboa notes in a 2005 interview that despite its excellent reception at international film festivals, winning the 2005 Sundance Grand Jury prize and enjoying a successful premier in Portugal, *O herói* at the time was not available in Angola; it was later distributed on DVD. The economy of internal production and consumption of a film like *Kangamba* no longer has to make the case for internationalist intervention that it did even at the end of the Angolan collaboration in the late 1980s. The limitations with national production and consumption for a film like *O herói*—Gamboa's 2012 film *O grande Kilapy* was filmed entirely in Brazil and, like *O herói*, employed a number of Brazilian actors (Gamboa 2013)—suggest that the cultural packaging of grappling with the wartime legacy is as contested as its method.

While both films present a nostalgia for the solidarities of the past, *Kangamba* ultimately constructs a vertical hierarchy of power/right that privileges a single mode—heroic nostalgia—embodied in the national patriarch, where the will of the "pueblo," the people, is assumed to be in line with the leftist ideology that linked Cuba to the MPLA. And yet, in the early twenty-first century context of its production, the allegiance no longer functions as it did in the 1970s and 1980s. The majority MPLA party, a synecdoche in the film for the Angolan people, is increasingly the object of critique for corruption and abuse. Neat divisions between Cold War superpowers and the Third World, between imperialists and anti-colonialists, no longer so easily organize the geopolitical context of the early twenty-first century, and Cuba's internationalist missions are increasingly seen as opportunistic economic enterprises necessary to the country after the economic crisis of the 1990s. *O herói*, which ironizes and criticizes postrevolutionary neocolonial exploitation and three decades of destructive civil divides, serves to put into relief how *Kangamba* perhaps even undermines its historical referent of radical popular collaboration in failing to update its politics for a post–Cold War world where the enemies and allegiances have shifted. In *Kangamba*, the possibility of this ideological collaboration remains buried in the past, where in *O herói* by contrast, it's renewed and presented as a possibility for the future, if only in a limited way, by confronting the inheritances of the recent war and of contemporary corruption.

The two films together emphasize the importance of the Angolan war and the Cuba-Angola allegiance as a definitive example of anticolonial solidarity in the South Atlantic. As Hatzky points out, the overwhelming focus on the Cold War superpowers as the only independent actors in the limited historiography of this interaction obscures the radical nature of third-world allegiance in the mid–twentieth century (2015, 7). The two films nonetheless represent divergent viewpoints on how to negotiate the legacy of South-South alliances once the global enthusiasm for utopian idealism founded in revolutionary orthodoxy has faded away. It cannot be ignored that *Kangamba*'s defense of Cuba's ongoing internationalist collaboration is nonetheless advanced via allegiance to one side of a violent civil conflict, and produced at a moment when concerns over postwar reconciliation have saturated the public sphere in twenty-first-century Angola. While *Kangamba*'s investment in a narrative of continuity between Cuba's twentieth-and twenty-first-century forms of international assistance might imply an ongoing criticism of the neoliberal and exploitive models of engagement and "development" that so often guide relationships between sites in the Global North and South, the film fails to interrogate these two conflicting contexts. *O herói*'s complex engagement with the larger national and international narratives that so thoroughly occupy intellectual debates in and about Angola in film and literature posits localized mini-narratives as a method for grappling with the inheritances of the war that have relevance because they are so divorced from the unrealized promises of the revolutionary period. This example of postrevolutionary disappointment, therefore, provides an important representation of nodes of personal contact and ironic distancing from broad ideological framing of international relations that are lost in the orthodox point of view of which *Kangamba* is an example, and thus provide an important perspective on how historical ideas of solidarity demand both critique and revision as the global context in which they are embedded changes.

NOTES

1. See Peters (2012), Millar (2012), and Hatzky (2015).

2. Translation by Cubanow.net.

3. I have not been able to confirm whether *Cuito Cuanavale*, the third film of the trilogy mentioned in press materials at the time of the releases of *Sumbe* and *Kangamba*, will be another fictional film. At the time this article was composed, no such film has been listed as a coming release or as "in production" on the website of the ICAIC. A documentary and multimedia project, *Cuito Cuanavale: Una gesta más allá del tiempo*, directed by Olivia Marín Álvarez and Susana Pérez Gil, is available online and was shown following *Kangamba* by the Cuban Embassy in India in Delhi on May 11, 2014 (CubaMINREX 2014).

4. For a thorough discussion of Cuba's film history, including films made about movements in Latin America, Africa and elsewhere in the world during the 1960s and 1970s, see Chanan (2004) and Fornet (2001).

5. See Mahler's contribution to this volume for a more complete discussion of the Three Worlds theory and its implications for cinema and visual culture.

6. For more on Cuban internationalism, see Krull (2014), Díaz-Briquets (1989), and *The International Journal of Cuban Studies* 5 (1), a special issue dedicated to the topic.

7. A similar episode takes place in París's *Caravana*.

8. There are interesting differences between the portrayals of UNITA soldiers in *Kangamba* and in París's 1990 *Caravana*. While in *Caravana* Savimbi and the UNITA soldiers are vilified as murderous and violent, in *Kangamba* the portrayal of the opposition party is much more neutral, even approaching sympathy, in casting them as unfortunate puppets of a cruel South African regime.

Adrift Between Neoliberalism and the Revolution

Cape Verde and the South Atlantic in Germano Almeida's *Eva*

Luís Madureira

One might reduce the plot of Cape Verdean author Germano Almeida's *Eva* to a series of performances of the paradox between the unique event and its inevitable, obsessive repeatability, the compulsive reproduction of a singular event that each reiteration defers or deflects in turn. The novel's four central characters remain apparently caught, either consciously or unconsciously, in a structure of desire that compels them unceasingly to replicate the same actions in an effort to live out a singular, absolutely irreproducible experience. In the close reading of the novel that follows, I suggest that this compulsive performativity relates directly to a sustained interrogation of the contradictory and often fractious dialogic entanglements that inform the constitution (or "performances") of Cape Verdean identity (or identities) within a broad South Atlantic cultural and geopolitical space that encompasses not only Portugal, the former colonial power, but also Brazil and continental Africa. Often, these identitarian pathways lead us into meandering alleys, at times even dead ends, as though the process of identity formation (and sexual and political apprenticeship, by analogy) represented in the novel were consistently divested of all teleological certainty.

On a broader yet related note, a similar artifactual or undecidable formation comes arguably to define Cape Verde's location in the South Atlantic, as it is referenced in the novel. Identities and symbolic meanings invariably emerge as fragile and contingent in this novel, often ephemeral, becoming on occasion thoroughly undone. *Eva* thus consistently refuses to fix identity in unequivocal terms, and muddles the corporeal signs of absolute alterity that we routinely and reflexively imagine to be located in the bodies of "others." Eva is the perplexing and contradictory central figure around which this aporia is elaborately staged. I should like to pursue the implications, which these recurrently inconsistent cues about Eva's selfhood, this deliberate undoing of fixed identity constructs and unraveling of clear-cut allegorizations, carry for the brittle articulation of a viable postcolonial and postrevolutionary Cape Verdean identity, and relatedly of the archipelago's location in the Global South Atlantic.

Eva tells the story of two Cape Verdean men (Reinaldo and Luís Henriques), who meet and trade stories about the woman they both love (Eva). The action takes place in contemporary Lisbon, which alternates with the Cape Verdean capital (Praia) and 1970s Lisbon as the setting of episodes in the life of Eva, a Portuguese woman who moves to Cape Verde in order to marry Luís Henriques. For reasons that are revealed only in the final pages of the novel, the latter never returns home from Lisbon, where he and Eva had met a few months prior to the April 25, 1974, revolution that toppled Portugal's nearly five-decade-old dictatorship and ushered in a new era of decolonization in many of Portugal's South Atlantic colonies, including Cape Verde. The plot develops from what the extended dialogue between the two men reveals (and occludes), as well as the narrator-protagonist Reinaldo's interior monologue. It is supplemented by what Eva and her deceived husband separately narrate to Reinaldo, invariably recollected from his narrative point of view.

Although both Reinaldo and Luís Henriques are former colonized subjects, their drawn-out and often competing accounts of Eva at times resemble a somewhat dissonant reproduction at the level of discourse of a masculinist struggle between colonizer and colonized. The possession of Eva's body emerges as the terrain of dispute. One of the tasks of this chapter is to read against the grain of these contending masculinities, while concomitantly seeking to pay heed to the troubling ways in which this male rivalry unfolds in the novel, with the aim of uncovering the ground of the utopian political ties between the postcolony and former metropolis (between North and South Atlantic, in the broad sense).

Almeida himself acknowledges that this intricate and often imbricated latticework of exuberant narrations, omissions, tergiversations, and untruths cannot but produce an inchoate or "approximate" portrait of Eva: "We don't know if he's lying or telling the truth, when Luís Henriques talks about Eva" (2006b). "We also don't know to what extent Eva has been lying or inventing stories [about Luís] to the narrator." To complicate matters further, Almeida concedes that it is "no coincidence" that Eva is a Portuguese woman. If the novel contains a "message," he contends, it resides precisely in her Lusitanian provenance, which, in his eyes, points to the "affirmation of Cape Verde [as] the most multiracial country in the world, even more than Brazil." Here the Cape Verdean novelist appears to corroborate Phillip Rothwell's assertion that "if ever a part of the Portuguese Empire embodied the myth [of lusotropicalism], it was Cape Verde, with its high incidence of miscegenation when compared with other Portuguese colonies" (2009, 403). As the necessary initial step in the labor of disentangling this troubling relation between an essentially masculinist sexuality and the politics of miscegenation, an overview of lusotropicalism's fraught connection to the Cape Verdean colonial context is in order.

Beginning in the early 1950s, this myth of Portuguese colonial domination was to become, not only the official colonial doctrine of Portugal's authoritarian regime, but also what a historian of the Portuguese expansion has fittingly called a *prêt-à-penser* (Léonard 1999, 30). Loosely based on Brazilian sociologist Gilberto Freyre's theories regarding the central function of miscegenation in Portugal's colonial experience as a whole and the formation of Brazil in particular, the official version of lusotropicalism projects an image of Portugal as a "pluri-continental" yet "united and indivisible" nation dispersed across the globe. It constructs Portugal as the fountainhead of an exemplary (and uniquely humane) mode of colonization, which, in contrast to that of other European powers, was characterized by tolerance and openness. This euphemistic vision of empire was ratified by the constitutional revisions of 1951, whereby the African colonies were redefined as formally integrated into the national "body." Portugal itself was reclassified as an "Afro-European" power and the colonies became, as a result, integral and organic parts of the metropolis. Alluding to Paul Gilroy's signature concept, Portuguese anthropologist Miguel Vale de Almeida has coined the ironic phrase "*Atlântico pardo*" ("the Brown Atlantic") to designate this broad "hegemonic narrative" of an alleged miscegenation project in Brazil, as well as its ultimate failure in Africa, notwithstanding the proliferation of colonial discourses affirming the opposite (2007, 29–30).

The phrase retains a trace of the blend of imperialist bluster and authoritarian parochialism underpinning many of the dictator Salazar's (1889–1970) emblematic pronouncements on Portugal's supposed expansionist aptitude. Speaking on the eve of World War II, about a decade before lusotropicalism was to emerge as Portugal's ruling colonial idea, the autocrat describes "the small Lusitanian rectangle" as willingly ensconced in a far-flung "corner of Europe, almost detached from [the continent] and projecting itself boldly out to sea, an Atlantic country par excellence," endowed with "the Atlantic style" ("*feição atlântica*") that defines its "heroic efforts as a builder of empires" (*Boletim* 1939, 20, 25).[1] Barely two decades later, Salazar was appending the crucial lusotropicalist characteristic of miscibility to this peculiarly Lusitanian colonizing impetus. In an interview published in *Life* magazine that I have also cited and examined elsewhere,[2] he depicted the Portuguese mode of being in the tropics (or the South Atlantic) as undergirded by "a natural penchant" (*um pendor natural*) toward multiracialism, a vocation for establishing contacts with other peoples and cultures entirely devoid of any notion of superiority or racial discrimination: "What distinguishe[d] Portuguese Africa," Salazar (in) famously declared, was the preeminence that "we Portuguese" had always accorded to "the enhancement and ennoblement of man under the aegis of civilizing principles brought to peoples distant from us in every respect, regardless of their color and creed" (1962, 6–7).

According to this plausive dominant narrative of empire, Portugal represented something like the Atlantic exception to the North/South divide. Unsurprisingly, as a discursive space, the "lusotropical Atlantic" differs markedly from an imagined Global South Atlantic, or Gilroy's "Black Atlantic," whose groundwork is an incredulity in Western modernity's egalitarian potential and a related belief in the emancipatory possibilities of cultural expressions unstably linked to transatlantic political and social movements. Indeed, in an early anticolonial critique of what he calls "*à la fois un concept, une théorie, un système et une méthode de colonisation*," the Angolan nationalist Mário Pinto de Andrade asserts unequivocally, in effect, that "in the tropical countries under Portuguese rule, at the very least in Africa, a marriage of two cultures, a form of contact which would incidentally be desirable, has never existed, but rather a relation of power exercised by a dominant culture over a dominated one" (1955, 30, 34). Lusotropicalism therefore constitutes a Western Iberian variation of the Eurocentrism that Derrida discerns (without naming) in the familiar and reiterative "autobiography of Europe," that is, the narrative that insistently designates the continent as "an advance" ("*une avancée*")—the vanguard of geography and history" (1991, 50).

As I argue elsewhere,[3] and as Claudia Castelo has more recently reaffirmed, it is hardly a coincidence that the Portuguese *Estado Novo* should choose to appropriate Freyre's "concept" as a theory or methodology of colonization precisely in the wake of World War II (2011, 272). As Slaughter and Bystrom argue appositely in the introduction to this volume, despite the intensification of "transatlantic bonds" among empires both once and future, this is concomitantly a geopolitical moment in which self-determination was increasingly becoming the order of the day. In Robert Young's considerably more elegant and succinct formulation of an argument I belabor in an early piece,[4] "lusotropical hybridity is the opposite of any form of contestation by the subaltern or oppressed, and it offers them no form of agency or means of resistance" (2006a, 115). It is, moreover, as Angela Gilliam argues, a narrativization of white male privilege, in which "the sexual violence against black women is romanticised [and] the inequality between men and women is both eroticised and racialised" (1998, 65). "The *mestiçagem* narrative," she contends elsewhere, "disembodies women's potential for power and authority in their own lives," eliding "the predatory sexuality that affected the lives of indigenous and Black women throughout the [southern] hemisphere" (2003, 100).

Cape Verde's "embodiment" of this enduring myth was not nearly as seamless as Rothwell would have it, however. Paradoxically, in the "scientific travelogue" (or "suggestions for a voyage in search of the Portuguese constants in character and action," to quote its subtitle), which Freyre produces in the wake of his official tour of the Portuguese colonies at the invitation of Portugal's colonial minister in 1951–52, the Brazilian sociologist pointedly excludes Cape Verde from lusotropicalism's "new civilizational complex" (1961, 293). After his brief visit to the archipelago, while acknowledging Cape Verde's historical primacy as "the test cauldron for [lusotropicalism's] ethnic adventure," Freyre finds only a "vague kinship" between Cape Verde's ethnic and cultural makeup and "the luso-tropical populations and cultures" present in northeastern Brazil, for instance (1953, 290). He obtains the "impression of a population sociologically and even ethnically related to the Portuguese or Brazilian; but too dominated by the legacy of African culture and race for its kinship with the Portuguese and Brazilian to be any more than the exoticism of its appearance and costumes" (1953, 292). Rather than "embody" lusotropicalism, then, or confirm the principle that Freyre formulates elsewhere ("It is as if every . . .

land fertilized by even a single drop of Portuguese blood or enlivened by a smattering of Portuguese culture is a land predisposed for the flowering of [the] lusotropical complex of civilization" [n.d., 139]), Cape Verde, in Freyre's eyes, traces a limit. It constitutes the exception to the lusotropicalist rule due in large measure to its cultural location in the South Atlantic. What the archipelago needs in order fully to exemplify lusotropicalism is a "greater European presence," which would infuse Cape Verde with a "new vigor," a superior or North Atlantic "value creative activity," "an invigoration of the ["sociologically European" side of its] culture" (1953, 303–304).

As prominent Cape Verdean scholars and intellectuals suggested at the time, Freyre's peremptory dismissal of Cape Verde's experience of cultural miscegenation, an experience which, much like that of Caribbean island societies and cultures is, as Germano Almeida insists, quintessentially Creole, is startling. In a 1956 response to Freyre's critique, for example, Baltazar Lopes, one of the leading figures of the 1936 *Claridade* movement, characterized the Brazilian sociologist's interpretation of island culture as "marred by journalistic haste," and betraying a tendency toward "simplistic generalizations" as well as dwelling on "insignificant details" (quoted in Medina 2000, 57). Ironically, Freyre's Cape Verdean critics take the eminent Brazilian scholar to task chiefly for having overlooked the indelible Portuguese component of Cape Verdean identity. "How could it occur to anyone, moderately informed about Cape Verdean matters, that the Cape Verdean is more African than Portuguese," queries Baltazar Lopes (quoted in Medina 2000, 58). In a similar vein, in his "indirect refutation" of Freyre's cultural interpretation (Medina 2000, 59), Cape Verdean poet Gabriel Mariano regards as especially meaningful the fact that "a [people] of predominantly Black blood should be, from a cultural standpoint, predominantly Lusitanian" (1991, 53). In essence, Cape Verdean intellectuals take Freyre to task for his insertion of the archipelago in the South Atlantic. The counternarrative they offer to lusotropicalism amounts to its reincorporation in the North.

Eva's author appears to subscribe, in the main, to this view. For instance, he stipulates that to assume a specifically Cape Verdean identity in the colonial era "was not essential": "To be Portuguese did us no harm whatsoever. . . . [During the transition to self-rule] we didn't think the assertion of independence excluded the assertion of a Portuguese identity (*portugalidade*)":

> We didn't feel colonized by Portugal, as happened with other colonies, because the colonial machine in Cape Verde was operated by Cape

> Verdeans: the administrator, the outpost chief, even the governor, at a given time, were all Cape Verdean. So whether we should like Portuguese identity or not was not a question we posed to ourselves. Even with respect to the desire for independence, we were struggling not against the settler, not against the white man . . . but rather for a land where we could lead the life we deserved, with a [functioning] school system, health care, work . . . things that were lacking [during colonial rule]. (Almeida 1998a)

In this broad sense, Cape Verdean identity oscillates between a "phenotypic" Africanness and a cultural *portugalidade*. For Almeida, in effect, at the very moment that Cape Verde emerges as a nation, its "identity" is constitutively fractured, unmoored, essentially at odds with itself. Such a construct seems to trouble, if not fundamentally to undo the conventional notion of identity as "an indelible mark or code somehow written into the bodies of its carriers" (Gilroy 2001, 103–104). Not only does otherness *not* threaten the putative uniformity of Cape Verdean identity, but it is at once ineradicably inscribed in the bodies of those who possess it and indefinable, ambivalent, always prone to be misidentified or mistaken for its other(s). In this light, even if we could readily insert the archipelago into a "Lusophone [cultural] matrix" (Arenas 2011, 1–43), attempting to plot its exact coordinates might well send us adrift.

It is with a comparable sense of disorientation that the novel opens, as the two men, searching for a tavern on the Rua da Mãe d'Água,[5] conclude that they had become "irremediably lost" (Almeida 2006a, 7, 10). Needless to say, they never locate the watering hole they seek. There is doubtless something symbolic about an opening scene in which two former colonized subjects become "irremediably lost" in meandering, "exotically named alleyways and dead ends" (8) located at the very heart of the former metropolis, or imperial "mother city," in search of a street called Water Mother,[6] while incessantly discussing a shared lover (Eva) christened after the biblical mother of humanity and whom the two men insist on literally and figuratively linking with motherhood and fertility. If this surfeit of maternal tropes connotes a putatively "matricial" Lusitanian culture, then the attempt to rejoin it—a kind of "postcolonial" inversion of Amílcar Cabral's renowned demand to "return to the source" of "the culture of the people who are undertaking the struggle" against colonial domination (1973, 4), this effort appears to be defined by deferral and diversion. Lisbon's topography seems as elusive and resistant to Reinaldo's and Luís's intoxicated attempts to navigate it as Eva is to their (discursive) efforts to delimit and define her. Perhaps fittingly, the woman who holds such fascination over the two men is described as "Eva of all our deliriums[7]" (Almeida 2006a, 8). At one point, Reinaldo, the narrator, asks her "half in gest," "Tell me who you really are, Eva of a thousand people?" (183). Eva repeatedly claims that, "she doesn't have many certainties" (114), professing to contain multiple egos, "so contradictory [that we] are unable to distinguish their signs" (155).

Despite this slipperiness and indeterminacy, she first appears to Reinaldo as a kind of hyperbolic mother figure: "We met . . . [when] she was pregnant, a scandalously big and protuberant pregnancy . . . It was at a beach . . . she was wearing a bikini . . . carrying that belly of hers like a menacing battering ram" (Almeida 2006a, 115–116). In one of several detailed descriptions of Eva's ample physical attributes, Reinaldo insists on employing the word "tits" (*mamas*) to refer to her "beautiful" breasts "because tit gives an idea of plenitude, of abundance, of . . . a sort of fertility goddess surrounded by her sons" (95). The narrator's descriptions of Eva's conflictive relationships with Luís, her older lover, and with her husband are likewise placed under the sign of motherhood.[8] Placing under erasure, for now, my preceding remarks concerning the undecidablity of Eva's symbolic meaning, one could reduce her to a masculinist symbol of motherhood, of a perdurable Lusitanian "cultural matrix"—to "a modern, perverse echo of the Portuguese explorer," as Rothwell asserts (2009, 404), a lusotropical mother or globalized female counterpart to Freyre's sixteenth-century lusotropical patriarch. Her oversize, incongruously bellicose pregnant belly would thus denote the conquest by miscegenation that lusotropicalism arguably constitutes. The first discordant note that arises in relation to this construction are the two men's repeated attempts to subdue her, at times in a disturbingly violent manner. Hence, when Reinaldo narrates his first encounter with Eva to Luís, he "opts to tell him a half-lie" (Almeida 2006a, 199). He "confesses" that, upon watching Eva emerge from the water like an "enormous siren with a misshapen belly," he becomes sexually excited to an "insane and incomprehensible" degree: "what I felt like doing at that moment was grab her from behind and rape her right there in the middle of that sun-bathing crowd as if I myself were a savage sea horse" (199). The untruth to which Reinaldo refers is presumably his subsequent dissembling claim that this was the last time he "ever looked at Eva like a woman" (199). We can probably assume therefore that this troubling rape fantasy is the truthful "half" of his anecdote.

Its putative mendacity notwithstanding, the episode belongs to a wider pattern that both lovers obsessively reenact throughout the novel. After

Eva gives birth to her first son, and, in Reinaldo's sexist formulation, is "restored" to her former splendor, he muses: "I began to imagine her being touched by an expert male . . . until she lay vanquished on a bed, quivering with lustful desire" (Almeida 2006a, 116–117). Reinaldo's prolonged wooing of Eva is in some ways reducible to an overpowering desire to dominate her: "I would put her in a horizontal position. . . . Even if it were only once! Yet, in so manly (*macho*) a fashion that she would never forget me and . . . would run after me like a bitch in heat" (71–72). And, according to Reinaldo again, Eva herself freely admits his irresistible supremacy over her: "I wanted to hand you my soul so you could mold it as you mold my body with your hands" (162–163). Even after they finally consummate their affair, Reinaldo admits that he had trouble controlling his need to dominate her, above all because Eva was the one woman on earth "who could proclaim herself free" (178).

On the other hand, Eva characterizes Luís Henriques (who is around ten years older than she, a girl "of sixteen, seventeen," when they initially meet) as the "man who had made her a woman" and taught her "everything" (Almeida 2006a, 47). Henriques exalts the supreme pleasure of "molding a soul" (254), conceding his pleasure at treating Eva as a kind of blank page upon which he could write everything he "thought, dreamed, desired, projected" (252). He claims to have been inspired in his soul-fashioning efforts by an excerpt from one of Salazar's speeches that he had encountered some years prior (256). Expressing his begrudging admiration for the autocrat's erudition and "scandalously" refined rhetorical skills (254), Henriques alleges to have deemed the fragment "execrable" (256) until he witnesses Eva's relieved and elated reaction at the loss of her virginity, or her "first communion," in her own words: "At that moment, [Salazar's] words came back to me and I thought how I wanted to mold that beautiful girl lying there naked beside me, in order to turn her into a glorious woman. . . . And in fact I did throw the gates of life wide open for her, and she learned to be free, and assert and exercise her freedom" (256). Luís may well be misremembering the episode, since the speech he recites was delivered when the future dictator was still a young seminarian, and did not become widely available until after the fall of the dictatorship in April 1974.[9] He seems nonetheless to be wresting from the dictator the role that Freyre attributes to Portugal: "the Author" of the archipelago's "historical existence" (1953, 288).

Whether these inaccuracies result from Luís Henriques's defective memory or a propensity to stretch the truth, there is a neat symmetry between Salazar's restrictive shaping of the Portuguese "soul" and the Cape

Verdean's ostensible empowerment, or emancipation of Eva. If this pedagogic relationship contains any allegorical links with the colonial relation, they reside in the formative influence that the revolutionary tricontinentalism of the national liberation movements exerted over the young officers (many of whom were veterans of Portugal's protracted colonial wars) who led the April 1974 coup that toppled the autocratic regime, setting in motion the ensuing decolonization process. As C. L. R. James argued:

> It used to be the ideas growing out of the political developments of western civilization which were taken up by leaders in Africa. Today something new has emerged. Portugal, which dominated Africa for 500 years has not only lost control over them; but revolutionary developments in Africa have effected the future of Portugal itself. . . . Instead of movements from Europe stimulating revolutionary developments in Africa, revolutionary struggles in Africa have unleashed movements of tremendous importance in Europe itself. (1992, 377–378)

Thus, Luís's "pedagogy of liberation" would reproduce in a broad sense this inversion of the trajectory of emancipatory ideals, and more specifically, the Portuguese military officers' revolutionary political formation. Arguably in accordance with this hypothetical allegorization of anticolonial revenge, Eva, if one is to believe Reinaldo's account, gladly assumed "the role of Luís Henriques's disciple" (Almeida 2006a, 106). She tacitly recognizes that she had learned all she still knew from him (47), fantasizing (again, in Reinaldo's somewhat unreliable retelling) about being "vanquished, subdued" until she was left "sapped" and seemingly dead (57). By the same token, Reinaldo's rape fantasy would be refigured as a sort of metaphorical retribution for and reversal of the sexual violence of colonial rule. As a possible reinforcement of this allegorical link, in *Aventura e rotina*, Freyre cites the poet Carlos Queiroz's description of the Portuguese countryside landscape as thoroughly "feminine" (Queiroz 1940, 92).[10] Thus, to grasp Eva as a modern perverse replica of the lusotropical patriarch, as Rothwell claims, the two men would need to be seen as reproducing the predatory sexuality which, for Angela Gilliam, the lusotropicalist narrative generates while willfully eliding (2003, 11). Such allegorical reading could not fail to address the insuperable contradictions, and indeed undeniable offensiveness of turning sexual violence into a metaphor for anticolonial struggle. As Achille Mbembe asserts in a critique of Fanon's legitimation of anticolonial violence, power in this context is conceptualized as "a masculinist prerogative"; as a result, resistance becomes inscribed in "the framework of a war between men": "to wrestle one's body from the property of a racist state or to confront it as an irretrievably corporeal and physical phenomenon is often reduced to a mere recapturing of one's balls. It is evident that in such a calculus of manhood, women's bodies are still assigned to the status of territories as well as superfluous and interchangeable assets" (2011, 27). We would therefore need seriously to question, "at what point does resistance become unethical? Are there ethical limits to resistance?" (Young 2011, 57).

This allegorical structure is further eroded when we look more closely into Cape Verde's unique colonial situation. The avowed goal of the anticolonial armed struggle waged by Amílcar Cabral's PAIGC (the African Party for the Independence of Guinea[-Bissau] and Cape Verde) was independence for both Guinea and Cape Verde, and the PAIGC established itself as the island nation's ruling party after independence, maintaining the unity between the two former colonies as one of its ideological pillars until 1980. Despite this ostensibly common history of struggle, and as Almeida has maintained, Portugal's colonization of the archipelago differed fundamentally from that of Guinea-Bissau, in particular, and its other African colonies, in general:

> In the 60s and 70s we [Cape Verdeans] had to learn in a great hurry that we were also part of the wretched of the earth, that we likewise belonged to the great mass of humanity half-human, half-beast called "natives," as we were taught in some book, although, to our great intellectual sorrow, the turmoil described either in *Cry, the Beloved Country* or in *The Native Son* certainly had nothing to do with our reality of islanders lost in the Atlantic. . . . Our mere situation as colonized compelled us to be always and for all times on the side of the oppressed the world over, although it was true that the colonizer in Cape Verde [was] almost exclusively represented by Cape-Verdean officials. (1998b, 15)

In contrast to the populations of Angola, Guinea-Bissau, and Mozambique, Cape Verdeans did not directly experience "the burden of the Portuguese colonizer," Almeida contends; for this reason, they never observed "the cult of their independence" (2006b). As a reactionary compatriot informs the narrator of one of Almeida's earlier novels, many Cape Verdeans (including Almeida himself) fought the independence wars "on side of the Portuguese" (1999, 77). In this way, the kind of intellectual conversation that purportedly elicited the South-North reversal in the global emancipatory movement, which C. L. R. James hails as part and parcel of "the new world we are living in"[11] (1992, 378), was at best improbable in Cape Verde. Beyond its exceedingly disturbing gender politics, the tropological link between Reinaldo's and Luís Henriques's desire violently to subjugate Eva and a presumed retribution against colonialism as "rape" is ultimately as unfounded in the reality of colonialism in Cape Verde as is Henriques's recollection of an apocryphal presidential speech in the political context of the *Estado Novo*.

This incongruity is intensified by Reinaldo's only partially acknowledged condescension toward the other colonized from former Portuguese Africa. In an imagined encounter with an Angolan who may or may not have had an affair with Eva, Reinaldo addresses him by the racist term *grunho* ("coon"), while Luís Henriques employs the equally derogatory term *negragem* (roughly translatable as "nigger trash") to designate immigrants from Portugal's other former African colonies (Almeida 2006a, 241). As a cynical compatriot reminds the protagonist of another novel by Almeida, in the other Portuguese African colonies Cape Verdeans "were often treated as whites, many of them, in fact, behaved worse toward the blacks than did the whites (*mandrongos*) themselves" (1999, 75). Ultimately, these ambivalent and contradictory figurations call into question Freyre's hurried assessment of the archipelago's population as excessively dominated by the legacy of African race and culture. They also appear to suggest a key variation on the colonizer-colonized binary. Writing in 1959, the poet Gabriel Mariano insists, in a pointed response to Freyre, that "in Cape Verde there was a certain deviation from what the Portuguese carried out in [the rest of] Africa" as well as colonial Brazil, where "the white man always played the leading role" (1991, 53). By contrast, Mariano asserts:

> In Cape Verde . . . *the mulatto acquired* early on a great freedom of movement and [played] the role that the kingdom-born Portuguese carried out in Brazil. That is: *the condition of master, of leader in the structuring of Cape Verdean society, shifted to the mulatto* . . . The capacity to assimilate the exotic and the reproduction of new cultural forms cited as the dominant facet of the Portuguese experience in Africa seems to me to have shifted in Cape Verde to the mulatto. It was he who took charge of receiving and recreating elements from European civilization. And it was [in] the *funco*, not in the *sobrado*[12] . . . that the black man's and the mulatto's appropriation of Portuguese civilizational elements and expressions was accomplished. . . . In Cape Verde the "colored" element was transformed from mere servant to owner, *to actual master in the ethnic and cultural adventure of his homeland.* (1991, 53, 54; my emphasis)

Mariano's formulation operates a cunning dialectical turn not only upon Freyre's Eurocentric ascription of lusotropicalism's agency exclusively to the dominant "authorial" role of the white slave master or colonizer, but it posits a South Atlantic variant of Hegel's well-known master-slave dialectic. The inescapable implication is that Freyre was unable to recognize Cape Verde's cultural and physical miscegenation as "lusotropical" precisely because it did not rest on the supremacy of white masters over black and mulatto subordinates (Medina 2000, 60).[13] If, however, one reads Reinaldo's, and especially Luís Henrique's attempts to dominate or "mold" Eva as symbolic of Mariano's form of mulatto mastery, then Eva's body is once again reduced to the status of a territory over which "a war between men" is waged, or competing modes of patriarchy are played out. As with women of color in the lusotropicalist narrative, Eva is bereft of any form of agency or means of resistance. At the same time, the Cape Verdean's cultural agency evoked by Mariano restores, in the last instance, the ascendancy of colonial culture, since "from a cultural standpoint," Cape Verdeans ostensibly consider themselves "predominantly Lusitanian" (1991, 53). This "mastery" thus emerges as a kind of aporetic relation, drifting uncertainly between the North and South Atlantic.

A similarly elusive command defines the two men's obsessive efforts to control Eva, whom Reinaldo somewhat inconsistently regards as "a creature who had the right to belong to no one, to have no masters," to "assert herself as a public woman, public in the sense that she should have remained forever free," "a Portuguese geisha," "a compassionate goddess" (Almeida 2006a, 160). If earlier in the novel Reinaldo associates Eva with motherhood and deific fertility (95), here her figural divinity attaches to their diametrical opposite. Although still figured as a "compassionate goddess," Eva appears as at least provisionally "liberated" from the tropological burden under which her two lovers insist on placing her almost from the onset of the narrative.

She remains nevertheless a figure, a figure, moreover, that is nearly as archetypal and stereotypically feminine as maternity and fecundity: Liberty. At the same time, Eva also comes to register a kind of figural limit or a boundary to figuration itself. And this figural instability further unsettles the allegorical reading I have been outlining. Each time she assumes a supplementary symbolic meaning, she also recurrently eludes or diverts Reinaldo's and Luís Henriques's successive efforts to trope her. For example, by describing her as "a Portuguese geisha," Reinaldo simultaneously ratifies her Lusitanian identity and splits or "Orientalizes" it. In effect, the conventional, even physical signs of Eva's Portuguese identity are consistently loosened. Thus, Eva is surprisingly tall for "the standard of Portuguese women of her generation" (Almeida 2006a, 84), her lips are "fleshy like a mulatto woman's" and have nothing in common with "the sort of fine line that European women generally have" (95). It is as though "the desire to fix identity in the body is inevitably frustrated by the body's refusal to disclose the required signs of absolute incompatibility people imagine to be located there" (Gilroy 2001, 104). Yet Eva's identitarian undecidability is not restricted to the recalcitrant lineaments of her body. Upon meeting an Angolan who assumes that she is Portuguese, for example, Eva retorts that, having spent almost half her life in Cape Verde, she no longer know exactly what she is (Almeida 2006a, 77). She speaks Creole fluently (119), and since her arrival in the archipelago, has, according to Reinaldo, assumed Cape Verdean nationality and a commitment to "build the nation" (223). Indeed, Luís Henriques recalls that immediately after the April Revolution, Eva "embraced the anticolonial cause with such violence that she behaved much more as one of us than one of them" (257). Given these indeterminacies, then, the allegorical reading of sexual violence as anticolonial revenge becomes increasingly untenable.

As Paul Gilroy argues, identities "are formed through relationships of exteriority, conflict, and exclusion. Differences can be found within identities as well as between them. The Other, against whose resistance the integrity of an identity is to be established, can be recognized as part of the self that is no longer plausibly understood as a unitary entity but appears instead as one fragile moment in [a series of] dialogic circuits" (2001, 109–110). Occasionally, despite its troubling figurations of gender relations, the novel endeavors to narrativize precisely this fragile motility, rehearsing a series of often-conflicting identity constructs only promptly to unravel them. As we have seen, among the binaries it consistently displaces is the classical colonizer/colonized. In this sense, and especially from the vantage point of the neoliberal dispensation prevailing in the archipelago around the turn of the last millennium, the fierce confrontations that marked the transition to independence in Cape Verde appear both excessive and somewhat incongruous. For Reinaldo, the strident affirmation of a radical Cape Verdean identity immediately after independence constitutes a form of social violence whose indelible and lasting impact he recognizes in "the painful stories" he hears from the Cape Verdean exiles who chose to seek refuge in the former metropolis at the time of independence because they deemed the archipelago an integral part of "the Motherland" (Almeida 2006a, 21).

His attitude toward his interviewees seems deeply ambivalent. On the one hand, he admits experiencing "an almost perverse pleasure" in confronting his invariably sour and nostalgic compatriots, in whose imagination the archipelago had remained virtually unchanged since 1975, with the "proud success" of Cape Verde nearly three decades after independence: its "achievements in education, health and the GDP," the economic liberalism fostering opportunities undreamed-of by those who witnessed "the birth of this country . . . out of nothing" (Almeida 2006a, 22, 21), and the fact that in a little more than twenty-five years Cape Verde had taken "a greater leap forward" than in centuries of Portuguese presence (26). On the other hand, perhaps precisely in the light of this ostensibly flourishing economic liberalism, and as Almeida remarks elsewhere, "for those people who always lived as Portuguese and saw Cape Verde as a little slice of Portugal, independence represented in fact a breach, a form of psychological violence. We shall only make peace with History when we accept that these folks also have a place in our society" (2006b). What in hindsight makes the infliction of this psychological violence even more absurd is that the new revolutionary leaders who assumed political control of the archipelago in 1975 soon fell prey to an "undisguised arrogance" of power, which led many of them to assume an elitist attitude and "behave like the country's new overlords" (Almeida 2006a, 18). As a character from one of Almeida's early satirical novel asserts more cynically, aside from a slight change in "the people who ruled, everything stayed the same following the substitution of colonial power by national power" (1989, 190).

Admittedly "lost" amidst all the material he collects, Reinaldo "dreams" of writing a book that would be both "a tribute to all those of us who opted to remain in Cape Verde and assume all the risks and uncertainties of a problematic independence in which the world did not believe," as well as a kind of atonement for those whom his generation had, "with the radicalism that is proper to youth, not only prevented from expressing themselves but even from living in peace in a what was also their homeland" (Almeida 2006a, 21–22). As one of the young radicals who vituperated against and occasionally destroyed the property of those they branded "two-legged dogs sell-outs to the Portuguese,"[14] Reinaldo feels personally responsible for the social violence he dreams of expiating, particularly when he interviews Dr. Rocha, a pro-Portuguese former lawyer who was the victim of one such act of vandalism. Nevertheless, not entirely unlike the makeshift sense of "African belonging" that Cape Verdeans must hastily fashion for themselves during the decolonization period (Almeida 1998b, 15), this overwrought radicalism, too, is partly redeemed by what Achille Mbembe regards as the essential political meaning of decolonization: "the active will to community," the collective task of "standing up for oneself and establish a legacy . . . the quest for a future that would not have been written in advance" (2013, 10), what Almeida himself describes as "the tremendous effort to establish ties of solidarity with unknown brothers in suffering" (1998b, 15).

It is to this global emancipatory project, the international or tricontinental, anti-imperial, anticolonial, and antidictatorial struggles across the Global South, which Slaughter and Bystrom survey in the introduction, that Eva commits with exuberant and untrammeled enthusiasm after the April 1974 Revolution, according to Luís Henriques. This utopianism allegedly afflicts Eva as a fit of "that anarchic and healthful folly from . . . the decade when people believed they could change the world, give the land back to those who worked it, do away with man's exploitation by man, equal rights for men and women, crazy stuff like that, but which sustained our reason for being and struggling for years" (Almeida 2006a, 96). In this heady and fleeting epoch of decolonization, the story of the metropolitan left coincided with the story of anticolonial liberation. The South Atlantic flowed into the North, joined in a global emancipatory current. This Utopian vision and revolutionary ethos aimed to undo (yet were ultimately cancelled out by) the unrestrained economic liberalization already asserting itself at the height of the popular uprising in Portugal, and that would sweep through the archipelago a few decades later. As Eva recounts to Reinaldo, the multitude that gathers spontaneously on April 25 before the gates of the political prison at Caxias, shouting, "Long Live Liberty! Long Live Democracy! Long Live the People United!" could not have foreseen that by the time the signature axiom "will never be defeated" was appended to their catchphrases, the people had already been "defeated once again and once again caught in the vice of the forces of capital" (220).

In a considerably less celebratory tone, Reinaldo himself later acknowledges that "the liberalization of our trade" (whose essential political-economic meaning for Cape Verde one might reduce to a turn away from the Global South and toward the North) allowed a few Cape Verdeans "to grow fatter but each day impoverished the country a little more" (Almeida 2006a, 37). From Reinaldo's perspective, Eva must perform a correlate abdication, which, in hindsight, renders all the more futile the struggles over ideological and identitarian purity that marked the transition from colony to nation: compelled to adapt to and subsist "in this liberal new world of 'everyone for himself,' which she ended up joining so as not to starve," Eva obstinately refuses to relinquish outright "the principles and ideals that shaped [her] generation" (114–115).

In a more sardonic appraisal of Eva's obdurate militancy, Reinaldo labels her an "an active capitalist" suffering from "passive communism syndrome," since she apparently attempts to compensate for her growing affluence by intensifying her rhetoric in favor of the disenfranchised, "for whom she didn't do a damned thing anyway since her whole business catered to the well-to-do in the land" (Almeida 2006a, 91). At the same time, however, Reinaldo credits her "last remnants of leftism" with strengthening her will to continue toiling in "the rampant capitalist system" prevalent in Cape Verde" (56). Yet, despite having become superannuated in the face of this unrestrained capital accumulation, and as Eva's refusal wholly to surrender to the implacable logic of global capital perhaps indicates, the ideals of decolonization subsist as the nostalgic reminder and remainder of a once compelling utopian configuration of the Global South Atlantic, a promise of social justice that has been indefinitely deferred, if not absolutely abjured.

Hence, despite his cynicism, Reinaldo shares with Eva the tendency selectively to crystallize decisive elements from the convulsive decades of tricontinental struggle against global capital, and wax nostalgic about what is ultimately an idealized radical past. In at least two different moments and in almost the same words, Reinaldo explains to both Luís Henriques and Eva "how the generation to which [they] belonged had been a privileged one" (Almeida 2006a, 217). Unlike his own succeeding generation of alleged "office leftists" and "passive communists," who "found everything already done," Eva and her older lover had encountered worthy causes to militate for.[15] For Phillip Rothwell, this kind of yearning for political relevance and meaning would belong to a broader structure of nostalgia, which in the last instance deprives those willfully locked in it of any desire to let go of "specters [that] become complicit terms in an act against possible futures" (2009, 407). For Rothwell, in effect, nostalgia (*saudade* in Portuguese), "the quintessence of both the Portuguese and Cape Verdean emigration narrative" (2009, 407), plays a crucial role in the novel (2009, 406). Broadening Žižek's (2002) Lacanian axiom concerning the conscious forgetting of "historical traumas" to encompass memory as a whole, Rothwell sums up his critique of nostalgia in the novel thus: "what we do not remember properly exercises a horrific, immobilizing power over us" (2009, 407). Rothwell seems to be suggesting that lusotropicalism, consistently displaced, occluded, and always deferred, insistently returns in the guise of nostalgia for the lost empire. Eva would be the sign and symbol of this obsessive recurrence. As Reinaldo himself might concur, Rothwell maintains that in spite of "her formally anticolonial stance," Eva remains in thrall to the North, blithely engaging in "the post-independence neoliberal colonisation process" (2009, 409). Eva's politico-economic trajectory would therefore mirror that of the archipelago, whose "special partnership" with the European Union, for instance, recognizes and ratifies Cape Verde's increasing interest in closer links with the European Union, in particular with the EU's outermost regions in the North Atlantic.[16] If Eva is indeed a figure of neoliberal (re) colonization, then what is the role and significance of her gender in this figuration? As I move toward the conclusion of my analysis, I should like to explore in more detail the implications (and limitations) of this claim.

As Rothwell notes, of the several allusions to nostalgia that pervade the novel the key one is perhaps an episode in which Eva and Reinaldo take turns reciting "the poem *Saudade* by Pablo Neruda" (Almeida 2006a, 246). Although frequently attributed to Pablo Neruda in sundry websites,[17] the "poem" is neither a poem nor authored by Pablo Neruda. It is in fact a fragment from a monologue drunkenly delivered by one of the principal characters (the poet Afonso Henriques) in a Brazilian *telenovela* titled *Fera ferida* (Wounded Beast), which initially ran on TV Globo between 1993 and 1994.[18] Reinaldo claims to have elected to declaim Neruda's apocryphal verses to Eva in order to lighten her somber mood. As he tells Luís Henriques, he recites the poem to console Eva after she confesses to him that she misses Luís Henriques. Reinaldo deems Luís Henriques unworthy of her love, who responds by declaiming the final lines of the poem with a nostalgic sigh. Claiming to know the text almost by heart, he recalls taking turns with Eva reciting the same lines in the "terrible days" that followed the commemoration of Cape Verde's independence, when the pair had made a "spectacle" of themselves by getting into a bitter and "embarrassing" public fight.

Whether or not Reinaldo and Eva may have memorized a text they both believed to be a Pablo Neruda poem, the fact remains that in 1975, neither Luís Henriques nor Eva could have recited "verses" that would be produced only around two decades later. In other words, the incident narrated by Luís Henriques could not have occurred. The two recitation situations are nevertheless specular opposites. While Reinaldo speaks the "verses" gazing into Eva's "sad eyes" (Almeida 2006a, 247), she and Luís Henriques, as the latter tells it, have their backs to one another as they recite the same lines. If the former instance indicates closeness, the latter prefigures separation. In effect, for Luís Henriques, the episode "is in some ways related" (248) to the reason why he never joins Eva in Cape Verde. It adumbrates the incident he acknowledges probably having converted into the proverbial "last drop that spilled the cup" (248). When he, Eva and a younger Cape Verdean "disciple" share the same bed, Eva and the younger man furtively have sex, while Luís pretends to be asleep with his back to her and Eva herself keeps her back to the younger man. What Luís Henriques regards as unforgivable is not Eva's unfaithfulness per se, but the fact that on the following day she does not disclose her illicit act to him, as he had wished and expected. As he explains to Reinaldo, had Eva told him what happened, the "secret" would have turned into another mutually shared "complicity," or perhaps into the starting point for a reinvigorated bond between them. Instead, the incident left him wondering, "How many men would she end up sleeping with in Cape Verde, as naturally as she had done with this one here" (265)?

Eva had revealed the occurrence to Reinaldo, insisting that at the time she had ascribed it "no special importance." She considered it "merely an amusing game" to do for the nameless young man what Luís Henriques had done for her, "to throw open the gates of life for him" (Almeida 2006a, 264).[19] Privy to such confidential information, Reinaldo might reasonably regard it as yet another "proof of his superiority over" Luís in Eva's eyes (179). His arrogance is nevertheless short-lived. As Luís Henriques will soon inform him, Reinaldo doesn't know all about Eva.[20] Alternately defining it as a "kind of depravity," an "aberration" (269), and a "tragedy" (272), Luís Henriques discloses that, "Eva enjoys sexual cruising," as Rothwell puts it (2009, 404). This is the "tragic" and allegedly irresistible drive that, according to Luís, "really began to surface when she decided to become an entrepreneur": "Inexplicable impulses lead her to approach men she meets casually in the hotel bars she frequents, sometimes even on the street" (Almeida 2006a, 272).

For Rothwell, Eva's compulsive hypersexuality is unequivocally the "result of her consumption by global capital;" it is ultimately what converts her into "a modern perverse echo of the Portuguese explorer" (2009, 404).[21] One could plausibly assert, however, that Eva's globalized promiscuity echoes not only the Portuguese explorer but also the libidinous Cape Verdean migrant that Jorge Barbosa evokes in a famous 1941 poem "Brother," for instance;[22] or even the oversexed protagonist of Almeida's own *As memórias de um espírito* (2001).[23] Ultimately, however, Rothwell's analysis stands or falls on the reliability of Luís Henriques as a narrator. And since, by Almeida's own admission, whether or not Luís Henriques is lying about Eva remains an open question, Rothwell's reading, albeit compelling, remains merely one among several possible hermeneutic paths laid out before us.

What if Luís Henriques is indeed lying? What if the "tragic" version of Eva that he "cruelly" unveils to an ever more anguished Reinaldo is as apocryphal as the Neruda poem he alleges to have declaimed almost twenty years before it was even written? Tellingly, his account of transatlantic sexual "depravity" confirms (and transposes onto a global plane) the suspicion that Eva's surreptitious sexual encounter with his young "disciple" had aroused in him. And the structure of his emotional estrangement from Eva reproduces that of their political rift after the April Revolution. Therein lies perhaps the key to an alternate reading of Eva's alleged hypersexuality. Just as Luís Henriques, after teaching Eva that faithfulness has nothing to do with sexuality, is unable to cope with the concrete results of his sexual education, so is he, despite allegedly having taught her to assert and exercise her freedom, ultimately incapable of immersing himself in the insurrectionary tumult that will absorb her in April 1974. When Eva and Luís join the ecstatic Lisbon throngs clamoring for liberty, she is "shocked" to realize that "the man of her life [was] shitting his pants with fear and incapable of staying in the people's midst and mingling with them at that moment of unrepeatable joy" (Almeida 2006a, 225). As she compares her Luís Henriques "who spoke of the people not only as if he were one of them, but rather as if he himself personified the people" with the man standing before her, she cannot but begin to gauge "the profound distance that can fall between our most beautiful words and the acts we embody them with" (225). As Luís himself admits to Reinaldo, alluding to the revolutionary theories bandied about on the eve of the April Revolution, "Personally, what I felt above all was the uneasiness of someone who was practicing a religion in whose God I did not believe" (211). By contrast, "Eva felt like a fish in water" (216) among the tumultuous masses. Before the gates of the political prison in Caxias, just as the *Estado Novo*'s political dissidents are about to be released, she realizes she will "never again be able to experience a night like that," that it was "the most glorious time of her life" (220). Indeed, as Luís Henriques acknowledges, it is precisely on April 25 that he irretrievably loses Eva, not to another lover, but to the Revolution: "my own Eva, the one whose character, intelligence, whose soul I thought I had molded in the image and likeness of the woman I always dreamed for myself, to wit, submissive, obedient, sensible, thinking with my head, I lost her on the night of April 25 and I was never able to find her again . . . she had died or rather purely and simply committed suicide" (221).

Significantly, with this concession, Luís Henriques discloses his apostasy with respect to the revolutionary ideals for which he so passionately (and hypocritically) militates. Rather than the "glorious woman," who learned to assert and exercise her autonomy, the free spirit who would brook no effort to possess or dominate her, he yearns for "a kind of blank page" upon which to inscribe everything he "thought, dreamed, desired, projected" (Almeida 2006a, 252). It is at the very instant that Eva's actions begin fully to "embody" his emancipatory doxa, and she concomitantly recognizes the insurmountable gap between his most stirring words and the acts she embodies them with, it is at that moment that Eva "dies" or commits suicide in the eyes of Luís Henriques. In this context, the reference to suicide acquires a broader political signification since it remits us to another of Eva's radical transformations, her unreserved commitment to the anticolonial cause and the Global South, and de facto forfeiture of her homeland, as well as her subsequent contribution to Cape Verde's nation-building project. At this precise and ephemeral moment, Eva appears to heed Amílcar Cabral's famous call for the petty bourgeoisie to commit class suicide.[24] This, according to Reinaldo, is exactly what Cape Verde's nationalist leaders (as well as Luís Henriques and Reinaldo) fail to do after independence.[25] It is this wider (or global) political dimension of Eva's "suicide" that Luís Henriques empties out when he reduces it to an instance of personal loss. In a similarly reductive sense, Eva's "pedagogic" coitus with the nameless young man reproduces her symbolic death on a sexual plane.

In the end, then, the hypersexual Eva that Luís Henriques either invents or reveals to Reinaldo "actualizes" the figure of "the public woman"—a sort of archetypal and conventionally feminine symbol of Liberty—into which Reinaldo had transformed her earlier in the novel. Significantly, whereas Reinaldo's trope is celebratory, Luís Henriques places his figuration under the sign of depravity, aberration, and tragedy. We might legitimately ask, therefore, whether in the "supreme pleasure" she can experience only in the arms of strangers, Eva would seek compulsively to duplicate the matchless and anonymous intimacy of the insurgent multitudes on the night of April 25. It is as though the political sublime that is April 25 lapses into the Sisyphean absurdity of Camus's Don Juan. Precisely because she loves each of her innumerable lovers "with the same passion and each time with [her] whole self," she must obsessively repeat her sexual quest (Camus 1985, 97). Exhibiting a behavior held as "typically masculine," "she accumulated the men" she met: "I love them all, because each one has his own and un-substitutable place" (Almeida 2006a, 231). As Torrente Ballester's Leporello observes of his fabled companion, "For my master 'woman' does not exist, only each single woman, different from the rest, unmistakable" (1998, 259).[26]

Eva's professed sexual addiction is thus the last in a long series of tropes she comes to embody in the novel. It constitutes not just a "sexualization," but arguably (and *pace* Rothwell) a commodification of her revolutionary tricontinentalism. For, in the final analysis, Eva's serial consumption of male bodies, her globalized Don Juanism, would perform a conjunctural shift from liberatory politics to economic neoliberalism that mirrors (and is enabled by) not only her own "forced" immersion into "the liberal new world," but Cape Verde's (and indeed Lusophone Africa's) own transition from revolutionary nationalism to neoliberalism. In this way, her personal "tragedy" would rejoin the global turn that Reinaldo twice signals in the text as fundamentally "tragic" (Almeida 2006a, 96).[27] Presumably the tragedy of the total and precipitous collapse of the late Second World's alternative to global capitalism resides in capital's untrammeled hegemony in the post-Soviet era. As Ella Shohat points out analogously in a classical piece on postcolonialism, "the collapse of Second World socialism . . . has not altered neocolonial policies, and on some levels, [it] has generated increased anxiety among . . . Third World communities . . . concerning their struggle for independence without a Second World counter-balance" (1992, 111).

To accept uncritically Luís Henriques's account of her "tragedy" is, to a certain extent, to assume the irrevocable foreclosure of that revolutionary vision. Yet, as we have seen, despite the neoliberal diversion of this "active will to community" (Mbembe 2013, 10), in spite of the betrayal of what Almeida himself defines as the tremendous effort to establish ties of solidarity with unknown brothers in suffering, Eva refuses to renounce it altogether. She tenaciously holds on its "remnants" (Almeida 2006a, 56), and in fact, according to Reinaldo, it is these very vestiges that sustain her in the face of the rampant neoliberalism that has overrun the archipelago. If there is a nostalgic theme pervading the novel, then, it seems to reside in what Alistair Bonnet identifies, in a different context, as "a yearning for the political drama and moral clarity of the era of socialist revolutionary anticolonial struggle" (2010, 87). On the one hand, the reduction of the utopian dream of tricontinentalism to a nostalgic residue signals its abrogation, or at least its ineluctable desuetude. On the other hand, its survival suggests its persisting relevance to what Achille Mbembe calls "the quest for a future that would not have been written in advance" (2013, 10). Eva's nostalgic utopianism thus broadly resembles Deleuze and Guattari's gloss of Nietzsche's *Untimely*: "the unhistorical vapor that has nothing to do with the eternal, the becoming without which nothing would come about in history but that does not merge with history" (1994, 112). Rather than a modern, perverse avatar of the sixteenth-century Portuguese explorer, rather than a mother figure or even a symbol of Liberty, Eva could perhaps be more productively grasped as the sign of this (un)historical becoming. The irresistible attraction she continues to exert over Reinaldo and Luís

Henriques, notwithstanding her multiple betrayals, would in this way become closely bound with the lure that the moribund political project Mbembe associates *grosso modo* with the decolonization of the global south insistently retains for the collective refashioning of a viable alternative to the current neoliberal dispensation, or "special partnership" with the North Atlantic. In this way, the political enthusiasm that tricontinentalism entailed, and whose tragic abdication Reinaldo bemoans, does not designate that utopia's irrevocable annulment as much as its abiding conjunction with the present historical moment. As with Deleuze and Guattari's understanding of revolution as a "self-referential" concept or event, to define the tricontinental revolution Eva "embodies" as a

> Utopia of immanence is not to say that it is a dream, something that is not realized or that is only realized by betraying itself. On the contrary, it is to posit revolution as plane of immanence, infinite movement and absolute survey, but to the extent that these features connect up with what is real here and now in the struggle against capitalism, relaunching new struggles whenever the earlier one is betrayed. . . . As concept and as event, revolution is self-referential or enjoys a self-positing that enables it to be apprehended in an immanent enthusiasm without anything in states of affairs or lived experience being able to tone it down, not even the disappointments of reason. Revolution is absolute deterritorialization even to the point where this calls for a new earth, a new people. (1994, 100–101)

Yet if Eva figures this "immanent enthusiasm," she does so only to the extent that her figuration is incomplete. As I indicated earlier, Eva also marks a limit to figuration itself, persistently deflecting Reinaldo's and Luís Henriques's consecutive attempts to reduce her tropologically. In resisting rhetorical closure, Eva paradoxically comes close to denoting a revolution whose sign resides outside the historical, but which also denotes "the becoming without which nothing would come about in history." At the same time, while this partial figuration would displace a troubling conversion of the sexual possession of Eva into a metaphor for anticolonial struggle, Eva's putative agency in this political drama remains under erasure in the novel. As noted, Mbembe points out in his critique of Fanon's defense of anticolonial violence that resistance or the revolution appears to be inscribed in the framework of a war between men (2011, 27). I close with a question concerning whether this new earth and new people to come "might be posited beyond the strictures of gender" (Mbembe 2011, 27).

NOTES

1. I discuss this speech at greater length in Madureira (2009).

2. See Madureira (2008).

3. See Madureira (2007), Chapter 2.

4. See Madureira (1994).

5. The street name could be translated as Headwaters or Reservoir Street, literally, Water Mother Street.

6. Although considerably beyond the scope of this essay, it would be intriguing to explore the resonances between this metropolitan aquatic "idol" and the deity known in the English-speaking world as Mami Wata (or Mammy Water), which is revered throughout much of West Africa as well as parts of Central and Southern Africa and indeed the Diaspora. In the context of Luso-African literary and cultural production, a figure that comes readily to mind as the *mãe d'água*'s potential foil is the water spirit Kianda of Angolan mythology. In Angolan novelist Pepetela's *O desejo de Kianda* (*The Return of the Water Spirit*), for instance, Kianda reappears uncannily in a central square of the capital city Luanda at the crucial historical juncture that marks Angola's headlong plunge into the second brutal stage of the civil war and insertion into a no less ruthless phase of neoliberal globalization. Interestingly, the water spirit's reemergence symbolizes a kind of vengeful return of a forsaken (or repressed) spirit of collectivity and solidarity. (I thank Joseph Slaughter for suggesting the link with Mami Wata.)

7. Literally, disorientations. All translations from the novel that follow are my own.

8. The former, for example, ends up "allowing himself to be coddled [by Eva's] maternal tenderness" (127). When she and Luís Henriques resume their romantic involvement, many years after their breakup, she forgives him "as a mother forgives a misbehaving son who humbly returns home with his hands clasped in prayer" (58). And upon meeting Zé Manel, the man she will eventually marry, she grasps "his two hands with maternal gentleness" (147). Ironically, Eva, who is the mother of two sons, regards her two lovers as so similar in personality and character that they could have "issued from the belly of the same mother" (267). It is perhaps no accident, in this light, that Reinaldo's previous lover ("a forty-something *mulatta*" [154]), with whom he "lived out a passionate love affair so unbridled that [he] had no time to crack open a single book" while he was a university student in Brazil (155), was not only and like Eva an older woman, but a mother figure as well: "She could be my mother [and] I ended up falling (*perdido*) for [this] mommy (*mamã*)" (155). As a Brazilian, she is a "mother" who hails from one of the fundamental vertices of the lusotropical "triangle."

9. Henriques admits experiencing a guilty "pleasure," during his years of self-professed clandestine opposition to the authoritarian regime of Salazar's successor Marcelo Caetano, in reading the despot's ornate discourses "behind the backs" of his left-leaning comrades (254). Closing his eyes "as if praying inside a church," he commands Reinaldo's attention and proceeds to recite the fragment in Salazar's "effeminate" voice: "'to mold a soul, what a great achievement! What an extraordinary achievement to shape a character, an individual, a body, an intelligence'" (255). Interestingly, Luís Henriques omits the last clause of the quoted fragment: "as this poor Nation of Portugal demands [from us] in order to become great!" (quoted in Galvão 1975, 43). Following Luís Henriques's spirited impersonation of the "monkish" dictator, Reinaldo conveys his regret at never having heard "the original" (255). It is highly unlikely, however, that his older compatriot would have been able to hear this particular speech because, as far I know, it was never included in his collected speeches editions published during Salazar's lifetime. The fragment is probably excerpted from a 1959 "Open Letter" to Salazar (*Carta aberta ao dr. Salazar*), by Henrique Galvão (1895–1970), a Portuguese military officer, writer and statesman, who began his career as an enthusiastic imperialist and ardent supporter of Salazar's *Estado Novo* regime, but went on to become one of its most vociferous and uncompromising opponents. According to Galvão, the fragment comes from a speech that Salazar, as "a twenty-year old seminarian" (1975, 43), delivered to (or "heaved upon") the students of a high school in the city of Viseu, that is, more than two decades before a military junta would appoint him as Portugal's chief of state. Galvão discerns in the autocrat's juvenilia a glimpse of his later skillful and sedulous mutilation of "the souls and characters of present-day Portuguese," an undertaking for which History should reserve for him the epithet of "Castrator," Galvão concludes (1975, 43). Since the Portuguese political police (PIDE) almost immediately seized the book's first three (1959) editions, and a subsequent 1960 Venezuelan edition was likewise promptly apprehended, it is somewhat improbable that Luís Henriques would have come across the passage before the April 1974 revolution. And if he had discovered Salazar's quote in Galvão's book, there would obviously have been little need to hide it from his dissident friends, quite the contrary, in fact, given its "subversive" source. The inspirational citation he purports to have remembered before the collapse of the Portuguese dictatorship only became widely available after *Carta aberta* was reissued as a "previously unpublished" [*inédito*] text in 1975.

10. "Our landscapes are feminine. . . . One of the reasons is that a large part of the charm is recondite, almost secret. The landscape is also feminine in its art of seduction and its inconstancy" (Queiroz 1940, 23–24).

11. "Portuguese soldiers have said that in their contacts with African fighters in Angola and Mozambique, either the prisoners they captured or when they themselves were taken prisoner, they talked to one another, they exchanged ideas and they found that the average Portuguese peasant was not in a very different situation from the peasants in Africa whom they were fighting" (James 1992, 378).

12. *Funco*: traditional Cape Verdean dwelling constructed with lava slices; *sobrado*: the wood-floored house belonging to the whites.

13. Reinaldo may be indicating precisely this disavowed racism when he evokes Brazil's "veiled, yet fierce racism, albeit sifted through an appearance and a discourse of equality that, at the end of the day, made it more cruel and humiliating than South African apartheid" (16–17).

14. In Creole in the original: "*Catchor de dôs pé vendido aos tugas*."

15. "Besides May 68, they had the April 25 [Revolution] and the independences that came in its wake, to say nothing of the Vietnam War, the invasion of Prague, Allende's and Pinochet's Chile, etc." (96).

16. Dubbed as "a political approach that goes beyond the ordinary donor-beneficiary relationship, thus meeting other mutual interests in the areas of security and development," with the objective of defining "a new model for EU-Cape Verde cooperation," the agreement was signed in 2007 by the president of the European Commission, Durão Barroso, who was a former prime minister of Portugal.

17. See, for example: *Pensador*. "Saudade, Pablo Neruda." Although in his own reading of the passage, Rothwell refers to the lines that are purportedly quoted directly from "Neruda's poem," he also appears to miss that the entire dialogue, in which he discerns "the pair's competing interpretations of *saudade*," never departs from the text of the "poem," as Reinaldo insists (247). The exchange is in fact an almost ritualistic recitation from memory of the entire "poem": "*Saudade* is escorted solitude! / Saudade is when *the lover has gone away, but love lingers on.* / It is to love a past that hasn't yet gone by. / It is *above all* to reject a present that pains us, / but it is also not to see a future that invites us. . . / Saudade is *to continue* feeling that something exists when it exists no more. . . / And *for that reason* it is the hell of those who have lost, / the pain of those left behind,/ the taste of death on the lips of those who remain. / Only one person can desire to feel saudade: the one who never loved. / The greatest suffering *is* to have no one to yearn for [to feel saudade for], / to go through life and not to live. / The greatest suffering is never to have suffered" (My italics) (247).

18. With a few minor variations, Afonso Henriques's monologue is the same as "Neruda's poem," but it ends with the phrase "I confess that I have lived" ("*Falsas atribuições*"). Curiously, Afonso Henriques's last sentence

("*Confesso que vivi*") glosses the title of Neruda's memoir (*Confieso que he vivido*). Might that be the source of the false attribution? The character of Afonso Henriques, who happens to share his name with that of Reinaldo's interlocutor (whose full name is Luís Afonso Henriques), is loosely modeled on the Brazilian novelist and journalist Afonso Henriques Lima Barreto (1881–1922), whose texts are adapted and interwoven into the *novela*'s convoluted plot.

19. Significantly, "to throw open the gates of life" is virtually the same phrase Luís Henriques uses to describe to Reinaldo the lesson he imparts to Eva: "I did throw the gates of life wide open for her (*abri-lhe de par em par as portas da vida*), [and] I taught her and she learned that faithfulness has nothing to do with sexuality" (256).

20. "Now I know that Eva continues to surprise us both, it's as though for each of us she's a different person, or had a private secret space" (269).

21. On the other hand, by lapsing into "the lusotropical mistake" of seeing "love where there is a staging of complicity and exclusion" (409), Reinaldo suffers "the most devastating blow possible to one who felt himself to be the accomplice to, and not the target of, cruelty" (408). As to whether Reinaldo's blow is as shattering as Rothwell indicates, the fact remains that Reinaldo resumes his relationship with Eva upon his return to the archipelago, as the following derisive aside about Luís Henriques's excessively punctilious mannerisms suggests: "It appears that he has been like that forever, since he was a child, as Eva made clear to me when I arrived [back] in Cape Verde and told her about all his pompous airs" (226). Indeed, in *A morte do ouvidor* (The Magistrate's Death, 2010), Reinaldo and Luís Henriques meet once again in the Cape Verdean capital following the encounter related in *Eva*, in order to collaborate in the writing of an historical novel set in the seventeenth century. Eva and her two former lovers not only renew their friendship ties, but Luís Henriques gets to know Eva's husband, whom he considers "an extraordinary person, a healthy, marvelously candid person. And their two sons are happy and friendly boys [who] are already calling me Uncle Henrique" (2010, 133). It seems as thought the blow was considerably less shattering than Rothwell argues.

22. "You crossed oceans/. . . And with the sensual impulse of our people/loved women from foreign lands" (1941, 84).

23. "He had an array of women he would pick from in each of the countries where he had been stationed" (2001, 192).

24. "In order to truly fulfill the role in the national liberation struggle, the revolutionary petty bourgeoisie must be capable of committing suicide as a class in order to be reborn as revolutionary workers, completely identified with the deepest aspirations of the people to which they belong" (Cabral 1966).

25. "The so-called class suicide that Cabral had so steadfastly endorsed and defended as the condition for a dignified post-independence national society seemed increasingly beyond the intent of a good number of those who ruled Cape Verde at the time" (*Eva* 18).

26. Luís Henriques quotes both Camus and Torente Ballester repeatedly throughout the novel.

27. "For me the destruction of the socialist world will endure in Universal History as the twentieth century's greatest tragedy"; "the crumbling of the Soviet Union . . . should be understood as a tragedy for leftist humanity" (217–218).

A Sweet Sweet Tale of Terror

Rita Indiana Hernández Writes the Dominican Republic into the Global South Atlantic

Maja Horn

Columbus's crossing of the Atlantic and accidental arrival in the Americas on the island that he would name "Hispaniola" catapulted it into the center of a new Atlantic world. Indeed, soon after 1492 Hispaniola was at the forefront of events that would come to shape Atlantic history. The first European settlement of the so-called new world was founded on Hispaniola, and not long after, "Hispaniola received the first blacks to ever to arrive on the western hemisphere. It inaugurated both the colonial plantation and New World African slavery, the twin institutions that gave blackness its modern significance" (Torres-Saillant 2010, 2). Yet, the meaning that "blackness" would come to assume on the eastern and western parts of the island diverged notably. In the late eighteenth century, Hispaniola was formally divided between French and Spanish colonial powers, and this division eventually evolved into what are today the Dominican Republic and the Republic of Haiti.[1] Though these neighboring Global Southern nations emerged out of a shared Atlantic history, their relation is nowadays described mainly as one of stark difference, if not of conflict, rather than of commonality.

Recent developments on the island of Hispaniola have called international attention to their troubled relation. In the fall of 2013 the Dominican supreme court issued a ruling that effectively denationalized approximately 200,000 people of Haitian descent in the Dominican Republic (as well as anyone else born to two noncitizen parents). This ruling has sparked international concern and on March 24, 2014, the Inter-American Commission on Human Rights (IACHR) held a hearing in Washington, D.C., about its effects and consequences. While the Dominican supreme court's ruling is not explicitly directed at Haitian immigrants and Dominicans of Haitian descent it is clearly mainly aimed at them and emerges out of a long history of anti-Haitian official discourse and sentiments.

Unfortunately, this current turn of events, as well as Dominican-Haitian relations more broadly, are addressed in the international media as well as by scholars less familiar with the country in often very reductive terms. Carlos U. Decena has incisively critiqued how the international media and outside observers portray the supreme court ruling and the anti-Haitianism and Dominican racial beliefs that are thought to underlie it, namely the presumed self-denial of Dominicans' own blackness and the concurrent racist attitudes toward presumably darker-skinned Haitians. Such accounts tend to depict Dominican racial attitudes as both deeply pathological and ultimately "historically anachronistic"—inherently "unmodern" in ways that, at least implicitly, uphold the United States as the harbinger of a more commendable racial modernity (Decena 2014). This is in fact a longstanding tendency. As Silvio Torres-Saillant notes in his authoritative *Introduction to Dominican Blackness*, Dominican articulations of race are generally treated in "either of two ways: omission or trivialization" (2010, 2). Trivializing accounts point to the "oddity of an African-descended people unable to come to terms with their own blackness" in a way that often "borders on caricature" and that presents Dominicans' "self-identity as delusional" (2010, 1–2).[2] A recent special issue of the *Black Scholar* on "Dominican Blackness" echoes Torres-Saillant's critique of how "the bulk of US academic and mainstream output on blackness in the Dominican Republic" has shown "a strange inability to let go of narratives emphasizing Dominican self-hatred, negrophobia, and anti-Haitianism" even "when investigators find a recognizable (to them) embrace of African origins and black identity" (Chetty and Rodríguez 2015, 2). Such renderings of Dominican racial beliefs and anti-Haitianism ignore the work of many Dominican scholars as well as of Dominican writers and artists, both on an off island, who have long addressed these in more historically informed and complex ways that offer explanations beyond suggestions that a whole people is steeped in delusions. Prominent among them is the Dominican writer and musician Rita Indiana Hernández (b. 1977), who is considered one of the most important creative and critical voices of her generation.

Hernández addresses and problematizes Dominican views of Haitians and the racial and nationalist beliefs that underwrite these already in her debut novel, *La estrategia de Chochueca* (1999). In a more recent novel, *De nombres y animales* (2013), Dominican-Haitian everyday life relations in fact take center stage. In this chapter, however, I want to foreground a much less known performance piece and text by Hernández that—while it has yet to receive any scholarly attention—offers her most historical engagement with Dominican-Haitian relations and the island of Hispaniola. I argue that *Sugar/Azúcal* (2003) suggests how the complex South-South relations of the two nations on Hispaniola may be usefully considered through the lens of a shared South Atlantic history. Indeed, Hernández's work, and Dominican-Haitian relations more broadly, can serve as a promising point of departure for conceptualizing South-South relations in the Atlantic world and the politics that may emerge out of these—including in relation to knotty issues of race—that are not captured by the too general concept of the "Global South" or by Paul Gilroy's (1993) generative articulation of the "black Atlantic." Specifically, I suggest that alongside the two critical-cultural strategies that according Gilroy emerge out of the history of the Black Atlantic, the "politics of fulfillment" and "the politics of transfiguration," other forms of resistant politics emerge particular to colonial and postcolonial locales and their encounters with modernity in the Global South.

The oft-circulated narrative of the two nations of Hispaniola locked in a perpetual fight, as suggested, for example, by the title of Michelle Wucker's book *Why the Cocks Fight: Dominicans, Haitians, and the Fight for Hispaniola* (2000), has been questioned and revised in various ways in the past few decades. Historian April J. Mayes outlines usefully in *The Mulatto Republic: Class, Race, and Dominican National Identity* (2014) a few of the scholarly approaches to apprehending Dominican-Haitian relations in more complex ways. Mayes points in particular to the work of a new generation of Dominican scholars, the so-called *nueva ola*, that emerged after the end of the Trujillo dictatorship in 1961 and challenged established views of Dominican-Haitian relations as one of inherent and longstanding antagonism that had been cemented by the Rafael L. Trujillo dictatorship (1930–61) and the Joaquín Balaguer years (1966–78, 1986–96).[3] This generation of scholars revised prevailing understandings of key moments in the history of Dominican-Haitian relations, including prevalent accounts of Haiti's unification of the island (1822–44), and thereby complicated the narrative of deep-seated historical antagonism that had become dominant in the twentieth century. Similarly, a group of anthropologists and sociologists, including Carlos Andújar, Martha Ellen Davis, Carlos Esteban Deive, Franklin Franco Pichardo, June Rosenberg, and Dagoberto Tejeda Ortiz, among others, began highlighting the importance of Afro-Dominican histories, practices, and beliefs that had remained largely unacknowledged in official historical accounts. They reveal some of the cultural and religious continuities across the border of Hispaniola that challenged prevalent views of their inherent difference, namely that "Haitians practiced voodoo, Dominicans Catholicism; Haitians spoke Creole, Dominicans Spanish; Haitians were black, Dominicans were of mixed race or white. More than this, Haitian culture and society were seen as an extension of Africa, whereas Santo Domingo clung to its pure Spanish origins" (San Miguel 2005, 39).

Indeed, part of the broader project of revising dominant historical narratives surrounding Dominican-Haitian relations included scholars turning to the fissures within the national community, noting the role that specific Dominican classes and intellectual circles played in consolidating and upholding this narrative. Scholars highlighted the "the substantial divergence and distance between official state anti-Haitianism and the quotidian, lived experience of ethnic and racial difference among non-elite Dominicans" (Mayes 2014, 6). Foregrounding these internal fissures and the divergences and differences within the Dominican national community is an important corrective but also raises the hardly resolved question of "how (or whether) Dominican elites managed to impose their ideology beyond their class . . . among working-class and lower-middle-class Dominicans" (Mayes 2014, 3). This question resurfaced also in the discussions surrounding the 2013 Dominican supreme court ruling when it was noted that among some of the outspoken advocates of this ruling were Dominicans perceived as clearly "black" by observers.

How racist and anti-Haitian beliefs variously traffic in the Dominican imaginary is shown in Hernández's novel *La estrategia de Chochueca* (1999). In it, the young female protagonist recounts how she had been taught to fear Haitians through popular sayings such as "*los haitianos se comían a los niños*" (the Haitians ate children), (1999, 19). Such popular sayings speak to how anti-Haitian views extended beyond official state discourses and came to shape popular Dominican views in varying degrees as well. However, once the young protagonist witnesses how the many Haitians working in construction in Santo Domingo built "*la mitad de la ciudad con sus brazos*" (half of the city with their own arms), she dismisses these popular sayings (Hernández 1999, 19). Hernández's novel thus critically points to the disjuncture between the reality of Haitian migrants' social marginality in the country and the paranoid racialized narratives and myths that circulate about them.

Hernández's novel *De nombres y animales* (2013), published in Spain, similarly shows the disjuncture between widespread anti-Haitian sentiments and actual interactions and experiences of Dominicans with Haitians. The novel addresses these popular anti-Haitian beliefs as well as the discriminatory action of state institutions, namely the police, to show how they both forestall a stronger integration of Haitians and people of Haitian descent into Dominican civil society.

Beyond the scholarly and literary probing into the fissures *within* the Dominican national community and imaginary to understand its racial and anti-Haitian imaginary, other scholarly approaches have also looked *outside* the national borders to account for these. As Mayes describes, for some "Dominican anti-Haitianism . . . responds to shifts in regional and global power" (2014, 6). Silvio Torres-Saillant, Ginetta Candelario, and Anne Eller, as well as many of the contributors to the aforementioned *Black Scholar* special issue, foreground the role of outside views, and of the United States specifically, in shaping Dominican racial discourses. They show the notable role that imperial US practices played in consolidating the notion that Haitians were "more African" than Dominicans and in encouraging Dominicans to racially self-differentiate themselves from Haitians as a way of gaining a "foothold among the 'civilized nations'" (Eller 2014, 88). The role that the United States played in fomenting and consolidating such racial identifications, of course, remains thoroughly unacknowledged in current US critiques of Dominican racial beliefs and Dominican-Haitian relations.[4]

The necessary consideration of Dominican-Haitian relations in the context of US imperialism and broader geopolitical issues is evinced also in Hernández's public response to the Dominican supreme court ruling in an editorial for the Spanish newspaper *El País* in October 2013. There Hernández critiques the recent ruling and how Haitian migrants are treated by the Dominican bureaucracy and their purposeful marginalization in Dominican civil society; yet, the entire piece is more broadly framed as a response to the US televangelist preacher Pat Robertson. Robertson infamously declared the 2010 earthquake to be a direct result of Haiti's pact with the devil to secure its independence from France in 1804.

Robertson argued that the comparably greater prosperity of the Dominican Republic is evidence of this nation's more commendable Christian inclinations. Hernández in her editorial ultimately reverses this logic to argue that it is Dominicans' treatment of Haitians in their country that is "devilish."

> Queremos que construyan nuestras casas, iglesias y puentes, queremos que corten nuestra caña y que limpien nuestra mierda, pero sin formar parte de la sociedad civil, víctimas de una ilegalidad irreparable, para cuya superación nos abren cada vez más caminos los países del Primer Mundo, adonde los dominicanos acudimos de la misma forma, en cientos de miles. Pat, dime ahora, ¿de qué lado de la isla viven los diabólicos? (Hernández 2013)

> We want them to build our houses, our churches and bridges, we want them to cut our sugar cane and that they clean our shit, but without forming part of civil society, victims of an irreparable illegality, for surmounting which ever more paths are opened up to us by First World Countries, where we Dominicans show up in the same way, in hundreds of thousands. Pat, tell me now, on which side of the island do the diabolic live?

Thus, Hernández squarely places the blame here on Dominicans for their treatment of Haitians; yet, at the same time, she also insists on placing these Dominican-Haitian relations in the context of highly overdetermined outside ideologies and the racialized and civilizational dichotomies that they superimpose on the two nations of Hispaniola. Hernández furthermore emphasizes the shared experience of Haitians and Dominicans with mass migration and illegality as they try to escape from Hispaniola where living conditions for the majority of people are often dire on both sides of the border. Hernández's editorial thus indexes a much larger geopolitical and cultural dynamic, driven by the Global North, that both Haiti and the Dominican Republic are embedded in and that has profoundly noxious and far-reaching effects. The legal drama unfolding on the island, according to Hernández's editorial, hence cannot be divorced from North-South power dynamics and the racial, economic, political and social inequalities that shape these.

Both approaches that pay attention to the racial and ideological fissures within the Dominican Republic as well as approaches that note how these cannot be divorced from broader North-South relations, are essential for understanding Dominican-Haitian relations. However, in addition to these lenses, I argue for the importance of considering these two nations'

South-South relations within the frame of the South Atlantic. Neither approaches that foreground primarily the national context—which arguably emerged out of European (mainly Spanish and French) colonialism and hence foregrounds *North* Atlantic history—nor the ones that foreground North-South dynamics (especially between the United States and the island) sufficiently consider how these conflictive South-South relations may be thought in the context of their shared *South* Atlantic connections and history.

The most generative critical framework for thinking shared Atlantic connections, particularly in relation to race, beyond nationalist approaches, is Paul Gilroy's concept of the "black Atlantic" developed in *The Black Atlantic: Modernity and Double Consciousness* (1993). In this work, Gilroy foregrounds the "vernacular cultures of the black Atlantic diaspora" (1993, 38), or what he calls "the stereophonic, bilingual, or bifocal cultural forms originated by, but no longer the exclusive property of, blacks dispersed within the structures of feeling, producing, communicating, and remembering that I have heuristically called the black Atlantic world" (1993, 3).

Gilroy's capacious articulation usefully allows us to turn to shared affinities, beyond nationalist and black essentialist forms, produced by the black Atlantic history and experience. As he states, the black Atlantic indexes a "desire to transcend both the structures of the nation state and the constraints of ethnicity and national particularity" (Gilroy 1993, 19).

A fundamental part of this project, written from the vantage point of the black experience in Britain, are for Gilroy "the affinities and affiliations which link the *black of the West* to one of their adoptive, parental cultures: the intellectual heritage of the West since the Enlightenment" (1993, 2, my emphasis). While Hispaniola, and the Caribbean and Latin America more broadly, are geographically certainly part of the "West," we may ask what particular relation their position in the colonial and postcolonial South creates with the "intellectual heritage of the West." Their "affinities and affiliations" with this heritage arguably differs qualitatively and ideologically from Euro-American locales that more readily can lay claim to this heritage. The black diasporic experience in the Global South occurs in contexts that have a much more tenuous claim to the Enlightenment project, and to "modernity" more broadly, than the Global North. In these colonial and postcolonial contexts, "blackness" thus also intersects with these legacies differently and in ways that are not fully captured by Gilroy's "black Atlantic" framework, which foregrounds the experience of the black diaspora in Northern regions (Britain and the United States in particular) that more readily lay claim to "modernity." The more tenuous relation of the colonial and postcolonial South to "Western modernity," and how this refracts the black diasporic experience in particular ways, suggests that it may be useful to consider the "black South Atlantic" as a specific analytical lens for this region.

Other scholars have also pointed to some of the limitations of Gilroy's concept of the black Atlantic. For example Sibylle Fischer, who also discusses Gilroy's work in relation to Hispaniola, addresses how his particular perspective and the aspects it privileges sidelines the "non-Anglophone areas of the Atlantic," which "are only nominally included in his study" (2004, 35).[5] In the introduction to this volume, Joseph R. Slaughter and Kerry Bystrom echo this observation, similarly observing that Gilroy's black Atlantic was "largely situated in the North" and "primarily Anglophonic" (this volume). I want to add that it is not only specific differences between Anglophone and Hispanophone, Lusophone, or Francophone worlds of the Atlantic that recede in Gilroy's study; more broadly, the relation that Gilroy traces between "blacks in the West" and "Western modernity" is not exactly the same as the relation between blacks in the colonial and postcolonial West and these regions' more fraught relation with "Western modernity."

Considering Dominican-Haitian relations through a Global South Atlantic lens, and Dominican racial beliefs within a black South Atlantic context, does not necessarily offer a radically new understanding of these, but it provides an important added lens. While the "global" in "Global South Atlantic" accounts for how outside forces, in particular Global Northern ones, have inevitably shaped Hispaniola's colonial and postcolonial history, the "South Atlantic" reminds us of the island's shared black Atlantic history as well as of how both countries, despite their presumed differences, have had to negotiate a much more tenuous relation to the Western Enlightenment project, and to modernity more broadly, than North Atlantic contexts. At least on the Eastern side of the island, in the Dominican Republic, negotiations of race cannot be divorced from Western notions "modernity" and of the desire to be "modern"—themselves inevitably Eurocentric and racially tinged—and the concomitant rejection of what is perceived as antimodern.

In the context of recent developments a Global South Atlantic framework would help to account for Dominican racial beliefs and anti-Haitianism in less reductive and simplistic ways. Specifically, it foregrounds a shared Atlantic history and black Atlantic experience on Hispaniola as a point of departure, hence countering conventional accounts that posit an inherent racial and ethnic incommensurability between them. Furthermore, this framework allows us to consider how this shared black Atlantic experience was shaped and reshaped differently in the vortex of colonial and imperialist forces particular to the Global South and under the aegis of an always (presumably) lacking or lagging modernity vis-à-vis European–North American locales. Indeed, the very perception of the Global South's "lacking/lagging" in modernity is deeply wound up with the perceived racial otherness of the peoples of the Global South. Hence the Global South has largely had to maneuver the contradictory space of laying claim to a modernity whose ideological basis presupposes their racial otherness and cultural inferiority and finding ways of making these commensurate, as Rita Indiana Hernández's work shows. I would in fact argue that perhaps the principal ideological difference between the Global North and the Global South is how Western modernity's inherent contradictions, in particular in relation to race, had to be made commensurate in the non-white colonial and postcolonial South in more urgent, practical, and all-encompassing (nationalist) ways than in the North that traditionally has perceived itself as dominantly white. The results of this ideological negotiation and lived contradiction can have particularly noxious results, as has been the case for the Dominican Republic. At the same time, this Global South Atlantic context should give pause to portrayals of Dominican racism as inherently more "backward" and "antimodern" vis-à-vis a presumably more commendable US racial modernity, which reproduces this well-known North-South dynamic.

How Dominican-Haitian relations may be approached through a Global South Atlantic lens is modeled, I suggest, in Rita Indiana Hernández's most sustained engagement with the Dominican Republic's racial history and relation with Haiti, the performance piece and performance text and catalogue *Sugar/Azúcal: A Sweet Sweet Tale of Terror* (2003). This performance piece was conceived and first performed by Hernández in Norway at the Kunsternes Hus in Oslo in 2003. The Kunsternes Hus in Oslo had organized an exhibit of contemporary art from Haiti and the Dominican Republic that for the opening event brought some of these Haitian and Dominican artists together, including Hernández. The exhibit and the accompanying documentary were undertaken to place the artistic visions of the two sides of the island, perceived by the organizers as starkly different, in dialogue with each other. In the words of the curator, Inghild Karlsen,

> There are many things that distinguish these two countries: language, history, religion, political systems, ethnic backgrounds and skin colors. Even so, their artists have shown remarkable openness and determination to hear about each other, to meet and to make this exhibition a reality. It is a spirit that holds promise for the future of the two countries. (2013)

It is in this context of spending several weeks with a group of Dominican and Haitian artists outside of Hispaniola and partaking in an exhibit that took their presumed differences as a point of departure, that Hernández developed the performance piece *Sugar/Azúcal*. Yet, while the piece traces conflictive Dominican-Haitian historical relations, it takes as its points of departure the two nations' shared origin in the Global South Atlantic.

After its premiere in Oslo in 2003, the performance piece was also performed in Santo Domingo, as well as in San Juan, Puerto Rico, in 2004. The Spanish Cultural Center in Santo Domingo (Centro Cultural de España) sponsored a publication of the performance text, which was accompanied by a foreword and afterword by this chapter's author. The performance itself featured Hernández, wearing a black ski mask, declaring a series of monologues and poems while at the same time slides of her, again wearing a black ski mask, were projected behind her (see Figure 3). The pictures, taken in various places in Oslo, responded often humorously to cues in the text. These visual images thus refracted the spoken performance and produced a doubling of Hernández's figure as they mediated, interrupted, and reframed her live performance. This dynamic of outside meanings and views erupting into the present and complicating, if not destabilizing, her live performance, speaks, at least obliquely, to the difficulty of the colonial and postcolonial Caribbean claiming a singular and stable identity and self-narrative in the face of its own cultural multiplicity as well as vis-à-vis the pervasive presence of external forces and outside views that produced this multiple reality in the first place.

The performance piece interweaves various discourses around the theme and person of *Sugar/Azúcal*. Hernández performs *Sugar/Azúcal* as a sort of female Caribbean superhero (Figure 4), who narrates the colonial and postcolonial histories of sugar on Hispaniola—from the earliest plantations to the contemporary moment. Hence, sugar is both the object and the subject of Hernández's performance and highlights thereby both a long racialized history of oppression and exploitation—of objectification—in which the sugar economy played a principal role, as well as the

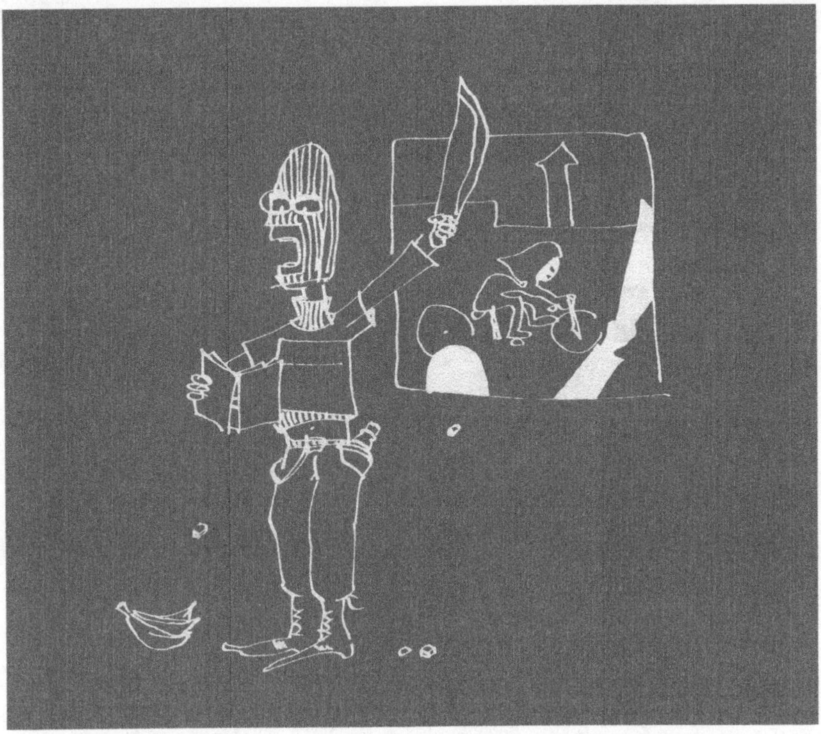

Figure 3. *Sugar's Performance*. Artwork by Rita Indiana Hernández.

particular forms of agency, survival, and subject formation that this history produced.

The various narrative strands in the published performance text include a historical timeline that runs on the right edge of various pages and traces how Hispaniola's history has been shaped by the sugar economy and the Atlantic slave trade triangle, and how these have put Haitians and Dominicans into close but also unequal contact for many centuries. Some of the timeline's events and themes are then expanded upon in the rest of the text/performance through short episodic pieces that elaborate them further. Importantly, this timeline's very first entry is "*1516, el primer trapiche aparece en la Española*" (1516, the first sugar mill appears on Hispaniola), hence giving the establishment of the sugar industry a foundational role in the history of the island. In turn the very last entry on the timeline reads, "*1514, se discute la necesidad de importar negros directamente desde Africa y no*

Figure 4. *Sugar as a Caribbean Superhero*. Artwork by Rita Indiana Hernández.

de España, pues estos últimos conocían el castellano y podían hablar entre ellos y urdir trampas" (1514, the need for importing blacks directly from African and not from Spain was discussed, since the latter knew Spanish and could communicate with each other and plot traps). The timeline's closing entry thus focuses on how the Atlantic slave trade and the forms of racial oppression and control fostered by the sugar plantation economy were integral to the history of Hispaniola. Moreover, the timeline is historical in content but not chronological, given that it begins in 1516 and ends in 1514, with in-between dates stretching to the late twentieth century. The island's historical trajectory, according to this timeline, which jumps chronologically back and forth throughout, is thus firmly placed within and determined by the framework of the Atlantic world. Moreover, the fact that the timeline, from its first to its last entry, retrogresses two years, from 1516 to 1514, gestures to a historical circularity that proffers a notable challenge to views of Hispaniola's trajectory as one of inevitable progress and insists that the Atlantic framework remains as important to understanding the present as understanding the past.

Not solely the initial Spanish colonial influence but a broader web of European influences on Hispaniola is traced by the timeline. For example, other entries on the timeline read that in "*(1716) Francia llega tarde a la producción de azúcar*" ([1716] France arrives late to the production of sugar). And in "*1878, Alemania se ubica como el mayor productor de azúcar*" (1878, Germany takes on the place of the major producer of sugar). These entries attest to how various European powers at different times drove the demand and trade of sugar during both colonial and postcolonial times on the island; Hispaniola was thus already part of a globalized economy, in which, as much of the Global South, it found itself at a disadvantage vis-à-vis Northern interests. Indeed, these entries reveal how various European influences were formative on the entire island of Hispaniola, and not limited to the eastern or western side, or to what are now the Dominican Republic and the Republic of Haiti. This is a critical move by Hernández's piece, since conventionally the Dominican Republic is viewed primarily in relation to Spanish colonialism and Haiti in relation French colonialism. In contrast, shared Global North-South dynamics that affect both sides of Hispaniola are foregrounded here that are not captured by primarily "nationalist" historical approaches that focus primarily on each side's relation with their colonizing powers.

Hernández's performance piece and text further suggests how Hispaniola's South Atlantic historical context produced determinative and long-lasting racial realities and imaginaries. Among the earliest historical references alluding to the racialized imaginary that took shape on the island are: "*1519, plaga de hormigas*" (1519, ant plague) and "*1521, otra plaga*" (1521, another plague). The relevance of these ant plagues is more fully fleshed out in the performance text's closing episode. This narrative episode reproduces part of Fray Bartolomé de Las Casas's famous sixteenth-century account of an ant plague on Hispaniola. The text tells how at a time when the indigenous population was already significantly decimated and African slaves had begun to replace their labor force, the Spanish colonizers were looking forward to the riches that the sugarcane harvest would bring. Yet, these hopes were destroyed by a massive ant plague that devoured everything in the black ants' path. This well-known Las Casas episode has been widely interpreted as an expression of the racial paranoia emerging on Hispaniola as whites were being outnumbered by an increasing black population; indeed, as the timeline marks with another entry, such fears resulted in that in "*1543, la población blanca no se atreve a salir al campo si no es en grupos de 50 o 60 personas armadas*" (1543, the white population does not dare to go to the countryside unless they are in groups of 50 to 60 armed people). Thus, since the earliest colonial times a racial imaginary emerged, particularly among the elite, that relied on a series of racial suppressions and displacements produced by the economic and social consequences of European colonization and the Atlantic slave trade.

The particular unreality produced by this racial imaginary is condensed in one of the several one-sentence slogans in the performance text: "*El último slogan de la voracidad hiperreal del azucal, una contagiosa institución que te invita: apúntale a las hormigas*" (the last slogan of the hyperreal voracity of sugar, a contagious institution that invites you: aim at the ants) (Figure 5). Here the sugar economy and the reality it instituted are explicitly tied to racialized forms of displacement and paranoia that lead to false perceptions of threat and misdirected defenses. The literal and most devastating effect of such misdirected threats produced by this racialized imaginary and its particular suppressions was the 1937 massacre of thousands of Haitians and Dominicans of Haitian descent on the Dominican side of the border during the Trujillato (1930–61). The timeline entry that refers to the massacre is preceded by three entries addressing Dominican-Haitian relations that are, importantly, chronologically regressive again: "*1949, Trujillo manda construir ingenio Catarey*" (1949, Trujillo orders to build the sugar mill Caterey), "*1936, un intenso movimiento de inmigración clandestina de braceros haitianos se desarrolla en la frontera con la anuencia, dirección y control de miembros del Ejercito Dominicano*" (1936, an intense clandestine migration movement of Haitian workers develops at the border with the consent, direction and control of members of the Dominican military), "*1801, Toussaint unifica la isla*" (1801, Toussaint unifies the island). It is after these three entries that the timeline places the entry that in "*1937, 20,000 haitianos son ejecutados en territorio dominicano, los únicos ciudadanos haitianos cuya vida es respetada durante la masacre son los empleados en los bateyes de las corporaciones azucareras*" (1937, 20,000 Haitians are executed on Dominican territory, the only Haitian citizens whose life was respected during the massacre were the employees in the sugar corporations' towns). This reverse historical sequence deftly links Dominican state support of the sugar industry, especially by Trujillo, to the need for a migrant Haitian labor force to sustain it, overlaid against a previous historical backdrop when Haitians had ruled the Dominican Republic in the nineteenth century, yet in the context of a very different power dynamic when Haitians were politically and militarily dominant. It is against these backdrops and in relation to the different power dynamics that they index that the tragedy of the 1937 massacre of thousands of Haitians and Dominicans of Haitian descent is introduced. The massacre is thus presented as emerging out of a particular history of racial suppressions and disavowals fostered by elite and state forces.

Figure 5. *Sugar Slogan*. Artwork by Rita Indiana Hernández.

This noxious dynamic is brought into the late twentieth century by the first narrative episode in the performance text. This episode recounts how in 1984 the Dominican state tried to encourage Dominicans through television commercials to volunteer to harvest sugar cane, because Haitian workers "were suddenly too costly." A "celebrity brigade slept over in the cane [field] and one could see them on TV every night," including a "Swedish model dressed up as a sweaty cane cutter, chopping down the cane while some little yellow arrows with signs explained the names of the movements that the machete was performing."[6] The official state "face" for this initiative is here a blonde Swede, a figure deeply at odds with the reality of cane historically always having been cut by darker-skinned workers, many of Haitian or Anglo-Antillean origin. Such racial displacements and transferences are figuratively represented by the narrator herself, who recounts how, beginning that summer, she would easily faint or "black out" easily ("*se me pone negrecito*"). The blood sugar low that that leads to her fainting figuratively alludes here to the county's concurrent danger of facing a "sugar low" (without a labor force to harvest the cane). Similarly, alongside the state's disavowal of blackness, the narrator tells of her own "change in color" from "going black" to, in the end, being told "girl you sure are pale" when she is about to faint. Dominican racial disavowals, or "changes in color," are closely associated in this scene with physical illness and debility.

This linking of a history of elite and state racial unease with bodily disease is reinforced by the historical time line, which includes entries that mark the date of the discovery of insulin and of medical tests for sugar in urine. Such references suggest how, beyond the economic realm, the pervasiveness of the sugar economy and its racialized effects impact the physical constitution of subjects and create perilous physiological imbalances. These "gut wrenching" effects are literalized in another brief narrative episode in which the descent through the colon is narrated as a dizzying roller coast ride: "*Este roller coaster invertido . . . contiene una caida de bienvenida de 100 piés, seguida por una vertiginosa sensación acorazonada, una torcedura en línea y varios descensos*" (this inverted roller coaster . . . contains a one hundred feet welcoming drop, followed by a vertiginous arrival sensation, an inline twist and several descents) (Figure 6). This turbulent intestinal ride of the colon invariably evokes, at least in Spanish, its homonym Cristobal "Colón," who, of course, plays a key role in the creation of the South Atlantic world and the new and vertiginous racial imaginaries that it produced.

The "objectifying" history and forces of colonialism and sugar production on Hispaniola, traced creatively by Hernández, produce particular Caribbean subjectivities and strategies, including resistant ones. Alongside the noxious effects of the racialized sugar economy, *Sugar/Azúcal* highlights subjects and forms of subjectivity that emerged to contest these forces. The timeline, for example, includes an entry for the legendary Boukman ceremony, the religious ritual that is said to have incited the slaves' uprising that would eventually lead to the Haitian Revolution and to Haitian independence in 1804.[7] Also mentioned is the iconic Afro-Cuban singer Celia Cruz, who often marked her performances with the exclamation "*Azúcar*" and repurposed the call for "sugar" into a spirited onstage Caribbean battle cry. Most important, however, there is the protagonist "Azucal" herself, a comic-heroic subject produced by Hispaniola's colonial and postcolonial historical trajectory. "Azucal" is presented as a wannabe swashbuckling postcolonial super hero. At the same time she is an ambivalently raced and gendered subject, a notably androgynous figure with the "*color de hormiga*" (the color of ants), but who is represented by the

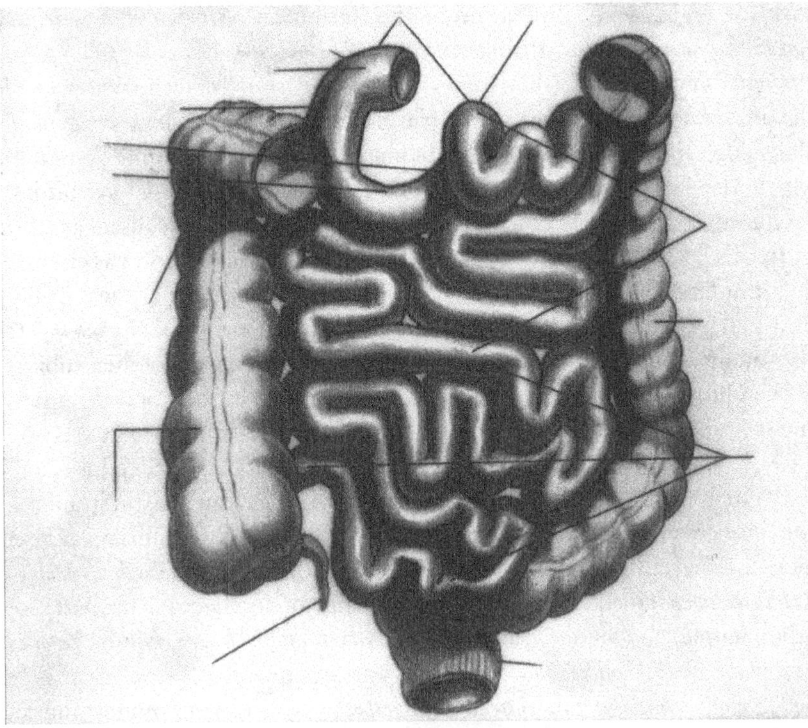

Figure 6. *Sugar's Intestinal Ride*. Artwork by Rita Indiana Hernández.

lighter-skinned Hernández donning a black ski mask (Hernández 2003). The black mask and its uncomfortable evocation of both black minstrelsy and of a masked assailant, of racial and violent "terror," forestalled receptions of this performance piece as simply "comedic," despite its several comic moments. The performance thereby spoke effectively but also uneasily about Dominican racial ambivalences and denials as well as to the impact that outside views and constructions of racial otherness have had on such forms of "masking" race on Hispaniola.

Indeed, "sugar" never aims solely at the constraints of an impoverished postcolonial Caribbean, or at an exceptionalist Dominican racial imaginary, but always also at the Global Northern powers and mechanisms that helped produce and continue to reproduce this "othered" and racialized Caribbean. The long poetic text declared by "Azucal" includes as much allusions to tourism, if not sex tourism, about tourists snorkeling the Atlantic to come see and taste Caribbean "sugar," as well as references to anthropologists who come to probe the Caribbean's African roots: "*te tan entrevistando a ti y a tus African ancestors todo el tiempo. Y si es verdad que tus African ancestors at all*" (they interview you and your African ancestors all the time. And if its true that your African ancestors at all). These are evoked alongside critiques of a broader exploitative capitalist economic system in which the Caribbean as an exporter of primary materials, agricultural products, and of people tends to be at a significant economic disadvantage.

In this deeply unequal context the Caribbean subject emerges as embedded in a larger desiring economy and forms of being that are not of her own making. She wants to be "*la gran cosa*" (the big thing), "*personaje*" (a personality), who wants "*la fama*" (fame) but who, as a postcolonial subject in the Global South, does not have access to the resources, opportunities, and positions as those in the Global North. Instead, "Azucal" has to rely on a whole set of "cannibalistic procedures" or secondhand procedures and forms of appropriation—echoing other South American artistic strategies and movements—that allow her to make do in the Caribbean. These include subverting property relations, such as through "*el robo de la propiedad intelectual de otras personas*" (the stealing of intellectual property of other people), "*samplear*" (sampling), "*tomar prestado dinero, música, zapatos o cualquier electrodoméstico de alguien que ya te está invitando a cenar o que ya te está proporcionando alguna clase de favor especial*" (borrowing money, music, shoes or any domestic electronic machine from someone who is already inviting you to dinner or who is already doing you a special favor). These also include habits and practices of "superstition," "bad memory," "improvising," "underachieving," and "oral traditions" that go against the grain of guiding Western norms of behavior centered on rationality, historical continuity, strategic action, achievement, and the written word. Also included are characteristics such as "being a fan," "being poor" and "being hellen keller or barney," referring to forms of subjectivity that in different ways fall outside normative notions of the autonomous and the "proper" and fully "able" human subject. Overall, these satirical *and* serious takes on Caribbean strategies of survival assert how key Western values, including those of originality, authorship, ownership, and autonomy are both more historically fraught and remain more difficult to access in the colonial and postcolonial Caribbean while at the same time questioning the primacy of these in the first place. In sum, "Sugar Azúcal" shows us some of the particularities of Atlantic history in the colonial and postcolonial South and how it places subjects and nations in a different, and in fact contradictory, relation to what has come to be known as Western modernity and the values attached to it. This relation is neither one of unequivocal embrace nor, importantly, one of outright rejection of the values and the desires they index.

This ambivalent relation in fact gestures to other forms of politics, in addition to the politics that emerge, according to Paul Gilroy, out of the "black Atlantic" history. Gilroy compellingly defines these as a "politics of fulfillment," which proffers "the notion that a future society will be able to realize the social and political promise that present society has left unaccomplished," and the "politics of transfiguration," which "emphasizes the emergence of qualitatively new desires, social relations, and modes of association within the racial community of interpretation and resistance *and* between that group and its erstwhile oppressors" (1993, 37). With regard to the first, the West's unfulfilled "social and political promises" (for example of equality), certainly also remain unfulfilled in the colonial and postcolonial Atlantic South; yet, I suggest that this region's relation to these promises is inherently different, given that these promises did not emerge out of these contexts, which lay outside their purview when they were formulated in the "West." Indeed, the question of what the unfulfilled "social and political promises" proper to the Caribbean are (beyond those inscribed promised by Western modernity) remains less settled than in the "West." Hernández's piece suggests that the Caribbean subject "Azucal" does not simply forgo these promises, but neither does she push them to their realization or fulfillment (as Gilroy's politics would strive to do). Instead, she claims these promises and desires but inhabits them differently, "cannibalistically," as the text suggests. It is this inhabiting of Western modernity's promises with a colonial and postcolonial difference, that perhaps can be described as a "politics of transfigured promises [of Western modernity]" in the Global South Atlantic context. This is to say that the promises of Western modernity and the question of their fulfillment in what is thought of as the non-Western world (or perhaps more accurately the Global South) pose themselves necessarily in transfigured ways and through negotiations that differ from the Global North.

Gilroy's "politics of transfiguration," which takes place in "the racial community" and between it and the "erstwhile oppressor," in turn is complicated in the Caribbean context in a different way, arguably especially so in the Hispanophone Caribbean, where the determination of who is "within the racial community" and who are the "erstwhile oppressors" is rarely simple nor a straightforwardly drawn line. This racial line is often mightily more messy in non-European and non–North American contexts with a proliferation of racial categories and gradations that do not neatly fit into a black and white binary that can demarcate more clearly who is "within" and who is "outside" *the* racial community. The politics that one may glean from "Azúcal" here is then what may be called "a politics of fulfillment of *old* social relations and modes of association" that have persisted despite their denial by an elite state apparatus. These "old social relations and modes of association" include many forms of Dominican-Haitian commonality and solidarities as well as everyday Afro-Dominican and popular practices that contradict and fly in the face of official Dominican racial narratives. Yet, these relations are not easily circumscribed by a clearly delimited racial community, which makes naming and circumscribing these in terms that are *both* racial and not solely racial an ongoing critical challenge.[8] Thus, the particular ways in which the Global South Atlantic inhabits the insides and outsides of Western modernity, as Azúcal's desiring economy reveals in Hernández's performance piece, produce strategies of resistance and forms of politics distinct from those envisioned by Gilroy. Rather, these strategies of resistance and forms of politics emerge out of the very ambivalence of imagining postcolonial futures based on promises that were formulated without these regions and peoples in mind, if not in contraindication to them. While this particular geopolitical context has had profoundly noxious and racially toxic effects, as I have shown, it also produces its own possible emancipatory paths and politics, not only in the Dominican Republic but also in the postcolonial Global South Atlantic world more broadly.

NOTES

1. With "the 1777 Aranjuez Treaty . . . the Spanish and French agreed on a formal partition of the island into two geographically discrete colonial spaces" (Torres-Saillant 2010, 32).

2. "Analysts of racial identity in Dominican society have often imputed to Dominicans heavy doses of 'backwardness,' 'ignorance' or 'confusion' regarding their race and ethnicity" (Fennema and Loewenthal 1989, 209; see also Sagás 1993; Torres-Saillant 2010, 5).

3. Mayes includes among them "Dominican historians such as Roberto Cassá, Frank Moya Pons, Franklin Franco Pichardo, Orlando Inoa, Raymundo González, Carlos Doré Cabral, Rubén Silié, José Chez Checo, María Filomena González, and Emilio Cordero Michel" (2014, 4).

4. According to Candelario, "the representation of Dominicans and the Dominican Republic as a nation with a minimal degree of 'pure blackness,' . . . should be understood as part of a geopolitically framed racial project of U.S. imperialism that intersected unevenly but importantly with Dominican nation-building projects through anti-Haitianist discourses and ideologies" (2007, 14). Similarly, Torres-Saillant, notes that "it is not inconceivable, for

instance, that the texture of negrophobic and anti-Haitian nationalist discourse sponsored by official spokespersons in the Dominican state may have drawn significantly from North American sources dating back to the first years of the republic" (2010, 8).

5. Sibylle Fischer also critiques how "slavery, slave resistance and radical anti-slavery receive only perfunctory treatment" in Gilroy's work, as he shifts from "history to memory" (2004, 36, 35). She furthermore critiques how in Gilroy's work "modernity . . . remains the master's domain" and the "contestatory potential is ultimately derived from the memory of premodern traditions" (Fischer 2004, 36). She finds that this does not allow us to "discern the discontinuities that are constitutive of the history of the black Atlantic and thus of Western modernity," and "we will find it difficult to understand how the gaps and silences in hegemonic concepts of modernity ever came into being" (Fischer 2004, 37). While the task of tracing these gaps and silences in the emergence of Western modernity is essential, my focus here is on how the hegemonic Western concept and ideal of modernity was negotiated in colonial and postcolonial contexts.

6. This episode appears both in Spanish and in English side-by-side.

7. As David Patrick Geggus describes, in *Haitian Revolutionary Studies*, "vodou (loosely defined as supernatural beliefs of African origin) is generally thought to have contributed organization, leadership, and ideological/emotional inspiration to the slave revolution. With regard to the organizational element, the key factor is the famous Bois Caïman ceremony, where the leader Boukman is believed to have taken a blood oath with his fellow conspirators immediately before the slave uprising" (2002, 77).

8. In their introduction to the *Black Scholar*'s special issue on Dominican blackness, Raj Chetty and Amaury Rodríguez also pinpoint the challenged posed by "questions of cultural and political struggle that may not articulated with black struggle in an explicit or recognizable way, or that that may eschew a politics of black self-affirmation in favor of other modes of struggle" (2015, 3).

Carioca Orientalism
Morocco in the Imaginary of a Brazilian *Telenovela*

Waïl S. Hassan

If Orientalism represents a discourse of Western mastery over the "Orient," as Edward Said argued, what happens when it "travels" to another part of the imperialized world? What, for example, are the contours of Brazilian Orientalism? If not driven by imperial or foreign policy imperatives, what are its ideological investments? I address these questions by focusing on the representation of Morocco and Islam in *O Clone* (The Clone), a specimen of the highly popular genre of the *telenovela* (or *novela*, as it is often called for short), Latin America's answer to US soap operas. I argue that the *novela* depicts Morocco as both a locus of otherness (different religion, strange customs and sexual mores) and solidarity (another part of the Third World, a partner in the anti-imperial struggle). It is the repository of authentic spirituality but also antimodern and tradition-bound. These paradoxes speak to the problematics of identity in twenty-first century Brazil and reveal Brazilian Orientalism to be a tertiary construct in which the traditional East/West divide of Euro-American Orientalism is triangulated in its "southern" variety. Differently put, the South-South relationship between Brazil and Morocco (and the Arab world in general) is mediated by the "northern" discourse of Orientalism. Like the construct of the

"South Atlantic," it is intelligible only with reference to its northern counterpart, from which it derives and at the same time deviates.

Brazilian *novelas* share certain characteristics with US soap operas. Both genres originated with the birth of radio and television, both were first sponsored by soap companies, and both use melodramatic plots with tangled storylines involving romantic affairs (frequently of the forbidden-love variety), family secrets, coincidences, missed encounters, secrets and revelations, sensational traps set by villains and narrow escapes by the innocent, occasional supernatural elements, and episodes ending with a pregnant pause or cliffhanger, often with a close-up shot on one of the main characters. Media scholars are also quick to point out differences. Unlike US soap operas, which can run for decades, Brazilian *novelas* average 180–200 episodes airing five or six days a week over a period of six to eight months, at the end of which all storylines come to a happy conclusion. Settings in Brazilian *novelas*, especially those aired in prime time, can be very elaborate, often using picturesque outdoors settings, unlike their studio-bound US counterparts, and consequently production costs tend to be significantly higher. Moreover, whereas in the United States the highest-paid actors work in Hollywood, in Brazil the most sought-after, and the biggest, stars are those who populate the *novelas*. And while US soaps continue to be broadcast during the daytime, targeting mainly housewives (something that accounts for their decline over the past few decades as more women work outside the home and as younger generations of women spend less time watching them with their mothers), Brazilian *novelas* are broadcast during prime time, with three or four new ones running consecutively from 6:00 or 7:00 p.m. to around 10:00 p.m., and occasionally with a late-night *novela*, as well. Their audiences are, consequently, rather diverse and very large. They participate in the production of the national self-image and even play a role in national elections (Porto 1998). And while with few exceptions soap operas are produced for a US market, Brazilian *novelas* enjoy wide circulation oversees (Mattelart and Mattelart 1990, 9–10; Lopez 1995, 258–261; Martín-Barbero 1995; Tufte 2000, 97–98).

Another crucial difference has to do with the use of *novelas* as a vehicle for often-progressive social commentary, ranging from simple instructions on how to fight the spread of mosquitos bearing the dengue virus, for example, to controversial issues such as racism, artificial insemination, urban violence, street children, child labor, human trafficking, and, in the case of *O Clone*, human cloning, substance abuse, and post-9/11 Islamophobia. The results are sometimes dramatic. Witness, for instance, the spike in organ and blood donations as a result of emphasizing their shortage in *novelas* like *Corpo e alma* and *Laços de família*, or the 570 percent increase in calls to drug treatment centers when the subject of substance abuse and chemical dependency was broached in *O Clone* (Andaló 2003). This educational aspect of *novelas* often also goes hand in hand with commercial product placement, in what has been described as "social merchandising"—a type of "entertainment education" that aims at achieving profit. The educational function is rooted in the leftist politics of many of the major *novela* writers, who work for Rede Globo, Brazil's largest television network and the driving force in *novela* production. As Michèle and Armand Mattelart explain,

> The links between television fiction writers and critical intellectual circles become obvious when one examines the shelves of their personal libraries. Latin American literature stands next to works by historians, anthropologists, economists, and sociologists of the continent. For each screenplay, documentation is carried out by a historian, a sociologist, or an anthropologist. What emerges, at least among some writers, is an intellectual context nourished by the memory of oppression, a memory which cannot be understood without referring to the historical commitment of Latin American intellectuals to the people. (1990, 84–85)

But since the primary goal of the corporate network for which those leftist writers work is profit, their "social consciousness is filtered by the mediations and constraints implied by the production of texts in a particular political and industrial context," which leaves "the trace of a calculation" on their work (1990, 85). This calculation allows authors and network to collaborate in a joint venture that Samantha Nogueira Joyce expresses in this way: "while SM [social merchandising] programs aim to educate, the network's first priority is to profit from the EE [entertainment-education] message" (2012, 88). In other words, for authors to reach wide television audiences with their socially conscious message, they rely on the resources of a corporate network that seeks to profit from the enormous popularity of those authors' creations. Clearly, this calculation, or compromise, has implications for the representation of Arabs and Muslims that involves, for example, the fetishization of goods and services marked as "Arab," which promotes a certain exoticism, at the same time as the *novela* informs the viewers about a foreign culture.

Related to the social consciousness that characterizes Brazilian *novelas* is their responsiveness both to audience feedback and to national and international events. As an "open genre" in which composition runs parallel to broadcast, *novela* writers take into account the input of audiences who write to the network and participate in online forums, focus groups, and opinion polls. The comments of social organizations, churches, activists, politicians, advertisers, media critics, and talk show hosts also feed into the writing process (Mattelart and Mattelart 1990, 41–44; Barbosa 2005, 38).[1] Several scholars have focused on this aspect of the genre, arguing, for example, that *novelas* "should . . . be viewed not only as a form of entertainment but also as an important source of symbolic representation of national identity" (Porto 2011, 64), and showing how real and fictional events often vie for space in the public arena. For example, the murder of Danielle Perez, star of the *novela Corpo e alma*, by her costar and onscreen lover Guillerme de Pádua, hours after the episode aired in which her character broke up with his, brought a fictional intrigue to an abrupt, bloody, real-life conclusion, plunging the country into weeks of heated debates about the legal system and the social role of television, debates that eclipsed the ongoing Senate impeachment of the nation's president, Fernando Collor (Hamburger 2005, 7–15).

All of this renders incomplete any inquiry into Brazilian Orientalism that does not take into account how it manifests itself in one of the most successful *novelas* in the history of Brazilian television. With a primary focus on the thorny topics of human cloning and drug addiction, the *novela* also featured a "forbidden love" story between a Brazilian man and Moroccan woman that introduced Muslim culture as a third thematic thread. In the immediate aftermath of the terrorist attacks of 9/11, what was originally intended as a subsidiary theme became the main focus of the *novela* and the dominant theme in online discussions of it (Barbosa 2005). In fact, as John Tofik Karam reports, *O Clone* quickly dampened the suspicion of Muslims that initially resulted from the 9/11 attacks in the United States, as the Brazilian public became enchanted with the *novela*'s representation of Muslims (2007, 14).

O Clone first aired on Brazil's Globo TV network from October 1, 2001, to June 15, 2002.[2] Written by Glória Perez and directed by Jayme Monjardim, and with enormous production costs reaching up to $150,000 per episode (Mazziotti 2006, 64), the *novela* had the largest audience in Brazilian television history at the time and was followed on 65 percent of television sets on average, and 75 percent for final episodes, in the greater São Paulo area (Mattos and Castro 2002).[3] The *novela* was also exported to sixty-two countries (Mazziotti 2006, 124), including a Spanish-dubbed version entitled *El Clon* that began to air in January 2002 in several Latin American countries and in the United States by the Spanish-language network Telemundo. In January 2010, a Spanish remake began in Colombia, a joint production by Globo and Telemundo. Glória Perez won several national and international awards for Best Author and Best Telenovela, including awards from the Arab-Brazilian Chamber of Commerce, the Brazilian Institute for the Development of Citizenship, the Ministry of Foreign Relations, Rio de Janeiro's Anti-Drug Council and the Brazilian Alcohol and Drugs Association, with numerous other awards going to the *novela*'s principal actors (Barbosa 2005, 93–94).

If this tremendous success was not fully anticipated by Globo's executives, they had nonetheless "prepared several lines of merchandise to be released within weeks of the [*novela*'s] first airing. Items included attached wrist and finger bracelets [like the ones worn by its leading Moroccan character Jade (Giovanna Antonelli)], 'Moroccan' leather sandals, and Middle Eastern music CDs" (Karam 2007, 131). This example of social merchandising by the network was echoed by an explosion of interest in things perceived as Arab, like belly dancing, such that "enrollments in São Paulo belly dancing academies . . . 'increased by as much as 80 percent'" (130). Likewise, event planners enjoyed a boom in demand for Arab-themed parties like the ones seen on television, complete with "Arab" (i.e. Lebanese, Syrian, and Palestinian) dishes, Egyptian and Lebanese music, and belly dancers who were almost always Brazilian (131).[4] This "clonomania" also spread to the 2002 Carnival, which featured numerous parade dancers dressed in costumes worn by the *novela*'s principal characters (Ghazouani 2002). Needless to say, tourism to Morocco increased as well (Mazziotti 2006, 69).

Here we have many of the hallmarks of Orientalism: the collapsing of widely divergent cultural customs into an undifferentiated exotic norm, the fascination with a cultural Other construed as radically different, the consumption frenzy of Arab exotica, and the touristic appeal generated by wide-angle camera and aerial shots of the deserts of the Sahara and the medina of Fes, where nearly half of the *novela*'s action takes place, and where Brazilian characters regularly travel on vacation. In fact, the homogenization of diverse cultural customs is matched by the deliberate collapsing of distinct geographies into one picturesque norm, since the *novela* gives the impression that the medina rises out of the sands, whereas Fes is located in the northern, agricultural part of Morocco, with the Sahara lying hundreds of miles to the east and the south.

Nevertheless, a number of factors differentiate this kind of Orientalism from the familiar European and US varieties. European Orientalism, as Edward Said argued, is wedded to an ideology of colonial mastery that constructs a hierarchy of superior and inferior cultures. Brazilian Orientalism is, of course, derived from the European, but it answers to different ideological imperatives that give it a unique character. European Orientalism posits the Aristotelian self-identity of "East" and "West" and their absolute difference from one another that Rudyard Kipling famously memorialized when he declared that "East is East and West is West and never the twain shall meet." On this view, the East defines the West, and vice versa, through the logic of the excluded middle, the one being what the other is not. Consequently, as scholars like Martin Bernal and Maria Rosal Menocal have argued, the idea of Europe and of "the West" required an effort of historical reconstruction that suppressed or purged African, Arab, and Asian contributions to its civilization, which is depicted as descended directly through a tunnel of time from ancient Greece (Hassan 2011, 7–13).

Nothing can be further from the idea of racial and cultural *mistura*, or the mixing of Amerindians, Africans, and Europeans, popularized by Gilberto Freyre during the 1930s as the defining characteristic of Brazilian identity. To be Brazilian, on this view, is to carry the physical and cultural traces of that mixing, and to recognize oneself as its product. As Freyre writes in his influential book, *The Masters and the Slaves: A Study in the Development of Brazilian Civilization* (1933): "Every Brazilian, even the light skinned fair haired one carries about him on his soul, when not on soul and body alike . . . the shadow or at least the birthmark of the aborigine or the Negro. . . . In our affections, our excessive mimicry, our Catholicism which so delights the senses, our music, our gait, our speech, our cradle songs—in everything that is a sincere expression of our lives, we almost all of us bear the mark of that influence" (278). Elaborating this theme of mixture but with reference to Arab influence, Josimar Melo writes: "Much of what is in the Brazilian is not European, nor indigenous, nor even the result of direct contact with black Africa. . . . It is still much of the Moor which persists in the intimate life of Brazilians through colonial times." He concludes, "we are all a bit Arab" (quoted in Karam 2007, 15).

Is Brazil "Western," then? And what are the investments of Brazilian Orientalism? The answer to the first question is twofold. On the one hand, I would argue, nobody is "Western," in Kipling's sense, because strictly speaking "the West" is an ideological fiction. On the other hand, if we ask whether, in the worldview of the *novela*, Brazil is Western, the answer would have to be yes because a Brazil in dialogue with Islam appears more Western, and that is a desirable self-image for many among Brazil's intellectual elite, even though it does not quite fit with the idea of mixture and cultural anthropophagy. Thus, as it negotiates Brazilian identity in relation to Islam and Arabs, the *novela* unselfconsciously reveals certain anxieties about Brazil's identity and place in the world.

As early as July 2001, Glória Perez declared that, as she had done earlier with gypsies in another *novela*, *Explode Coração* (1996), *O Clone* would help "Muslims undo a series of preconceptions that weigh on their shoulders" (quoted in Klein 2001).[5] This she hoped to accomplish by portraying Muslim families for the first time—and here it is important to note that throughout the twentieth century, Arab immigrants in Brazilian literature and popular culture had been predominantly depicted as male *turcos*, in what became the stereotype of the pack peddler and clever merchant who worshipped money and cheated his clients. This figure is misidentified as a Turk throughout the Americas because early Arab immigrants carried Ottoman passports. By portraying Muslim families, Perez was breaking new ground. Moreover, one year before *O Clone* first aired, and as part of the extensive research that prominent primetime *novela* writers normally do when tackling a social issue, Perez enlisted the help of Muslim community leaders in Rio de Janeiro and São Paulo, who advised her on questions of Islamic law and social practices related to marriage, divorce, and the like ("Xeque apói" 2001). Less than two weeks after 9/11 and a week before the much-anticipated first episode aired, Perez was asked whether the suspicion hanging over Muslims in general was going to lead her to diminish the role of Islam in the *novela*—and rumors had been circulating that some actors even withdrew from the cast (Mattos and Castro 2002). She responded, "We have to say no to prejudice, to stop feeding this ignorance by showing ordinary people. Terrorism exists in all countries and among all peoples, and Muslims are people like us" (quoted in Dionisio). Days later, one of Perez's consultants, Sheikh Jihad Hassan, agreed. Asked whether he thought that the representation of Islam in the *novela* would be a good thing after 9/11, he replied, "Yes, now more than ever, it is important to show our real values and that a Muslim family is like any other, with its positives and negatives. . . After the attacks, people are curious, [but] without being able to understand what is a personal error and what a [whole] people thinks. The public will have the chance to criticize or to praise our culture . . . that is a positive [thing]" (quoted in "Xeque apóia" 2001).

Yet Perez's virtuous intent and the advice of Muslim authorities that she solicited as she wrote the *novela* failed to intercept many problematic representations drawn from classic Orientalism, stereotypes having to do with male authority, polygamy, the status of women, and a host of other Orientalist obsessions like the veil and belly dancing that one finds in a Flaubert or a Delacroix, as well as the depiction of Morocco as a primitive country stuck in the past. All of this is evidence of Perez's indebtedness to Orientalism, something that melodramatic form and *novela* conventions only reinforced. This led Morocco's ambassador in Brazil, Abdelmalek Cherkaoui Ghazouani, to respond with great indignation. On June 17, 2002 (two days after the last episode aired), he published an article in the major daily newspaper *Folha de São Paulo*, in which he said that, despite the sympathetic portrayal of his country and the popularity of some of the Moroccan characters, *O Clone* was "a gross falsification, transmitting mediocre images and a simulacrum of the reality of an Arab-Muslim culture." The *novela*, he argued, "showed a Morocco that was very distant from reality, a country that can only exist in its authors' imagination" (Ghazouani 2002).

Before commenting on this contradiction between Perez's progressive intent and the odd manner of its realization, it might be helpful to give a brief summary of two of the main narrative threads in the *novela*. Set in 1981, *O Clone* opens with Dr. Albieri (Juca de Oliveira) giving a lecture on the potential of therapeutic cloning and emphasizing that researchers must abide by medical ethics. Albieri had just succeeded in cloning a sheep, fifteen years before Dolly the Sheep was born in Scotland, so the *novela* claims precedence for Brazilian scientists in this area, in keeping with similar claims in this and other *novelas* that, for example, Brazilian medicine is as good, if not better, than elsewhere. Such claims are part of the genre's production of national identity and Brazil's self-image as a nation in possession of the natural and human resources necessary for becoming a major world power. Earlier in life, Albieri was crushed by the premature death of his fiancée, and since then he has been obsessed with cloning as a way of conquering death. A little later in the first episode, he is shown standing in front of the pyramids of Giza with the twins Diogo and Lucas (Murilio Benício), his godsons and the children of his close friend the millionaire businessman Leônidas Ferras (Reginaldo Faria). Albieri tells them that just as the ancient Egyptians tried to conquer death through mummification, the twenty-first century will achieve immortality through cloning. When Diogo, Albieri's favorite, later dies in a helicopter accident, the geneticist is again devastated and decides to make Diogo live again by cloning Lucas, whose genetic makeup is identical to that of his twin brother. Albieri accomplishes this in the fertility clinic he owns by taking a cell from Lucas during a routine exam and injecting its DNA into the egg of an unsuspecting patient, Deusa (Adriana Lessa), who wishes to become pregnant through artificial insemination. A healthy child is born, whom he names Léo, after his friend Leônidas, who is technically the baby's biological father. For the next twenty years, and until the story line resumes in 2001, Albieri keeps the existence of the clone a secret for fear of ruining his professional career. He is proud nonetheless at having been the first scientist in the world to create a healthy human clone, and whenever a lesser breakthrough in Europe or the United States is celebrated in the international media, he is tempted to reveal his accomplishment to the world. As he says to his wife Edna (Nívea Maria), who tries to dissuade him from confessing to the Medical Ethics Council (to which his deed has been denounced by a colleague who discovers the secret), "Can you imagine that I, a Third World scientist, I was able to do first what the more advanced nations of the world are just beginning to try?" (episode 183). Despite Albieri's confession, the Ethics Council dismisses the charge, finding it highly implausible, so he goes on to tell his life story to a Portuguese journalist who intends to publish his biography. By then, the story of the clone Léo has taken many turns and become known to Leônidas, who files a lawsuit to have his paternity recognized and to erase Deusa's name from the birth certificate in order to have his wife be recognized as the mother, even though she had died many years before Léo's birth. Such legal conundrums, not to mention the grave psychological and emotional damage suffered by Léo, Deusa, and the rest of their relatives, illustrate the *novela*'s message that human cloning represents a violation of ethical, social, and religious norms. At the same time, of course, the *novela* is also celebrating Albieri's achievement as evidence that Brazil can compete with "the more advanced nations of the world." These complicated ideological investments are matched by the similarly contradictory representation of Morocco and Islam, which give Brazilian Orientalism a unique character.

The theme of Islam enters into the story from the first episode and quickly begins to intertwine with that of cloning. Immediately after the first scene in which Albieri is introduced, the Moroccan teenage girl Jade (Giovanna Antonelli) appears in a conservative one-piece bathing suit on a Rio de Janeiro beach, glancing wistfully at Brazilian lovers in much less modest apparel. Flashbacks show Jade in arguments with her mother, who forbids her to go to nightclubs with her Brazilian girlfriends or to spend the night at their houses. Jade protests that she does not like feeling different from her peers, but her mother tells her that one day she will go back to Morocco, where she will be like everyone else. Jade returns home to find her mother breathing her last. What follows is the first of a long list of mini-lessons offered throughout the *novela*, explaining Muslim customs: Jade informs her Brazilian neighbor who offers to help her that she needs to remain by herself in order to perform the ritual washing of the dead, to be carried out only by family members. Accurate or not, such explanations are examples of "entertainment education," and they sometimes go to great lengths.[6] In this case, Jade is shown washing the naked body of her dead mother, in what would have been, in any production made in an Arab or Muslim country, an unthinkable scene. Indeed, the scene gives an unexpected twist to the odalisque theme from nineteenth-century Orientalist art. This connection would have been somewhat forced if, throughout the *novela*, Jade and other young and attractive Moroccan women were not frequently referred to as *odaliscas*, in unequivocal evocation of French painters like Ingres and Delacroix, who painted so many female nudes in harem settings. Such paintings not only claim to show naked female Muslim bodies that are otherwise covered, but often also dramatize the act of revelation to the viewer, who is invited to appreciate the fact of breaking a taboo: partially drawn curtains (e.g., in Delacroix's *Odalisque alongée sur un divan*, and many others), female figures with their back turned to the viewer as though unaware of being gazed at (as in Ingres's *Baigneuse Valpinçon* and *Grande odalisque*), tondi that simulate seeing through a peephole (as in Ingres's *Bain turc*), among other effects (Yeazell 2000, 27–29). Here, the scene of Jade washing her mother's naked corpse is shot omnisciently from above, before another camera shot fades in showing the same scene reflected through an Oriental-frame mirror, further dramatizing the act of looking. Emblematic of the *novela*'s approach, this "entertainment education" mini-lesson on Islamic ritual is couched within a specifically French-Orientalist frame. This contradictory approach to the representation of Morocco and Islam throughout the *novela* betrays not the least awareness of the hegemonic nature of Orientalist discourse, treating it instead as a privileged and authoritative form of knowledge. The macabre irony of the scene also indexes the belatedness of Brazilian Orientalism, as the opium-intoxicated and/or oblivious Oriental nudes of nineteenth-century French paintings return as aestheticized corpses in Brazilian *telenovelas*.

Jade is next seen arriving in Fes, where she is met at the airport by her cousin Latifa (Letícia Sabatella) and her uncle Ali's middle-aged housekeeper, Zoraide (Jandira Martini), only to be separated from them and lost in the narrow, crowded, labyrinthine alleys of the medina. She then meets Uncle Ali (Sténio Garcia), who is now her guardian, her father having died years earlier. A few episodes later, Albieri takes Lucas with him to visit his old friend Ali, whom he met decades earlier when they were students at a Brazilian university. Lucas leaves the two elder men and wanders by himself through the house in total innocence of local customs—that is, he walks into the parts reserved for women and forbidden to males who are strangers to the family. He comes face to face with Jade in a revealing belly dancing outfit and dancing in front of a cheering audience of household women. At the moment he first sees her, she is covering her face with a veil—and colored, diaphanous veils are fetishized in the *novela*. When their eyes meet, she stops dancing, drops the veil, and falls silent, while the other women scurry out of the room screaming. The scene dramatizes, once again, the dialectic of coverage and revelation enacted in the scene of washing the dead mother and in the harem paintings mentioned above. Needless to say, Lucas and Jade instantly fall in love at that dramatic moment, which is to be recalled several times in flashbacks throughout the rest of the *novela*.[7]

This event occurs in the first part of the *novela*, which takes place in 1981, and the love story of Lucas and Jade extends over the next two decades, when the action resumes in 2001. Predictably, the families of the two youngsters oppose their union: Ali does not permit his niece to marry a non-Muslim and warns her that "Occidentals" are fickle and unreliable, while Leônidas considers his son's plan to convert to Islam so as to marry Jade to be foolish and immature, given the cultural differences between them, and continues to berate his son for preferring music to a career in business. Lucas and Jade make the first of numerous plans to run away together in defiance of their families, but in each case, Lucas fails to fulfill his part, often abandoning Jade as she waits for him with her suitcase. Eventually, she consents to marrying Saíd (Dalton Vigh), one of two half-Moroccan, half-Brazilian brothers born and raised in Brazil. The couple has a daughter, Khadija. Lucas also marries Maysa (Daniela Escobar), the girlfriend of his deceased twin brother, and gives in to his father's wishes by working with him in his company. Lucas and Maysa have a daughter, Mel (Débora Falabella), who later as a teenager becomes a drug addict and a central figure in the *novela*'s treatment of chemical dependency. Mel's involvement with drugs also becomes one more complicating factor in the love story of Lucas and Jade, both of whom have become estranged from their respective spouses, and once again occasioning a last-minute desertion of the Moroccan woman by the Brazilian man.

Clearly then, this story deviates from Orientalist narrative described by Gayatri Chakravorty Spivak as "White men saving brown women from brown men" (1999, 287). Lucas is portrayed as weak, indecisive, timid, rebellious yet powerless to oppose his strong-willed father, and hardly capable of rescuing even himself. In fact, Lucas's role in the story differs greatly from the Orientalist script identified by Spivak: unlike his European or American counterparts, he is not there to "liberate" Jade from her

Moroccan captivity and whisk her away to freedom in Brazil, as it were. On the contrary, on one occasion he deserts her in Brazil after having said to her, "I will never leave you," after which she decides to return to Morocco. This confirms what she had said to him earlier: "Brazilians are different from us. You don't follow the rules . . . each [of you] follows his own head, each does what he wants" (episode 13). What underwrites the scene, then, is not the discourse of Western freedom vs. Oriental oppression of women, but an autocritique of what is presented as Brazilian unreliability or irresponsibility vs. Oriental self-discipline. This complete reversal of the Orientalist norm reveals the self-critical function of Brazilian Orientalism, which does not serve to justify nonexistent imperialist interests.

In another deviation from Orientalist tales, the narrative as a whole discards the motif of geographical remoteness, common among European travel narratives of the colonial era, in which the length and/or difficulty of the journey is part of the imaginative reproduction of space. Here, by contrast, the traffic between Brazil and Morocco is constant and easeful, visually signaled by a shot of the Rio de Janeiro and Fes airports, and belying the fact that there are no direct flights between the two cities. The main characters are always following each other from one country to the other, as Saíd and his brother Mohamed (Antônio Calloni), who respectively marry Jade and Latifa, resettle in Brazil and establish successful businesses there, and as Brazilians go to Morocco on vacation, or in the case of Lucas and later also his clone, Léo, in pursuit of Jade. Likewise, Leônidas frequently goes to Morocco on romantic getaways, and Albieri finds it a suitable place for soul searching. Moreover, the *novela* also misleadingly gives the impression of significant Moroccan immigration to Brazil. The principal Moroccan characters are all fluent in Portuguese. They either studied there in their youth, like Ali; had Brazilian mothers and were partially raised in Brazil, like Mohamed, Saíd, and their older sister, Nazira (Eliane Giardini); or were born and raised in Morocco but spoke Portuguese at home with their Brazilian mother and grandparents, like Saíd's second wife, Ranya (Nívea Stelmann), and her sister Amina (Ingra Liberato). All of this gives the impression of far more extensive contact and intimate relations between the two countries than actually exist.[8]

And yet, as a mark of the contradictory nature of this carioca Orientalism, Moroccans and Brazilians remain fundamentally alien to each other. At every turn, the Moroccans express their shock and disapproval at the dress and behavior of Brazilians, to whom they often refer simply as "Occidentals," while the Brazilians meet Moroccan customs with incomprehension. In fact, from the very beginning, Islam and Muslims are presented as completely alien to Brazil, where they do not fit because they refuse to mix with Brazilians, even those who have lived there for decades. The defining feature of Jade and her like-minded niece Samira (Sthefany Brito), both of whom are born and raised in Brazil, is that they are split between cultures: They seek romantic love and want to complete their education in order to have a professional career, but these "Western" desires, as they are labeled in the *novela*, run into stiff opposition from the Moroccan patriarchs who insist that "love is born from living together," within arranged marriages and not in romantic affairs, and that women have no place outside of the home. The opposite sentiments are expressed by Latifa and Khadija (Carla Diaz), who are Jade's Moroccan-born and raised cousin and daughter, respectively: They do not understand the need for formal education, since they are to be married to rich men whom they will learn to love and who will give them "a lot of gold, God willing," as Khadija repeats ad nauseam in almost every episode. This cultural-geographical determinism dictates what women believe depending on where they are born, and it is completely unmitigated—in keeping, one must say, not only with Orientalist binarism but also with the generic norms of *telenovelas*, in which devices like parallels, contrasts, and cyclical repetitions structure the plot, and where characters tend to be two-dimensional and drawn in contrastive pairs—rich and poor, heroes and villains, extroverts and introverts, honest and dishonest, hard workers and parasites, and so on. *O Clone* contains several such pairs: the two pious Moroccan uncles are liberal Ali and fanatical Abdu (Sebastião Vasconcellos); the Ferras twins are outgoing Diogo and withdrawn Lucas; the two lawyers working for Leônidas are recovering addict and alcoholic though competent Lobato (Osmar Prado), who is short and bald, and fitness fanatic yet incompetent Tavinho (Victor Fasano), who is tall and handsome. Other examples abound. Within this aesthetic, "Orient vs. Occident" is a self-evident and irresistible formula.

However, two features differentiate this binarism from that found in Euro-American Orientalism. First, difference does not automatically denote negativity or inferiority. It is explicitly presented as neutral, but when it carries a charge, it may be negative, as we would expect, or positive, as a function of leftist critique that seeks to disrupt common assumptions. As Albieri puts it, "It's another culture, a way of seeing the world, neither better nor worse than ours. It is different" (episode 70). Similar statements are made by several Moroccan and Brazilian characters, always in reaction to members of one or the other group expressing surprise or puzzlement at the attitudes or behaviors of people from the other culture. Mutual incomprehension can lead to tense or hilarious situations (a rich source of dramatic and comic effects), but such situations almost always end in extended explanations of cultural differences. Othering flows in both directions, and the dramatization of that reinforces the culturally relativist message of the *novela*.

More radically, audience assumptions about difference are frequently undermined in the service of social critique. For example, one Brazilian character, Laurinda (Totia Meireles) asks Latifa if she would not prefer to have been born Brazilian so that she would not have to get permission from her husband before leaving the house. Latifa's reaction is instantaneous: "God forbid! I wouldn't want that at all! Brazilian women's lot is sad, really sad. . . . You don't have a man to take care of you, no. You live in fear of getting fat, fear of having cellulite, and you can't take your eyes off your husband or he'll run away. Isn't that so?" Stunned by this totally unexpected response, Laurinda cannot help but agree (episode 42).[9] Later in the same episode, the idea of Muslim women's imprisonment is emphasized when Jade, who has just hatched a new plot to run away, must steal her own passport from Saíd's safe, where he keeps it locked, and even then, she is prevented from boarding a plane at the airport without written permission from her husband. Yet the episode as a whole makes a double critique: What Muslim women lose in freedom, they gain in protection and security, and what Brazilian women gain in personal freedom, they lose in terms of insecurity and anxiety, since their husbands or boyfriends would leave them if they become less attractive or the moment they find a more desirable woman. The character of Lidiane (Beth Goulart) embodies that anxiety to a pathetic, if comic, extreme: When she is not in the gym or at a fashion show, she keeps calling her husband Tavinho to see where he is and what he is doing, always justifying that by saying, "A handsome man is a Karma; I am suffering," to the amusement and occasional despair of her friends and teenage children. Meanwhile, her husband seems to justify her fears, for he spends his time on the beach flirting with young women and answers her incessant calls with annoyance, tells her he is at work or about to enter a tunnel, then hangs up.

The treatment of gender in the *novela* shows that while there are striking contrasts between Brazil and Morocco, the situation of women in both cultures is precarious, and that is something that the two have in common. This leads to the second difference between Euro-American and Brazilian Orientalisms: Whereas the one insists that "East is East and West is West and never the twain shall meet," in the Brazilian variety, the twain do meet. Despite stark differences, there are similarities. Take music and dancing. As already mentioned, the *novela* fetishizes belly dancing and presents Muslim women as bedroom belly dancers. If on the street they are covered from head to toe, indoors they don skimpy two-piece outfits and dance provocatively to their mesmerized husbands. Girls learn to dance from an early age as well; in fact, Khadija is dancing when she first appears at age eight or nine (episode 57). And if modest women from good families dance only to their husbands, professional dancers are hired by pious and respectable patriarchs to animate the lavish weddings they organize and the numerous parties they throw in honor of every visiting guest and every departing or returning traveler—in short, for whatever excuse. And far from seeing a contradiction, as many conservative Muslims in the real world in fact do, between modesty and the sexually provocative dance, the two pious Moroccan elders, liberal Ali and fanatical Abdou, equally enjoy the spectacle and often join the dancer at the center of the festivities. Happy Muslims, indeed!

But so are the inhabitants of the neighborhood of São Cristóvão, where Mohamed lives with Latifa and their children after they settle in Rio de Janeiro, and where street parties break out on every national holiday and often spontaneously as well. The neighborhood bar owner, Dona Jura (Solange Couto), receives a steady stream of celebrities who drop by to sample her savory pastries—from soccer legend Pelé to superstars of Brazilian music like Zeca Bagodinho, Beth Carvalho, Jorge Aragão, and Raul de Barros. On those occasions, neighborhood residents dance in the street well into the night. As far as music, dancing, and partying go, Moroccans have nothing over Brazilians. Both groups, in their own way and after their manner of tune, are party animals. When they join together in the same festivity, as in the wedding of Moroccan Mustafá (Perry Salles) and Brazilian Noêmia (Elizângela), they play both kinds of music and teach each other how to dance differently (episode 190).

The more substantive difference, in this respect, can be noted not between Brazilians and Moroccans, but between the working-class residents of São Cristóvão and their rich counterparts who inhabit the villas and mansions of Zona Sul, the city's upscale south side. The latter are neither so cheerful nor so musical. Their broken homes and dysfunctional marriages produce troubled teens who often fall prey to drug addiction. In fact, this narrative thread also revolves around another "forbidden love," that of Mel and Xande (Marcello Novaes), the son of Dona Jura and Mel's onetime bodyguard. This love story, like that of Lucas and Jade, Samira and Zé Roberto, and Mustafá and Noêmia, eventually has a happy ending, so that the *novela* addresses both cultural and class differences, ultimately showing that neither barrier is insurmountable.

Thus, unlike Euro-American Orientalism, the play of difference and similarity in the Brazilian variety disturbs intuitive assumptions about Self and Other. It disperses rather than consolidates. Moreover, this Brazilian Orientalism has a tertiary, not a binary, structure. Even though it recycles the East/West division, it simultaneously undercuts it both explicitly by emphasizing what Morocco and Brazil have in common, and implicitly by suggesting that the two merge into one pole on the vertical axis that binds South and North (Atlantic) together.

In the final analysis, this Brazilian Orientalism involves anxiety about Brazil's own cultural identity as a postcolonial nation that differentiates itself from the erstwhile "mother country" of Portugal through the concept of *mistura*, yet whose intellectual elites have historically looked to Europe, particularly France, and more recently to the United States, as the embodiment of completed progress and civilization, ideals seen to be still unrealized in what Stefan Zweig called "the land of the future," which seems unable to rid itself of internal contradictions. Brazil may be the product of the "mixture" of Amerindians, Europeans (with substantial Moorish heritage), Africans, and to a lesser extent Asians, but it self-identifies as culturally Western, while geopolitical and economic realities place it in the Third World, the Global South. These paradoxes are embedded in what I would venture to say is the original purpose behind Perez's decision to insert Islam in a *novela* about human cloning, long before 9/11 turned the spotlight on Muslims, and her choice of Morocco over Lebanon or Syria, from which most Arab immigrants in Brazil came. As mentioned earlier, the theme of cloning unfolds in a Faustian narrative of a Brazilian geneticist and advocate of medical ethics who sacrifices his ideals. Mixed with what is represented in the *novela* as his atheistic desire to play God is his ambition to accomplish a feat that his European and US colleagues deem impossible, which is to create a healthy human clone. The moral dilemma which Dr. Albieri embodies—the dictates of ethics vs. the ambition of science—encodes an anxiety about Brazilian identity as a Catholic country that risks losing its spiritual moorings as it strives to realize its promised, though seemingly forever-delayed, prominence on the world stage.

Within this difficult equation, Islam figures as a spiritual ballast where Catholicism apparently falters. The counterweight to Albieri's atheistic hubris is not the Catholic priest, Padre Matiolli (Francisco Cuoco), who is introduced into the story halfway through the *novela*, almost as an afterthought (episode 126), but the pious Muslim Ali, who in the first episode criticizes "the West" for claiming that God is dead, then from the third episode onwards debates religion, science, and faith with Albieri. Ali is the wise old man of the *novela*, spreading his pearls of wisdom in almost every episode, and whenever he is shown praying (as in his first appearance in episode 1) or when he pronounces on matters of spiritual or philosophical weight, or quotes Kahlil Gibran, Gregorian chants play in the background, signaling to the viewers that he speaks truths common to both religions.[10] In this way, Ali serves as the moral and spiritual compass orienting the rest of the characters or indexing their deviation from the standards of behavior that the *novela* upholds. In fact, he is given the last word, for it is his voice that ties all the narrative threads together in the final episode, and he is the last to speak in it. Ali is the counterbalance both to Albieri's atheism and to the religious extremism of the other Moroccan patriarch, Abdu (and by implication, perhaps, the kind of fanaticism responsible for the terrorist attacks of 9/11). Indeed, Ali represents an Islam that is more Catholic than Catholicism.

Without a history of colonial or imperial interests in the Middle East, Brazilian Orientalism is derived from the European variety and adapted to the country's own historical experience. This necessarily alters the derivative discourse's ideological functions and restricts the scope of its imaginative geography. Given the demographics of Arab immigration in Brazil and the fact that many Brazilians of Syrian-Lebanese descent have emphasized their Christianity as a factor in their easeful integration into Brazilian society (Karam 2007, 114–116), the *novela* had to bring Muslims to Brazil from elsewhere in the Arab world. This leaves exactly two other Arab countries on the landscape of Brazilian Orientalism at this point: Egypt and Morocco—the former because of its ancient monuments and the latter for its well-known historic connection to Portugal and Spain.[11] As mentioned, Egypt figures in the first episode of the *novela*, in a scene in which Albieri stands with the Ferras twins in front of the pyramids and describes human cloning as a continuation of the ancient Egyptians' efforts to defeat death, as he puts it. This is Egypt as the cradle of civilization, anchoring both the continuity and the contrast between ancient and modern. As for contemporary Egypt, it becomes a frequent reference for the Moroccan characters in the *novela* as the source of the best belly dancers (e.g., Abdu wants Ali to contract the famous Egyptian dancer Fifi Abdu to dance in Saíd and Jade's wedding, depicted in episode 15). Yet paradoxically, modern Egypt is also a breeding ground for subversive feminists: To think or speak "like the feminists of Cairo" is a frequent accusation (and stock phrase) uttered by conservative Moroccan males like Abdu and

Mohamed to describe women like Jade or Nazira, who do not conform to what is presented as the more authentically Islamic (i.e., patriarchal) norms of Morocco. This contrast between Egypt and Morocco is emphasized with the appearance of an Egyptian Don Juan named Zein (Luciano Szafir), who is nicknamed "Pharaoh's curse" (episode 140) by the Brazilians whose wives he has seduced. Zein opens an exotic new nightclub called Nefertiti, decorated to look like an Egyptian temple and where employees are dressed as ancient Egyptians; it is a place that his childhood friend Mohamed would not enter because it serves alcohol.

In the discursive economy of the *novela*, this modern and Westernized Egypt serves to set off Morocco as both archaic and authentic, traditional and unadulterated by modernity—that is, the ideal counterpart to "mixed" Brazil that, in its quest for modernity, risks losing its bearings. If, unlike their Arab Christian counterparts, Muslims' supposed resistance to mixing disqualifies them as Brazilians, it also maintains their grasp on precisely those religious and social values that, as Ali says in the first episode, "the West" is losing: faith in God, acceptance of death as part of life, family values, financial support of female relatives, self-discipline, and other positive qualities that the *novela* attributes to Islam and Muslims while dramatizing their absence in Brazil. The country's ideal Other then becomes Morocco, and particularly Fes, whose medina, home to the Moroccan characters, is described as "the oldest place in the Orient" (episode 71). Yet because so much of Brazilian culture has its roots in Moorish Iberia, as Gilberto Freyre affirms time and again in *The Masters and the Slaves*, Morocco is also an intimately familiar Other. What Maysa says to Saíd is highly emblematic of the relationship between Brazil and Morocco: "To me you are strange and at the same time very intimate [i.e., intimately familiar]" (episode 95). That this statement is spoken during the course of an extramarital affair that the two of them have in revenge against Lucas and Jade, their respective spouses, underscores the deep anxiety that Morocco stirs in the *novela*'s Orientalist imaginary, an anxiety about the very nature of "mixing," the defining characteristic of the Brazilian self-image. For if Morocco is at once Brazil's Other and a mirror reflecting its shortcomings, that locus of pure, "unmixed" or unadulterated spiritual values must also represent a challenge to the fundamental characteristic of Brazilian culture and society—the mixture of races, ethnicities, religions, and cultures. The flipside of *mistura* is contamination, fear of which animates dualistic ideologies of dominance. If, in the final analysis, the *novela* seems ever so subtly and implicitly to suggest that the very source of Brazil's strength may also be its weakness, that is because the ideological investments of European Orientalism haunt the progressive proclamations of its carioca variety.

As such, behind the façade of exoticism and cultural relativism erected by a *tour de force* throughout the *novela* stands an uncanny specter—strangely familiar and deeply troubling. It is perhaps for this reason that the theme of Morocco and Islam is couched within another highly troubling concern with human cloning. The clone embodies a similarly insoluble paradox: the human ambition for (forbidden) knowledge and immortality, which involves a rejection of death and desire for eternal life; but he also represents a violation of the natural process of genetic mixing and change, of which death is part. Not surprisingly, the priest Matioli calls the clone Léo a "laboratory Adam" and accuses Albieri of having committed the Original Sin all over again, adding that all humanity will have to pay for this (episode 179). In the very first episode, as noted earlier, Ali condemns "the West" for "defying God" and for saying that "God is dead," and counsels Jade not to cry anymore out of grief for her dead mother because "dying is part of the destiny of human beings. It is written [in the Qur'an] that every soul has to taste death." Ali and Matioli appear together in one scene in which they are in complete agreement with each other on this issue: "it is written in all the [sacred] books" (episode 187). As such, Albieri is a modern day Prometheus, a Faustus, or a Frankenstein, at the same time that he is also, in his own view, carrying the torch of discovery, pushing the frontiers of knowledge, and evidencing Brazil's potential as a great world power.

This age-old dilemma also encodes the choice between stasis and change—between, on the one hand, the archaism of reproducing or copying inherited forms, clinging to tradition, puritanism and, in its extreme form, fundamentalism; and on the other hand, dynamic change with the times, modernization, receptivity to, and incorporation of, the new. In Orientalist terms, this is the duality of Orient and Occident. Tradition-bound Morocco, its serenity troubled only by its restrictive gender norms, versus modernizing Brazil, contending with all manner of social, political, ethical, and spiritual challenges in the process of realizing its national motto of "Order and Progress." In *O Clone*, this remains an insoluble dilemma. On the one hand, the Romeos and Juliets of the Global South are all united at the end and live happily ever after, in violation of Kipling's binarism but in observance both of the norms of melodrama and of the progressive intent of the author to combat anti-Muslim prejudice. On the other hand, cloning continues to haunt the narrative, without a substantive answer being given to the more challenging questions it unleashes about Brazil's self-image. In the final episode, Albieri and the clone Léo disappear in a desert storm in Morocco, which erases from the world what is presented as a gross violation of social, ethical, and spiritual norms, much as the icy plains of the North Pole rid the world of Frankenstein and his monster. This is a redemptive Orient, though of course no less Orientalized than the Orient of nineteenth-century Europe. In both cases, the Orient is an ideal Other, but while that Other serves to consolidate Europe's identity as a superior colonial power, Glória Perez's carioca Orientalism exposes the anxieties and dilemmas that continue to trouble Brazil's self-image.

NOTES

1. Thomas Tufte explains, "The narrative is not concluded when the telenovela goes on air, but unfolds in a process dependent on audience response. Typically, when a telenovela starts, 24 chapters are filmed [four weeks of broadcast], the author has written 15–20 more and thereafter seeks to keep about 20 chapters ahead of the chapter on air" (2000, 87).

2. The original broadcast totaled 221 episodes of varying length, as is typical of Brazilian *novelas*. In preparation for export to other countries, the series was reedited to a total of 250 episodes of about 50 minutes each. Reference here is made to the rerun of the latter version on Globo Internacional (for North America), between April 1, 2012, and March 15, 2013.

3. Ratings had begun to be recorded seven years earlier by the Instituto Brasileiro de Opinião Pública e Estatística (IBOPE).

4. On the appropriation, by Brazilian women and Arab men, of belly dancing as a "universal feminine" activity that nonetheless excludes Arab women, see Karam (2010).

5. All translations from Portuguese are mine unless a published translation is listed in the Works Cited.

6. Here and throughout the *novela*, the accuracy of information given on Islamic practices varies greatly, from correct to wildly inaccurate. Such practices themselves often differ widely by region, country, class, sect, and so forth, and it appears that Perez's sources gave her answers based, in some cases, on generic *shari'a* laws that are practiced only in Saudi Arabia or Taliban-era Afghanistan (e.g., public floggings and amputations) rather than in Morocco specifically. In other cases, she seems to have completely misunderstood certain rules or even made them up (e.g., the idea that women lose custody of children, even infants, if they are divorced, or that a divorced woman must continue to live with her husband for three months after a divorce, as happens with Jade). However, it must also be noted that sometimes she takes pains to explain that practices such as female genital mutilation, which are believed by many to be Islamic, were banned by the Prophet Muhammad (episode 9).

7. This scene is repeated exactly twenty years later (with Jade wearing the same belly dancing outfit, which she nostalgically takes out of the closet), but this time with Léo, Lucas's clone, who retraces his original's steps into the forbidden part Ali's house (episode 167). Such repetitions are among the conventions of the *novela* genre.

8. For example, Jeffrey Lesser reports that of the estimated 107,135 Middle Eastern immigrants to Brazil between 1884 and 1939, only 328 were Moroccans (2013, 124).

9. The same conversation is repeated with different characters in episodes 71 and 195.

10. One of the ironies of Perez's Orientalism is the conflation of Gibran with Islam, another is the contradiction between the staunchly patriarchal family structure attributed to Muslims and the anticonformist message of the lines that Ali, himself an exemplary patriarch, often quotes from Gibran's *The Prophet*: "Your children are not your children. / They are the sons and daughters of Life's longing for itself. / They came through you but not from you and though they are with you yet they belong not to you, / And though they are with you yet they belong not to you" (1923, 17). I have written at length about Gibran's concoction of Hindu and Christian ideas into a highly marketable pop spiritualism that relies on the mystique of the East (Hassan 2011, 59–77).

11. Dubai emerges in Brazilian popular culture a bit later—for example, in Glória Perez's wildly popular *novela* of 2009, *Caminho das Índias* (The Way of [or to] the Indies), which takes place between India and Brazil. In this *novela*, Indians and Brazilians transit in Dubai on their way to either country, and a large Indian expatriate community works there. Rich Brazilians also go to Dubai to forget their troubles and to wallow in luxury. This, however, is a glitzy cosmopolitan city with a dizzying skyline of ultramodern, futuristic architecture, hardly the image of tradition or of the Orient.

ACKNOWLEDGMENTS

This volume grew out of a seminar on "The Global South Atlantic" held at the annual convention of the American Comparative Literature Association in April 2013. We would like to thank the original participants in the seminar for inspiring the multiyear collaborative work visible in these pages: Odette Casamayor-Cisneros, Jason Frydman, Yogita Goyal, Jaime Hanneken, Waïl Hassan, Isabel Hofmeyr, Kathryn Lachman, Justin Neuman, Taiwo Osinubi, Rachel Price, and Julie-Francoise Tolliver. We thank Juan Orrantia for allowing us to use his wonderful image of Amílcar Cabral's birthplace on our cover. We would also like to thank our editor, Tom Lay, as well as Eric Newman, Gregory McNamee, and the rest of the staff of Fordham University Press for its trust in this project and the exceptionally helpful editorial support. Our two anonymous readers gave extensive commentary that made the project richer for their interventions.

Kerry Bystrom would additionally like to thank Eduardo Cadava, Arcadio Diaz-Quiñones, and Tim Watson for their warm acceptance of an unconventional doctoral project across the South Atlantic; and the many colleagues who challenged me to develop the comparative aspects of my research, including Eleni Coundouriotis, Richard A. Wilson, Sarah Nuttall, Isabel Hofmeyr, Pamila Gupta, Meg Samuelson, Liz Gunner, Simon Gikandi, Monica Popescu, Kathryn Lachman, Tom Keenan, Nicole Caso, Drew Thompson, Brenda Werth and Florian Becker. Special thanks to Christian Crouch, who was a key advisor in Atlantic studies. And of course to Joey Slaughter, who inspired this whole project in a graduate seminar at Columbia long ago and proved a rigorous and extremely generous coeditor.

Joseph Slaughter would like to thank Kerry Bystrom for initiating this project and asking him to join forces with her to see it to fruition. In addition to the participants in the ACLA seminar already mentioned, I want to acknowledge the students in my Global South Atlantic seminar at Columbia University. I also want to recognize the vital importance of the Ethnic and Third World Literatures (E3W) program at the University of Texas at Austin, my faculty mentors (Mia Carter, Barbara Harlow, Gerry Heng,

José Limón, Ben Lindfors, and César Salgado) and my numerous student colleagues. Together, we never imagined that the literatures and historical conditions of Africa, Latin America, and other places around the Global South were somehow incomparable. Literary and critical trends come in and out of fashion, but the serious and committed work done under the E3W rubric throughout the 1990s (and beyond) remains salient and continues to challenge my thinking and the reigning paradigms of our day. Like Kerry, I can trace my own investments in comparative Third World studies to the intellectual and political excitement of a formative graduate seminar: Barbara Harlow's "Poetry and Partition," which confirmed for me the necessity and legitimacy of doing historically responsible literary scholarship across borders, languages, and contexts that might be connected by common systems, experiences, and desires that are too often ignored or overlooked for other insalubrious reasons. Thank you, Barbara.

Works Cited

ʿAbd al-Nāṣir, Taḥiyya (Tahia Abdel Nasser). 2011. "al-Arshīf al-ʿArabī fī al-Waqiʿiyya al-Siḥriyya." *Alif: Journal of Comparative Poetics* 31: 185–214.

Abi-Mershed, Osama. 2010. *Apostles of Modernity: Saint-Simonians and the Civilizing Mission in Algeria*. Stanford: Stanford University Press.

Abramson, Pierre-Luc. 1999. *Las utopías sociales en América Latina en el siglo xix*. Translated by Jorge Alberto and Luis Padin Videla. Mexico City: Fondo de Cultura Económica.

Achebe, Chinua. 1990. *Hopes and Impediments: Selected Essays*. New York: Anchor Books.

Acosta, Abraham. 2014. *Thresholds of Illiteracy: Theory, Latin America and the Crisis of Resistance*. New York: Fordham University Press.

Adebayo, Mojisola. 2012. *Moj of the Antarctic: An African Odyssey*. In *Plays One*. London: Oberon Books.

African National Congress. 2012. "The Second Transition? Building a National Democratic Society and the Balance of Forces in 2012." *African National Congress*. http://www.anc.org.za/docs/discus/2012/transition.pdf. Accessed August 31, 2016.

Airiau, Athénase. 1860. *Canal inter-océanique par l'isthme du Darien, Nouvelle Grenade (Amérique du Sud). Canalisation par la colonisation*. Paris: Chez France.

Alexis, Jacques Stéphen. 1956. "Du réalisme merveilleux des Haïtiens." *Présence Africaine* 8–10: 245–271.

Alford, Terry. 2007. *Prince among Slaves*. New York: Oxford University Press.

Allen, Richard. 2008. "The Constant Demand of the French: The Mascarene Slave Trade and the Worlds of the Indian Ocean and Atlantic during the Eighteenth and Nineteenth Centuries." *Journal of African History* 49: 43–72.

Almeida, Ana Carolina Lima, Clinio de Oliveira Amaral, and Marcelo Santiago Berriel. 2013. "Le Moyen Âge est-il arrivé aux Amériques?" *Editions papiers laboratoire*. https://goo.gl/FyJZNN Accessed August 16, 2013.

Almeida, Germano. 1989. *O meu poeta*. Lisbon: Caminho.

———. 1998a. "Temo pelo futuro do meu país." Interview with António Loja Neves. *Expresso*, September 12.

———. 1998b. "Uma forma de identidade africana." *Estórias Contadas*, 13–17. Lisbon: Caminho.

———. 1999. *Dona Pura e os camaradas de abril*. Lisbon: Caminho.

———. 2001. *As memórias de um espírito*. Lisbon: Caminho.

———. 2006a. *Eva*. Lisbon: Caminho.

———. 2006b. "Germano Almeida e uma mulher feliz na escolha de amar vários homens." Interview with Ana Dias Cordeiro. *A Semana*, April 22. https://www.goo.gl/Dp2VIq. Accessed April 5, 2013.

———. 2010. *A morte do ouvidor*. Lisbon: Caminho.

Almeida, Miguel Vale. 2007. "O Atlântico pardo." *Trânsitos coloniais: Diálogos críticos luso-brasileiros*, edited by Cristiana Bastos, Miguel Vale de Almeida, Bela Feldman-Bianco, 23–37. Campinas: Universidade Estadual de Campinas.

Alryyes, Ala. 2011. "Introduction." In Said, *Muslim American Slave*, 3–46.

Álvarez, Santiago, dir. 1965. *Now*. Havana: ICAIC.

———. 1968. *El movimiento panteras negras*. Havana: ICAIC.

Andaló, Paula. 2003. "Lágrimas, amores, traiciones . . . y mensajes de salud." *Revista Perspectivas de Salud* 8:1. https://www.goo.gl/XwAzY9. Accessed June 3, 2013.

Anderson, Benedict. 1983. *Imagined Communities: Reflections on the Origin and Spread of Nationalism*. Revised edition. London: Verso, 2006.

Anderson, Clare. 2000. *Convicts in the Indian Ocean: Transportation from South Asia to Mauritius, 1815–53*. London: Macmillan.

———. 2012. *Subaltern Lives: Biographies of Colonialism in the Indian Ocean World, 1790–1920*. Cambridge: Cambridge University Press.

Andrade, Mário Pinto (Buanga Fele). 1955. "Qu'est-ce que le lusotropicalismo?" *Présence Africaine* 9 (5) (October–November): 24–35.

Appadurai, Arjun. 2001. "Grassroots Globalization and the Research Imagination." In *Globalization*, edited by Arjun Appadurai, 1–21. Durham, N.C.: Duke University Press.

Apter, Emily. 2013. *Against World Literature: On the Politics of Untranslatability*. New York: Verso.

Arenas, Fernando. 2011. *Lusophone Africa: Beyond Independence*. Minneapolis: University of Minnesota Press.

Arendt, Hannah. 1958. *The Origins of Totalitarianism*. New York: Meridian.

Armillas-Tiseyra, Magalí. 2014. "The Dictator and His Objects: The Status of the Fetish in the African Dictator Novel." In *Unmasking the African Dictator: Essays on Postcolonial African Literature*, edited by Gichingiri Ndigirigi, 125–140. Knoxville: University of Tennessee Press.

Armitage, David. 2002. "Three Concepts of Atlantic History." In *The British Atlantic World, 1500–1800*, edited by David Armitage and Michael J. Braddick, 11–29. New York: Palgrave Macmillan.

———. 2001. "The Red Atlantic." *Reviews in American History* 29 (4): 479–486.

Arrais, Amador. (1589) 1974. *Diálogos*. Introduction by M. Lopes de Almeida. Porto: Lello and Irmão.

Arthur, Paige. 2009. "How 'Transitions' Reshaped Human Rights: A Conceptual History of Transitional Justice." *Human Rights Quarterly* 31 (2): 321–367.

Asturias, Miguel Ángel. 1946. *El señor presidente*. Edited by Alejandro Lanoël-d'Aussenac. 10th ed. Madrid: Cátedra, 2014. English: *The President*. Translated by Frances Partridge. Long Grove, Ill.: Waveland Press, 1963.

Austin, Allan. 1984. *African Muslims in Antebellum America: A Sourcebook*. New York: Garland.

Ayala, César J. 1999. *American Sugar Kingdom: The Plantation Economy of the Spanish Caribbean, 1898–1934*. Chapel Hill: University of North Carolina Press.

Baderoon, Gabeba. 2009. "The African Oceans: Tracing the Sea as Memory of Slavery in South African Literature and Culture." *Research in African Literatures* 40 (4): 89–107.

Bailyn, Bernard. 2005. *Atlantic History: Concept and Contours*. Cambridge, Mass.: Harvard University Press.

Baldwin, James. 1985. "Princes and Powers." *The Price of the Ticket: Collected Nonfiction 1948–85*. New York: St. Martin's Press.

Ballan, Mohamad. 2014. "The Transference of 'Reconquista' Iconography to the New World: From Santiago Matamoros to Santiago Mataindios." *Wordpress*, Feb. 11. https://goo.gl/bziKLx.

Barbosa, Elizabeth. 2005. *The Brazilian Telenovela "El Clon": An Analysis of Viewers' Online Vicarious and Virtual Learning Experiences*. Diss. Lynn University.

Barbosa, Jorge. 1997. "Irmão." In *50 Poetas Africanos*, edited by Manuel Ferreira, 166–168. Lisbon: Plátano Editora.

Barchino, Matías. 2007. "Últimas noticias sobre la presencia de Miguel de Cervantes en Guatemala." In *Territorios de La Mancha: Versiones y subversiones cervantinas en la literatura hispanoamericana*, edited by Matías Barchino, 123–130. Cuenca: Ediciones de la Universidad de Castilla–La Mancha.

Barnard, Rita. 2000. "*The Smell of Apples*, *Moby-Dick* and Apartheid Ideology." *Modern Fiction Studies* 46 (1): 207–226.

———. 2004. "On Laughter, the Grotesque, and the South African Transition: Zakes Mda's *Ways of Dying*." *NOVEL: A Forum on Fiction* 37 (3): 277–302.

Barnett, Anthony. 1982. *Iron Britannia: War over the Falklands*. London: New Left Review.

———. 2012. "The Falklands Syndrome: The 30 Year Legacy of Iron Britannia." *Open Democracy Net*, 12 June 2012.

Baschet, Jérôme. 2011. *La civilisation féodale: De l'an mil à la colonisation de l'Amérique*. Paris: Flammarion.

———. 2013. "Ce monde qui n'était pas encore le nôtre et qui s'est emparé des Amériques." Editions papiers—laboratoire. https://goo.gl/NlVnYo. Accessed December 12, 2013.

Bayoumi, Moustafa. 2003. "Moving Beliefs: The Panama Manuscript of Skeikh Sana See and African Diasporic Islam." *interventions* 5(1): 58–81.

Behr, Mark. 1995. *The Smell of Apples*. New York: Picador.

———. 1996. "South Africa: Living in the Fault Lines." *Common Sense* 11 (1). https://www.goo.gl/8ukq5O.

Benjamin, Walter. 1999. *The Arcades Project*. Translated by Howard Eiland and Kevin McLaughin. Cambridge, Mass.: Harvard University Press.

Berkoff, Steven. 1987. *Sink the Belgrano!* London: Faber & Faber.

Berman, Jessica. 2011. *Modernist Commitments: Ethics, Politics, and Transnational Modernism*. New York: Columbia University Press.

Besteman, Catherine. 2002. "Conclusion: Political Violence and the Contemporary World." In *Violence: A Reader*, edited by Catherine Besteman, 299–313. Basingstoke: Palgrave Macmillan.

Bhabha, Homi K. 1990. "Introduction: Narrating the Nation." In *Nation and Narration*, edited by Homi K. Bhabha, 1–7. New York: Routledge.

———. 1994. *The Location of Culture*. London: Routledge.

Bilbao, Francisco. 1941. *La América en peligro*. Santiago: Ercilla.

Blok, Anton. 2000. "The Enigma of Senseless Violence." In *Meanings of Violence*, edited by Göran Aijmer and Jon Abbink, 23–38. New York: Berg.

Blue, Sarah A. 2013. "Internationalism's Remittances: The Impact of Temporary Migration on Cuban Society." *International Journal of Cuban Studies* 5 (1): 41–60.

Blum, Hester. 2013. "Introduction: Oceanic Studies." *Atlantic Studies* 10 (2): 151–155.

Blyden, Edward W. 1871. "Arabic Manuscript in Western Africa." In *The People of Africa*, edited by Edward W. Blyden, Taylor Lewis, Theodore Dwight, et al., 69–73. New York: Anson D. F. Randolph and Co.

Blyden, Edward W., Taylor Lewis, Theodore Dwight, et al., eds. 1871. *The People of Africa: A Series of Papers on Their Character, Condition, and Future Prospects*. New York: Anson D. F. Randolph and Co.

Boelhower, William Q. 2008. "The Rise of the New Atlantic Studies Matrix." *American Literary History* 20 (1/2): 83–101.

Bolaño, Roberto. 2000. *Nocturno de Chile*. Barcelona: Anagrama.

Bolaños, Álvaro Félix. 2008. "Hispanism and Its Literary Icon's Exclusions: Moors and Indians in Reading Don Quixote Today." *Romance Quarterly* 55 (4): 255–278.

Boletim Geral das Colónias. 1939. (*Dedicado à viagem de sua Excelência o Senhor Presidente da República à África acompanhado de sua Excelência o Senhor Ministro das Colónias*). 15 (173) (November).

Bonnet, Alistair. 2010. *Left in the Past: Radicalism and the Politics of Nostalgia*. New York: Continuum.

Boraine, Alex, Janet Levy, and Ronel Scheffer, eds. 1994. *Dealing with the Past: Truth and Reconciliation in South Africa*. Cape Town: IDASA.

Borgwardt, Elizabeth. 2005–2006. "'When You State a Moral Principle, You Are Stuck with It': The 1941 Atlantic Charter as a Human Rights Instrument." *Virginia Journal of International Law* 46 (3): 501–562.

———. 2007. *A New Deal for the World*. Cambridge, Mass.: Harvard University Press.

Bound, Graham. 2012. *Fortress Falklands*. Barnsley: Pen & Sword Military.

Boxer, Charles R. 1952. *Salvador de Sá and the Struggle for Brazil and Angola, 1602–1686*. London: Athlone Press.

Bramley, Vincent. 1991. *Excursion to Hell: Mount Longdon, A Universal Story of Battle*. London: Bloomsbury.

———. 1994. *Two Sides of Hell*. London: Bloomsbury.

———. 2006. *Forward into Hell*. London: John Blake Publishing.

Branche, Jerome. 2006. *Colonialism and Race in Luso-Hispanic Literature*. Columbia: University of Missouri Press.

Braudel, Fernand. 1995. *The Mediterranean and The Mediterranean World in the Age of Philip I* (Volume 1). Berkeley: University of California Press.

Brásio, Fr. António. 1959. "Do último cruzado ao padroado régio." *Studia*: 125–153.

Brásio, Fr. António, ed. 1952. *Monumenta Missionária Africana*. 2nd series, vol. 1. Lisbon: Agência Geral do Ultramar.

———. 1982. *Monumenta Missionária Africana*, 1st series, vol. 13. Lisbon: Academia Portuguesa da História.

Brathwaite, Kamau. 2002. *MR: Magical Realism*. New York: Davacou North.

Breto, R.G. 1984. "South Africa-Chile-Israel Connection." *Journal of Palestine Studies* 13 (3): 188–90.

Brink, André. 1983. *Mapmakers: Writing in a State of Siege*. London: Faber and Faber.

Brito Vieira, Mónica. 2003. "*Mare Liberum* vs. *Mare Clausum*: Grotius, Freitas, and Selden's Debate on Dominion over the Seas." *Journal of the History of Ideas* 64 (3): 361–377.

Brooke, Thomas Henry. 1824. *A History of the Island of St Helena from its Discovery by the Portuguese to the Year 1823*. London: Kingsbury, Parbury and Allen.

Brownlie, Ian. 1970. "An Essay in the History of the Principle of Self-Determination." In *Studies in the History of the Law of Nations*, edited by C. H. Alexandrowicz, 90–99. The Hague: Martinus Nijhoff.

Burton, Julianne. 1997. "Film and Revolution in Cuba. The First Twenty-Five Years." In *New Latin American Cinema*, edited by Michael T. Martin, 2:123–142. Detroit: Wayne State University Press.

Bustos, Dalmiro M. 1982. *El otro frente de la guerra: los padres de las Malvinas*. Buenos Aires: Ramos Americana Editora.

Butalia, Nivriti. 2014. "Remembering Nobel laureate Gabriel Garcia Marquez." *Khaleej Times*, April 19. https://www.goo/gl/CGq2Iw.

Butler, Judith. 1997. *Excitable Speech: A Politics of the Performative*. New York: Routledge.

Bystrom, Kerry. 2014. "Literature, Remediation, Remedy (The Case of Transitional Justice)." *Comparative Literature* 66 (1): 25–34.

Cabral, Amílcar. 1966. "The Weapon of Theory." https://www.goo.gl/MKhYfb. Accessed June 2014.

———. 1973. *Return to the Source. Selected Speeches of Amílcar Cabral*. Edited by Africa Information Service. New York: Monthly Review Press.

Campbell, Gwyn. 2004. "Introduction: Slavery and Other Forms of Unfree Laour in the Indian Ocean World." In *The Structure of Slavery in the Indian Ocean, Africa and Asia*, edited by Gwyn Campbell, vii-xxxii. London: Frank Cass.

Campbell, Roy. 1930. "Rounding the Cape." https://www.goo.gl/DMkTol. Accessed July 20, 2014.

Camus, Albert. 1985. *Le mythe de Sisyphe: Essai sur l'absurde*. Paris: Gallimard.

Candelario, Ginetta E. B. 2007. *Black Behind the Ears: Dominican Racial Identity from Museums to Beauty Shops*. Durham, N.C.: Duke University Press.

Cañizares-Esguerra, Jorge, and Benjamin Breen. 2013. "Hybrid Atlantics: Future Directions for the History of the Atlantic World." *History Compass* 11 (8): 597–609.

Cantel, Raymond. 1959. *Les sermons de Vieira: étude du style*. Paris: Hispano-Americanas.

Cardoso, Jerônimo. 1586. "Carta ao geral da Companhia." *Monumenta Missionária Africana*, 1st series, vol. 15. Dated 6 September. Lisbon: Agência Geral do Ultramar.

Carpentier, Alejo. 1949. "De lo real maravilloso americano." In *Tientos y diferencias*, 66–80. Barcelona: Plaza & Janés Editores, 1984. English: "On the Marvelous Real in America." Translated by Tanya Huntington and Lois Parkinson Zamora. In *Magical Realism: Theory, History, Community*, edited by Lois Parkinson Zamora and Wendy B. Faris, 89–108. Durham, N.C.: Duke University Press, 1995.

———. 1966a. "El realismo en la literatura latinoamericana." In *La cultura en Cuba y en el mundo*, edited by Daniel García Santos, 205–213. Havana: Editorial Letras Cubanas, 2003.

———. 1966b. "Encuesta sobre literatura revolucionaria" (*Bohemia*, La Habana, 20 de Julio de 1966). In *Entrevistas*, edited by Virgilio López Lemus, 140–142. Havana: Editorial Letras Cubanas, 1985.

———. 1975. "Lo barroco y lo real maravilloso." In *Tientos y diferencias*, 103–119. Barcelona: Plaza & Janés Editores, 1984. English: "The Baroque and the Marvelous Real." Translated by Tanya Huntington and Lois Parkinson Zamora. In *Magical Realism: Theory, History, Community*, edited by Lois Parkinson Zamora and Wendy B. Faris, 74–88. Durham, N.C.: Duke University Press, 1995.

———. 2010. *Ecué-Yamba-Ó*. Madrid: AKAL.

Casanova, Pascale. 2004. *The World Republic of Letters*. Translated by M. B. DeBevoise. Cambridge, Mass.: Harvard University Press.

Castells, Manuel. 2011. "A Network Theory of Power." *International Journal of Communication* 5: 773–787.

Castelo, Claudia. 2011. "Uma incursão no lusotropicalismo de Gilberto Freyre." *História Lusófona* 6 (September): 261–280.

Castro, Fidel. 1975. "Discurso Pronunciado por el Comandante en Jefe Fidel Castro Ruz, Primer Secretario del Comité Central del Partido Comunista de Cuba y Primer Ministro Del Gobierno Revolucionario, en la Clausura del Primer Congreso del Partido Comunista de Cuba, Celebrado en el Teatro 'Carlos Marx', El 22 de Diciembre de 1975, 'Año Del Primer Congreso.'" Speech presented at the First Congress of the Communist Party of Cuba, Havana, Cuba, December 22. https://www.goo.gl/pdo9VM.

Césaire, Aimé. 1972. *Discourse on Colonialism*. Translated by Joan Pinkham. New York: Monthly Review.

———. 1995. *Cahier d'un retour au pays natal / Notebook of a Return to a Native Land*. Translated by Mireille Rosello and Annie Pritchard. Northumberland: Bloodaxe Books.

Chakrabarty, Dipesh. 2010. "The Legacies of Bandung: Decolonization and the Politics of Culture" in *Making a World After Empire: The Bandung Moment and Its Political Afterlives*, edited by Christopher J. Lee, 45–68. Athens: Ohio University Press.

Chanan, Michael. 1997. "The Changing Geography of Third Cinema." *Screen* 38 (4): 372–388.

———. 2004. *Cuban Cinema*. Minneapolis: University of Minnesota Press.

Chaunu, Huguette, and Pierre Chaunu. 1954. "Autour de 1640: Politiques et économies atlantiques." *Annales. Historie, Sciences Sociales* 9 (1): 44–54.

———. 1955–1959. *Séville et l'Atlantique 1504–1650*, Paris: S.E.V.P.E.N.

Chaunu, Pierre. 1961. "Brésil et Atlantique au XVIIe siècle." *Annales. Historie, Sciences Sociales* 16 (6): 1176–1207.

Chetty, Raj, and Amaury Rodríguez. 2015. "Introduction: The Challenge and Promise of Dominican Black Studies." *The Black Scholar* 45 (2): 2–9.

Chevalier, Michel. 1853. "Sobre el progreso y porvenir de la civilización." *Revista Española de Ambos Mundos* 1: 1–10.

Childers, William. 2012. "Cervantes in Moriscolandia." *Cervantes: Bulletin of the Cervantes Society of America* 32 (1): 277–290.

Christiansë, Yvette. 1999. *Castaway*. Durham, N.C.: Duke University Press.

———. 2003. "Passing Away: The Unspeakable (Losses) of Postapartheid South Africa." In *Loss: The Politics of Mourning*, edited by David Eng and David Kazanjian, 372–395. Berkeley: University of California Press.

———. 2007. *Unconfessed*. Cape Town: Kwela.

———. 2009. *Imprendehora*. Cape Town: Kwela/Snail Press.

Civantos, Christina. 2006. *Between Argentines and Arabs: Argentine Orientalism, Arab Immigrants, and the Writing of Identity*. Albany: State University of New York Press.

———. 2015. "The View from Beyond: Diaspora and Intertextuality in Ilyās Khūrī's *Majma' al-asrār*." *The Journal of Arabic Literature* 46 (2–3): 193–215.

Clancy Smith, Julia. 2009. "Exoticism, Erasures and Absence: The Peopling of Algiers, 1830–1900." In *Walls of Algeria: Narratives of the City through Text and Image*, edited by Zeynep Celik, Julia Clancy Smith, and Frances Terpak, 19–61. Seattle: University of Washington Press.

Cockram, Gail. 1970. *Vorster's Foreign Policy*. Pretoria: Academia.

Cohn, Deborah N. 1999. *History and Memory in the Two Souths: Recent Southern and Spanish American Fiction*. Nashville: Vanderbilt University Press.

Collis, Christy. 2007. "Mawson and Mirnyy Stations: The Spatiality of the Australian Antarctic Territory, 1954–61." *Australian Geographer* 38 (2): 215–231.

Collis, Christy, and Quentin Stevens. 2007. "Cold Colonies: Antarctic Spatialities at Mawson and McMurdo Stations." *Cultural Geographies* 14: 235–254.

Committee on Africa, the War, and Peace Aims. 1942. *The Atlantic Charter and Africa from an American Standpoint*. Camden, N.J.: Haddon Craftsmen, Inc.

Conrad, Joseph. 1897a. *The Nigger of the "Narcissus": A Tale of the Forecastle*. New York: Doubleday.

———. 1897b. "A Smile of Fortune: Harbour Story." In *'Twixt Land and Sea*. New York: Doubleday.

Cooper, Brenda. 1998. *Magical Realism in West African Fiction: Seeing with a Third Eye*. New York: Routledge.

Corbalán, Ana. 2005. "Entre la aversión y el deseo: Aproximación a la mirada del otro en las páginas de Don Quijote." *Letras Hispanas: Revista de Literatura y Cultura* 2 (2): 75–85. http://www.modlang.txstate.edu/letrashispanas/

previousvolumes/vol2-2/contentParagraph/0/content_files/file5/aversion .pdf.

Coronil, Fernando. 2008. "Elephants in the Americas? Latin American Postcolonial Studies and Global Decolonization." In *Coloniality at Large: Latin America and the Postcolonial Debate*, edited by Mabel Moraña, Enrique Dussel, and Carlos A. Jáuregui. Durham, N.C.: Duke University Press.

Cortes Lopez, José Luis. 1991. "Felipe II, III y IV, Reyes de Angola y protectores del reino del Congo (1580–1640)." *Studia Histórica* 9: 223–246.

Cross, H.E. 1978. "Commerce and Orthodoxy: A Spanish Response to Portuguese Commercial Penetration in the Viceroyalty of Peru, 1580–1640." *The Americas* 35 (2): 151–167.

CubaMINREX/ Embacuba-India. 2014. "Embajada de Cuba presenta Kangamba y Cuito Cuanavale en el Instituto Cervantes de Nueva Delhi." Ministerio de Relaciones Exteriores de la República de Cuba. https://www.goo.gl/8gohQf.

Cunard, Nancy, and George Padmore. 2002. "The White Man's Duty: An Analysis of the Colonial Question in Light of the Atlantic Charter." In *Essays on Race and Empire*, edited by Maureen Moynagh, 127–177. London, Ontario: Broadview.

Cunliffe, John, and Andrew Reeve. 1996. "Exploitation: The Original Saint-Simonian Account." *Capital and Class* 20: 61–80.

Curtin, Philip D. 1967. *Africa Remembered: Narratives by West Africans from the Era of the Slave Trade*. Madison: University of Wisconsin Press.

———. 1968. "Epidemiology and the Slave Trade." *Political Science Quarterly* 83 (2): 190–216.

———. 1969. *The Atlantic Slave Trade: A Census*. Madison: University of Wisconsin Press.

Damrosch, David. 2003. *What Is World Literature?* Princeton, N.J.: Princeton University Press.

Daniel, John. 2009. "Racism, the Cold War, and South Africa's regional security strategies 1948–1990." In *Cold War in Southern Africa: White Power, Black Liberation*, edited by Sue Onslow, 35–54. New York: Routledge.

Danilevicz Pereira, Analúcia. 2013. "The South Atlantic, Southern Africa and South America: Cooperation and Development." *Austral: Brazilian Journal of Strategy and International Relations* 2 (4): 313–345.

Dash, J. Michael. 1998. *The Other America: Caribbean Literature in a New World Context*. Charlottesville: University Press of Virginia.

Daulatzai, Sohail. 2012. *Black Star, Crescent Moon: The Muslim International and Black Freedom Beyond America*. Minneapolis: University of Minnesota Press.

Davis, Forrest. 1941. *The Atlantic System*. New York: Reynal and Hitchcock.

de Alencastro, Luiz Felipe. 2000. *O trato dos viventes: Formação do Brasil no atlântico sul, séculos XVI e XVII*. São Paulo: Companhia das Letras.

———. 2006. "Le versant brésilien de l'Atlantique Sud." Annales 61 (2): 339–382.

———. 2007. "Brazil in the South Atlantic: 1550–1850." Translated by Emilio Sauri. *Mediations* 23 (1): 125–174.

———. 2013. "The Portuguese Missionaries and Early Modern Antislavery." In *Slavery and Antislavery in Spain's Atlantic Empire*, edited by Josep M. Fradera and Christopher Schmidt-Nowara, 43–73. New York: Berghahn Books.

———. 2014. "La traité des noirs et la construction de l'Atlantique ibérique." In *La péninsule ibérique et le monde: Années 1470–années 1640*, edited by Françoise Dartois, 167–184. Paris: PUPS.

———. 2015. "Introduction: The Ethiopic Ocean—History and Historiography, 1600–1975." In *The South Atlantic: Past and Present*, edited by Luiz Felipe de Alencastro, 1–79. Dartmouth, Mass.: Tagus Press.

de Armas, Frederick. 2011. *Don Quixote among the Saracens: A Clash of Civilizations and Literary Genres*. Toronto: University of Toronto Press.

de Camões, Luís. 1572. *The Lusiad or The Discovery of India, an Epic Poem*. Translated by William Julius Mickle. London: George Bell.

de Castro, Aníbal Pinto. 1997. "Os sermões de Vieira: Da palavra dita à palavra escrita." In *Vieira Escritor*, edited by Margarida Vieira Mendes, Maria Lucília Pires, and J. Costa Miranda, 79–94. Lisbon: Cosmos.

de Freitas, Serafim. (1625) 1983. *De justo imperio Lusitanorum asiatico*. Lisboa: Instituto Nacional de Investigação Científica.

de la Fuente, Alejandro. 2001. *A Nation for All: Race, Inequality, and Politics in Twentieth-Century Cuba*. Chapel Hill: University of North Carolina Press.

de la Hoz, Pedro. "Kangamba u otra dimensión de la épica." *Cubacine* 12 (2). https://www.goo.gl/XUVFJe.

de Oliveira, Fernando. 1555. *Arte da Guerra do Mar*. Coimbra.

de Silva, Chandra Richard. 1974. "The Portuguese East India Company 1628–1633." *Luso-Brazilian Review* 11 (2): 152–205.

De Witte, C. M. 1958. "Les bulles pontificales et l'expansion portugaise au XVe siècle." *Revue d'Histoire Ecclésiastique* 53: 443–471.

Decena, Carlos U. 2014. "Triangulating Racial Formations, or Theorizing Dominicana in the African Diaspora." Conference Presentation. Chicago: Latin American Studies Association.

DeLoughrey, Elizabeth. 2010. "Heavy Water: Waste and Atlantic Modernity." *PMLA* 125 (3): 703–712.

Deleuze, Gilles, and Felix Guattari. 1994. *What Is Philosophy?* Translated by Hugh Tomlinson and Graham Burchell. New York: Columbia University Press.

Derrida, Jacques. 1980. "The Law of Genre." Translated by Avital Ronell. *Critical Inquiry* 7 (1): 55–81.

———. 1991. *L'autre cap*. Paris: Éditions de Minuit.

Dimock, Wai Chee. 2006. "Genre as World System: Epic and Novel on Four Continents." *Narrative* 14 (1): 85–101.

Diouf, Sylviane A. 1998. *Servants of Allah: African Muslims Enslaved in the Americas*. New York: New York University Press.

Dionisio, Rodrigo. 2001. "Muçulmanos ganham destaque em *O Clone*." *Folha de São Paulo*, September 23. https://www.goo.gl/xSxxTF. Accessed August 30, 2012.

Dirlik, Arif. 2007. "Global South: Predicament and Promise." *The Global South* 1 (1): 12–23.

Dodds, Klaus. 2012. *The Antarctic: A Very Short Introduction*. Oxford: Oxford University Press.

Dodds, Klaus-John. 1994. "Creating a Strategic Crisis out of a Communist Drama? Argentine and South African Geo-graphs of the South Atlantic." *European Review of Latin American and Caribbean Studies* 56: 33–54.

Domínguez García, Javier. 2008. *De Apóstol Matamoros a Yllapa Mataindios: Dogmas e ideologías medievales en el (des)cubrimiento de América*. Salamanca: Ediciones Universidad de Salamanca.

———. 2008. *Memorias del futuro: Ideología y ficción en el símbolo de Santiago Apóstol*. Madrid: Iberoamericana; Frankfurt: Vervuert.

Dorfman, Ariel. 2010. "Whose Memory? Whose Justice? A Meditation on How and When and If to Reconcile." Nelson Mandela Foundation. https://www.goo.gl/JPM5TT. Accessed August 31, 2016.

Doyle, Laura. 2014. "Inter-Imperiality." *Interventions: International Journal of Postcolonial Studies* 16 (2): 159–196.

Du Bois, W. E. B. 1997. *The Souls of Black Folk*. Edited by David W. Blight and Robert Gooding-Williams. Boston: Bedford Books.

Dwight, Theodore. 1871. "Condition and Character of Negroes in Africa." In *The People of Africa*, edited by Edward W. Blyden, Taylor Lewis, Theodore Dwight, et al., 43–61. New York: Anson D. F. Randolph and Co.

Edwards, Brent Hayes. 2003. *The Practice of Diaspora: Literature, Translation, and the Rise of Black Internationalism*. Cambridge, Mass.: Harvard University Press.

Eggers, Dave. 2006. *What Is the What: The Autobiography of Valentino Achak Deng*. New York: McSweeney's.

El Attar, Heba. 2008. "Orientalismo hispanoamericano en *Crónica de una muerte anunciada* de Gabriel García Márquez y *La Turca* de Jorge Luis Oviedo." *Hispania* 91 (4): 914–924.

Eller, Anne. 2014. "'Awful Pirates' and 'Hordes of Jackals': Santo Domingo/The Dominican Republic in Nineteenth-Century Historiography." *Small Axe* 44: 80–94.

El-Outmani, Ismail. 1994. "La maqama en al-andalus." In *La sociedad andalusí y sus tradiciones literarias*, edited by Otto Zwartjes, 105–126. Amsterdam: Rodopi.

Eltahawy, Mona. 2000. "What They're Reading in Egypt." *The Guardian*, March 9.

Eltis, David and David Richardson. 2010. *Atlas of the Transatlantic Slave Trade*. New Haven: Yale University Press.

Enfantin, Prosper. 1868. "5ième enseignement d'Enfantin, 7 decembre 1831." In *Oeuvres de Saint-Simon et d'Enfantin*, edited by E. Dentu, 14:205–210. Paris: Libraire de la Société des Gens de Lettres.

Ercolani, Patrick. 2013. "Why Are Immigrants Being Deported for Minor Crimes?" *The Atlantic*, November 20.

Escudero, Lucrecia. 1996. *Malvinas: El gran relato. Fuentes y rumores en la información de guerra*. Barcelona: Gedisa.

Espinosa, Julio García. 1979. "For an Imperfect Cinema." Translated by Julianne Burton. *Jump Cut* 20: 24–26.

Esponera Cerdán, Alfonso. 2003. "Bartolomé de las Casas y la esclavización de los negros, según las aportaciones de I. Pérez Fernández O. P." *Studium*, 43 (1): 87–100.

Ette, Ottmar. 2006. "Chronicle of a Clash Foretold? Arab-American Dimensions and Transareal Relations in Gabriel García Márquez and Elias Khoury." In *ArabAmericas: Literary Entanglements of the American Hemisphere and the Arab World*, edited by Ottmar Ette and Friederike Pannewick, 215–260. Frankfurt: Vervuert/Madrid: Iberoamericana.

———. 2010. "¿Quién mató a Santiago Nasar? Indicios arabamericanos en una crónica de cuatrocientos años de soledad." In *Indicios, señales y narraciones. Literatura policíaca en lengua española*, edited by Enrique Rodrigues-Moura, 209–230. Innsbruck: Innsbruck University Press.

Falola, Toyin, and Kevin D. Roberts. 2008. "Introduction." In *The Atlantic World, 1450–2000*, edited by Toyin Falola and Kevin D. Roberts, ix–xiv. Bloomington: Indiana University Press.

"Falsas atribuições." 2015. *Recanto das letras*. http://www.recantodasletras.com.br/artigos/3524813. Accessed June 12, 2014.

Fanon, Frantz. 1963. *The Wretched of the Earth*. Translated by Richard Philcox. New York: Grove Press, 2004.

———. 2008. *Black Skin, White Masks*. Translated by Richard Philcox. New York: Grove Press.

Faris, Wendy B. 2004. *Ordinary Enchantments: Magical Realism and the Remystification of Narrative*. Nashville: Vanderbilt University Press.

Feres Júnior, João. 2010. *Histoire du concept d'Amérique latine aux Etats-Unis*. Paris: L'Harmattan.

Ferreira, Carolin Overhoff. 2011. "Ambivalent Transnationality: Luso-African Co-Productions after Independence (1988–2010)." *Journal of African Cinemas* 3 (2): 221–245.

Fig, David. 1979. "South Africa's Expansion of Relations with Latin America 1966–1977: Some Initial Observations." York: Collected Papers of the Centre for Southern African Studies at the University of York.

———. 1983. "South African Interests in Latin America." *South African Review* 1984: 239–255.

Fischer, Sibylle. 2004. *Modernity Disavowed: Haiti and the Cultures of Slavery in the Age of Revolution*. Durham, N.C.: Duke University Press.

Fleitas, Miguel. 1976. *La guerra en Angola*. Film. ICAIC; FAR; MPLA.

Fleming Figueroa, Leonor. 2007. "El espacio literario: Territorios 'manchados' en la narrativa latinoamericana (García Márquez, Rulfo, Onetti, Tizón)." In *Territorios de La Mancha: Versiones y subversiones cervantinas en la literatura hispanoamericana*, edited by Matías Barchino, 281–290. Cuenca: Ediciones de la Universidad de Castilla–La Mancha.

Fogwill, R. E. 1983. *Los pichiciegos: Visiones de una batalla subterránea*. Buenos Aires: Ediciones de la Flor.

———. 2007. *Malvinas Requiem*. Translated by Nick Caistor and Amanda Hopkinson. London: Serpent's Tail.

Forced Apart (By the Numbers): Non-Citizens Deported Mostly for Nonviolent Offenses. 2009. Human Rights Watch, April 15. https://www.goo.gl/RHJTuF.

Fornet, Ambrosio. 2001. "Apuntes para el cine cubano de ficción." *Temas* 27: 4–16.

Foster, Kevin. 1999. *Fighting Fictions: War, Narrative and National Identity*. London: Pluto.

Foucault, Michel. 1997. *Society Must Be Defended: Lectures at the Collège de France, 1975–76*. Edited by Mauro Bertani and Alessandro Fontana. Translated by David Macey. New York: Picador.

———. 2007. *Security, Territory, Population. Lectures at the Collège de France, 1977–78*. Edited by Michel Senellart. Translated by Graham Burchell. Basingstoke: Palgrave MacMillan.

Fowles, John. 1982. "The Falklands, and a Death Foretold." *The Georgia Review* 36 (4): 721–728.

France, Jules de. 1857a. "Alger, San Francisco, Panama." *El Panameño*, June 26.

———. 1857b. "Fertilité de l'Algérie." *El Panameño*, June 21.

Francis, Richard. 1986. *Swansong*. Glasgow: William Collins and Sons.

Franco, Jean. 2002. *The Decline and Fall of the Lettered City: Latin America in the Cold War*. Cambridge, Mass.: Harvard University Press.

Frank, Andre Gunder. 1968. *Capitalisme et sous-développement en Amérique Latine*. Translated by Guillaume Carle and Christos Passadeos. Paris: Maspero.

Freedman, Lawrence. 1983. "Bridgehead Revisited: The Literature of the Falklands." *International Affairs* 59 (3): 445–452.

———. 2007. *The Official History of the Falklands Campaign. Vol. 2, War and Diplomacy*. 2nd ed., rev. London: Routledge.

Freud, Sigmund. (1919) 1955. "The Uncanny." In *The Complete Psychological Works of Sigmund Freud*, vol. 17. Translated by James Strachey. London: Hogarth Press.

Freyre, Gilberto. 1933. *The Masters and the Slaves: A Study in the Development of Brazilian Civilization*. 2nd ed., 1986. Translated by Samuel Putnam. Berkeley: University of California Press.

———. 1953. *Aventura e rotina: Sugestões de uma viagem à procura das constantes portuguesas de caráter e ação*. Rio de Janeiro: José Olympo.

———. 1961. *O Luso e o trópico*. Lisbon: Comissão Executiva para a Comemoração do V Centenário da Morte do Infante Dom Henrique.

———. N.d. *Um brasileiro em terras portuguesas*. Lisbon: Livros do Brasil.

Friedman, Susan Stanford. 2013. "Why Not Compare?" In *Comparison: Theories, Approaches, Uses*, 15–33. Baltimore: Johns Hopkins University Press.

———. 2011. "Why Not Compare?" *PMLA* 126 (3): 753–762.

Frobert, Ludovic. 2011. "French Utopian Socialists as the First Pioneers in Development." *Cambridge Journal of Economics* 35: 729–749.

Frydman, Jason. 2014. *Sounding the Break: African American and Caribbean Routes of World Literature*. Charlottesville: University of Virginia Press.

Fuentes, Carlos. 1993. "Augusto Roa Bastos: El poder de la imaginación." In *La geografía de la novela*, 91–102. Mexico City: Fondo de Cultura Económica.

Fukuyama, Francis. 1992. *The End of History and The Last Man*. New York: Free Press.

———. 2014. "At the 'End of History' Still Stands Democracy." *Wall Street Journal*, June 6.

Galvão, Henrique. 1975. *Carta Aberta ao dr. Salazar. Um documento inédito de Henrique Galvão*. Lisbon: Arcádia.

Gamboa, Zézé. 1998. *Dissidence*. VHS. Fábrica d'Imagens; Garance Production; RTP.

———. 2004. *O herói*. DVD. David & Golias.

———. 2005. "'Como Angola está, eu não podia fazer um filme alegre,' Zezé Gamboa." Interview by Paulo Spranger. Diário de Notícias/angonoticias.com. http://www.angonoticias.com/Artigos/item/3874.

———. 2012. *O Grande Kilapy*. Film. David & Golias; Raíz Produções Cinematográficas; Gamboa & Gamboa.

———. 2013. Entrevista: Zézé Gamboa. Um golpe entre Angola e Paraíba. Interview by Ivonete Pinto. *Orson: Revista dos Cursos de Cinema do Cearte UFPEL*. https://www.goo.gl/IJZojA.

Gamerro, Carlos. 1998. *Las islas*. Buenos Aires: Norma Simurg.

Games, Allison. 2006. "Atlantic History: Definitions, Challenges, and Opportunities." *American Historical Review* 111 (3): 741–757.

García Añoveros, Jesús María. 2000. "Luis de Molina y la esclavitud de los negros africanos en el siglo XVI. Principios doctrinales y conclusiones." *Revista de Indias* 60 (219): 307–329.

García Calderón, Francisco. 1913. *Latin America: Its Rise and Progress*. Translated by Bernard Miall. London: T. Fisher Unwin.

García Márquez, Gabriel. 1967. *Cien años de soledad*. Buenos Aires: Sudamericana.

———. 1970. *One Hundred Years of Solitude*. Translated by Gregory Rabassa. New York: Harper and Row.

———. 1975a. *El otoño del patriarca*. Buenos Aires: Sudamericana.

———. 1975b. *The Autumn of the Patriarch*. Translated by Gregory Rabassa. New York: Harper and Row.

———. 1981a. *Crónica de una muerte anunciada*. New York: Vintage.

———. 1981b. *Qiṣṣat Mawt Muʿlan*. Translated by Ṣāliḥ ʿAlmānī. Damascus: al-Madāq.

———. 1989. *Sard Aḥdāth Mawt Muʿlan*. Translated by ʿAbd al-Munʿim Salīm. Beirut: Dār al-ʿAwda.

———. 1990. *Waqāʾiʿ Mawt Muʿlan*. Translated by Kāmil ʿUwayd ʿĀmirī. Baghdad: al-Maktaba al-ʿĀlamiyya.

García Márquez, Gabriel, and Mario Vargas Llosa. March 20, 1967. Box 10, Folder 7, Mario Vargas Llosa Papers, Archives of Latin American Writers and Intellectuals, Manuscripts Division, Department of Rare Books and Special Collections, Princeton University Library.

García Márquez, Gabriel, and Plinio Apuleyo Mendoza. 1982. *El olor de la guayaba: conversaciones con Plinio Apuleyo Mendoza*. Barcelona: Bruguera.

García Ramos, Juan Manuel. 2007. "*El Quijote* y *Cien años de soledad*: Paralelismos." In *Territorios de la Mancha: Versiones y subversiones cervantinas en la literatura hispanoamericana*, edited by Matías Barchino, 335–342. Cuenca: Ediciones de la Universidad de Castilla–La Mancha.

García Usta, Jorge. 1997. "Árabes en Macondo." *Deslinde* 21: 122–139.

Gates, Henry Louis, Jr. 1989. *Figures in Black: Words, Signs, and the "Racial" Self*. New York: Oxford University Press.

———. 2008. "Third World of Theory: Enlightenment's Esau." *Critical Inquiry* 34 (2): s191–s205.

———. 2011. *Black in Latin America*. New York: New York University Press.

Gaylard, Gerald. 2005. *After Colonialism: African Postmodernism and Magical Realism*. Johannesburg: Wits University Press.

Geggus, David Patrick. 2002. *Haitian Revolutionary Studies*. Bloomington: Indiana University Press.

German Marshall Fund of the United State and the OCP Policy Center. 2014. *Atlantic Currents: An Annual Report on Wider Atlantic Perspectives and Patterns*. Washington, D.C.: German Marshall Fund of the United States and the OCP Policy Center. Available: http://www.gmfus.org/file/3537/download.

Ghazouani, Abdelmalek Cherkaoui. 2002. "'O cloné e o simulacro." *Folha de São Paulo*, June 17. https://www.goo.gl/Rj6Eaj. Accessed March 22, 2013.

Ghazoul, Ferial. 1996. *Nocturnal Poetics*. Cairo: American University of Cairo Press.

Ghosh, Amitav. 2008. *Sea of Poppies*. London: John Murray.

Gibran, Kahlil. 1923. *The Prophet*. New York: Knopf.

Gikandi, Simon. 1996. "Introduction: Africa, The Diaspora and the Promise of Modernity." *Research in African Literatures* 27 (4): 1–6.

Gilliam, Angela. 1998. "The Brazilian *mulata*: Images in the Global Economy." *Race and Class* 40 (1) (July): 57–69.

———. 2003. "Globalization, Identity and Assaults on Equality in the United States: An Initial Perspective for Brazil." *Souls* 5 (2) (Spring): 81–106.

Gilmore, Glenda. 2008. *Defying Dixie: The Radical Roots of Civil Rights: 1919–1950*. New York: Norton.

Gilroy, Paul. 1993. *The Black Atlantic: Modernity and Double Consciousness*. Cambridge, Mass.: Harvard University Press.

———. 2001. *Against Race: Imagining Political Culture Beyond the Color Line*. Cambridge, Mass.: Belknap Press.

Gleijeses, Piero. 1996–97. "Havana's Policy in Africa, 1959–76: New Evidence from Cuban Archives." *Cold War International History Project Bulletin* (Winter): 5–18.

Gomez, Michael. 1998. *Exchanging Our Country Marks: The Transformation of African Identities in the Colonial and Antebellum South*. Chapel Hill: University of North Carolina Press.

———. 2005. *Black Crescent: The Experience and Legacy of African Muslims in the Americas*. New York: Cambridge University Press.

Gordimer, Nadine. 2010. *Telling Times: Writing and Living, 1954–2008*. New York: Norton.

Gosse, Van. 1993. *Where the Boys Are: Cuba, Cold War America, and the Making of a New Left*. London: Verso.

Goyal, Yogita. 2014. "Introduction: Africa and the Black Atlantic." *Research in African Literatures* 45 (3): v–xxv.

Gqola, Pumla Dineo. 2010. *What is Slavery to Me? Postcolonial/Slave Memory in Post-apartheid South Africa*. Johannesburg: Wits University Press.

Graf, Eric Clifford. 2007. *Cervantes and Modernity*. Lewisburg, Pa.: Bucknell University Press.

Grant, Douglas. 1968. *The Fortunate Slave: an Illustration of African Slavery in the Early Eighteenth Century*. Oxford: Oxford University Press.

Grovogui, Siba N'Zatioula. 1996. *Sovereigns, Quasi Sovereigns, and Africans: Race and Self-Determination in International Law*. Minneapolis: University of Minneapolis Press.

Gruzinski, Serge. 2004. *Les quatre parties du monde: Histoire d'une mondialisation*. Paris: La Martinière.

Gúber, Rosana. 2004. *De "chicos" a "veteranos": Memorias argentinas de la guerra de Malvinas*. Buenos Aires: Antropofagia.

Guenther, Irene. 1995. "Magic Realism, New Objectivity, and the Arts During the Weimar Republic." In *Magical Realism: Theory, History, Community*, edited by Lois Parkinson Zamora and Wendy B. Faris, 33–74. Durham, N.C.: Duke University Press.

Guevara, Che. 1967. *Message to the Tricontinental*. Special supplement of *Tricontinental*. April.

Gupta, Pamila. 2010. "Introduction: Islandness in the Indian Ocean." In *Eyes across the Water: Navigating the Indian Ocean*, edited by Pamila Gupta, Isabel Hofmeyr, and Michael Pearson, 275–285. Pretoria: UNISA Press.

Guridy, Frank Andre. 2010. *Forging Diaspora: Afro-Cubans and African Americans in a World of Empire and Jim Crow*. Chapel Hill: University of North Carolina Press.

Haggard, H. Rider. 1929. *Mary of Marion Isle*. London: Hutchinson.

Hall, Stuart. 1995. "Whites of Their Eyes: Racist Ideologies and the Media." In *Gender, Race, and Class in Media*, edited by Gail Dines and Jean M. Humez, 18–22. Thousand Oaks, Calif.: Sage.

Hamber, Brandon, and Richard A. Wilson. 2002. "Symbolic Closure through Memory, Reparation and Revenge in Post-conflict Societies." *Journal of Human Rights* 1 (1): 35–53.

Hamburger, Esther. 2005. *O Brasil antenado: A sociedade da novela*. Rio de Janeiro: Jorge Zohar Editor.

Hammond, Andrew. 2006. *Cold War Literature: Writing the Global Conflict*. New York: Routledge.

———. 2012. *Global Cold War Literature: Western, Eastern and Postcolonial Perspectives*. New York: Routledge.

Hanekom, Wouter Pierre. 2014. "A History of Tourism, Leisure and Adventure in the Antarctic and Sub-Antarctic, c. 1895 to Present." MA thesis, University of Stellenbosch.

Hardt, Michael, and Antonio Negri. 2000. *Empire*. Cambridge, Mass.: Harvard University Press.

Harlow, Barbara. 1992. *Barred: Women, Writing and Political Detention*. Hanover, N.H.: Wesleyan University Press.

Harris, Robert. 1983. *Gotcha! The Media, The Government and the Falklands Crisis*. London: Faber.

Harrow, Kenneth W. 2013. *Trash: African Cinema From Below*. Bloomington: University of Indiana Press.

Hart, Stephen. 2005. *Gabriel García Márquez: Crónica de una muerte anunciada*. London: Grant & Cutler.

Hassan, Waïl S. 2011. *Immigrant Narratives: Orientalism and Cultural Translation in Arab American and Arab British Literature*. New York: Oxford University Press.

Hatzky, Christine. 2015. *Cubans in Angola. South-South Cooperation and Transfer of Knowledge, 1976–1991*. Translated by Christine Hatzky. Madison: University of Wisconsin Press.

Haydar, Paula. 1996. "Preface." In Elias Khoury, *The Kingdom of Strangers*, v–viii. Translated by Paula Haydar. Fayetteville: University of Arkansas Press.

Hemer, Oscar. 2012. *Fiction and Truth in Transition. Writing the Present Past in South Africa and Argentina*. Münster: Lit Verlag.

Hernández, Rita Indiana. 1999. *La estrategia de Chochueca*. Puerto Rico: Isla Negra, 2003.

———. 2003. *Sugar/Azúcal*. Performance text. Santo Domingo: Centro Cultural de España.

———. 2013. "Magia negra." *El País Internacional*, October 9.

———. (2013) 2014. *De nombres y animales*. Spain: Editorial Periférica.

Hernández Lefranc, Harold. 2011. "Santiago Mataindios: Las apariciones del apóstol Santiago en la conquista de América." July 30. http://www.preguntasantoral.es/2011/07/santiago-mataindios/

———. 2006. "El trayecto de Santiago Apóstol de Europa al Perú." *Investigaciones Sociales* 10 (16): 51–92.

Hespanha, António Manuel. 2001. "Luís de Molina e a escravização dos negros." *Análise Social* 35 (157): 937–960.

Heyns, Michiel. 1996. "Fathers and Sons: Structures of Erotic Patriarchy in Afrikaans Writing of the Emergency." *Ariel* 27 (1): 81–104.

———. 2000. "The Whole Country's Truth: Confession and Narrative in Recent White South African Writing." *Modern Fiction Studies* 46 (1): 42–66.

Higgins, D. S. 1981. *Rider Haggard: The Great Storyteller*. London: Cassell.

Hoffman, Ross. 1945. "Europe and the Atlantic Community." *Thought* 20 (1): 21–36.

Hofmeyr, Isabel. 2007. "The Black Atlantic Meets the Indian Ocean: Forging New Paradigms of Transnationalism for the Global South—Literary and Cultural Perspectives." *Social Dynamics* 33 (2): 3–32.

Holland, Tom. 2012. "Islam & Influence." *Literary Review* 403 (October). https://literaryreview.co.uk/islam-influence.

Howkins, Adrian. 2008. "Defending Polar Empire: Opposition to India's Proposal to Raise the "Antarctic Question" at the United Nations in 1956." *Polar Record* 44 (228): 35–44.

Huish, Robert, and Sarah A. Blue. 2013. "Understanding the Place of Cuban Internationalism." *International Journal of Cuban Studies* 5 (1): 6–9.

Humphrey, Michael, and Estela Valverde. 2008. "Human Rights Politics and Injustice: Transitional Justice in Argentina and South Africa." *International Journal of Transitional Justice* 2 (1): 83–105.

Hunwick, John O. 2003–4. "I Wish to be Seen in Our Land Called Afrika: Umar b. Sayyid's Appeal to be Released from Slavery (1819)." *Journal of Arabic and Islamic Studies* 5: 62–77.

Hurrell, Andrew. 1983. "The Politics of South Atlantic Security: A Survey of Proposals for a South Atlantic Treaty Organization." *International Affairs* 59 (2): 179–193.

Hutcheon, Linda. 1988. *A Poetics of Postmodernism: History, Theory, Fiction*. New York: Routledge.

Ibawoh, Bonny. 2014. "Testing the Atlantic Charter: Linking Anticolonialism, Self-determination, and Universal Human Rights." *The International Journal of Human Rights* 18 (7 and 8): 842–860.

International Preparatory Committee of the First Solidarity Conference of the Peoples of Africa, Asia and Latin America and the Cuban National Committee. "Background of Tricontinental Conference to be Held in Havana." In *Towards the First Tricontinental Conference*. 1965.

Izquierdo, Jaisy. 2011. "Para que zumbe en la memoria." *Juventud Rebelde*, July 16. https://www.goo.gl/D8OYwn.

Jackson, Richard L. 1988. *Black Literature and Humanism in Latin America*. Athens: University of Georgia Press.

James, C. L. R. 1938. *The Black Jacobins: Toussaint L'Ouverture and the San Domingo Revolution*. New York: Vintage, 1989.

———. 1992. "Black People in the Urban Areas of the United States." In *The C. L. R. James Reader*, edited by Anna Grimshaw, 375–378. Wiley-Blackwell.

Jameson, Fredric. 2005. *Archaeologies of the Future: The Desire Called Utopia and Other Science Fictions*. New York: Verso.

———. 2013. *The Antinomies of Realism*. New York: Verso.

Jameson, J. Franklin. 1925. "Autobiography of Omar ibn Said, Slave in North Carolina, 1831." *American Historical Review* 30 (4): 787–795.

Johnson, Carroll B. 2009. *Transliterating a Culture: Cervantes and the Moriscos*. Edited by Mark Groundland. Newark, Del.: Juan de la Cuesta.

Joseph, Peniel E. 2006. *Waiting 'Til the Midnight Hour: A Narrative History of Black Power in America*. New York: Henry Holt.

Joset, Jacques. 1991. "Autores *Traduttori Traditori*: *Don Quijote* y *Cien años de soledad* (I)." In *Actas del X Congreso de la Asociación Internacional de Hispanistas*, edited by Antonio Vilanova, 737–744. Barcelona: Promociones y Publicaciones Universitarias (PPU).

———. 1992. "Autores *Traduttori Traditori*: *Don Quijote* y *Cien años de soledad* (II)" In *On Cervantes: Essays for L. A. Murillo*, edited by James A. Parr, 105–117. Newark, Del.: Juan de la Cuesta.

Joyce, Samantha Nogueira. 2012. *Brazilian Telenovelas and the Myth of Racial Democracy*. Lanham, Md.: Lexington Books.

Judy, Ronald. 1993. *(Dis)forming the American Canon: African-Arabic Slave Narratives and the Vernacular*. Minneapolis: University of Minnesota Press.

Kahin, George McTurnan. 1956. *The Asian-African Conference: Bandung, Indonesia, April 1955*. Ithaca, N.Y.: Cornell University Press.

Kantorowicz, Ernst. 1997. *The King's Two Bodies: a Study in Medieval Political Theology*. Princeton: Princeton University Press.

Karam, John Tofik. 2007. *Another Arabesque: Syrian-Lebanese Ethnicity in Neoliberal Brazil*. Philadelphia: Temple University Press.

———. 2010. "Belly Dancing and the (En)Gendering of Ethnic Sexuality in the 'Mixed' Brazilian Nation." *Journal of Middle East Women's Studies* 6 (2): 86–114.

Karlsen, Inghild. 2003. "Introduction." In *etter Columbus.com*, 4–9. Exhibit catalogue. Oslo: Kunsternes Hus.

Karpat, Kemal. 1985. "The Ottoman Emigration to America, 1860–1914." *International Journal of Middle East Studies* 17 (2): 175–209.

Khoury, Elias (Ilyās Khūrī). 1996. *The Kingdom of Strangers*. Translated by Paula Haydar. Fayetteville: University of Arkansas Press.

———. 1994. *Majma' al-Asrār*. Beirut: Dār al-Ādāb.

———. 1993. *Mamlakat al-Ghurabā'*. Beirut: Dār al-Ādāb.

———. 2000. *Yālū*. Beirut: Dār al-Ādāb.

Kline, Carmenza. 2002. *Violencia en Macondo. Tema recurrente en la obra de García Márquez*. Bogotá: Fundación General de la Universidad de Salamanca.

Klein, Cristian. 2001. "Islamismo chega ao horário nobre." *Folha de São Paulo*, July 1. https://www.goo.gl/j7jVRH. Accessed August 27, 2012.

Klose, Fabian. 2013. *Human Rights in the Shadow of Colonial Violence: The Wars of Independence in Kenya and Algeria*. Translated by Dona Geyer. Philadelphia: University of Pennsylvania Press.

Kohan, Martín. 2002. *Dos veces junio*. Buenos Aires: Sudamericana.

Kohan, Martín, Oscar Blanco, and Adriana Imperatore. 1993. "Trashumantes de neblina, no las hemos de encontrar. De cómo la literatura cuenta la Guerra de Malvinas," *Espacios*, December 13, 1993: 82–86.

Kon, Daniel. 1984. *Los chicos de la guerra: Hablan los soldados que estuvieron en Malvinas*. Buenos Aires: Galerna.

Kourouma, Ahmadou. 1998. *En attendant le vote des bêtes sauvages*. Paris: Éditions du Seuil.

———. 2001 (1998). *Waiting for the Vote of the Wild Animals*. Translated by Carrol F. Coates. Charlottesville: University of Virginia Press.

Krull, Catherine, ed. 2014. *Cuba in a Global Context: International Relations, Internationalism, and Transnationalism*. Gainesville: University Press of Florida.

Kubayanda, Josaphat. 1990. "Dictatorship, Oppression, and New Realism." *Research in African Literatures* 21 (2): 5–11.

Kutzinski, Vera M. 1993. *Sugar's Secrets: Race and the Erotics of Cuban Nationalism*. Charlottesville: University Press of Virginia.

Labou Tansi, Sony. 1979. *Le vie et demie*. Paris: Éditions du Seuil.

———. 2011. *Life and a Half*. Translated by Alison Dundy. Bloomington: Indiana University Press.

Langer, Jessica. 2011. *Postcolonialism and Science Fiction*. New York: Palgrave Macmillan.

Las Casas, Bartolomé. 1989. *Brevísima relación de la destrucción de África: Preludio de la destrucción de Indias* (1540–54). Edited and with notes by Isacio Pérez Fernández. Salamanca: San Esteban.

Lawson, Mark. 2002. "Our Own Vietnam." *The Guardian*, 25 February.

Leane, Elizabeth. 2007. "Isolation, Connectedness and the Uses of Text in Heroic-Era Antarctica: The Cases of Inexpressible and Elephant Islands." *Island Studies Journal* 2 (1): 67.

———. 2012. *Antarctica in Fiction: Imaginative Narratives of the Far South*. Cambridge: Cambridge University Press.

Lee, Christopher J. 2010. "Between a Moment and an Era: The Origins and Afterlives of Bandung." In *Making a World After Empire: The Bandung Moment and Its Political Afterlives*, edited by Christopher J. Lee, 1–42. Athens: Ohio University Press.

Lenin, Vladimir. 2010. *Imperialism: The Highest Stage of Capitalism*. London: Penguin.

Léonard, Yves. 1999. "O império colonial salazarista." In *História da Expansão Portuguesa*, edited by Francisco Bethencourt and Kiri Chaudhuri, 5:10–30. Lisbon: Círculo de Leitores.

Lesser, Ian O. 2010. "Southern Atlanticism: Geopolitics and Strategy for the Other Half of the Atlantic Rim." *Brussels Forum Paper Series*. Washington D.C.: German Marshall Fund.

Lesser, Jeffrey. 2013. *Immigration, Ethnicity, and National Identity in Brazil, 1808 to the Present*. New York: Cambridge University Press.

Levallois, Michel. 2001. "Le 'mariage arabe' d'Ismaïl Urbain." *Etudes Littéraires* 33 (3): 109–117.

Lionnet, Françoise, and Shu-mei Shih, eds. 2005. *Minor Transnationalism*. Durham, N.C.: Duke University Press.

Lipschutz, Alexandre. 1966. "Problèmes agraires de l'Amérique latine. Survivances coloniales et précoloniales." *Annales. Économies, Sociétés, Civilisations* 21 (4): 779–814.

Liss, Sheldon B. 1984. *Marxist Thought in Latin America*. Berkeley: University of California Press.

Lodge, Tom. 2003. *Politics in South Africa: From Mandela to Mbeki*. Bloomington: Indiana University Press.

López, Alfred J. 2007. "Introduction: The (Post)Global South." *The Global South* 1 (1): 1–11.

Lopez, Ana M. 1995. "Our Welcomed Guests: Telenovelas in Latin America." In *To Be Continued : Soap Operas Around the World*, edited by Robert C. Allen, 256–275. London: Routledge.

Lorcin, Patricia M. 1999. *Imperial Identities: Stereotyping, Prejudice and Race in Colonial Algeria*. New York: Tauris.

Lorenz, Federico G. 2006. *Las guerras por Malvinas*. Buenos Aires: Edhasa.

Lund, Joshua. 2006. *The Impure Imagination: Toward a Critical Hybridity in Latin American Writing*. Minneapolis: University of Minnesota Press.

L'union agricole d'Afrique. 1846. *Nouveau système de colonisation de l'Algérie*. Lyon: Imprimérie de Lyon Boitel.

Lynch, Hollis R. 1970. *Edward Wilmot Blyden: Pan-Negro Patriot, 1832–1912*. New York: Oxford University Press.

MacDonald, Ian P. 2016. "The Cybogre Manifesto: Time, Utopia, and Globality in Ngũgĩ's *Wizard of the Crow*." *Research in African Literatures* 47 (1): 57–75.

Madureira, Luís. 2007. *Imaginary Geographies: Narratives of Discovery and Empire*. Lewiston, N.Y.: Edwin Mellen Press.

———. 2009. "La poetización del atlántico y el dilema del compromiso: José Saramago, Pablo Neruda y Fernando Pessoa." *Iberoamericana* 35 (228): 841–864.

———. 2008. “Nation, Identity and Loss of Footing: Mia Couto’s ‘O Outro Pé da Sereia’ and the Question of Lusophone Postcolonialism.” *Novel: A Forum on Fiction* (Spring/Summer): 200–229.

———. 1994. “Tropical Sex Fantasies and the Ambassador’s Other Death: The Difference in Portuguese Colonialism.” *Cultural Critique* 28 (Fall): 149–174.

Mahler, Anne Garland. 2015. “The Global South in the Belly of the Beast: Viewing African American Civil Rights through a Tricontinental Lens.” *Latin American Research Review* 50 (1): 95–116.

Mancing, Howard. 1981. “Cide Hamete Benengeli vs. Miguel de Cervantes: The Metafictional Dialectic of Don Quijote.” *Cervantes: Bulletin of the Cervantes Society of America* 1 (1–2): 63–81.

Mandela, Nelson. 1991. “We Will Ensure That the Poor and Rightless Will Rule the Land of Their Birth.” In *How Far We Slaves Have Come! South Africa and Cuba in Today’s World*, edited by Nelson Mandela and Fidel Castro, 17–28. New York: Pathfinder.

———. 1994. *Long Walk to Freedom*. Boston: Little, Brown.

Mariano, Gabriel. 1991. “Do funco ao sobrado, ou, O mundo que o mulato criou.” *Cultura Caboverdeana: Ensaios*, 39–61. Lisbon: Vega.

Marques, João Francisco. 1997. “A cronologia da pregação de Vieira.” In *Vieira Escritor*, edited by Margarida Vieira Mendes, Maria Lucília Pires, and J. Costa Miranda, 117–134. Lisbon: Cosmos.

Marques Pereira, Nuno. 1988. *Compêndio narrativo do peregrino da América* (1728). Rio de Janeiro: Academia Brasileira de Letras.

Marr, Timothy. 2006. *The Cultural Roots of American Islamicism*. New York: Cambridge University Press.

Martin, Gerald. 1989. *Journeys through the Labyrinth: Latin American Fictions in the Twentieth Century*. New York: Verso.

Martín-Barbero, Jesús. 1995. “Memory and Form in the Latin American Soap Opera.” In *To Be Continued: Soap Operas Around the World*, edited by Robert C. Allen, 276–284. London: Routledge.

Marx, Karl. 1973. *Grundrisse: Foundations of the Critique of Political Economy*. Translated Martin Nicolaus. New York: Penguin.

Massip, José. 1976. *Angola, Vitória da esperanza*. Film. ICAIC.

Matar, Nabil. 2009. *Europe Through Arab Eyes: 1578–1727*. New York: Columbia University Press.

Mattelart, Michèle, and Armand Mattelart. 1990. *The Carnival of Images: Brazilian Television Fiction*. Translated by David Buxton. New York: Bergin & Garvey.

Mattos, Laura, and Daniel Castro. 2002. “Termina amanhã ‘O Clone,’ maior audiência dos últimos seis anos.” *Folha de São Paulo*, June 13. https://www.goo.gl/6PWoMv. Accessed March 20, 2013.

Mauro, Frédéric. 1960. *Le Portugal et l'Atlantique au XVIIe siècle (1560–1760)*. Paris: S.E.V.P.E.N.

Maximin, Daniel. 1995. *L'île et une nuit*. Paris: Seuil.

Mayes, April. 2014. *The Mulatto Republic: Class, Race, and Dominican National Identity*. Gainesville: University Press of Florida.

Mazziotti, Nora. 2006. *Telenovela: Industria y prácticas sociales*. Bogotá: Norma.

Mbembe, Achille. 2001. *On the Postcolony*. Berkeley: University of California Press.

———. 2011. "Fragile Freedom." In *Experiences of Freedom in Postcolonial Literatures and Cultures*, edited by Annalisa Oboe and Shaul Bassi, 13–31. New York: Routledge.

———. 2012. "Rule of Property Versus Rule of the Poor?" *Mail & Guardian* June 15. https://www.goo.gl/GFJkG3. Accessed September 30, 2014.

———. 2013. *Sortir de la grande nuit: Essai sur l'Afrique decolonisée*. Paris: La Découverte/Poche.

McGuinness, Aims. 2003. "Race and Sovereignty: Searching for 'Latin' America in the 1850s." In *Race and Nation in Modern Latin America*, edited by Nancy Applebaum, Anne Macpherson, and Karin Alejandra Rosenblatt, 87–107. Chapel Hill: University of North Carolina Press.

———. 2007. *Path of Empire: Panama and the California Gold Rush*. Ithaca, N.Y.: Cornell University Press.

McGuirk, Bernard. 2007. *Falklands-Malvinas: An Unfinished Business*. Seattle: New Ventures.

McLaren, Joseph. 2008. "From the National to the Global: Satirical Magical Realism in Ngugi's *Wizard of the* Crow." *The Global South* 2 (2): 150–158.

Medina, João. 2000. "Gilberto Freyre Contestado: o lusotropicalismo criticado nas colónias como alibi colonial do salazarismo." *Revista USP* 45 (March): 48–61.

Melville, Hermann. 1851. *Moby Dick; or The Whale*. http://www.gutenberg.org/ebooks/2701.

Meyer, Stefan G. 2001. *The Experimental Arabic Novel: Postcolonial Literary Modernism in the Levant*. Albany: State University of New York Press.

Millar, Lanie. 2012. "'A Friendship Forged With Blood': Cuban Literature of the Angolan War." *Romance Notes* 52 (3): 325–332.

Miller, John C. 1972. "The Imbangala and the Chronology of Early Central African History." The Journal of African History 13 (4): 549–574.

Molina, Luis. 1733. *De justitia et jure*. Geneva: Bousquet.

Molina, María Elena. 2008. "Guerra de Malvinas: La literatura argentina y el desafío de la autocrítica." *Especulo. Revista de estudios literarios* 39. Madrid: Universidad Complutense.

Monaghan, David. 1998. *The Falklands War: Myth and Countermyth*. New York: St. Martin's Press.

Monteiro, D. Antonio de Castro Xavier. 1993. "Como se ensinava o Direito das Gentes na Universidade de Coimbra no século XVI." *Anais da Academia Portuguesa da História* 33: 9–36.

Monteiro, John Manuel. 1994. *Negros da terra: Indios e bandeirantes nas origens de São Paulo*. São Paulo: Companhia das Letras.

Moorman, Marissa. 2001. "Of Westerns, Women, and War: Re-Situating Angolan Cinema and the Nation." *Research in African Literatures* 32 (3): 103–122.

Moreiras, Alberto. 2001. *The Exhaustion of Difference: The Politics of Latin American Cultural Studies*. Durham, N.C.: Duke University Press.

Morgan, K. S. 1982. *The Falklands Campaign: A Digest of Debates in the House of Commons, 2 April to June 1982*. London: Her Majesty's Stationery Office.

Moretti, Franco. 2000. "Conjectures on World Literature." *New Left Review* 1: 54–68.

Moudileno, Lydie. 2006. "Magical Realism: *Arme miraculeuse* for the African Novel?" *Research in African Literatures* 37 (1): 28–41.

Moya, Eduardo. 2011. *Sumbe*. Film. ICAIC.

Muhana, Adma. 1997. "Quando não se escreve o que se fala." In *Vieira Escritor*, edited by Margarida Vieira Mendes, Maria Lucília Pires, and J. Costa Miranda, 107–116. Lisbon: Cosmos.

Mukherjee, Pablo. 2007. "Doomed to Smallness: Violence, V. S. Naipaul, and the Global South." *Yearbook of English Studies* 37 (1): 209–226.

Nairn, Allan. 1986. "South Africa's War Machine," *Multinational Monitor* 7 (7). https://www.goo.gl/ZoWbNL.

Ngũgĩ wa Thiong'o. 1980. *Devil on the Cross*. Portsmouth: Heinemann.

———. 1986. "The Language of African Fiction." In *Decolonizing the Mind: The Politics of Language in African Literature*, 63–86. Portsmouth: Heinemann.

———. 2006. *Wizard of the Crow*. New York: Pantheon.

———. 2012. *Globalectics: Theory and Politics of Knowing*. New York: Columbia University Press.

———. 2014. Foreword. In *Unmasking the African Dictator: Essays on Postcolonial African Literature*, edited by Gichingiri Ndigirigi, vii–viii. Knoxville: University of Tennessee Press.

Novaro, Marcos, and Vicente Palermo. 2003. *La dictadura militar 1976–1983: Del golpe de estado a la restauración democrática*. Buenos Aires: Paidós.

Nuttall, Sarah. "Telling 'Free' Stories? Memory and Democracy in South African Autobiography since 1994." In *Negotiating the Past: The Making of Memory in South Africa*, edited by Sarah Nuttall and Carli Coetzee, 75–88. Oxford: Oxford University Press.

O'Donnell, Guillermo. 1996. "Letter to the Editor." *Common Sense* 11 (2), https://www.goo.gl/iTfk6z.

O'Neill, Peter D., and David Lloyd, eds. 2009. *The Black and Green Atlantic: Cross-Currents of the African and Irish Diasporas*. New York: Palgrave Macmillan.

Onslow, Sue. 2009. "Introduction." In *Cold War in Southern Africa: White Power, Black Liberation*, edited by Sue Onslow, 1–8. New York: Routledge.

Organization of American States. 1966. Council. *Report of the Special Committee to Study Resolution II.1 and VII of the Eighth Meeting of Consultation of Ministers of Foreign Affairs on the First Afro-Asian-Latin American Peoples' Solidarity Conference and Its Projections ("Tricontinental Conference of Havana"): New Instrument of Communist Intervention and Aggression* 2. Washington D.C.: Pan American Union.

Ortiz, Fernando. 1995. *Cuban Counterpoint: Tobacco and Sugar*. Translated by Harriet de Onís. Durham, N.C.: Duke University Press.

Padmore, George. 1942. "Crisis in the British Empire." *The Crisis* 49 (7): 216.

Palés Matos, Luis. 1993. *Tuntún de pasa y grifería*. San Juan: University of Puerto Rico.

Paranguá, Paulo Antonio. 1997. "Cuban Cinema's Political Challenges." In *New Latin American Cinema*, edited by Michael T. Martin, 2:167–192. Detroit: Wayne State University Press.

París, Rogelio. 1990. *Caravana*. VHS. ICAIC; Laboratório Nacional de Cinema.

———. 2008. *Kangamba*. DVD. ICAIC; MINFAR.

París, Rogelio, and Cecilia Crespo. 2010. "Rogelio, Aprendiz . . ." *Revista Cine Cubano* 18/19. https://www.goo.gl/6W9qFf.

Pelayo, Rubén. 2001. *Gabriel García Márquez: A Critical Companion*. Westport, Conn.: Greenwood Press.

Pepetela. 1995. *O Desejo de Kianda*. Lisbon: Dom Quixote.

Perera, Suvendrini. 2009. *Australia and the Insular Imagination: Beaches, Borders, Boats, and Bodies*. New York: Palgrave Macmillan.

Perez, Glória. 2001–2002. *O Clone*. Dir. Jayme Monjardim. 250 episodes. Globo Internacional. April 1, 2012–March 15, 2013. Television.

Peters, Christabelle. 2012. *Cuban Identity and the Angolan Experience*. New York: Palgrave McMillan.

Phelps, Teresa. 2004. *Shattered Voices: Language, Violence and the Work of Truth Commissions*. Philadelphia: University of Pennsylvania Press.

Picon, Antoine. 2002. *Les Saint-simoniens. Raison, imaginaire et utopie*. Paris: Belin.

Pitman, Thea, and Andy Stafford. "Introduction: Transatlanticism and Tricontinentalism." *Journal of Transatlantic Studies* 7 (3): 197–207.

Pocock, Tom. 1993. *Rider Haggard and the Lost Empire: A Biography*. London: Weidenfeld and Nicolson.

Polakow-Suransky, Sascha. 2010. *The Unspoken Alliance: Israel's Secret Relationship with Apartheid South Africa*. New York: Pantheon.

"Polar Air Bases." 1948. *News Review*, January 15. National Archives of South Africa, Pretoria Depot, SAB, BLO 287, PS 16/4, Vol. 1.

Popescu, Monica. 2008. "Licence for Shooting: South African Literature, the Media, and the Cold War." *Scrutiny2: Issues in English Studies in Southern Africa* 13 (1): 92–104.

———. 2010. *South African Literature Beyond the Cold War*. New York: Palgrave MacMillan.

Popescu, Monica, Cedric Tolliver, and Julie Tolliver, eds. 2014. "Special Issue: Alternative Solidarities: Black Diasporas and Cultural Alliances During the Cold War." *Journal of Postcolonial Writing* (50) 4.

Porto, Mauro. 1998. "Telenovelas and Politics in the 1994 Brazilian Presidential Election." *Communication Review* 2 (4): 433–459.

———. 2011. "Telenovelas and Representations of National Identity in Brazil." *Media, Culture & Society* 33 (1): 53–69. http://mcs.sagepub.com/content/33/1/53.

Prashad, Vijay. 2007. *The Darker Nations: A People's History of the Third World*. New York: New Press.

———. 2012. *The Poorer Nations: A Possible History of the Global South*. London: Verso.

Press, Karen. 2009. "An Introduction to *Imprendehora* by Yvette Christiansë." https://www.goo.gl/PBt3bS. Accessed July 20, 2014.

Puccini, Darío. 1989. "Utopía y antiutopía en Gabriel García Márquez." *Nuevo Texto Crítico* 2 (3): 83–116.

Quayson, Ato. 2006. "Fecundities of the Unexpected: Magical Realism, Narrative, and History." In *The Novel*, volume 1, *History, Geography, and Culture*, edited by Franco Moretti, 725–754. Princeton: Princeton University Press.

Queiroz, Carlos. 1940. *Landscapes of Portugal*. Lisbon: National Secretariat of Information.

Quinn, Mary B. 2013. *The Moor and the Novel: Narrating Absence in Early Modern Spain*. New York: Palgrave Macmillan.

Rabia, Abdelkader. 1981. "Gabriel García Márquez et sa fortune dans les pays arabes." *Recherches et Études Comparatistes Ibéro-Françaises de la Sorbonne* 3: 95–103.

"Raḥīl Ghābrīyil Ghārsīyā Mārqīz . . . Riwāʾī Amrīkā al-Lātīniyya wa-Sāḥiriha." 2014. *Al-Ḥayāt*, April 17. http://alhayat.com/Articles/1860736/

Rama, Ángel. 1976. *Los dictadores latinoamericanos*. Mexico City: Fondo de Cultura Económica.

Rasmussen, Kim Su. 2011. "Foucault's Genealogy of Racism." *Theory, Culture & Society* 28 (5): 34–51.

Reclus, Onésime. 1906. *Le partage du monde*. Paris: Librarie Universelle.
Régnier, Philippe, ed. 1989. *Les Saint-simoniens en Egypte, 1833–51*. Cairo: Banque de L'Union Européenne.
———. 1991. *Le livre nouveau des Saint-Simoniens. Manuscrits d'Emile Barrault, Michel Chevalier, Charles Duveyrier, Prosper Enfantin, Charles Lambert, Léon Simon et Thomas Ismaÿaul Urbain*. Paris: Editions du Lerot.
Richards, Colin. 2010. "Feeding the Hand that Bites: South African Art and the Valparaiso Biennial of 1987." Africa South Art Initiative, December 20. https://goo.gl/jS7r2e.
Rieder, John. 2008. *Colonialism and the Emergence of Science Fiction*. Middletown, Conn.: Wesleyan University Press.
Roa Bastos, Augusto. 1974. *Yo el Supremo*. Edited by Carlos Pacheco. Caracas: Biblioteca Ayacucho.
———. 1986. *I the Supreme*. Translated by Helen Lane. New York: Knopf.
Roberts, Brian Russell, and Keith Foulcher, eds. 2016. *Indonesian Notebook: A Sourcebook on Richard Wright and the Bandung Conference*. Durham, N.C.: Duke University Press.
Robichon, François. 1985. "Le panorama, spectacle de l'histoire." *Le Mouvement Social* 131: 65–86.
Rodriguez, Besenia. 2005. "'De la esclavitud yanqui a la libertad cubana': U.S. Black Radicals, the Cuban Revolution, and the Formation of a Tricontinental Ideology." *Radical History Review* 92: 62–87.
Roh, Franz. 1995. "Magic Realism: Post-Expressionism." Translated by Wendy B. Faris. In *Magical Realism: Theory, History, Community*, edited by Lois Parkinson Zamora and Wendy B. Faris, 15–32. Durham, N.C.: Duke University Press.
Roht-Arriaza, Naomi. 2005. *The Pinochet Effect: Transnational Justice in the Age of Human Rights*. Philadelphia: University of Pennsylvania Press.
Rojas, Rafael. 2009. *El estante vacío*. Barcelona: Anagrama.
Romano, Ruggerio, and Stanley J. Stein. 1984. "American Feudalism." *Hispanic American Historical Review* 64 (1): 121–134.
Romulo, Carlos P. 1956. *The Meaning of Bandung*. Chapel Hill: University of North Carolina Press.
Rosenberg, Fernando J. 2006. *The Avant Garde and Geopolitics in Latin America*. Pittsburgh: University of Pittsburgh Press.
———. 2007. "Afecto y política de la cosmópolis latinoamericana." *Revista Iberoamericana* 72 (215–216): 467–479.
Rosny, Léon de. 1859. "Amérique et Orient." *Revue Orientale et Américaine* 1: 1–3.
Rothwell, Phillip. 2009. "Lusotropical Legacies in Germano Almeida's Eva, or Cruelty as a Staged Performance." *Forum for Modern Language Studies* 45: 401–410.

Rousset, Thierry Jean-Marie. 2012. "Breaking Glass: An Analysis of Tristan da Cunha as Robinsonade." Abstract for XXXII SCAR and Open Science Conference, Portland, Oregon, July 16–19. https://www.goo.gl/JAcu98. Accessed July 20, 2014.

Ryan, Connor. 2013. "Regimes of Waste: Aesthetics, Politics, and Waste from Kofi Awoonor and Ayi Kwei Armah to Chimamanda Adichie and Zeze Gamboa." *Research in African Literatures* 44 (4): 51–68.

Sabine, Mark. 2011. "Rebuilding the Angolan Body Politic: Global and Local Projections of Identity and Protest in O Herói/The Hero (Zézé Gamboa, 2004)." *Journal of African Cinemas* 3 (2): 201–219.

Said, Edward. 1978. *Orientalism*. New York: Pantheon Books.

———. 1983. *The World, the Text, and the Critic*. Cambridge, Mass.: Harvard University Press.

Said, Omar ibn. 2011. *A Muslim American Slave: The Life of Omar ibn Said*. Translated and edited by Ala Alryyes. Madison: University of Wisconsin Press.

Salazar, Oliveira. 1962. "Problemas portugueses em África-Entrevista concedida pelo Presidente do Conselho, Prof. Dr. Oliveira Salazar, à revista norte-americana *Life*." *Boletim Geral do Ultramar* 38: 3–16.

Samper, José María. 1860a. "La Confederation Grenadine et sa population (première article)." *Revue Orientale et Américaine* 5: 157–162.

———. 1860b. "La Confederation Grenadine et sa population (deuxième article)." *Revue Orientale et Américaine* 6: 115–127.

———. 1860c. "La Confederation Grenadine et sa population (troisième article)." *Revue Orientale et Américaine* 7: 242–254.

San Miguel, Pedro. 2005. *The Imagined Island: History, Identity, and Utopia in Hispaniola*. Translated by Jane Ramírez. Chapel Hill: University of North Carolina Press.

Sangari, Kumkum. 1987. "The Politics of the Possible." *Cultural Critique* 7: 157–186.

Santos, Boaventura de Sousa. 2002. *Toward a New Legal Common Sense: Law, Globalization and Emancipation*. London: Reed Elsevier.

Sarlo, Beatriz. 1994. "No olvidar la guerra de Malvinas." In *Escritos sobre literatura argentina*. Buenos Aires: Siglo Veintiuno Editores, 2007.

Sartre, Jean-Paul. 1988. *What Is Literature? And Other Essays*. Translated by Bernard Frechtman. Cambridge, Mass.: Harvard University Press.

———. 1976. *Black Orpheus*. Translated by S. W. Allen. Paris: Présence Africaine.

"Saudade, Pablo Neruda." *Pensador*. http://pensador.uol.com.br/saudade_pablo_neruda. Accessed August 17, 2014.

Saunders, A. C. de C. M. 1982. *A Social History of Black Slaves and Freedmen in Portugal, 1441–1555*. Cambridge: Cambridge University Press.

Saussy, Haun. 2006. "Exquisite Cadavers Stitched from Fresh Nightmares: Of Memes, Hives, and Selfish Genes." In *Comparative Literature in an Age of Globalization*, edited by Haun Saussy, 3–42. Baltimore: Johns Hopkins University Press.

Sawyer, Mark Q. 2006. *Racial Politics in Post-Revolutionary Cuba*. New York: Cambridge University Press.

Scott, Shirley V. 2011. "Ingenious and Innocuous? Article IV of the Antarctic Treaty as Imperialism." *The Polar Journal* 1 (1): 51–62.

Seidman, Sarah. 2012. "Tricontinental Routes of Solidarity: Stokely Carmichael in Cuba." *Journal of Transnational American Studies* 4 (2): 1–25.

———. 2013. "Venceremos Means We Shall Overcome: The African American Freedom Struggle and the Cuban Revolution, 1959–79." Ph.D. dissertation, Brown University.

Senghor, Léopold. 1961. "Eloge de la Latinité." In *Liberté I. Négritude et Humanisme*, 354–357. Paris: Seuil.

Shih, Shu-Mei. "Comparison as Relation." In *Comparison: Theories, Approaches, Uses*, edited by Rita Felski and Susan Stanford Friedman, 79–98. Baltimore: Johns Hopkins University Press.

Shohat, Ella. 1992. "Notes on the 'Post-Colonial.'" *Social Text* 31–32: 99–113.

Siskind, Mariano. 2014. *Cosmopolitan Desires; Global Modernity and World Literature in Latin America*. Evanston, Ill.: Northwestern University Press.

Sivasundaram, Sujit. 2014. *Islanded: Britain, Sri Lanka and the Bounds of an Indian Ocean Colony*. Chicago: University of Chicago Press.

Slemon, Stephen. 1995. "Magical Realism as Postcolonial Discourse." In *Magical Realism: Theory, History, Community*, edited by Lois Parkinson Zamora and Wendy B. Faris, 407–426. Durham, N.C.: Duke University Press.

Smith, Eric D. 2012. *Globalization, Utopia, and Postcolonial Science Fiction*. New York: Palgrave Macmillan.

Smulders, Fritz. 1997. "Tradições manuscritas na obra de António Vieira." In *Vieira Escritor*, edited by Margarida Vieira Mendes, Maria Lucília Pires, and J. Costa Miranda, 53–63. Lisbon: Cosmos.

Solanas, Fernando, and Octavio Getino. "Towards a Third Cinema: Notes and Experiences for the Development of a Cinema of Liberation in the Third World." In *New Latin American Cinema*, translated by Julianne Burton and Michael T. Martin, 1:33–58. Detroit: Wayne State University Press.

Spivak, Gayatri Chakravorty. 1987. *In Other Worlds: Essays in Cultural Politics*. London: Methuen.

———. 1993. "Marginality in the Teaching Machine." In *Outside in the Teaching Machine*, 58–85. New York: Routledge.

———. 1999. *A Critique of Postcolonial Reason: Toward a History of the Vanishing Present*. Cambridge, Mass.: Harvard University Press.

———. 2003. *Death of a Discipline*. New York: Columbia University Press.

State President's Archive. 1928. National Archives of South Africa, Pretoria Depot, SAB, SPT 3/4/12, Vol. 1, 3/4307, Foreign Office, October 18.

Stavenhagen, Rodolfo. 1973. *Sept thèses erronées sur l'Amérique latine ou comment décoloniser les sciences humaines*. Paris: Anthropos.

Stern, Steve. 2006. *Remembering Pinochet's Chile: On the Eve of London, 1998*. Durham, N.C.: Duke University Press.

Stobie, Cheryl. 2008. "Fissures in Apartheid's 'Eden': Representations of Bisexuality in *The Smell of Apples* by Mark Behr." *Research in African Literatures* 39 (1): 70–86.

Stoler, Ann Laura. 1995. *Race and the Education of Desire: Foucault's* History of Sexuality *and the Colonial Order of Things*. Durham, N.C.: Duke University Press.

Studnicki-Gizbert, Daviken. 2005. "Revisiting 1640; or, How the Party of Commercial Expansion Lost to the Party of Political Conservation in Spain's Atlantic Empire, 1620–1650." In *The Atlantic Economy during the Seventeenth and Eighteenth Centuries: Organization, Operation, Practice, and Personnel*, edited by Peter A. Coclanis, 152–177. Columbia: University of South Carolina Press.

Sweet, James H. 2013. *Domingos Alvarez, African Healing, and the Intellectual History of the Atlantic World*. Chapel Hill: University of North Carolina Press.

Szok, Peter. 2012. *Wolf Tracks: Popular Art and Re-Africanization in Twentieth-Century Panama*. Jackson: University Press of Mississippi.

Takolander, Maria. 2007. *Catching Butterflies: Bringing Magical Realism to Ground*. Bern: Peter Lang.

Tan, See Seng, and Amitav Acharya. 2008. *Bandung Revisted: The Legacy of the 1955 Asian-African Conference for International Order*. Singapore: National University of Singapore Press.

Tietchen, Todd F. 2007. "The Cubalogues (and After): On the Beat Literary Movement and the Early Cuban Revolution." *Arizona Quarterly* 63 (4): 119–153.

Tóibín, Colm. 1996. *The Story of the Night*. London: Picador.

Tolliver, Cedric. 2014. "Introduction: Alternative Solidarities." *Journal of Postcolonial Writing* 50 (4): 379–383.

Torrente Ballester, Gonzalo. 1998. *Don Juan*. Madrid: Alianza Editorial.

Torres Caicedo, José María. 1875. *Mis ideas y mis principios*. Vol. 1. Paris: Imprenta Nueva.

Torres-Saillant, Silvio. 2010. *Introduction to Dominican Blackness*. The Dominican Monograph Research Series, CUNY. New York: Dominican Studies Institute.

Tresch, John. 2012. *The Romantic Machine: Utopian Science and Technology after Napoleon.* Chicago: University of Chicago Press.

Tricontinental. 1967–90. Havana: OSPAAAL.

Tricontinental Bulletin. 1966–88. Havana: OSPAAAL.

Truth and Reconciliation Commission, South Africa. 1998. "Final Report." Volumes 1–5. *Justice.gov.za.* http://www.justice.gov.za/trc/report. Accessed August 31, 2016.

Tufte, Thomas. 2000. *Living with the Rubbish Queen: Telenovelas, Culture and modernity in Brazil.* Luton: University of Luton Press.

Tutuola, Amos. 1984. *The Palm-Wine Drinkard and My Life in the Bush of Ghosts.* New York: Grove Press.

Ugarte, Manuel. 1978. *La nación latinoamericana.* Caracas: Ayacucho.

Vacs, Aldo César. 1984. *Discreet Partners: Argentina and the USSR Since 1917.* Pittsburgh: University of Pittsburgh Press.

Van der Watt, Susanna Maria Elizabeth. 2012. "Out in the Cold: Science and the Environment in South Africa's Involvement in the sub-Antarctic and Antarctic in the Twentieth Century." Ph.D. dissertation, University of Stellenbosch.

Vansina, Jan. 1975. *Kingdoms of the Savanna.* Madison: University of Wisconsin Press.

Vasconcelos, José. 1948. *La raza cósmica. Misión de la raza iberoamericana.* Mexico: Espase-Calpe.

Venn, Couze. 2009. "Neoliberal Political Economy, Biopolitics and Colonialism: A Transcolonial Genealogy of Inequality." *Theory, Culture & Society* 26 (6): 206–233.

Ventura, Maria da Graça A. Mateus. 2001. "Os Gramaxo. Um caso paradigmático de redes de influência em Cartagena das Índias." Cadernos de Estudos Sefarditas 1: 65–82.

Vieira, Fr. António. 1993. *Sermões: Obras completes do Padre António Vieira.* Vol. 4, edited and revised by Gonçalo Alves. Porto: Lello e Irmão.

Vieytes, Raúl. 1999. *Kelper.* Buenos Aires: Clarín/Aguilar.

Vila Vilar, Enriqueta. 1977. *Hispano-America y el comercio de esclavos: los asientos portugueses.* Seville: Escuela de Estudios Hispano-Americanos de Sevilla.

———. 1979. "Extranjeros en Cartagena (1593–1630)." *Jahrbuch für Geschichte von Staat, Wirtschaft und Gesellschaft Lateinamerikas* 16: 147–184.

Vine, David. 2009. *Island of Shame: The Secret History of the U.S. Military Base of Diego Garcia.* Princeton: Princeton University Press.

Vitalis, Robert. 2013. "The Midnight Ride of Kwame Nkrumah and Other Fables of Bandung (Band-doong)." *Humanity: An International Journal of Human Rights, Humanitarianism, and Development* 4 (2): 261–288.

Voisin, Georges. 1861. *L'Algérie pour les Algériens*. Paris: Michel Lévy Frères.

Von Eschen, Penny M. 1997. *Race Against Empire: Black Americans and Anticolonialism, 1937–1957*. Ithaca, N.Y.: Cornell University Press.

Warnes, Christopher. 2009. *Magical Realism and the Postcolonial Novel: Between Faith and Irreverence*. New York: Palgrave Macmillan.

Watt, Ian. 1957. *The Rise of the Novel: Studies in Defoe, Richardson and Fielding*. 2nd edition. Berkeley: University of California Press, 2001.

Weaver, Jace. 2014. *The Red Atlantic: American Indigenes and the Making of the Modern World, 1000–1927*. Chapel Hill: University of North Carolina Press.

Wenzel, Jennifer. 2009. *Bulletproof: Afterlives of Anticolonial Prophecy in South Africa and Beyond*. Chicago: University of Chicago Press.

Weschler, Lawrence. 1990. *A Miracle, A Universe: Settling Accounts with Torturers*. New York: Penguin.

Wheat, David. 2009. "The Afro-Portuguese maritime world and the Foundations of Spanish Caribbean Society, 1570–1640," Ph.D. thesis, Vanderbilt University.

———. 2011. "The First Great Waves: African Provenance Zones for the Transatlantic Slave Trade to Cartagena de Indias, 1570–1640." *Journal of African History* 52 (1): 1–22.

Whitfield, Esther. 2008. *The Dollar and "Special Period" Fiction*. Minneapolis: University of Minnesota Press.

Wicomb, Zoe. 1998. "Shame and Identity: The Case of the Coloured in South Africa." In *Writing South Africa: Literature, Apartheid, Democracy*, edited by David Attridge and Rosemary Jolly, 91–107. Cambridge: Cambridge University Press.

Williams, Laura Linford. 2005. "Malvinas Myths, Falklands Fictions: Cultural Responses to War from Both Sides of the Atlantic." Ph.D. dissertation, Florida State University.

Wilson, Richard Ashby. 2001. *The Politics of Truth and Reconciliation in South Africa: Legitimizing the Post-apartheid State*. Cambridge: Cambridge University Press.

Wittman, Richard. 2010. "Space, Networks, and the Saint-Simonians." *Grey Room* 40: 24–49.

Woodward, C. Vann. 2002. *The Strange Career of Jim Crow*. Oxford: Oxford University Press.

Wright, Richard. 1995. *The Color Curtain: A Report on the Bandung Conference*. Oxford: University Press of Mississippi.

Wucker, Michelle. 1999. *Why the Cocks Fight: Dominicans, Haitians, and the Fight for Hispaniola*. New York: Hill and Wang.

"Xeque apóia exposição do islamismo." 2001. *Folha de São Paulo*. September 23. https://www.goo.gl/meoq9Z. Accessed August 27, 2012.

Yeazell, Ruth Bernard. 2000. *Harems of the Mind: Passages of Western Art and Literature*. New Haven: Yale University Press.

Young, Cynthia. 2006. *Soul Power: Culture, Radicalism, and the Making of a US Third World Left*. Durham, N.C.: Duke University Press.

Young, Robert J. C. 2001. *Postcolonialism: An Historical Introduction*. Oxford: Blackwell.

———. 2004. *White Mythologies: Writing History and the West*. London: Routledge.

———. 2005. "Postcolonialism: From Bandung to the Tricontinental." *Historein* 5: 11–21.

———. 2006. "O Atlântico lusotropical: Gilberto Freyre e a transformação do hibridismo." In *Gilberto Freyre e os estudos latino-americanos*, edited by Joshua Lund and Malcom McNee, 99–121. Pittsburgh: Instituto Internacional de Literatura Iberoamericana.

———. 2011. "The Right to Resist." In *Experiences of Freedom in Postcolonial Literatures and Cultures*, edited by Annalisa Oboe and Shaul Bassi, 43–58. New York: Routledge.

Zamora, Lois Parkinson, and Wendy B. Faris. 1995. "Introduction: Faiquiri Birds and Flaubertian Parrot(ie)s." In *Magical Realism: Theory, History, Community*, edited by Lois Parkinson Zamora and Wendy B. Faris, 15–32. Durham, N.C.: Duke University Press.

Zarankin, Andres, and María Ximena Senator. 2005. "Archaeology in Antarctica: Nineteenth-Century Capitalism Expansion Strategies." *International Journal of Historical Archaeology* 9 (1): 43–56.

Žižek, Slavoj. 2002. *Welcome to the Desert of the Real! Five Essays on September 11 and Related Dates*. New York: Verso.

Zweig, Stefan. 1941. *Brazil: Land of the Future*. Translated by Andres St. James. New York: Viking.

CONTRIBUTORS

Luiz Felipe de Alencastro is Emeritus Professor, Université de Paris Sorbonne, and Professor and Director of the Center for South Atlantic Studies at the São Paulo School of Economics–FGV. He is the author of many publications, including *O trato dos viventes: Formação do Brasil no Atlântico Sul, séculos XVI e XVII* (2000); "Le versant brésilien de l'Atlantique-Sud: 1550–1850," *Annales* 61 (2): 2006; and "The Ethiopic Ocean: History and Historiography, 1600–1975," in *The South Atlantic: Past and Present*, Portuguese Literary & Cultural Studies 27 (2015).

Magalí Armillas-Tiseyra is Assistant Professor in the Department of Comparative Literature at the Pennsylvania State University. Specializing in African and Latin American literatures, she is particularly interested in theories of comparison and the intersection of large-scale frameworks—such as World Literature, the Global Anglophone, or the Global South—with local and regional specificities. The content of the essay in this volume is part of a larger project on the dictator novel in Latin American and African literatures.

Kerry Bystrom is Associate Professor of English and Human Rights and Associate Dean of the College at Bard College Berlin. She is author of *Democracy at Home in South Africa* (2016) and coeditor of collections including "Private Lives and Public Cultures in South Africa" (a special issue of *Cultural Studies*, with Sarah Nuttall) and "Oceanic Routes" (an ACLA forum in *Comparative Literature*, with Isabel Hofmeyr).

Christina E. Civantos is Associate Professor of Spanish and Arabic at the University of Miami (Florida). She holds a PhD in comparative literature from the University of California at Berkeley (1999) and researches and teaches modern Hispanic and Arabic literary and cultural studies, with a focus on postcolonial studies, nationalisms, the Arab diaspora in the Americas, and the politics of language. Her publications include *Between*

Argentines and Arabs: Argentine Orientalism, Arab Immigrants, and the Writing of Identity (2006) and *The Afterlife of al-Andalus* (forthcoming).

Jason Frydman is Associate Professor of English and Caribbean Studies at Brooklyn College, CUNY, and author of *Sounding the Break: African American and Caribbean Routes of World Literature*. His articles on transnational cultural production in the Americas have focused on storytellers such as Junot Díaz, Patricia Powell, and Vybz Kartel, genres from police procedurals to *telenovelas*, and geopolitical conjunctures including the Cold War and the War on Drugs.

Jaime Hanneken is Associate Professor in the Department of Spanish and Portuguese Studies at the University of Minnesota. Her research addresses questions of race and imperialism in Latin American and Francophone literatures and cultures in the nineteenth and early twentieth centuries. She is the author of *Imagining the Postcolonial: Discipline, Poetics, and Practice in Latin American and Francophone Discourse* (2015). Her current book project, *Tropologies of Latinité*, examines the spatial construction of race in France, Latin America, and Algeria between 1830 and World War II.

Waïl S. Hassan is Professor of Comparative Literature and English at the University of Illinois at Urbana-Champaign. A specialist in modern Arabic literature and intellectual history, he is the author of *Tayeb Salih: Ideology and the Craft of Fiction* (2003) and *Immigrant Narratives: Orientalism and Cultural Translation in Arab American and Arab British Literature* (2011). He has coedited *Approaches to Teaching the Works of Naguib Mahfouz* (2012) and *The Oxford Handbook of the Arab Novelistic Traditions* (forthcoming). He is the translator of Abdelfattah Kilito's *Thou Shalt Not Speak My Language* (2008) and Alberto Mussa's *Lughz al-qāf* (2015). He is currently writing a book on Arab-Brazilian literary and cultural relations.

Oscar Hemer is Professor in Journalistic and Literary Creation at Malmö University, Sweden. He holds a doctorate in social anthropology from the University of Oslo, Norway. He is also a writer of fiction and nonfiction.

Isabel Hofmeyr is Professor of African Literature at the University of the Witwatersrand and Global Distinguished Professor at New York University. Her recent books include *Gandhi's Printing Press: Experiments in Slow Reading* (2013) and *Ten Books that Shaped the British Empire: Creating an Imperial Commons* (2015), coedited with Antoinette Burton.

Maja Horn is Associate Professor of Spanish and Latin American cultures at Barnard College. She specializes in contemporary Hispanophone Caribbean literature, visual and performance art, gender and sexuality, and political culture and is the author of *Masculinity after Trujillo: The Politics of Gender in Dominican Literature* (2014).

Luis Madureira is Professor and Chair of the Department of Spanish and Portuguese, and Professor of African Cultural Studies at the University of Wisconsin-Madison. His research interests include Luso-Brazilian colonial and postcolonial studies, modernism and modernity in Latin America, Africa and the Caribbean, early modern and colonial studies, and theater and performance in Africa. He has published two books and several articles on these and related topics.

Anne Garland Mahler is Assistant Professor in the Department of Spanish, Italian, & Portuguese at the University of Virginia and an Andrew W. Mellon Fellow of the Institute of the Humanities and Global Cultures. She holds a Ph.D. from Emory University. She is the author of *The Color of Resistance: Race and Solidarity from the Tricontinental to the Global South* (forthcoming). Her articles have appeared in *Journal of Latin American Cultural Studies*, *Latin American Research Review*, and *Small Axe: A Caribbean Platform for Criticism*. Mahler serves on the founding executive committee of the Modern Language Association's Global South Forum.

Lanie Millar is Assistant Professor of Spanish in the Department of Romance Languages at the University of Oregon. She completed her PhD in comparative literature at the University of Texas at Austin. Her research focuses on contemporary Caribbean and Lusophone African literatures, especially those from Cuba and Angola. Her current research examines transatlantic solidarities and cultural connections forged through Cuba's participation in the war in Angola, and more broadly on the question of postrevolutionary "disappointment" in late twentieth- and twenty-first-century Cuban and Angolan narrative.

Joseph R. Slaughter is Associate Professor of English and Comparative Literature at Columbia University, where he teaches ethnic and Third World literatures (particularly African, Caribbean, and Latin American literatures of the South Atlantic), postcolonial literature and theory, human rights, and narrative approaches to international law. His book *Human Rights, Inc: The World Novel, Narrative Form, and International Law* won the 2008 René Wellek Prize for Comparative Literature and Cultural Theory. He is finishing two books: *New Word Orders*, on intellectual property and world literature, and *Pathetic Fallacies*, a collection of essays on human rights and the humanities.

INDEX